DB2: Maximizing Performance of Online Production Systems

Books from QED

Database

Migrating to DB2
DB2: The Complete Guide to Implementation and Use
DB2 Design Review Guidelines
DB2: Maximizing Performance of Online Production Systems
Embedded SQL for DB2: Application Design and Programming
SQL for DB2 and SQL/DS Application Developers
Using DB2 to Build Decision Support Systems
The Data Dictionary: Concepts and Uses
Logical Data Base Design
Entity-Relationship Approach to Logical Data Base Design
Database Management Systems: Understanding and Applying Database Technology
Database Machines and Decision Support Systems: Third Wave Processing
IMS Design and Implementation Techniques
Repository Manager/MVS: Concepts, Facilities and Capabilities
How to Use ORACLE SQL*PLUS
ORACLE: Building High Performance of Online Systems
ORACLE Design Review Guidelines
Using ORACLE to Build Decision Support Systems
Understanding Data Pattern Processing: The Key to Competitive Advantage
Developing Client/Server Aplications in an Architected Environment

Systems Engineering

Quality Assurance for Information Systems: Methods, Tools, and Techniques
Handbook of Screen Format Design
Managing Software Projects: Selecting and Using PC-Based Project Management Systems
The Complete Guide to Software Testing
A User's Guide for Defining Software Requirements
A Structured Approach to Systems Testing
Storyboard Prototyping: A New Approach to User Requirements Analysis
The Software Factory: Managing Software Development and Maintenance
Data Architecture: The Information Paradigm
Advanced Topics in Information Engineering
Software Engineering with Formal Metrics

Management

Introduction to Data Security and Controls
CASE: The Potential and the Pitfalls

Management (cont'd)

Strategic and Operational Planning for Information Services
Information Systems Planning for Competitive Advantage
How to Automate Your Computer Center: Achieving Unattended Operations
Ethical Conflicts in Information and Computer Science, Technology, and Business
Mind Your Business: Managing the Impact of End-User Computing
Controlling the Future: Managing Technology-Driven Change
The UNIX Industry: Evolution, Concepts, Architecture, Applications, and Standards

Data Communications

Designing and Implementing Ethernet Networks
Network Concepts and Architectures
Open Systems: The Guide to OSI and its Implementation

IBM Mainframe Series

CSP: Mastering Cross System Product
CICS/VS: A Guide to Application Debugging
MVS COBOL II Power Programmer's Desk Reference
VSE COBOL II Power Programmer's Desk Reference
CICS Application and System Programming: Tools and Techniques
QMF: How to Use Query Management Facility with DB2 and SQL/DS
DOS/VSE: Introduction to the Operating System
DOS/VSE: CICS Systems Programming
DOS/VSE/SP Guide for Systems Programming: Concepts, Programs, Macros, Subroutines
Advanced VSE System Programming Techniques
Systems Programmer's Problem Solver
VSAM: Guide to Optimization and Design
MVS/JCL: Mastering Job Control Language
MVS/TSO: Mastering CLISTS
MVS/TSO: Mastering Native Mode and ISPF
REXX in the TSO Environment

Programming

C Language for Programmers
VAX/VMS: Mastering DCL Commands and Utilities
The PC Data Handbook: Specifications for Maintenance, Repair, and Upgrade of the IBM/PC, PS/2 and Compatibles
UNIX C Shell Desk Reference

QED books are available at special quantity discounts for educational uses, premiums, and sales promotions. Special books, book excerpts, and instructive materials can be created to meet specific needs.

This is Only a Partial Listing. For Additional Information or a Free Catalog contact
QED Information Sciences, Inc. • P. O. Box 82-181 • Wellesley, MA 02181
Telephone: 800-343-4848 or 617-237-5656 or fax 617-235-0826

DB2: Maximizing Performance of Online Production Systems

W.H. Inmon

QED Technical Publishing Group
Boston • Montreal • London

Library of Congress Cataloging-in-Publication Data

Inmon, William H.
　　DB2 : maximizing performance of online production systems / W.H. Inmon.
　　　　p.　cm.
　　Bibliography: p.
　　Includes index.
　　ISBN 0-89435-256-3
　　1. Data base management.　2. IBM Database 2 (Computer system)
3. On-line data processing.　I. Title.　II. Title: DB two.
QA76.9.D3I5383　1988
005.75′65—dc 19　　　　　　　　　　　　　　　　　　　　88-18083
　　　　　　　　　　　　　　　　　　　　　　　　　　　　　　　CIP

© 1989, 1991 by QED Information Sciences, Inc. All rights reserved.
Printed in the United States of America
91 92 93　10 9 8 7 6 5 4 3 2 1

To T. F. Chang

Contents

Preface xv

Part I Introduction: Establishing the Production Environment 1

Chapter 1   The DB2 Environment   3
- Online, Interactive Environments   3
- The DB2 Environment   4
- The System Environment   4
- Program Flow   7
- Physical Structures   8
- Table Relationships   13
- Separation of Ad Hoc Processing   14
- Environmental Characteristics   16
- General Performance Considerations   18
- Summary   19
- Questions: The DB2 Environment   20

Chapter 2   From Logical to Physical Design in DB2   25
- Low-Level Design   28
- Mid-Level Design   28
- Transaction/Program Separation   33
- Control Database Design   35
- Thread Use, WFI   36
- Index Analysis   36
- Clustering Tables   36

- Very High Performance/Very High Availability   37
- Summary   38
- Questions: Logical to Physical Design   38

PART II   DB2 Database Online Performance Design   45

Chapter 3   DB2 Performance 1   47
- Database Design for DB2   47
- Conceptual Database Design   47
- From a Conceptual Model to a Physical Design   48
- Normalized Data Structures   49
- Indexing Data   54
- Questions: Database Design   58

Chapter 4   DB2 Performance 2   61
- Referential Integrity   61
- Multiple Occurrences of Data   63
- Questions: Database Design   69

Chapter 5   DB2 Performance 3   73
- Variable-Length Fields   73
- Control Databases   75
- Data Views   77
- Sequentially Accessing DB2 Data   79
- Questions: Database Design   82

Chapter 6   DB2 Performance 4   85
- Partitioning Databases   85
- Encoding of Data   87
- Summary   89
- Questions: Database Design   89

Chapter 7   DB2 Transaction Design for Performance: Part 1   91
- DB2 Performance in the Face of "Undesigned" Transactions   91
- Why Undesigned Transactions in DB2 Damage Online Performance   93
- What to Do about Undesigned Transactions   94
- Characteristics of Designed and Undesigned Transactions   96
- Data Driven Processes   97
- I/Os   97
- Data Contention   98
- Transaction Issues   98

- Examples: Designed and Undesigned Transactions   100
- Questions: Transaction Design   103

Chapter 8   DB2 Transaction Design for Performance: Part 2   105

- Static/Dynamic SQL   112
- Embedded SQL   112
- Summary   114
- Questions: Transaction Design   114

PART III   DB2 Application Design: Part I   117

Chapter 9   Data Structures and Data Relationships   119

- Standard Data Structures   119
- Application-Supported Relationships   119
- Multikeyed Relationships   125
- Multikeyed Cross-Reference Tables   127
- Secondary/Sparse Indexes   127
- Internal Arrays   128
- Stacks   129
- Logically Related Tables   130
- Key-Splitting   131
- Recursive Structures   133
- Summary   134
- Questions: Data Structures and Data Relationships   134

Chapter 10   Referential Integrity   137

- Application Responsibility   137
- Different Forms of Referential Integrity   138
- Deferred Referential Integrity   140
- Application Conventions   141
- Independent Audits   142
- Frequency of Audit   142
- Summary   143
- Questions: Referential Integrity   143

Chapter 11   The DB2 Batch Environment   145

- The Batch Window   145
- What Runs in the Batch Window   147
- I/Os and Joined Databases   147
- Parallel Sequential Runs   150
- Single Extract Processing   152

- Sorting Transactions into Primary Processing Sequence   153
- Ordering Batch Runs   154
- Consolidation of Update Requirements   154
- Peak-Period Processing   155
- Small Databases   156
- System Considerations   156
- Summary   157
- Questions: Batch Processing   157

Chapter 12   Testing DB2 Production Systems   161
Section 1   The DB2 Test Environment   161

- Input to Testing   162
- Stress Tests   163
- Stress-Testing and Service-Level Agreements   163
- Measuring the Stress Test   164
- Driver Programs   165
- Modularized Programs   166
- Separate Environments   166
- "Preliminary," "Full" Test Databases   167
- Testing Coordination Across Projects   168
- Administering the Test Environment   169
- Summary   171
- Questions: The DB2 Test Environment   171

Section 2   Testing Programs in DB2   176

- General Transaction/Program Control   177
- Single-Table Manipulation   177
- Referential Integrity   177
- Program Modularization   178
- Algorithmic Verification   179
- Data Access   179
- Recursive Relationships   179
- Continuous Time Span Rows   180
- Extract Processing   180
- Summary   182
- Questions: Testing Programs in DB2   183

PART IV   DB2 Application Design: Part II   187

Chapter 13   Bill of Materials Processing   189

- The Bill of Materials   189
- Recursive Relationships   190

- Continuity of the Level Count Field   193
- A Second Level Count Field   194
- The Generalized Recursive Structure   194
- A Simple Explosion   195
- Bill of Materials Explosion   195
- Implosions   197
- A Recursive Infinite Loop   197
- Other Bill of Materials Processing   198
- Algorithmic Differences   199
- Other Recursive Structures   200
- Differences between Levels   200
- Online/Batch Bill of Materials Processing   201
- Summary   201
- Questions: Bill of Materials Processing   201

Chapter 14   Denormalization   205
- Normalization of Data   205
- The Usage Matrix   208
- The Processing Frequency Anomalies   209
- Estimating Row Access Frequency   209
- Heuristic and Iterative Analysis   210
- Clustering Analysis   211
- Automated Tools   213
- Redundancy   213
- Internal Arrays   216
- Interleaving Data   216
- Other Options   217
- Summary   218
- Questions: Denormalization   218

Chapter 15   High Availability   221
- Importance of Design   221
- Recovery/Reorganization   222
- Phases of Recovery   222
- Reorganization—An Unload/Reload Process   223
- Estimating Downtime   224
- Probability of Downtime   225
- Reducing the Volume of Data   225
- Referential Integrity and High Availability   230
- Summary   230
- Questions: High Availability   231

Chapter 16 Extract Processing in DB2 235

- Extract Logic 235
- Designing the Extract Process 236
- Using the Extracted Data 236
- Granularity of Data 237
- The Right Level of Detail 238
- Less Extracted Detail 238
- The Hardware Environment 240
- The Piggyback Approach 242
- Incremental Changes 243
- Indexes and Extracted Data 243
- Periodic Loading 246
- Compacting Data 247
- Other Options 249
- A Final Note 250
- Questions: Extract Processing in DB2 250

Part V DB2 Technician's Part 255

Chapter 17 Detailed Design and Tuning 257

- Using an Index 257
- Indexing Variable-Length Columns 262
- Defining Variable-Length Fields 262
- Decimal Data Definition 263
- Index Space Considerations 263
- Updating Variable-Length Fields 265
- Nonstandard Indexes 266
- Edit Routines 267
- Row Size Greater Than 4Kb 268
- Questions: Detailed Design and Tuning 269

Chapter 18 An Introduction to Data Locking in DB2 273

- The Components of Data Locking 274
- Lock Components 275
- Locking Management 276
- A Typical Locking Sequence 277
- The Options for Locking Data 278
- The States of the Options 280
- The Unit of Recovery 284
- Some Rules of Thumb 285
- Cursor Stability/Repeatable Head 287
- Deadlock 289

- Summary   290
- Questions: Data Locking   290

Chapter 19   Archival Processing   295
- Criteria for Success   295
- Archival Media   296
- Primitive Archival Data   297
- Subject Orientation   298
- The Living Sample Environment   298
- Some Design Considerations—Time-Stamping Data   299
- Efficient Access of Archival Data   304
- Integrity and Access of Archival Data   307
- Foreign Keys in the Archival Environment   309
- Summary   310
- ALGO: Continuous Timespan Update Algorithm   310

Chapter 20   Strategic Positioning of DB2—High-Performance Systems   315
- High-Performance Levels   315
- The Banking Environment   316
- Hardware Configuration   318
- System of Record   319
- Peak-Period Processing Rates   320
- The Banking Life Cycle   323
- Extensibility of the Environment   325
- Key Structures   326
- Denormalization of High Performance Data   329
- Summary   330

Glossary   331

References   339

Answers   341

Index   367

Preface

IBM's Database 2 (DB2) product is a powerful tool with many capabilities. The possibilities for using DB2 are so numerous that DB2 can be used by the end user, the programmer, the manager, the decision support analyst, and the information center analyst. Indeed, DB2 has so many options that it can be the database management system (DBMS) to suit nearly all the processing needs for a very wide spectrum of users.

One very special usage of DB2 is the focus of this book—DB2 as a tool for production, online applications. It is recognized that DB2 has many other legitimate uses that will not be covered by this book. Instead, the focus will be almost entirely on the issues of production, online processing.

The issues of production, especially online processing, begin with performance and availability. *Performance*, of course, refers to the amount of time required for a user to complete a transaction. In the online environment, when the system either does not perform well or is unavailable, no other facets of the system matter. Consequently, the discipline that is required of the designer to achieve high performance and availability take precedence over other features of DB2 for processing in the online environment.

Online performance centers on the physical I/Os required to support the processing of online systems. The central issues of performance will naturally focus around the minimization and the effective use of I/Os.

I/Os are minimized by the proper construction of the production environment, by proper systems design, and by proper tuning of the system once constructed.

THE PHILOSOPHY OF THIS BOOK

This book assumes the philosophy that—

- if the online production environment is not properly constructed, then no amount of sound design or tuning will achieve, in the long run, adequate performance;
- if the application is not designed properly, then no amount of tuning will achieve, in the long run, adequate performance;
- if the online application has been properly constructed and the application has been properly designed, then tuning the application provides the fine touches to enhance performance.

The discussions throughout this book reflect the philosophy of creating good performance in the structured manner described.

This book conceptually divides into two major issues which, not surprisingly, correspond to the prioritization of the issues of performance:

- Establishing the DB2 online environment
- DB2 application design for performance and availability

WHO WILL FIND THIS BOOK VALUABLE?

This book benefits database designers, system developers, programmers, managers, consultants—in short, anyone interested in good performance and high system-availability for production systems in the online environment.

This is not a first course or a primer in DB2 concepts and facilities. It is assumed that the student has at least a working knowledge of the mechanics of DB2. This book addresses DB2 from the application perspective, not the system or technical perspective.

This book can be read in (at least!) two ways: as material that addresses some specific environments—such as the banking and manufacturing environments—or as material with discussions that address environments with high performance, large volumes of data and transactions. This book is not a replacement for existing technical literature. Instead, it is meant to be a complement to the large body of manuals and books that adequately discuss the mechanical workings of DB2. This book purposely does not repeat well-documented discourses on the technology of DB2. Instead, it addresses the application of that technology to the problems facing the developer who translates user requirements into a design.

PART I

Introduction: Establishing the Production Environment

Chapter 1 The DB2 Environment

- Online, Interactive Environments
- The DB2 Environment
- The System Environment
- Program Flow
- Physical Structures
- Table Relationships
- Separation of Ad Hoc Processing
- Environmental Characteristics
- General Performance Considerations
- Summary
- Questions: The DB2 Environment

Chapter 2 From Logical to Physical Design in DB2

- Low-Level Design
- Mid-Level Design
- Transaction/Program Separation
- Control Data Base Design
- Thread Use, WFI
- Index Analysis
- Clustering Tables
- Very High Performance/ Very High Availability
- Summary
- Questions: Logical to Physical Design

CHAPTER 1

The DB2 Environment

ONLINE AND INTERACTIVE ENVIRONMENTS

The differences between online and interactive processing are germane to the larger issue of establishing the DB2 online production environment. The online environment is the environment in which there is good, consistent online response time throughout the day. Each transaction in the online environment executes—from the initiation in the terminal to the processor and back to the terminal—in a matter of seconds. There is consistently good performance in the peak periods in the online environment. In a non-DB2 environment, typical online software is TPF (formerly ACP).

The interactive environment is one that combines some characteristics of the online environment and the batch environment. In the interactive environment, there typically is direct access to data and to the session manager, thus making the interactive environment appear as if it were online. But the interactive environment has other characteristics as well, such as the initiation and execution of long-running jobs, for example, sorts, merges, and compilations. During peak periods of processing, the interactive environment takes on the characteristics of a pure batch processor. VM/CMS or TSO are examples of software found in the interactive environment.

The effectiveness of the online environment is directly proportional to the response time achieved in the environment. The business justification for the online environment is especially sensitive to online response time, especially during peak period processing. The DB2 architect attempting to use DB2 for online processing should be very clear as to the differences between the environments—i.e., the online and the interactive environments. It should be understood that the purpose of this book is to address the usage of DB2 in the online environment, not the interactive environment.

THE DB2 ENVIRONMENT

Before the DB2 production environment can be defined and controlled, the production developer must first understand some of the basics of the DB2 environment. There are many aspects of the DB2 environment. The three most important to the production developer who desires to attain good, consistent online system performance are—

- the system environment,
- the execution of an SQL program, and
- the physical database environment.

Each of these aspects of DB2 will be described in an overview. The reader is invited to review these topics in depth in the materials referenced in the bibliography.

THE SYSTEM ENVIRONMENT

Terminal access to DB2 is achieved in conjunction with Information Management System (IMS), Customer Information Control System (CICS), and TSO. In addition, external software such as ORACLE can access the DB2 environment through one or the other of these facilities. The relationship of DB2 to these standard pieces of software is depicted by Figure 1-1.

In either IMS or CICS, DB2 is accessed through Structured Query Language (SQL) statements that are embedded in application code (i.e., in Cobol or PL-1 code). In TSO, DB2 is accessed through the Query Management Facility (QMF) facility. DB2-controlled data can also be loaded from an IMS database by means of the Data Extract Facility (DXT). When DB2 is accessed from IMS, it is accessed only from the control region (in other words, IMS batch cannot access DB2).

Chapter 1   The DB2 Environment   5

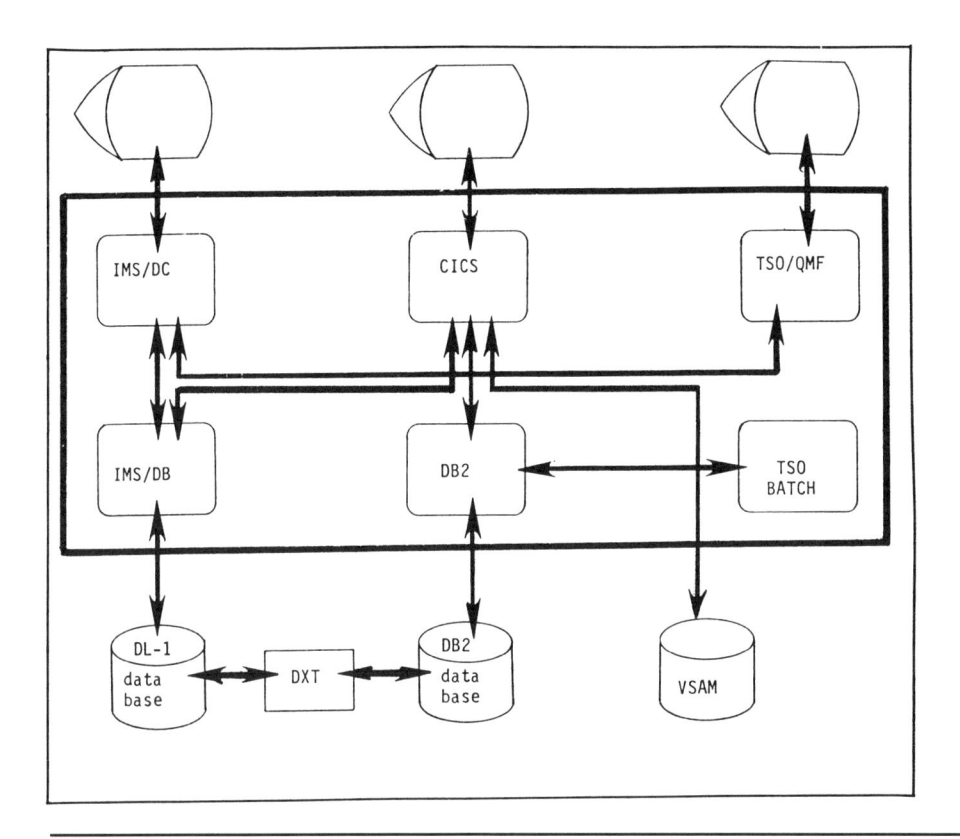

FIGURE 1–1. System environment of DB2.

Some Relevant Dynamics

An aspect of DB2 that is very important to performance is the inner dynamics of the management of data and the management of transactions. Understanding the structure and the dynamics of the components of DB2 that address the protection of data and transaction integrity, the flow of events, and the usage and access of data is essential to achieving online performance. These technical issues focus on, among other things, the way DB2 manages the locking of data.

An important component of DB2 is its locking facility. Locking of data prevents multiple online users from simultaneously updating the same data and creating erroneous results. Locking is an important factor in the number of online users that can access data concurrently and to online performance in general. DB2 uses the IRLM facility to manage all locks.

Locks can be held at various levels in DB2, such as tablespaces, pages, indexes, databases, plans, etc. The locking strategy for any given program is determined at the moment of BIND. Locks are held for a program as it goes into execution until a COMMIT, DEALLOCATION, or UNLOCK is issued.

The effects on performance of locking can be minimized by two types of DB2 databases, read-only and update databases. Locking is absolutely minimized when a program is accessing read-only databases. In addition to minimizing the conflicts with locks, separating data into read-only and update databases helps minimize the underlying data management of the databases. Read-only data can be very tightly packed, since the data and its indexes never have to be modified once created. Update data, of course, must address the issues of insertion, update, and deletion.

Some Relevant Details

Other technical details relevant to DB2 online performance are the following:

- The management and usage of indexes. Indexes can be added or deleted at any time in DB2. As a matter of practicality, indexes are not deleted or added during the online day, due to performance constraints. Indexes can be important to performance because their existence can cause queries to use less I/O than otherwise necessary.

- The access paths used in the location and access of data. DB2 decides internally which views and which access paths are to be used. The path is stored in a PLAN, which is used at execution time to determine the optimal method(s) to use in satisfying the calls issued by the query.

- The programs used to process against DB2 databases. Programs that can access DB2 can be written in APL, assembler, COBOL, Fortran, and PL-I and other language level interfaces.

If the DB2 production environment is to achieve adequate online performance during the peak period processing window, a certain amount of isolation of processing and data is required. This isolation is achieved through several facilities, such as the restricted usage of the DB2 catalogue during the online day.

PROGRAM FLOW

The program flow of SQL is illustrated by Figure 1-2.

Application source code is entered into a SQL precompiler. One of the outputs of the precompiler is a Database Request Module (DBRM), which is one of the inputs—along with table definitions—to the BIND process from which the PLAN is created, which determines the optimal access path. Modified source code is created that is input into the compile/link process from which a load module is executed. Once execution is initiated, data requests are satisfied in the Relational Data Store (RDS).

The requests for data flow from the RDS to the data manager, which translates set requests for data into actual database calls. From the data manager, the buffer manager is called. The buffer manager manipulates the different buffer pools. The media manager is called from the buffer manager and accesses data at the VSAM (ESDS) level.

Data is inserted into a table using either the SQL Insert facility, the DB2 Load utility or other utilities supplied by third party vendors.

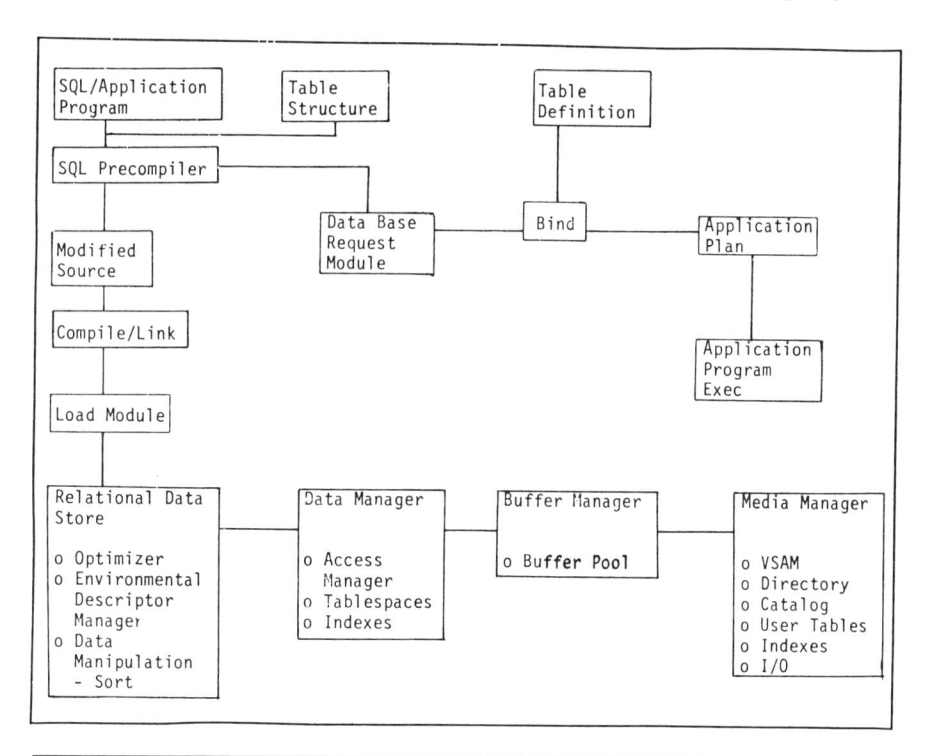

FIGURE 1–2. The program flow of SQL.

Data is committed to a database at a commit point. At a commit point the updates can be considered to be permanent. (Of course, prior to a commit point, the database updates can be backed out.)

The actual commit point depends upon the terminal access method the program is running in (i.e., IMS/DC, CICS, etc.). In IMS, for example, a commit point would be a SYNC point, a CHKP, a checkpoint, etc.

PHYSICAL STRUCTURES

The lowest unit of information in DB2 is the *field* or column. A field is defined by the database designer/administrator at the moment of physical database design. Each row contains one (or no) occurrences of a field or column. For multiple rows, the same fields in each row form a column. Fields contain the occurrence of a data element. For example, if a field name were part number, the field might contain the value of a part number—"1245pg".

DB2 gives the designer four physical formats for a field:

- Fixed length, no null values allowed
- Fixed length, null values allowed
- Variable length, no null values allowed
- Variable length, null values allowed

If a field can have null values, there is a prefix for the field. Figure 1-3 shows the different possibilities for field definitions.

In Figure 1-3, a P in the prefix for a field indicates the field contents are present, and an N indicates the contents are null. If a field cannot have null values, there is no field prefix for it. If a field is variable in length, it has a prefix indicating the length of the field. Note that a variable-length field that is nonnull may have a length of zero, which is the logical equivalent of being null.

Fields are defined into *rows* or *tuples*. A row is a group of related fields whose existence depends upon the key of the row. As an example, a row for a bank account activity might have a key of ACCOUNT/ACTIVITY DATE/ACTIVITY TIME and nonkey fields of AMOUNT, LOCATION, TELLER, PERSONAL IDENTIFICATION, etc. Rows can be fixed-length or variable-length. If a row contains only fixed-length fields, then the row is fixed in length. But if a row contains one or more variable-length fields, then the row is variable in length. Rows are combined together into pages. Figure 1-3 illustrates rows and pages.

Chapter 1   The DB2 Environment

```
┌─────────────────────────────────────────────────────────────┐
│  ┌──────────────────┐                                       │
│  │abcdefghij....    │  Fixed field length, no nulls allowed │
│  └──────────────────┘                                       │
│                                                             │
│  ┌─┬──────────────┐  ┌─┬────────────┐                       │
│  │P│abcdefgh....  │  │N│------------│  Fixed length fields, │
│  └─┴──────────────┘  └─┴────────────┘  null values allowed  │
│                                                             │
│  ┌─┬──────────────┐                                         │
│  │1│abcdefgh....  │  Variable length fields, no nulls allowed │
│  └─┴──────────────┘                                         │
│                                                             │
│  ┌─┬─┬────────────┐  ┌─┬─┐                                  │
│  │1│P│abcdefg...  │  │1│N│  Variable length fields, null    │
│  └─┴─┴────────────┘  └─┴─┘  values allowed                  │
│                                                             │
│        the types of fields supported by DB2                 │
└─────────────────────────────────────────────────────────────┘
```

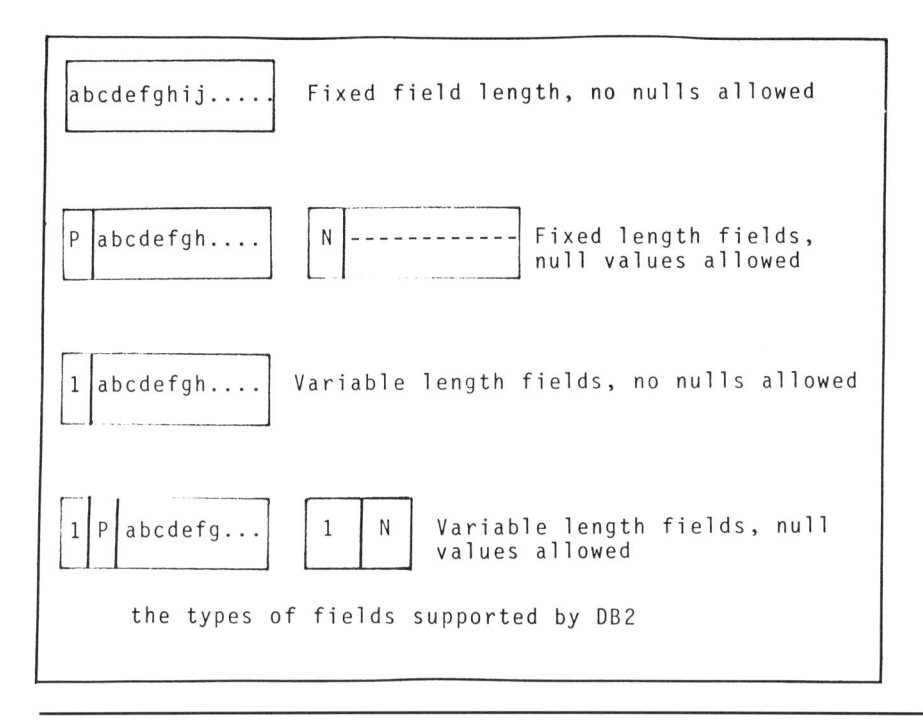

FIGURE 1–3. The types of fields supported by DB2.

A page is made up rows, or *tuples*. A tuple is made up of fields. The page shown in Figure 1-4 shows 10 tuples and three unused spaces where future tuples may be placed. The rows have a primary key—employee number, and four nonkey fields—hire date, starting salary, starting location, and supervisor. For a row to exist, only the primary key must exist. Other nonkey fields may be present or null. A page is either 4 kilobytes (KB) or 32KB in length. If a page is 32KB, it is made up of eight 4KB VSAM control intervals, or CIs, as shown in Figure 1-5.

Rows can be added or deleted one at a time, or they can be loaded and deleted en masse. Columns can be added to a row after the row is defined, but, even if the column that is added is fixed in length, the row is subsequently defined as variable in length. When a row is deleted, the space is marked as reusable. The space can be reused for the occurrence of another row or can be used for the extension of an existing variable length row.

Pages are physically organized into tablespaces. Tablespaces come in two forms—simple tablespaces and partitioned tablespaces. A simple tablespace can hold several types of tables together

Employee Number	Hire Date	Starting Salary	Starting Location	Supervisor
1908	Jun2183	--	Tallahassee	G Jones
2807	Aug0176	530	Shreveport	T Wynette
--	--	--	--	--
--	--	--	--	--
0019	Sep1765	980	Jackson	W Nelson
--	--	--	--	--
1007	Jan0166	500	--	G Jones
1108	Dec1580	--	Dallas	G Jones
1507	Jul2086	975	Shreveport	--
1807	Aug2184	1000	Oxford	G Jones
2106	Jul1979	997	--	T Wynette
0078	Feb2886	1065	Miami	W Nelson
1004	Aug2380	--	Gatlinburg	W Jennings

A page is made up of rows, or tuples. A tuple is made up of fields. The primary key for this page (or table) is employee number. Note that non-key data may exist for any field except for the primary key, but for a tuple to exist, the key must exist. Also note that any field may be a foreign key.

FIGURE 1-4. A page with tuples and spaces. The primary key for this page (or table) is employee number. Note that nonkey data may exist for any field except for the primary key, but for a tuple to exist, the key must exist. Also note that any field may be a foreign key.

or a single table. A simple tablespace may be segmented or not segmented. A partitioned tablespace holds only one type of table, but the table is divided into 2 to 64 units called *partitions*, as shown in Figure 1-6.

Simple tablespaces are good for small, interrelated tables, while partitioned tables are good for large tables. When a simple tablespace is segmented, it divides its space so that data of the same type, i.e., from the same table, is physically colocated together. By physically colocating data of the same type together, the amount of data locked by a deletion can be minimized. Figure 1-7 shows a segmented tablespace.

Data is organized into pages either randomly or sequentially. If

Chapter 1　　　　　　　　　　The DB2 Environment　　　　　　　　　　11

　　　　　　　　　　　　　a 32k page

　　　　　　　　　　　　　a 4k page

FIGURE 1–5. Pages of 32K and 4K with control intervals of 4Kb.

the data is stored randomly, it is said to be nonclustered. If data is stored sequentially, it is said to be clustered. Whether clustered or nonclustered there can be zero or more indexes pointing to designated fields. The index has three levels: the root-page level, the intermediate-page level, and the leaf-page level. The two top levels of indexes are used to point to the leaf pages in much the same way as master indexes are used to point to data in other systems.

The leaf pages actually point to the pages where rows reside. A direct access into the database uses three levels of indexing, while sequential access uses only the leaf page. If the data is clustered, the leaf page points to rows within one page and to rows in another page

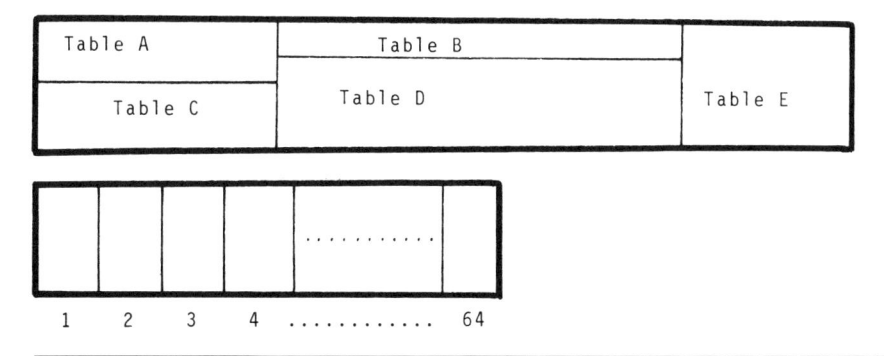

Table A	Table B	
Table C	Table D	Table E

1　2　3　4　. 64

FIGURE 1–6. A partitioned tablespace.

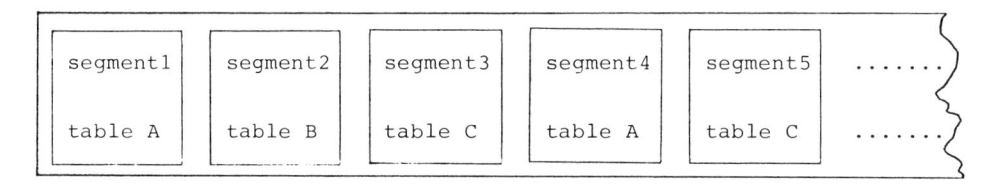

12 Introduction: Establishing the Production Environment Part I

segment1	segment2	segment3	segment4	segment5	....
table A	table B	table C	table A	table C	....

FIGURE 1–7. A segmented tablespace.

root page level
intermediate page level
leaf page level
data pages

clustered data   *non-clustered data*

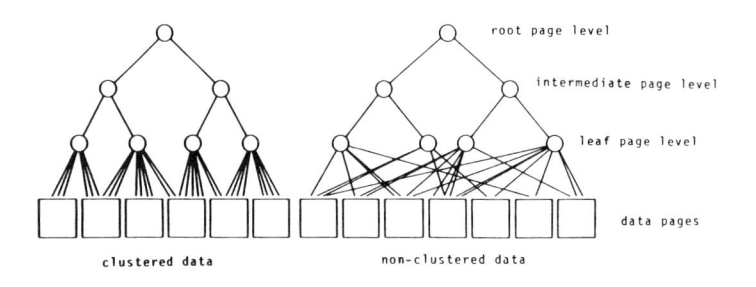

FIGURE 1–8. The index structure of DB2.

when the sequential order of the rows is interrupted by the physical boundaries of a page. But when data is not clustered, the leaf pages point to data in a random fashion. Figure 1-8 illustrates the different indexes in clustered and nonclustered data.

Ariz	Ariz	ArizSt	ArizSt	Ark	Ark	Ark	....
page02	page08	page97	page86	page93	page45	page83	......
entry02	entry07	entry02	entry08	entry03	entry10	entry15	.....

an index pointing to a page and a an offset within the page. To access the first index occurrence for Arkansas page 93 is located and the third entry in the prefix is used to actually locate the row that is being pointed to

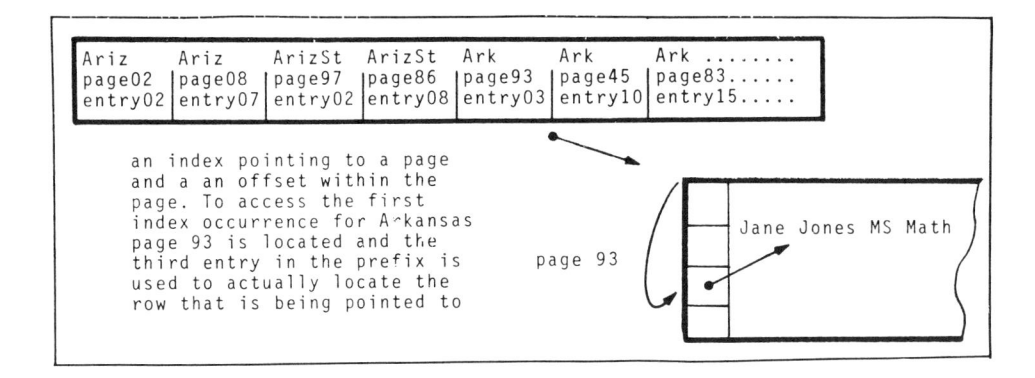

page 93

Jane Jones MS Math

FIGURE 1–9. An index pointing to a page and an offset within the page. To access the first index occurrence for Arkansas, page 93 is located, and the third entry in the prefix is used to actually locate the row that is being pointed to.

The pointer from the leaf page to the data page is in the form of a page/entry. The first part of the index pointer indicates which page the row can be found at. The entry is accessed to find the actual location of the row within the page. This indirect pointing to data allows data management to occur within the physical page without affecting the values in the index. For example, a row can be moved from one location to another within the page, and all that must be changed is the value of the location within the page. No index manipulation is necessary. The arrangement of indexes pointing into data is shown by Figure 1-9.

TABLE RELATIONSHIPS

Tables are related to each other in DB2 by means of *foreign keys*. Foreign key relationships (i.e., referential integrity) may be maintained by DB2 or the application. A foreign key is merely a field in a table that is likewise contained in another table and allows the two tables to be joined. Figure 1-10 shows a simple example of two tables that are related by a foreign key.

Figure 1-10 shows that customer and account tables are related by means of the account number. The account for M Robbins is shown to be Account 1250JA and relates to the second account shown in the account table. Note that in the structuring of data shown in the ex-

Customer	Name	Address	Phone	Account
459701872	M Robbins	123 Heaven Gate	777-1430	1250JA
570181760	J C Riley	1 Fast Lane	841-7781	16072
774182110	L Lynn	14 Jaybird	291-6604	17011B
⋮	⋮	⋮	⋮	⋮

Account	Date Opened	Balance	Domiciling Branch
1901K	Jul2081	1000.00	Oakland
1250JA	Aug1376	596.42	Pinole
1742AR	Mar1271	10513.13	Alameda
⋮	⋮	⋮	⋮

two tables connected by account number

FIGURE 1-10. Two tables connected by account number.

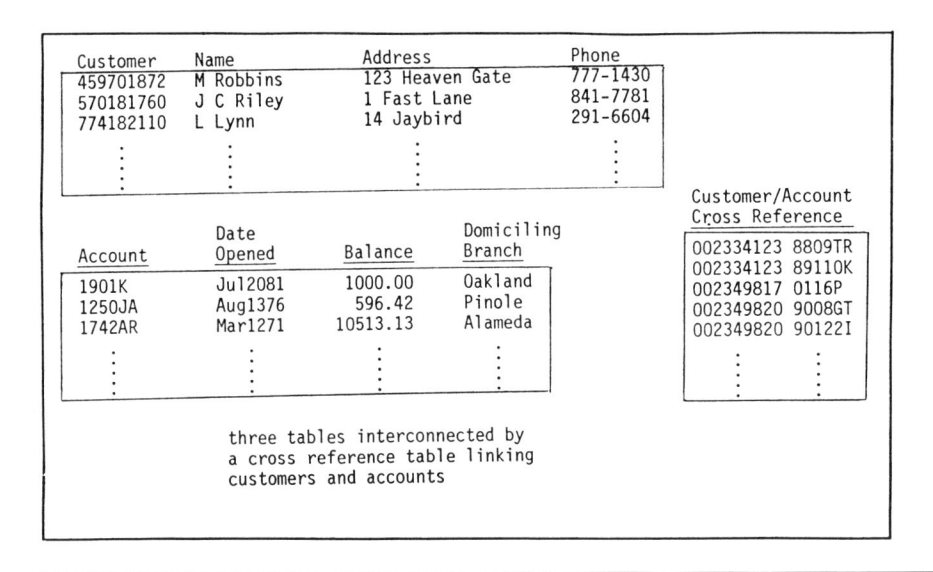

```
Customer   Name        Address          Phone
459701872  M Robbins   123 Heaven Gate  777-1430
570181760  J C Riley   1 Fast Lane      841-7781
774182110  L Lynn      14 Jaybird       291-6604
   ⋮          ⋮            ⋮               ⋮

                                              Customer/Account
            Date                 Domiciling   Cross Reference
Account     Opened    Balance    Branch       002334123 8809TR
1901K       Jul2081   1000.00    Oakland      002334123 89110K
1250JA      Aug1376    596.42    Pinole       002349817 0116P
1742AR      Mar1271  10513.13    Alameda      002349820 9008GT
   ⋮          ⋮          ⋮          ⋮          002349820 90122I
                                                   ⋮        ⋮

         three tables interconnected by
         a cross reference table linking
         customers and accounts
```

FIGURE 1-11. Three tables interconnected by a cross-reference table linking customers and accounts.

ample, a customer can have only one account. If more than one account per customer is desired, a structuring of data as shown in Figure 1-11 is necessary.

In either Figure 1-10 or Figure 1-11, there is easy access only from customer to account. The reverse direction—from account to customer—is not accommodated easily by the structure shown in the example. Only if there is an index on account number, making account number directly accessible, can reverse access be easily done.

The foreign key relationships in DB2 are actuated by application code, by DB2-supported referential integrity, or by DB2 views, which will be discussed later. The programmer must be aware of the relationships between databases and must actively build the relationships through application code or through DB2 referential integrity features.

SEPARATION OF AD HOC PROCESSING

To achieve good, consistent response time in the DB2 environment, it is necessary to separate short-running activities (such as normal online transactions) from long-running activities (such as ad hoc queries or relational joins and projects). In the same vein, workloads

State 1

Ad hoc and production ac-
tivities are mixed in the
same processor at the same
time. This configuration
yields good performance
only when there is a very
light load of activities.

State 2

Ad hoc activities are run during
off-peak hours while production
activities are run during the
peak period processing hours. In
such a fashion the same data can
be used to serve both environments.

State 3

Ad hoc activities are run on one
machine and production activities
are run on another. Different data
serves each environment, but there
is no conflict in peak period
processing.

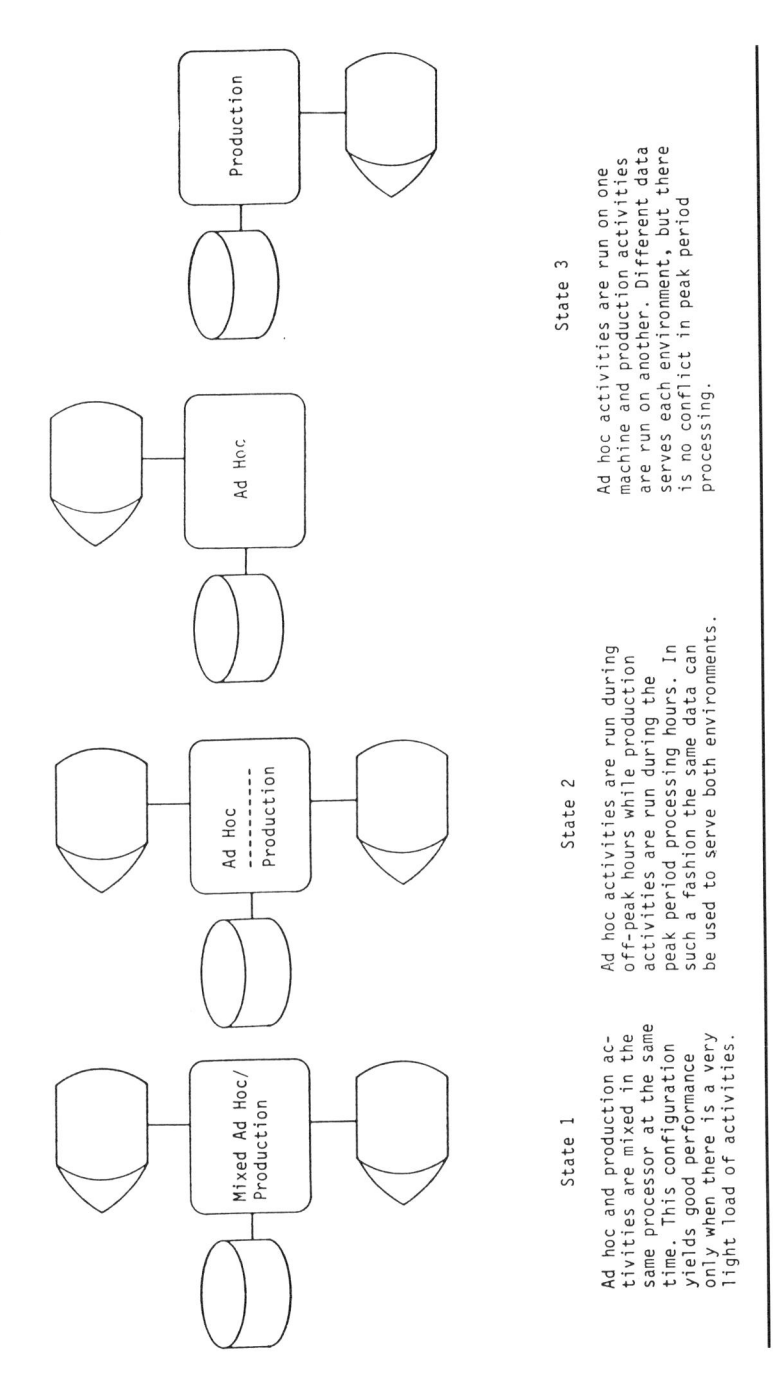

FIGURE 1–12. Possible configurations in the DB2 production environment.

whose resource consumption is predictable need to be separated from workloads whose resource consumption is unpredictable.

When long-running and short-running activities are allowed to mix with each other, the result is that the system runs at the speed of the slowest activity. It is thus essential that the DB2 production environment be properly configured before any online application and development begins. Figure 1-12 shows the different possibilities for environmental configurations.

In State 1 in Figure 1-12, ad hoc and production activities are run together in the same machine on the same data at the same time. As long as the total—ad hoc and online—activity is very light, there is no need to separate the different types of activities. But in the face of any significant amount of activity at all (as is typical of the production environment), performance degrades quickly.

In State 2 in Figure 1-12, ad hoc activities are run during nonpeak processing hours and production processing is run during peak-period processing hours (usually during the workday). This configuration allows DB2 to achieve its maximum performance during peak-period processing hours, but restricts the access of the end user doing DB2 processing to off hours.

In State 3 in Figure 1-12, ad hoc activities can be done during the daytime, and production processing can likewise be done during peak-period processing hours, but processing is done on separate machines. Of course, data must be periodically refreshed from the production to the ad hoc environment. But, in this state, optimum performance can be achieved, and ad hoc activities can be run during the daytime.

ENVIRONMENTAL CHARACTERISTICS

In State 2 and State 3 in Figure 1-12, the production online environment is separated from the ad hoc environment. It is in the production online environment that DB2 will achieve its highest levels of online performance. Then what exactly are the characteristics of the DB2 production environment?

1. No QMF access to data will be allowed. Only embedded SQL through either IMS or CICS will be allowed.
2. Only limited DXT processing will be allowed. Certain periods, such as from noon to 1:00 p.m. will be held open for DXT pro-

cessing. Otherwise, DXT processing will not be allowed until peak-period transaction processing is completed.

3. No access to DB2 data will be allowed other than through the standard teleprocessing (TP) monitors.
4. All embedded SQL transactions will be "designed." Chapter 3 contains a complete explanation of what is meant by designed. [Note: The terminology *designed* is somewhat artificial and is used to describe the way an online transaction must be configured. The terminology has a specific meaning in the context of this book. It has been suggested that other terminology for the same concept might be *calibrated*, or *online specific*.]
5. No database alterations—modifications and creations of indexes, additions of columns, etc.—will be allowed during the peak period for transaction processing.
6. All SQL commands used for production online processing will be precompiled.
7. Only limited views of data will be allowed for production online processing. The views allowed will be only for physical subsets of a table, not for views spanning one or more tables.
8. No sorting will be allowed during peak-period transaction processing.
9. No utilities will be run during peak-period processing hours.

During peak-period processing, the activities that are run are optimized for transactions moving through the system efficiently. Such is the discipline required to achieve adequate, consistent performance. But there are facets of the production online environment other than transaction processing. After peak-period processing, DB2 is allowed to process all of the activities otherwise disallowed. In such a fashion, the complete needs for database processing are accomplished.

Nonpeak-period processing turns into the traditional "batch window" in which lengthy batch processes are run without interfering with production online transaction processing. Typically, a batch window exists during off peak processing hours. One of the tasks of the designer is to determine how much batch window processing is to be done and what resources are required. If more batch window processing is to be done than there is adequate time for, the design of the application must be altered. One of the complications of batch window estimation is that ad hoc reporting requirements can vary widely from night to night.

GENERAL PERFORMANCE CONSIDERATIONS

Assuming that the discipline exists to create and maintain a DB2 production online environment, there are, nevertheless, upper limits of performance beyond which DB2 cannot perform. (Note: Every piece of online software has an upper limit, commonly referred to as the maximum transaction arrival rate, or MTAR). On a processor such as a 3090-200, DB2 under Release 2 can run up to 45 transactions per second, assuming that the discipline exists to create a production online environment. Subsequent releases of DB2 and other larger processors will improve on the transaction rate.

It should be noted that if the production online environment is not created and maintained with discipline, then the MTAR for DB2 drops substantially in whatever Release DB2 is on. The production environment is the environment in which the day-to-day transactions of the enterprise are run. The production environment is typified by the management of primitive data in a highly structured manner. Under normal conditions, unstructured processing such as that found in the the ad hoc reporting environment is not considered to be production.

The peak period arrival rate must be carefully estimated by the designer (in conjunction with the database administrator and system administrator) prior to the selection of DB2 as the DBMS of choice. If the peak-period processing rate exceeds the MTAR for DB2, then other high-performance software, such as IMS Fast Path or TPF, should be chosen for the application.

It is noted that peak-period processing is really a system parameter, not an application parameter. For example, if an application designer estimates a peak-period arrival rate for his or her application of 25 transactions per second, then DB2 will comfortably handle the workload. But if the application is to be run on a system that is already experiencing 30 transactions per second at peak period, then DB2 may not be the DBMS of choice or the application designer must find a less heavily loaded processor on which to run.

Peak-period estimation can be difficult. Some of the techniques for the estimation of the peak-period activity include—

- historical comparisons—what other systems have done in relation to the needs of the application to be built,
- analytical modelling—using software packages to simulate a typical day's activity, and

- paper-and-pencil estimates—using common sense and crude measurements to "guesstimate" peak period requirements.

Unfortunately each of these techniques has many pitfalls. For example, a concentrated focus on the technical environment and technical requirements may well yield a good understanding of the details of the technical needs, but the ultimate results achieved will be meaningless unless business needs are factored into the estimates as well. If the efficiency and polish of the new system will attract 50 percent more new customers, then the marginal workload required to handle new customers must be factored into peak-period resource requirements estimates. Focusing on technology and not on the business aspects as well can lead to grossly incorrect results.

SUMMARY

The first step in the establishment of the online production environment is to clearly outline what features and facilities of DB2 are to be used and what features and facilities are not to be used. The rigor demanded of the online environment to achieve good, consistent online performance is such that not all DB2 options are applicable.

The basis for performance in DB2 is the minimization of I/O. I/O consumption can be reduced (in some cases) by an awareness of the physical structures of DB2, the usage of data clustering, and the establishment and usage of table relationships.

Some of the specific limitations of the online production environment are the following:

- No QMF processing
- Limited DXT processing
- Online access of data through standard TP monitors
- The execution of only "designed" transactions
- No database structure changes during the online day
- Execution of precompiled SQL only
- Usage of limited views of data
- No sorting, summing, averaging, etc.
- No utility execution during the online day

QUESTIONS: THE DB2 ENVIRONMENT

1. DB2 runs in three modes. They are _____.
2. Consistent 2-to-3 second response time is characteristic of the _____.
3. Online access to data and a variety of ways to process the data are characteristic of _____.
4. Long sequential batch runs are typical of _____.
5. Production processing is done in _____.
6. Fast response time for production processing is typical of _____.
7. Is response time a large issue for interactive processing?
8. Is response time an issue for batch processing?
9. Besides performance, what else is important in the online production mode?
10. What is response time?
11. Name some of the components through which an online transaction passes.
12. Throughout the day, transactions are sent to the computer for execution. The time of day when the most transactions are being sent is called the _____.
13. Some typical (non-DB2) online transaction processors are _____.
14. Some non-DB2 interactive pieces of software are _____.
15. For the online production DB2 environment, how critical is consistency of response time?
16. DB2 can be accessed in batch through _____.
17. DB2 can be accessed online through _____.
18. DL-1 databases can be extracted by _____.
19. When IMS or CICS is used, SQL statements are embedded in _____.
20. Online transactions are prevented from accessing/updating the same data at the same time by the _____.
21. Name some levels that locks can be held at in DB2.
22. To minimize the effects of locking, DB2 has two types of databases. They are _____.

Chapter 1 The DB2 Environment

23. Locking strategy is determined at the moment of _____.
24. Locks are held until _____ is/are issued.
25. Read-only data will never be updated. Consequently, its data and indexes can be _____ packed.
26. Indexes CAN/CANNOT be added or deleted at any time.
27. The lowest unit of information in DB2 is the _____.
28. Fields are organized into _____.
29. Normally, a row holds _____ fields?
30. There are four physical formats for a field. They are _____.
31. If a field can have null values, it will have a _____.
32. Another name for a row is a _____.
33. Rows CAN/CANNOT be fixed-length or variable-length.
34. If a row contains _____ or more variable-length fields, it is a variable-length row.
35. Multiple rows (or tuples) are combined together to form _____.
36. A page IS/IS NOT in physically contiguous storage.
37. A row CAN/CANNOT span multiple pages.
38. Pages are processed in one of two types of buffers. The buffers are _____.
39. A row may be indexed by _____ or more fields.
40. Rows CAN/CANNOT be added and deleted one at a time.
41. Rows CAN/CANNOT be added and deleted en masse.
42. After a row is defined, no more columns can be added. (T/F)
43. When a row is deleted, the space is marked as _____.
44. Pages are arranged into _____.
45. There are two types of tablespaces. They are _____.
46. Simple tablespaces are good for _____.
47. Partitioned tablespaces are good for _____.
48. Partitioned tablespaces can have from two to _____ partitions.
49. Data is organized into pages either _____ or _____.
50. When data is stored sequentially in a page, it is said to be _____.

51. When data is stored randomly in a page, it is said to be _____.

52. When data is clustered, there is a _____ pointing to a field in the row.

53. A page can have _____ index(es) over which it is clustered.

54. Indexes have _____ levels.

55. The three levels of indexes are called _____.

56. The two top levels of indexes DO/DO NOT point into pages.

57. The _____ page level points to where data actually resides.

58. The pointer from the leaf page to the data is in the form of a _____ pointer.

59. The page portion of the page/entry pointer is used to point to the _____ where the data resides.

60. The entry portion of the page/entry pointer is used to point to an entry in the _____.

61. The page prefix ALLOWS/PREVENTS data manipulation in the page independent of the index.

62. Separate DB2 tables are related by means of _____.

63. A foreign key is a _____ between two or more tables.

64. DB2 CAN/CANNOT implement foreign keys at the system level.

65. DB2 implements foreign keys by means of _____.

66. The application programmer is responsible for _____ in the creation of foreign keys.

67. Normal online transactions can be characterized as SHORT-RUNNING/LONG-RUNNING activities.

68. Ad hoc queries can often be characterized as SHORT-RUNNING/LONG-RUNNING activities.

69. Online performance mandates the _____ of long-running and short-running activities.

70. Long-running processes DO/DO NOT belong in the online environment.

71. Long-running processes DAMAGE/ENHANCE online performance.

72. Long-running processes can be run during nonpeak period processing and not harm performance (a) in all circumstances, (b) in no circumstances, (c) under some circumstances. (d) under only very special circumstances.

73. Ad hoc and production activities can be run under separate versions of DB2 with no performance degradation (a) sometimes, (b) usually, (c) workload dependent.

74. QMF access to DB2 WILL/WILL NOT be allowed for the online production environment.

75. DXT processing WILL/WILL NOT be allowed for the online production environment.

76. Database modifications WILL/WILL NOT be allowed during online production processing.

77. SQL commands for the online environment will be (a) dynamic only (b) dynamic or precompiled (c) precompiled only.

78. Views of data across multiple tables WILL/WILL NOT be allowed for online production processing.

79. Sorting WILL/WILL NOT be allowed during online production processing.

80. Utilities WILL/WILL NOT be allowed during peak-period online processing.

81. During nonpeak-period online processing, large sequential jobs are run. They are run in the _____ window.

82. If the batch window is not carefully estimated, online performance MAY/MAY NOT be harmed.

83. If there is not adequate time for batch processing, one option is to _____.

84. If there is not adequate time for batch processing, another option is to _____.

85. The amount of batch processing DOES/DOES NOT vary widely from night to night.

CHAPTER 2

From Logical to Physical Design in DB2

Logical application design is done in many ways. Some people do structured design. Some people normalize data. Some people build entity-relationship diagrams. Each technique of logical design results in its own peculiar data structures and processing specifications.

Unquestionably, the most common result of logical database design is the creation of normalized tables of data. Normalized tables of data have (at the least!) the following attributes:

- The tables contain data elements
- The tables have a key
- The data elements in the tables directly depend on the key of the table for their existence
- There is nonredundancy of nonkey data across the normalized tables.

Normally, many tables are defined at the moment of logical design, and each table contains a modest amount of nonkey data. One of the pressing issues of design is the maintenance of the integrity of the logical model as the logical model passes from conceptual to physical designing. The integrity of the logical model refers to the degree to which the data maintains its logical form as data passes from logical design into physical design. When the structure and content of the logical design passes to the physical design with no changes, the integrity of the logical model has been maintained. When the structure and content of the logical model is significantly altered as design goes from logical to physical, then the degree of integrity that has been maintained is low.

After data elements are collected and normalized, it is common practice to assign physical attributes to each of the data elements. For example, account balance may be DECIMAL(15,2) and customer name may be CHAR(25).

In addition to database design, processing requirements are also collected for logical system design. The processing requirements may call for the merge of two large tables, the editing of another table, and the execution of multiple transactions against another table. The sequence of execution, the algorithms involved in execution, the input to each programming module, and the output from each module are commonly what is gathered up as logical program (or process) design.

There are many ways to arrive at the moment in time where logical design—logical database design and logical program design—passes into physical design—physical database design and actual program specifications. In some organizations, a formal methodology is used. In other organizations, logical design is done by practitioners that have been developing systems for a long time and use only the informal methodology that has evolved in their shop, using what techniques work best for them.

However formally or informally logical design is done, at some point, the design is ready to be transformed into a physical design in DB2.

Physical DB2 database design is important because data is related relationally and because data is accessed set-at-a-time in DB2, and these two characteristics pose special challenges for the developer. Two of the most fundamental issues of physical design in DB2 center around system performance and system availability.

Based on the levels of performance and availability that are desired, there are three levels of physical database and system design in DB2. The three levels of design are—

- the low performance/low availability level—where the maximum number of transactions to be handled is less than 10 transactions per second and where data can occasionally stay down for as much as 24 hours,
- the mid-level of performance/availability—where the maximum number of transactions to be handled is less than 25 transactions per second but more than 10 transactions per second, or where

data can occasionally be down for as long as 4 hours but not as long as 24 hours,
- the high level of performance/availability—where the maximum number of transactions to be handled is greater than 25 transactions per second or where data cannot be down for as much as 4 hours, even occasionally.

Note that the requirements for mid-level and high-level performance and availability involve two conditions. Meeting either of the conditions qualifies the design for mid- or high-level design considerations. Also note that the transaction rate that is referred to is a cumulative transaction processing rate; all transactions that will be running on the system are taken into account, not just the transactions that are being designed or developed.

Much processing in DB2 will not qualify for high- or mid-level design considerations. For example, decision-support processing usually does not meet the criteria for high- or mid-level design. And most, if not all, batch processing does not meet the criteria for high- or mid-level design considerations. Instead, the high- or mid-level physical design criteria are met almost exclusively by online, transaction processing.

Based on the quantified criteria that have been specified, the designer can create the following simple decision tree:

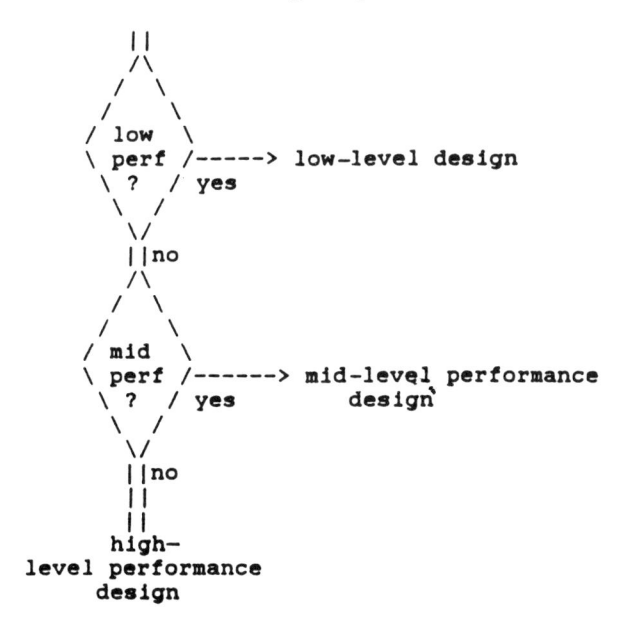

```
         | |
         /\
        /  \
       /    \
      / low  \
      \ perf /------> low-level design
       \  ? / yes
        \  /
         \/
         | |no
         /\
        /  \
       /    \
      / mid  \
      \ perf /------> mid-level performance
       \  ? / yes         design
        \  /
         \/
         | |no
         | |
         | |
        high-
   level performance
       design
```

LOW-LEVEL DESIGN

Low-level system design is simple. Normalized tables are simply turned into physical database designs. Each logical table becomes a physical table, separately defined to DB2. Each logical process requirement is literally turned into a program specification.

In general, indexes will be on the primary key of the table and secondary indexes will be on fields that require access in other than the sequence of the primary key. If data is to be clustered for a given table, then the clustering is done in the order of the primary key.

Program specifications may be drawn up from the general process design that has already been done. When there are no special considerations of performance or availability, the emphasis in program design is on the algorithms that may be translated into programs, the modularity of the resulting programs, and the adherence to the tenets of structured design.

When there is no need for advanced design techniques, the transformation of logical design into a physical design is very straightforward.

MID-LEVEL DESIGN

Several refinements to the general design process are included at mid-level design. The refinements are—

- primitive/derived data separation,
- table separation/consolidation,
- transaction separation,
- control database design,
- thread use, WFI,
- index analysis, and
- clustering analysis.

Primitive/Derived Data/Processing Separation

Primitive data is the detailed data used to run the day-to-day operations of the enterprise. *Derived data* is the data used for the management and direction of the enterprise. In general, derived data is summarized and is calculated either directly or indirectly from primitive data.

Primitive processing is that processing needed to support primitive data. The environment where most primitive data/processing resides is often called the *operational* or the *production* environment. *Derived processing* is that processing used to support derived data. The environment where most derived data/processing resides is called the *decision support* or the *end-user* computing environment.

In general, when primitive data is separated from derived data, the result is that day-to-day operational processing is separated from decision support processing. The separation of processing results in the establishment of two separate environments—the operational environment and the decision support environment. The operational environment is where most of the high-performance transaction processing is done. The decision support environment is where much bulk sequential processing is done. Large summarizations, large joins of tables, large database scans, etc. are done in the decision support environment. The separation of decision support processing from operational or production processing is very beneficial to the achievement of high performance in the operational environment.

The separation of the two types of processing usually has little impact on logical design. In most cases, processes fit naturally into either the primitive environment or the derived environment. In the worst case, the processes that are to be developed are put into one of the two environments. Usually, there is a general affinity between the processes that are in the two environments so that the fit is very natural. However, on occasion, processing requirements must be divided arbitrarily into either the primitive processing environment or the derived processing environment.

Achieving the goals of mid-level performance design requires that NO derived processing be mixed with primitive processing.

Table Separation/Consolidation

Oftentimes, major performance gains are possible in the physical separation or the consolidation of data. (For an in-depth discussion of this topic, refer to the chapter on Denormalization.

For example, when two or more tables are accessed together by a majority of the programs in the system and where the data in the two logical tables can be physically merged together in a meaningful way, then it may make sense to merge the two tables—physically—together. The physical merger of the two tables has the effect of allowing the data in the two tables to be accessed in the same I/O. If the tables are not physically merged, then separate I/Os are required in their access, and performance suffers.

There are several techniques for consolidation of data. Some of the techniques include—

- the simple merger of two or more tables,
- the creation of redundant nonkey data, and
- the creation of arrays in the same row of data.

Whenever these techniques are used, it must be remembered that many trade-offs are implicit to the technique. Some of the trade-offs that must be considered are—

- the extra space that might be required,
- the extra programming that might be required,
- the extra maintenance of programs that might be required,
- the additional complexity that is introduced, and so forth.

The performance advantage that may be gained by employing one or more of the techniques of data separation or consolidation must be weighed against all the disadvantages.

As a rule, when there is a performance gain of 20 percent or more in terms of reduction of I/Os, then the designer should seriously investigate separating or consolidating tables.

The integrity of logical design is not lost when tables are physically merged. However, when nonkey data is redundantly spread across multiple tables, there is a loss of integrity. In general, when nonkey data is redundantly spread across multiple tables at the moment of physical design—

- each redundant element should be considered individually,
- redundancy should be minimized as much as possible,
- there should be a single table where redundant nonkey data contains, by definition, the correct value for the contents of the data element. This table is often called the *system of record.*

Where logical design is translated into an array within a single physical row, there is actually little loss of integrity of logical design. Generally speaking, the only loss of integrity is that each occurrence of data cannot be accessed individually. However, arrays of data can be created from logical designs of data only under certain circumstances. Some of the criteria when a logical design may be translated into an array in a row at the moment of physical design are—

- when there are a regularly occurring number of occurrences of data in the array,
- when the occurrences of data in the array are created in an orderly fashion,
- when the occurrences of data in the array are accessed in an orderly fashion,
- when the occurrences of data in the array are deleted in an orderly fashion,
- when the occurrences of data in the array occupy only a small amount of space,
- when the occurrences of data in the array occupy the same amount of space per occurrence,
- when the occurrences of data in the array are created and accessed, but not created and updated.

The conditions that must be met for placing data in an array in the same row are stringent, so much so that only a few logical tables should ever be physically reduced to an array. Most logical designs will not be able to be physically translated into an array.

Another form of physical design that differs from the mere translation of the logical design into a physical design is the separation of data into several tables. As a simple example, consider a logical design that has grouped together the following data elements into the same table:

- Bank account number
- Date of account opening
- Location of account opening
- Domiciling location
- Account balance

While the data elements may be grouped together logically, they have a vastly different profile of utilization (i.e., probability of access).
There is very light utilization of most of the data elements, such

as date of account opening and domiciling location. However, there is very heavy utilization of the field—account balance—throughout the day. Every time a check is cashed, every time an ATM activity is serviced, every time a balance is queried, the data element—account balance—needs to be accessed. And the value in the account balance changes much more often than the values in the other data elements.

Because of the very different patterns of access of the data, it may make sense to create two tables at the physical design level from the single logical table. The tables would be the following:

Table 1
- Bank account number
- Date account opened
- Location of account opening
- Domiciling location

Table 2
- Bank account number
- Account balance

Once the tables are physically separated, they can be placed in different storage locations. The balance information can be placed in storage that is geared for fast access; the other data can be placed in storage that is not geared for fast access. In addition, because there is so little data in the balance table, there is a good chance that there will be more fortuitous buffer hits on the balance data because the balance of many accounts will be able to be held in main memory.

In general, when there is a performance gain of 20 to 25 percent or more in terms of less I/O, the designer should investigate the possibilities of separating data with very different probabilities of access.

But there is a reason other than performance why tables may need to be divided as the design passes from logical to physical. When tables are to contain lots of data, a major consideration is how long the table will take to recover or reorganize, or how long the table will take to have an index built on the rows in the table. In general, the smaller the table, the faster recovery and reorganization takes, and the quicker indexes may be built.

In order to physically reduce the amount of data in a table, the physical database designer may want to logically subdivide the data into a series of smaller tables without altering the logical design of the tables. For example, suppose a parts table has been specified at the logical level. The logical design of the parts table contains the following fields:

- Part number
- Unit of measure
- Description
- Quantity on hand

One way to subdivide the data is to create a chassis table, a drive train table, a body table, an interior table, and so forth. Each of these tables will be patterned after the same logical design. The difference in the tables is in the contents of the tables, not the structure of the tables. This subdivision is based on the contents of the parts table.

Another typical way to subdivide the parts table is to place all parts whose key begins with "0" in table A, all parts whose key begins with "1" in table B, all parts whose key begins with "2" in table C, and so forth. Each subdivision scheme has its own set of considerations. The net effect of these design considerations is to produce smaller tables (i.e., tables with a smaller amount of data therein contained). Smaller tables are more flexible and can be reorganized more frequently, yielding better performance.

The transformation of logical design to physical design then, in the case of high performance/high availability systems, may well be enhanced by either/both the separation/consolidation of tables at the moment of design.

As a guideline, if the table will contain either more than 100,000 rows or more than one spindle of data, then the designer should investigate the possibilities of splitting data.

TRANSACTION/PROGRAM SEPARATION

Transaction separation requires that program specification consider not just what function the transaction will accomplish but also what resources the program will use in accomplishing the function.

As a simple example of transaction separation, suppose a single transaction were specified to—

- locate the reservations record of a customer,

- determine if a room has been assigned,
- determine the cost of the room,
- determine if there is a corporate discount,
- check to see if there is a floor preference,
- determine whether the customer is an upscale customer,
- determine whether late arrival will be needed,
- verify form of payment.

If the program specification were to be run in a low-performance/low volume environment, then there would be no need to break up the transaction into small components. But if there is a need for high performance, there is a need to take the function that is accomplished and package the function differently. Note that the same function is going to be done in any case; the only thing that transaction separation does is to package the function differently.

For example, the function that is discussed could be packaged into the following discrete transactions:

Transaction 1

- locate the customer's reservations records
- determine whether a room has been assigned

Transaction 2

- determine room cost, corporate discount
- determine whether the customer is upscale

Transaction 3

- determine floor preference
- determine if late arrival is in order

Transaction 4

- determine form of payment

The net effect of breaking up the originally specified transaction into smaller component pieces is that system throughput is substantially enhanced.

As a rule of thumb, if any transaction does more than 50 GET-

PAGEs or more than 40 READPAGEs, then the designer should determine how to subdivide the transaction into units that conform to the suggested guidelines.

CONTROL DATABASE DESIGN

A *control* database is a database that is not directly related to the business function of an application. The logical design of the system may or may not have specified control databases as part of the logical design. Oftentimes, control databases creep into a design late into the game, almost as an afterthought.

Typical control databases include—

- audit databases,
- terminal control databases,
- security databases,
- forms control database, and so forth.

Control databases form an important part of a system design. There is nothing inherently wrong with control databases. However, control databases have a tendency to become a bottleneck if not implemented properly. Control databases can easily cause applications to become single-threaded because of the locking that DB2 does.

Where system performance and availability are issues, control databases need to be implemented carefully. Some of the techniques of implementation that may be used include—

- selective duplication of data,
- separation of data into very fine units of storage, and
- separation of control data into physically different tables.

The effect of separation of control data is that more users of data have access to more data a greater amount of time. In general, the logical design of control databases remains intact in the face of normal implementation techniques.

As a rule, if more than 30 percent of the transactions or programs in the system access the same control database, then some form of lessening the probability of contention must be formulated.

THREAD USE, WFI

In a CICS environment, thread reuse, or, in an IMS environment, WFI transaction specification, is probably in order for performance, sensitive processing. In either case, much system initialization does not have to be done every time a thread into DB2 is used. Of course, in an environment where high performance is not a priority, CICS thread reuse or IMS WFI transactions waste precious systems resources.

If the transaction arrival rate is greater than 10 per second, then thread reuse or WFI is suggested.

INDEX ANALYSIS

In a high-performance environment, indexes must be assigned very carefully in DB2. On the one hand, an index allows a table to be scanned selectively, thus reducing the amount of resources required for the fulfillment of set at-a-time processing. On the other hand, each index costs a fair amount of resources to build and maintain.

As a rule, a high-performance table will have one or two indexes defined for it based on the preponderance of processing going against the database. There may be a few other indexes against the database, but, as a rule, more than four indexes on a large, high-performance table is unusual.

A useful option is the sparse index (see chap. 1) that is possible in DB2 (built at the application level). Designed properly, the sparse index can save massive amounts of processing.

The assignment of indexes is otherwise not a large issue in the transformation of logical design into physical design.

CLUSTERING TABLES

Another consideration of large, high-performance tables is that of the clustering of data. Clustering data can save considerable I/O where data with like keys are accessed together. Of course, one of the limitations of clustering is that there can be only one order (key) in which clustering can be done. And another difficulty with clustering is that data management becomes more of an issue where the data that is clustered has insert and delete activities against the table.

Clustering of data is not a large issue in the transformation of logical design into physical design.

VERY HIGH PERFORMANCE/
VERY HIGH AVAILABILITY

Many of the considerations for very high performance systems are the same for high performance systems. The difference between the design of a high performance system and very high performance system is a matter of degree. If a high performance system has its data split into 5 partitions, a very high performance system may have its data split into 25 partitions. If a high performance system has its transactions divided into executable units that do no more than 50 physical I/Os per transaction, then a very high performance transaction has its transactions divided into units that do no more than 5 physical I/Os per transaction. Logical design is no more or no less compromised by very high performance design than by high performance design.

There are, however, some other considerations for very high performance systems. One question is whether the DB2 environment will be able to handle the workload under even the best of designs. As long as there is a need to process under a single processor (or a complex of tightly coupled dyadic or quadratic processors), there is a finite amount of traffic that DB2 can handle.

Generally speaking, DB2 peaks out at around 1.5 transactions per millions of instructions per second (MIPS) under the most streamlined of designs. This very raw measurement must be factored in light of many factors, such as the design of the database, whether dyadic processing or quadratic processing is occurring, and so forth.

If a single-image DB2 environment is not required, then the question becomes: How can the workload be divided to achieve the level of performance desired? In general, DB2, like other database management systems, can handle practically any workload as long as the workload can be split and divided among more than one processor or complex of processors.

The factors that determine whether DB2 workload-splitting can occur are generally related to the following:

- How easily the databases can be divided. If one or more databases must serve most or all of the processing that occurs, then applications are fairly well tied to a single processor. However, if data can be split across multiple machines, then the workload can likewise be divided across multiple machines. The finer the granularity of the data, the better the chance that data can be split over multiple processors.

- How easily the programs and transactions can be divided over multiple machines. After the issue of data is decided, the transactions and programs that use the data are considered next. In general, the more granular the transactions and programs, the better the chance that the processing workload will be able to be divided across multiple processors.

SUMMARY

There are three levels of database and process design, depending upon the characteristics of the system that is being built. The levels of design are the low level, the mid-level, and the high-performance levels of design. Generally speaking, if the performance level desired is less than 10 transactions per second, then standard, low-level design may commence. If transaction performance is between 10 and 25 transactions per second, then mid-level design may be done. And if performance requirements are above 25 transactions per second, then very high performance design is required.

Low-level design simply requires the translation of normalized tables into physical tables.

Mid-level design requires that at least the following areas be addressed:

- Primitive/derived data separation
- Table separation/consolidation
- Transaction separation
- Control database design
- Thread use, WFI
- Index analysis
- Clustering analysis

High-level performance design requires the same scrutiny and practices except that the design practices are carried to a greater extreme. In addition, the subject of workload-splitting becomes an issue as the workload increases.

QUESTIONS: LOGICAL TO PHYSICAL DESIGN

1. The most common practice in the conceptual design of data is _____.

Chapter 2 From Logical to Physical Design in DB2

2. In a normalized table, there are _____ and data _____.

3. In a normalized table, the elements of data directly depend on the key for their _____.

4. Across all the normalized tables in the organization, there IS/IS NOT redundancy of nonkey data.

5. Across all the normalized tables in the organization, there IS/IS NOT redundancy of key data.

6. The result of the process of normalization is the specification of MANY/FEW tables.

7. Usually each normalized table contains FEW/MANY data elements.

8. Normalization provides a foundation for PHYSICAL/LOGICAL design of a database.

9. The logical integrity of a design is maintained when the logical design passes to the physical design with NO/FEW/SOME/MANY/MINIMAL changes.

10. When the logical structure of the data is altered as physical design is done, there is A LOSS OF/NO LOSS OF integrity of design.

11. After normalization, _____ of data are assigned to each data element.

12. Give some examples of physical attributes.

13. There are two aspects to logical system design—data design and _____ design.

14. Name some activities of process design.

15. Name some formal development methodologies.

16. An organization may have FORMAL/INFORMAL/NO development methodologies.

17. The relational aspect of DB2 design—highly normalized tables—leads to poor performance when many tables must be _____ joined.

18. DB2 is oriented towards SET-AT-A-TIME/RECORD-AT-A-TIME processing.

19. Set-at-a-time processing lends itself to poor performance because _____ consumption tends to be so variable.

20. Two aspects of design that the physical designer must be concerned with are _____ and _____.

21. When the system is oriented toward low performance, normalized structures at the physical level of design are all right. (T/F)
22. A system that is oriented towards low performance will have no more than _____ transactions per second at peak processing.
23. A low-availability system can have outages of a database for up to _____ hours.
24. Peak-period processing includes (a) all transactions that will be running through the system at the moment of peak processing, (b) only those transactions that are being analyzed and designed.
25. A mid-level of performance is for transaction processing at peak period greater than 10 transactions per second and less than _____ transactions per second.
26. A mid-level of availability is for databases that can be down on occasion for up to _____ hours.
27. A high level of performance is for transaction processing at peak periods greater than _____ transactions per second.
28. A high level of availability is for databases that can be down for no more than _____, even occasionally.
29. Decision-support processing normally IS/IS NOT considered to be high performance processing.
30. Batch processing IS/IS NOT considered to be high-performance processing.
31. Nearly all high-performance processing is in the domain of _____ transaction processing.
32. Low levels of performance are satisfied by _____ design.
33. In low-level design, normalized tables are directly turned into _____ tables.
34. In low-level design, each process that has been specified is turned into a _____ specification.
35. In low-level design, tables may have MANY/SOME/FEW indexes.
36. In low-level design, tables are often clustered around the _____ of the table.
37. In low-level design, there ARE/ARE NOT special programming considerations that relate to performance.

38. Structured design IS/IS NOT a good practice in program specification for low-level programs.
39. Primitive data is detailed data used to run the day-to-day activities of the enterprise. Derived data ALWAYS/USUALLY/SOMETIMES stems from primitive data.
40. Consolidating tables of data reduces the amount of I/O needed to access multiple tables IN EVERY CASE/USUALLY/SOMETIMES.
41. Separating normalized tables CAN/CANNOT be used as a technique for the enhancement of physical design.
42. When arrays of data elements are created in a row, the _____ form of normalization is violated.
43. Transactions usually can be SEPARATED/CONSOLIDATED for better performance.
44. Thread reuse in CICS or _____ in IMS will reduce routine transaction overhead.
45. Too many indexes in a mid- or high-level design will hurt performance in two ways—_____ and _____.
46. Too few indexes hurt performance in that, on occasion, entire _____ must be scanned.
47. Primitive data is primarily associated with the _____ environment.
48. Derived data is primarily associated with the _____ environment.
49. Separating primitive and derived data DOES/DOES NOT have a large effect on logical design.
50. Primitive data and its associated processing requires a _____ use of computer resources.
51. Derived data and decision support processing is associated with a _____ pattern of utilization of computer resources.
52. Separating primitive data and processing from derived data and processing provides better performance in at least two ways—_____ and _____.
53. When two or more tables are frequently dynamically joined, physically consolidating the tables reduces the total amount of _____ needed to process against the tables.
54. If two tables are not often accessed together, it DOES/DOES

NOT make sense to physically consolidate the tables for enhanced performance.

55. If a normalized table contains data with very different patterns and probabilities of access, it may make sense to create _____ physical tables from the normalized table.

56. Another way denormalization for performance to occur is to selectively create _____ of nonkey data.

57. When more than one data element is created as an array in a row, MORE/LESS index entries are required to point to the table.

58. When more than one data element is created as an array in a row, an individual data element cannot be directly accessed through the index. (T/F)

59. Data elements can be placed into arrays under most normal conditions. (T/F)

60. When there are a stable number of occurrences of data, arrays of data elements in a row are a _____ idea.

61. The amount of space physically occupied by a data element IS/IS NOT a factor in the decision to place elements of data in an array.

62. In a typical banking environment, the data element "account balance" is frequently accessed, while the data element "location account opened" is infrequently accessed. It IS/IS NOT a good design practice to physically separate the data elements.

63. When account balance is separated from other data elements with which it is grouped as a result of normalization, the physical table that holds account balance CAN/CANNOT be placed in faster, more available storage.

64. The primary consideration of availability is the probability and length of time needed to _____ and _____ data.

65. The larger the table, the LONGER/SHORTER the time required for recovery and reorganization.

66. Physical subdivision of data INCREASES/DECREASES/DOES NOT AFFECT the total amount of data specified by a normalized design.

67. List some ways data can be physically subdivided.

68. Breaking a program up into fine pieces ENHANCES/HINDERS transaction performance.

Chapter 2   From Logical to Physical Design in DB2   43

69. When a program runs only a short while, only a _____ of data is locked by DB2, and the data is locked only a _____ of time.

70. Transactions can be broken up several ways. List three.

71. A control database hinders performance because of _____ probabilities.

72. Name some typical control databases.

73. When a transaction wishes to access data in a control database and the data is locked, the transaction _____.

74. Thread reuse in CICS and WFI in IMS allow transactions entering DB2 to not have to _____.

75. Thread reuse or WFI should be specified whenever a transaction is _____.

76. Very high performance can be accomplished by splitting the workload over multiple _____.

77. The designer should question whether or not DB2 is the right choice for a DBMS in the face of very high performance requirements. (T/F)

78. The techniques for achieving very high performance in DB2 are the same as the techniques for achieving high performance except to the degree to which the techniques are employed. (T/F)

PART II

DB2 Database Online Performance Design

Chapter 3   DB2 Performance 1

- Conceptual Database Design
- From a Conceptual Model to a Physical Design
- Normalized Data Structures
- Indexing Data
- Questions: Database Design

Chapter 4   DB2 Performance 2

- Referential Integrity
- Multiple Occurrences of Data
- Questions: Database Design

Chapter 5   DB2 Performance 3

- Variable-Length Fields
- Control Databases
- Data Views
- Sequentially Accessing DB2 Databases
- Questions: Database Design

Chapter 6   DB2 Performance 4

- Partitioning Databases
- Encoding of Data
- Summary
- Questions: Database Design

Chapter 7 DB2 Transaction Design for Performance: Part I

- DB2 Performance in the Face of "Undesigned" Transactions
- Why Undesigned Transactions in DB2 Damage Performance
- What to Do about Undesigned Transactions
- Characteristics of Designed and Undesigned Transactions
- Data Driven Processes
- I/Os
- Data Contention
- Transaction Issues
- Examples: Designed and Undesigned Transactions
- Questions: Transaction Design

Chapter 8 DB2 Transaction Design for Performance: Part II

- Creating Designed Transactions
- Static/Dynamic SQL
- Embedded SQL
- Summary
- Questions: Transaction Design

CHAPTER 3

DB2 Performance 1

DATABASE DESIGN FOR DB2

Once the production, online environment is established, good, consistent performance on a systemwide basis can become a reality. The next step in the achievement of good online performance is the translation of user requirements into a design in such a manner as to yield good performance. There are two facets in the design of high-performance systems—database design and transaction design. Both facets of design are necessary and equally important to achieve optimal online performance.

CONCEPTUAL DATABASE DESIGN

Most of the considerations of performance in database design occur during physical design. Consequently, this chapter discusses database design at the physical level almost to the exclusion of other aspects of design.

Prior to physical database design, the conceptual foundation for database design (which includes such activities as data modeling, entity relationship analysis, data item set derivation, and so forth) should be laid (for many reasons, among them performance). [Note: For a detailed explanation of conceptual database design, refer to *Information Systems Architecture*, Prentice-Hall, 1986, or to *Information Engineering for the Practitioner*, Yourdon Press, Prentice-Hall, 1988.]

The conceptual design activities that precede the physical database design should have accomplished (at the least!) the following:

- The consolidation of identical or similar data across broad functional areas
- The separation of primitive and derived data
- The organization of primitive data into major subject areas
- The definition of the interface between data and processes
- The recognition of commonality and the preservation of uniqueness of data and processing
- The definition of keys and foreign keys throughout the data structures
- The definition of the boundaries or limitations of the data model and the resulting databases
- Specific data characteristics, such as data definitions, data values, data representations, encoding, etc.

FROM A CONCEPTUAL MODEL TO PHYSICAL DESIGN

After the conceptual design is complete, the next design step is to use the conceptual design as input into physical design activities. Some activities of this intermediate step include—

- identification of the number of occurrences of data,
- identification of the volatility and growth of data,
- identification of the system response time requirements,
- estimation of the projected transaction workload, both in total and during peak-period processing,
- estimation of the amount of overnight batch processing to be done, both on the average and at peak periods,
- identification of annual or monthly periods of peak processing,
- creation/migration/conversion plan formulation, and
- identification of system availability requirements.

Once conceptual database design has been done and the transformation to the physical form of data has been undertaken, the details

Chapter 3   DB2 Performance

of physical database design (with an emphasis on performance) can commence.

NORMALIZED DATA STRUCTURES

Before the designer of a DB2 database begins to think about the technical details of specification of a physical database, a more strategic issue of database design must be considered.

The relational model of data, on which DB2 is based, calls for elements of data to be grouped together so that individual elements of data directly depend on their keys for their existence. In other words, if the key of the data for a specific occurrence of data does not exist, then the dependent data elements do not exist. This brief and untechnical explanation of normalization is best illustrated in terms of an example. Suppose the database designer is to structure the data found in Figure 3-1.

```
Unnormalized Data Elements
date employee attended school       net pay
school attended                     number of dependents
degree sought                       married/single?
major                               special deductions amount(1)
social security number              special deductions amount(2)
employee number                     special deductions amount(3)
cumulative FICA paid                special deductions amount(4)
cumulative annual pay               limits of deductibility(1)
cumulative annual state tax         limits of deductibility(2)
cumulative annual Federal tax       limits of deductibility(3)
date of hire                        limits of deductibility(4)
location of hire                    FICA per pay period
dependent(1) identification         state tax per pay period
dependent(2) identification         Federal tax per pay period
dependent(3) identification         insurer number
dependent(4) identification         liability limits
dependent(1) relationship           date of insurance coverage
dependent(2) relationship           accident coverage amount
dependent(3) relationship           illness coverage amount
dependent(4) relationship           death coverage amount
date of pay(1)
date of pay(2)
date of pay(3)
   :   :   :   :
date of pay(n)
```

FIGURE 3-1. Unnormalized data elements.

From the unnormalized set of data elements, a set of normalized data elements are created—in the case shown, normalized to the first normal form. The first level of normalization is shown with repeating groups removed in Figure 3-2.

The next level of normalization is achieved by grouping data in accordance with the direct existence dependency of the data, as shown in Figure 3-3.

The next level of normalization is achieved by recognizing indirect dependencies of data, as shown by Figure 3-4.

In the grouping of data found in Figure 3-4, any given data element will not exist if the key for the element does not exist. For example, in the Employee Base Table, if employee number 123 exists, then employee 123 will have a date of hire and a location of hire. But if employee 123 does not exist (or never has existed), then there will be no date of hire or location of hire for employee 123.

Figure 3-4 then shows the logical grouping of data according to the rules of normalization. The question then becomes: What if each of these normalized tables is turned into its own relational table? If each of the relational tables are turned into its own physical database, as is certainly technically feasible, what are the implications? The result of literally translating normalized data into physical database design is shown by Figure 3-5.

Figure 3-5 shows that when each of the tables is used as a basis for physical database design, that data tends to be spread across many

```
Normalized Data Elements - 1st Normal Form

date employee attended school      net pay
school attended                    number of dependents
degree sought                      married/single?
major                              special deductions amount
social security number             limits of deductibility
employee number                    FICA per pay period
cumulative FICA paid               state tax per pay period
cumulative annual pay              Federal tax per pay period
cumulative annual state tax        insurer number
cumulative annual Federal tax      liability limits
date of hire                       date of insurance coverage
location of hire                   accident coverage amount
dependent identification           illness coverage amount
dependent relationship             death coverage amount
date of pay
```

FIGURE 3–2. First level of normalization of data elements.

```
Normalized Data Elements - 2nd Normal Form

Employee Number                    (pay history relationship)
Date of Hire                       Pay Date
Location of Hire                   Net Pay
                                   FICA Paid
(dependent relationship)           State Tax Paid
Dependent's Id                     Federal Tax Paid
Dependent's Relationship
                                   (insurance relationship)
(pay relationship)                 Insurer Number
Cumulative FICA                    Liability Limits
Cumulative Pay                     Date of Coverage
Cumulative State Tax               Accident Coverage
Cumulative Federal Tax             Illness Coverage
                                   Death Coverage
(education relationship)
School                             (deduction relationship)
Degree                             Number Dependents
Date Attended                      Married/Single?
                                   Special Deduction Amounts
                                   Limits of Deductibility
```

FIGURE 3–3. Second level of normalization of data elements.

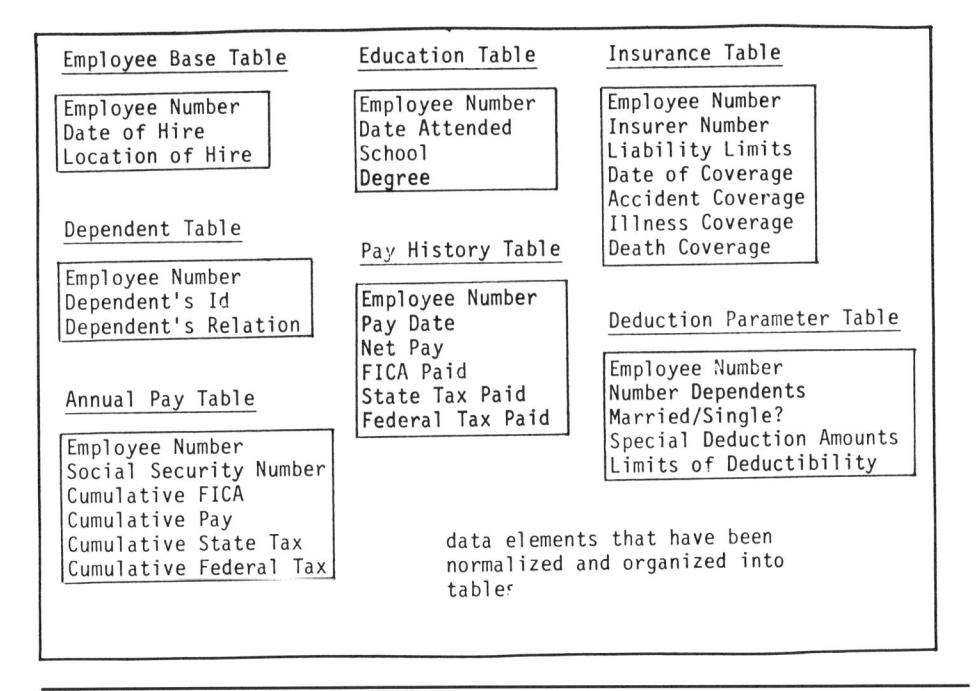

```
Employee Base Table      Education Table          Insurance Table

Employee Number          Employee Number          Employee Number
Date of Hire             Date Attended            Insurer Number
Location of Hire         School                   Liability Limits
                         Degree                   Date of Coverage
                                                  Accident Coverage
Dependent Table                                   Illness Coverage
                         Pay History Table        Death Coverage
Employee Number
Dependent's Id           Employee Number
Dependent's Relation     Pay Date                 Deduction Parameter Table
                         Net Pay
                         FICA Paid                Employee Number
Annual Pay Table         State Tax Paid           Number Dependents
                         Federal Tax Paid         Married/Single?
Employee Number                                   Special Deduction Amounts
Social Security Number                            Limits of Deductibility
Cumulative FICA
Cumulative Pay
Cumulative State Tax            data elements that have been
Cumulative Federal Tax          normalized and organized into
                                tables
```

FIGURE 3–4. Third level of normalization of data elements.

[Figure: Diagram showing cylinders labeled Base Employee Table, Annual Pay Table, Education Table, Deduction Parameter Table, Pay History Table, Dependent Table, and Insurance Table, illustrating the physical spread of data when normalized tables are directly translated into physical data bases.]

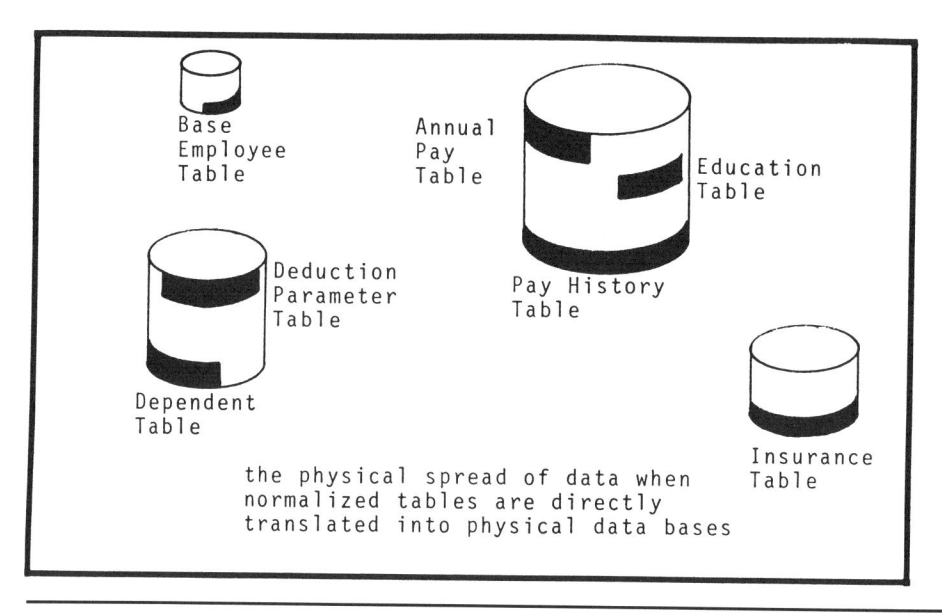

FIGURE 3-5. The physical spread of data when normalized tables are directly translated into physical databases.

physical locations. As long as there is no need to interrelate the data from one table to the next on a frequent basis, then there is no problem. But when data from one table needs to be related to data from another table (or tables) on a frequent basis, the result is much I/O, as each interconnection of data from one database to the next requires a physical I/O (unless, of course, a fortuitous connection of data is made in the buffer area). Figure 3-6 shows the connectivity of data across tables and the resulting I/O.

Figure 3-6 shows the I/O that must be done for each employee to satisfy simple payroll processing. From a performance perspective, the spread of data across different locations introduces much I/O.

A more efficient structuring of data would be to consolidate some of the tables shown in Figure 3-5 into a single table, even though the consolidation violates the rules of normalization. Figure 3-7 suggests one way that the data may be combined to enhance performance.

Figure 3-7 shows that three normalized tables of data have been combined into one. Because of the aggregation, the data will be stored in a single location on DASD. Upon accessing the data for any employee, ALL the data that is stored in the location will be available in the same I/O. The net result of storing unnormalized data together is the reduced need for I/O. The net effect of reducing the I/O re-

Chapter 3   DB2 Performance   53

```
Deduction                                          Annual
Parameter                                          Pay
Table                                              Table


                                            Pay History
                                            Table

    I/O must be done to three separate locations
    when a program wants to use a foreign key
    to relate data
```

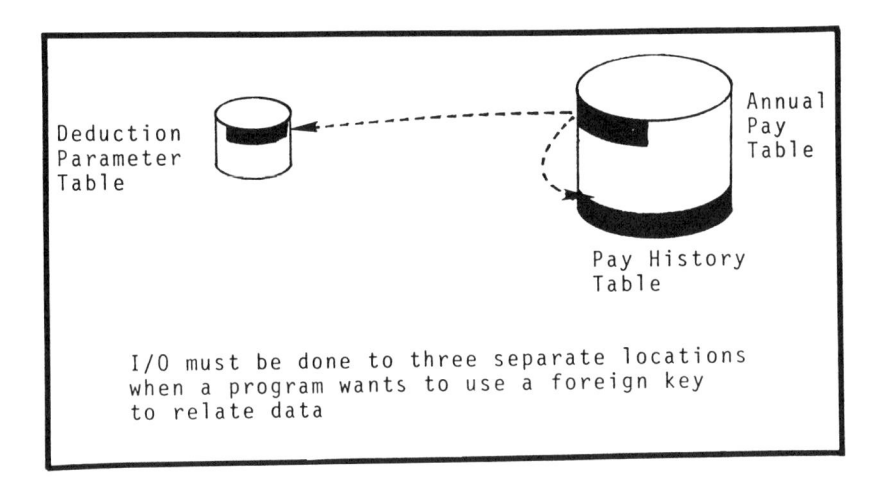

FIGURE 3–6. I/O must be done to three separate locations when a program wants to use a foreign key to relate data.

```
Base Employee Table
Employee Number
Date of Hire
Location of Hire
Number of Dependents
Married/Single?
Special Deductions
Limits of Deductibility
Social Security Number
Cumulative FICA            by grouping base data into a
Cumulative Pay             common table with deduction data
Cumulative State Tax       and annual pay data, the designer
Cumulative Federal Tax     has short circuited the need for
                           I/O that would otherwise be needed
                           to make inter-table connections if
                           data was separated into tables in
                           a normalized form
```

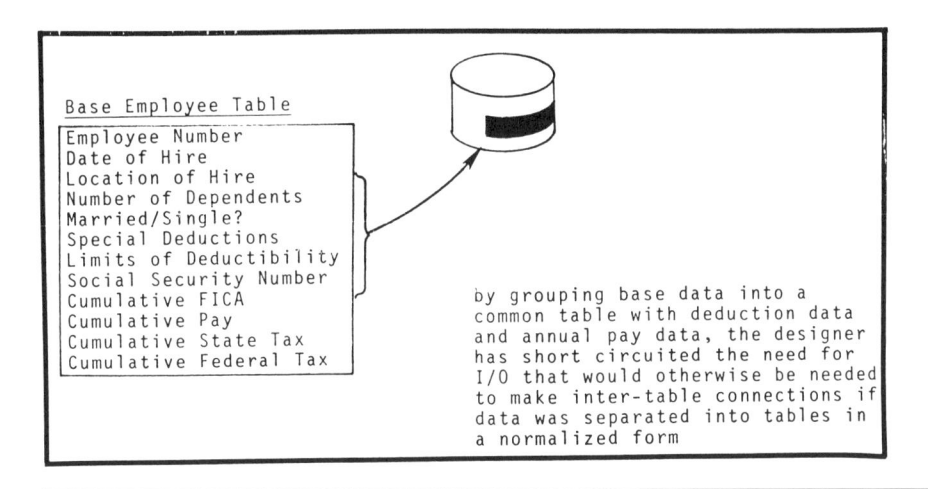

FIGURE 3–7. By grouping base data into a common table with deduction data and annual pay data, the designer has short-circuited the need for I/O that would otherwise be needed to make inter-table connections if data were separated into tables in a normalized form.

quired by a system is the enhancement of performance. Of course, when data is "denormalized," it should be "denormalized" to optimize the most frequently executed process or processes.

The designer should look at all the processes to be executed in the production environment and select the most frequently executed processes for analysis. Then the designer should denormalize the data to suit the needs of the most frequently run processes. The remaining processes that do not have data physically optimized for their execution will have to pay the penalty of I/O for the dynamic interconnectibility of relational data.

Of course, denormalization of data can be carried too far. There is nothing to say that all the data in Figure 3-5 cannot be arranged into a single table and into a single database. But if denormalization is carried to that extreme, another performance factor arises—that of locking of data and the probability of contention. When data is neatly tucked into small, highly-fragmented databases, there is little chance that two or more users will wish to access or update the same data at the same time. But when much data is conglomerated together, as happens in an extreme case of denormalization, then the odds are greatly improved that two or more users will wish to access/update the same data at the same time, thus introducing a negative performance factor.

INDEXING DATA

One of the biggest performance considerations of DB2 is selecting fields for indexing. The issue of indexing fields has two facets: In accessing data, indexes can greatly reduce I/O requirements, but in the change and update of data, indexes can cost I/O. The issue, then, of creating, maintaining, and using indexes is one of a trade-off between the access of data and the update of data.

To illustrate the potential I/O savings of an index, consider the simple relational table shown in Figure 3-8.

Figure 3-8 shows a table that contains an employee's educational history. Consider the I/O required to service the request to find all employees who attended Arizona University.

```
SELECT EMPLOYEE
FROM EMPTAB
WHERE SCHOOL = 'ARIZONA';
```

```
                    Employee Education Table
             Employee    Date
             Number      Attended    School        Degree    Major
             1456        1967        Yale          --        Math
             1456        1970        Arizona       BS        Math
Page 1       1456        1972        Arizona       MS        Com Sci
             1459        1981        Miami         BS        Business
               :           :           :             :         :

             1701        1968        UCLA          BS        Civ Eng
             1714        1979        Harvard       BS        English
Page 2       1714        1984        U Texas       PhD       English
             1743        1980        U Colo        BS        Anthro
             1752        1963        Boston Coll   BA        Spanish
               :           :           :             :         :

                an employee education table whose primary
                key is employee/date of attendance
```

FIGURE 3-8. An employee education table whose primary key is employee/date of attendance.

This request against an unindexed employee's data requires that all rows in all pages be queried. In short, if there are n pages, then n I/Os will be required to service the request.

But suppose the table in Figure 3-8 were indexed for each employee on school attended, as shown in Figure 3-9.

Figure 3-9 shows that with the index (which is highly condensed into a few blocks of data), the query of which employees went to Arizona University is easily answered. The "school attended" index is accessed and based upon the information found in the index; only those pages and rows that are appropriate are physically accessed. In short, instead of accessing all pages and randomly searching for data that fits the criteria, the index allows data to be precisely and directly accessed, thus greatly economizing on the I/Os required to satisfy a request.

But indexes can save I/O in other ways. Suppose the end user wished not to see the names of the employees that went to Arizona University but wished merely for a count of the employees that had attended Arizona University, as per the request—

```
                    Employee Education Table

         Employee    Date
         Number      Attended    School        Degree    Major
         1456        1967        Yale          --        Math
Page 1   1456        1970        Arizona       BS        Math
         1456        1972        Arizona       MS        Com Sci
         1459        1981        Miami         BS        Business
           :           :            :            :          :

         1701        1968        UCLA          BS        Civ Eng
         1714        1979        Harvard       BS        English
Page 2   1714        1984        U Texas       PhD       English
         1743        1980        U Colo        BS        Anthro
         1752        1963        Boston Coll   BA        Spanish
           :           :            :            :          :


         School Index

         Ariz    Ariz    Ariz    Ariz    ArizSt  ArizSt  .........
         page1   page1   page4   page10  page6   page8   .........
         entry1  entry2  entry2  entry6  entry4  entry6  .........

         Harv    Harv    Hofstr  Hofstr  IllSt   IllSt   .........
         page10  page2   page29  page81  page17  page6   .........
         entry4  entry2  entry2  entry3  entry7  entry8  .........

         an index on school allows the employee education table
         to be accessed directly based on the value of the school
         that the employee attended
```

FIGURE 3-9. An index on school allows the employee education table to be accessed directly based on the value of the school that the employee attended.

```
                  SELECT COUNT(*)
                  FROM EMPTAB
                  WHERE SCHOOL = 'ARIZONA';
```

In this case, the query can be satisfied entirely in the index without having to access the primary data. Much I/O is saved by satisfying this request in the index.

As useful as indexes are in the saving of I/O in the access of data, indexes have a corresponding cost, as the data that is indexed changes and needs to be updated. Consider the simple table in Figure 3-10.

The table in Figure 3-10 shows the department in which an employee works. There is an index on department that shows the department of an employee.

Consider the I/O that occurs when an employee changes departments. One I/O must be done to update the primary table; another I/O must be done to delete the index reference from the old department; and still another I/O must be done to the index to insert the reference to the employee's new department. In all, three I/Os were required to accommodate the change of departments. If there were no index by department, only one I/O would have been needed to accommodate the change in data. In general, when data that is indexed undergoes change, two I/Os per index are required to keep the data current.

Another consideration of indexes concerns indexing on data values that occur frequently. For example, in a personnel file, employees may be classified as exempt or nonexempt (having a field content of E or N). Creating an index on a commonly occurring value such as exempt or nonexempt is probably wasteful. When searches need to be done based on the value, it is most likely faster to actually access each page, row by row, than it is to access the data on an index.

```
                              Department/Employee Index
  Employee                          Employee
  Number    Department       Dept   Number   Page   Entry
  1456      43J              001A   0081     109    9
  1607      14BR             001A   0094     029    1
  1995      QA1              001A   0189     208    13
  0121      43J              001A   0971     018    4
   :         :                :      :        :     :
   :         :                :      :        :     :
```

a table showing the department in which an employee works and an index on the employees in a department

FIGURE 3–10. A table showing the department in which an employee works and an index on the employees in a department.

QUESTIONS: DB2 PERFORMANCE 1

1. Physical database design should be preceded by _____.
2. Some of the activities of conceptual database design are _____.
3. Some of the activities of the transition from conceptual database design to physical database design are _____.
4. Data normalization provides a discipline for the _____ of data elements.
5. Data normalization is a fundamental part of the _____ model.
6. The existence of nonkey data depends upon the existence of the _____.
7. First normal form requires that repeating data elements be _____.
8. Second normal form requires that _____ relationships between nonkey and key elements be formed.
9. Third normal form requires that _____ between groups of data be formed.
10. Normalized data can easily be translated into _____.
11. Normalized structures tend to lead to MANY/FEW tables of data.
12. The fine separation of data caused by normalization results in much _____.
13. To consolidate data and reduce system overhead, data can be _____.
14. Denormalization INTRODUCES/DOES NOT NECESSARILY INTRODUCE redundancy of data.
15. If data is consolidated fewer I/Os are used (a) always, (b) often, (c) seldom, (d) never.
16. Overconsolidation of data can hurt performance by increasing the chances of _____.
17. Overconsolidation of data can hurt performance by limiting the _____ path of popular data.
18. Indexing can help performance by allowing data to be accessed _____.
19. Without an index, search for a given value must be done _____.

Chapter 3 — DB2 Performance

20. Sequential searches for data do not harm performance in the face of LARGE/SMALL databases.
21. But most production databases are LARGE/SMALL.
22. _____ I/Os are required to access a single indexed row.
23. When data is _____ on an index, rows in the same page are sequentially ordered.
24. For clustered data, sequential access along the index requires one I/O for index-processing and _____ I/O(s) for subsequent page-processing.
25. When the last clustered row is read, the next _____ must be read to continue sequential processing.
26. When an index is used for clustering, _____ more clustered indexes on the same row may be created.
27. When a field that is indexed is altered, all _____ to the data must be changed.
28. Indexes trade off efficiency of access for efficiency of _____.
29. Some queries can be satisfied by processing in the _____.
30. When a value occurs MANY/FEW times, it may be more efficient to access the pages than the index.

CHAPTER 4

DB2 Performance 2

The designer must constantly be aware of the I/O requirements at update, creation, and deletion time, which are traded off for access efficiency.

REFERENTIAL INTEGRITY

Referential integrity is the capability of a system to keep the relationships between two occurrences of data synchronized in the face of change when data is interrelated by means of a foreign key. DB2 Release 2 depends upon the application programmer to implement and maintain referential integrity. In later releases of DB2, referential integrity can be managed by DB2. DB2, of course, uses primary keys and foreign keys in parent and dependent tables to relate different tables as shown in Figure 4-1.

Figure 4-1 shows three DB2 tables—a parts table, a supplier table, and a supplier/part number cross reference table. Consider what happens when part number 10087-pw is deleted from the parts table. For the system to remain "pure," all references to part number 10087-pw must be immediately deleted in all the tables that reference part number. In the example shown, the supplier/parts cross-reference would need to have the Jones Hardware reference for that part deleted. If the cross-reference is not deleted, then it will show that Jones Hardware is the supplier of a nonexistent part.

From a performance perspective, there are several options in

```
Part Number    Amount    Descriptor       U/M
1987ty-9         560     Manifold         Unit
776t-908       10700     Base Plate       Tub
66509-u           56     Housing Mold     Unit
10087-pw      600900     Bearings         Tub
9978-rtw12      6700     Platform Assem   Tray
   :              :         :              :


Supplier       Address            Contact    Phone
Jones Hdware   123 Main, Dallas   J Cash     555-1212
Emporium       90 Broad, Atlanta  J Carter   679-5142
Wilson St      13 First, Miami    R Acuff    998-0013
Pace Whse      1 S Jstreet, Denver R Clark   077-5519
   :              :                  :          :


Supplier/Part Number
Jones Hdware   10087-pw
Jones Hdware   66509-u
Jones Hdware   887-yt65
Jones Hdware   9987-trqe
Pace Whse      776t-908
Pace Whse      880-887rq
   :              :
```

three relational tables - a parts table, a supplier table, and a cross reference table from supplier to part.

FIGURE 4–1. Three relational tables: A parts table, a supplier table, and a cross-reference table from supplier to parts.

the management of referential integrity. One option is to delete all references to a part when the part is deleted as an integral part of the online transaction. Unfortunately, this might require much I/O in the middle of the online day, thus causing a major performance difficulty. However, repairing the logical inconsistency "on the spot" keeps the data of the system "pure."

If absolute purity (i.e., up to the second accuracy) is not required, then another strategy is to wait until the peak hours of processing have passed, and then repair the inconsistency in the database. The transaction that has deleted the part keeps track of the fact that it has executed successfully and is stored with other transactions that have likewise executed successfully. Then, during nonpeak hours, those transactions are batched together and run against the tables that relate to databases that have been updated during peak-hour processing. Figure 4-2 illustrates these two options.

MULTIPLE OCCURRENCES OF DATA

It is normal for there to be much data managed by a DBMS in a production environment. For example, a customer table may have 100,000 rows, or a parts table may have 10,000 parts. Such are the economies of handling production data under a DBMS. But occasionally data occurs in large enough numbers to require special design techniques. For example, suppose a bank has 100,000 customers and suppose each customer has, on the average, 25 banking activities each month. Now suppose the bank wishes to store 5 years' worth of history per customer in a DB2 database. The number of rows to be stored then are:

$$100,000 \times 25 \times 12 \times 5 = 150,000,000 \text{ rows}$$

This is a large number however implemented, the first question the designer should ask is:

> Is all the data necessary that will be held in such a large database?

An interesting analysis can be made of the probability of access of data. With 150,000,000 rows of data stored, how many will ever be used, and what is the cost of the storage? It is a good bet that much data, once stored, will never be accessed again. The next issue that must be settled is:

> Is the cost of storage effective from a business perspective?

A simple approach would be to create one row for each customer activity, as shown by the database design in Figure 4-3.

A word of explanation is in order for the table in Figure 4-3. The key is customer number, date, and activity number. Activity number is required to force uniqueness of the key. Without activity number, any customer doing more than one activity on the same day would create nonunique keys. While this approach to database design is straightforward, it carries with it some problems that can hamper system performance and availability. If the data is nonclustered, consider the number of index entries required. With one index entry for

64 DB2 Database Online Performance Design Part II

(Diagram)

table update ┊ integrity reparation

option 1 - foreign key reparation during peak processing hours - normally done at the expense of performance

---

transaction storage table update

peak period processing

transaction reparation during non-peak processing hours

option 2 - storing transactions that update, delete, or create foreign keys in a queue and repairing data base intgrity during off peak hours. This option leaves the data bases unsynchronized for a period of time, but enhances performance during peak period processing

---

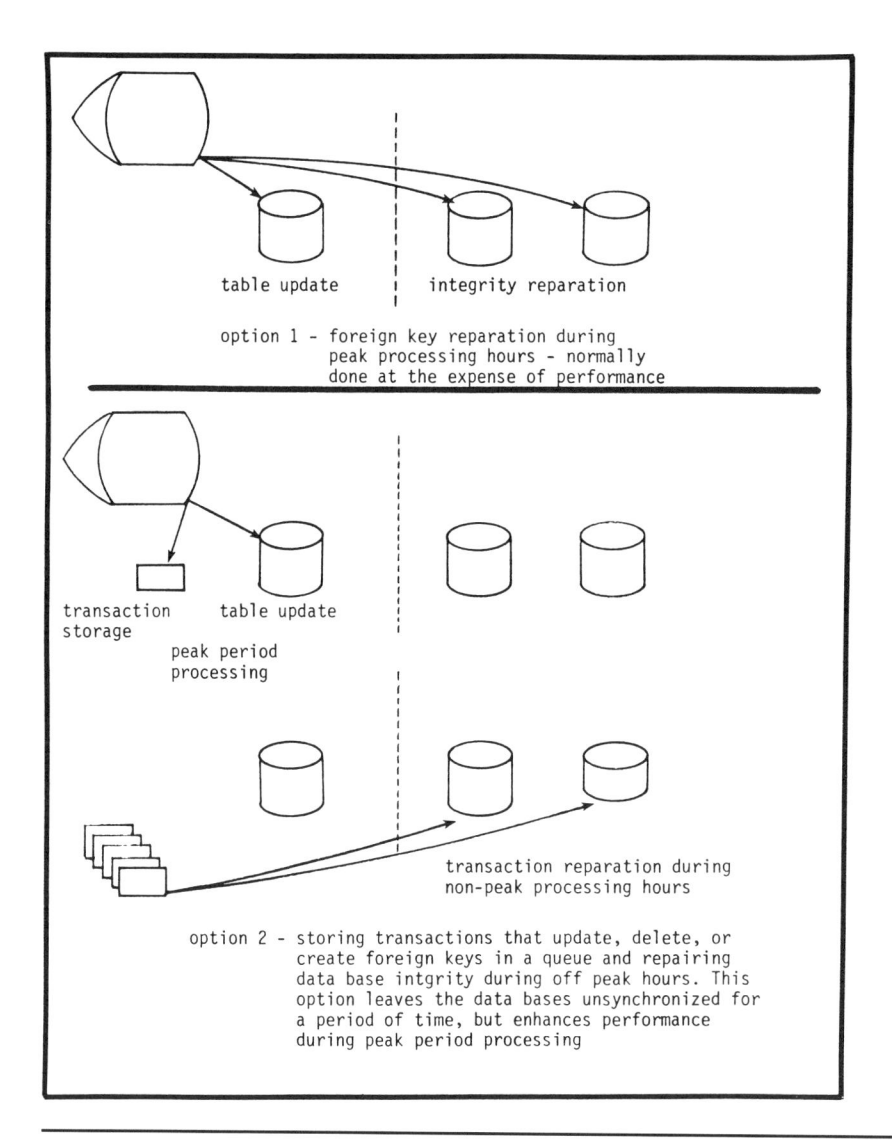

FIGURE 4–2. Option 2. Storing transactions that update, delete, or create foreign keys in a queue and repair database integrity during off-peak hours. This option leaves the databases unsynchronized for a period of time, but enhances performance during peak-period processing.

Customer Number	Year/ Month	Location	Group	1st Day	Amt	2nd Day	Amt	3rd Day	Amt	4th Day	Amt	5th Day	Amt
3341-0	Jun86	AZS	00001	12	136.90	12	1080.87	23	73.97	24	25.00	--	----
3981-8	Jun86	FRW	00001	11	760.00	14	458.00	14	12.50	15	100.00	16	167.98
3981-8	Jun86	FRW	00002	18	90.00	19	15.00	21	100.00	22	35.00	23	5.00
3981-8	JUN86	HGA	00001	15	1000.00	--	----	--	----	--	----	--	----
:	:	:	:	:	:	:	:	:	:	:	:	:	:

a different arrangement of customer activity data that packs the data into the table more tightly. The effectiveness of this approach depends on a knowledge about the customers data and the ability of the data base to be tailored

FIGURE 4-3. A simple design for the table for the banking activities of the customers of a bank.

each row, e.g., 150,000,000 index entries are required. And even if the table is clustered what about the number of index entries that will be required for indexing on nonkey fields?

Consider the work required of the system when the definition of a given field needs to be modified. The new definition of the data must be presented to the system. Then the field must be unloaded in its old format and reloaded in its new format. If the field has an index, the index must be recreated. In short, the volume of data to be manipulated in the redefinition of data presents its own special problems that are brought about solely by the existence of the volume of data.

Now consider what would happen if common usage of the data dictated that several days' banking activities for a customer needed to be accessed, as illustrated by the following request: For customer 1234, retrieve all banking activity for the week of July 20, 1986, to July 27, 1986. Locating the index records does not require a large amount of I/O because the index is tightly packed and contains several levels. But what about the I/O required to access the rows of data? The first row is in page 99, the next row is in page 32, the next in page 45, and so forth. (In other words, even though the index is compactly arranged and efficient to traverse in terms of I/O consumption, the data pointed to by the index is widely dispersed and requires much I/O) for its access). As long as the rows are not clustered, going from one row to the next requires one I/O per row (because each row is in a physically different page), and for a significant number of rows, the I/O consumed mounts quickly.

Now suppose the rows were clustered. This means that going from one row to the next does not require I/O unless, of course, a new page is encountered. And there are fewer index entries for the index pointing to the primary key. So clustering of data is the first step towards managing a large amount of data.

But there are other design options that can be utilized as well. One such option is depicted by Figure 4-4.

Several features of the design in Figure 4-4 enhance performance. The primary key of the table shown is customer number, year/month of activity, location, and group number. Following the key are up to five occurrences of data, showing the actual date of the month of the activity and the amount of the activity. When there are less than five occurrences of activities of the same key, null values are used. When there are more than five activities for a customer/year/month/location, then a new group of activities is created, thus building a new row with a unique key.

Some of the efficiencies of this structuring of data include the following:

- Many fewer index entries, regardless of whether the rows are clustered or not. Roughly one fourth of the index entries will be needed in the example shown.

- Data is compacted. Redundant occurrences of data, such as month and year, have been eliminated.

Customer Number	Year/Month	Location	Group	1st Day	Amt	2nd Day	Amt	3rd Day	Amt	4th Day	Amt	5th Day	Amt
3341-0	Jun86	AZS	00001	12	136.90	12	1080.87	23	73.97	24	25.00	--	----
3981-8	Jun86	FRW	00001	11	760.00	14	458.00	14	12.50	15	100.00	16	167.98
3981-8	Jun86	FRW	00002	18	90.00	19	15.00	21	100.00	22	35.00	23	5.00
3981-8	JUN86	HGA	00001	15	1000.00	--	----	--	----	--	----	--	----

a different arrangement of customer activity data that packs the data into the table more tightly. The effectiveness of this approach depends on a knowledge about the customers data and the ability of the data base to be tailored

FIGURE 4–4. A different arrangement of customer activity data that packs the data into the table more tightly. The effectiveness of this approach depends on a knowledge about the customer's data and the ability of the database to be tailored.

- Once a row is in the buffer, all five occurrences of data will be accessible in every case.

The effectiveness of the design depends greatly on the knowledge of a customer's habits. For example, if a customer frequents many different locations to execute banking activities, then this structuring of data may actually cost performance and space. But as long as customers are creatures of habit and have their own favorite tellers or ATMs, then the structuring of data, as depicted, saves space and I/O.

The selection of the number of occurrences that should fit into any row is not a random selection. The number of occurrences (in the case of the example shown in Figure 4-4) depends upon—

- the physical block size into which the row must fit,
- the number of occurrences of data—the average and the standard deviation,
- the pattern of access of data—random, sequential, etc.?
- the pattern of insertions and deletions, and
- the inability to directly index an occurrence once the occurrence has entered a row.

The designer then has a number of options that are available in the management of large numbers of rows.

Oftentimes when there is a large amount of data, it makes sense to organize data into collections that are active or inactive (i.e., archived). An active database is one that contains data with a high probability of access. An archival database is one that contains data with a low probability of access, usually containing nonrecent historical data. By separating the two types of data during design, the designer circumvents many problems during implementation.

One technique for the management of active and archival data is the placement of active data on the fastest storage device available and the placement of archival data on slower storage devices. In such a manner, the hierarchy of storage is matched with the usage of data.

One useful criterion for determining when data should be archived and when it should not be is whether it makes sense to update the data. Generally speaking, when data has the potential to be updated, it should not be archived, and when data does not need to be updated, it may be archived. This division of data fits ingeniously with the data management technology found in both the operational and archival environments (i.e., operational technology is geared for update, and archival technology is not.)

For a large collection of data, it is not unusual to have five percent of the data in the active database and 95 percent of the data in the archival database. The separation of data makes set-at-a-time processing of the active data viable.

As an example, suppose an insurance company wishes to create a five-year claim-history file. One approach is simply to create a single, large database. Another approach is to analyze what data will be needed the most. The active database typically will be made up of the claims of the last three months, all claims over $50,000, and all claims of selected clients. All other claims are shuffled off to the archival files. Of course, on a periodic basis, the data that is older than three months in the active file is sent to the archival file.

In some cases, a useful technique in the archiving of data, where data is stored in separate locations, is to create an I/O module that knows the location of data. In such a manner, the actual location is masked from the programmer.

But separating large amounts of data according to archival needs is only one way to break up large collections of data. Many other criteria can be used for separation. Some of them are the following:

- Separation by function. Instead of a parts database that contains many rows, several databases can be formed, each of which is smaller than the collective database, but which taken together, logically comprise the large collection of data. A drive train database, a body database, an interior database, a steering database, etc. can be created so that all of the assembly is represented, but is represented in different tables.

- Separation by key range. Suppose a parts database needs to be physically subdivided into smaller tables. One table contains parts whose key begins with "0." The next table contains keys whose first digit is "1," and so forth. In such a manner, a large database can arbitrarily be split into multiple other databases.

- Separation by date. Suppose an archival database is to be created. The archived data can be separated by year, by year/month, by year/month/day, and so forth. The granularity of the split depends on the amount of data and the usage of data.

- Separation by geographical division. A retail consumer vendor can either have a single, large, customer database or several smaller databases that segment the customers according to geographic lo-

cation. The retailer may have, for example, a Northern California database, a Southern California database, a Central California database, and so on.
- Separation by customer classification. A bank can have a single accounts database, or the bank may choose to have the accounts broken up by customer classification, such as commercial accounts, individual accounts (active), individual accounts (inactive), individual accounts—upscale, etc.

From the above examples, it is obvious that the database designer can segment large collections of data in many different ways. Given the set processing orientation of DB2, the segmentation has many advantages.

Some guidelines for the designer in the selection of the proper criteria for separation include the following:

- Are the categories chosen for separation mutually exclusive? If not, more than one occurrence of data may fit in multiple categories. (If an occurrence of data fits in more than one category, then the integrity of duplicate data must be maintained at the application level, something normally not desired.)
- Will the categorization effectively reduce the size of the databases? On occasion, subcategorization appears to reduce the size of the databases, but an analysis at the physical level shows that only a small reduction is being achieved. When the bulk of data is not reduced by subcategorization, nearly all data fits into a single subcategory.
- Will the subcategorization of one database fit with the subcategorization criteria of another database? For example, if in an insurance company all customers are subdivided by geographic region, it may be difficult to subdivide all accounts by another criterion, such as upscale, commercial, active, etc. customers.

QUESTIONS: DB2 PERFORMANCE 2

1. When data has interrelationships, the maintenance of the relationship is known as _____.
2. Referential integrity is done by the _____.
3. When two tables are related and one table has a row deleted, a corresponding row MAY/MUST be deleted.

4. Tables require relationships to be kept up to date instantaneously. (T/F)
5. Referential integrity may be maintained by overnight _____ processing in some cases.
6. Performance of large databases can be hindered because _____ of data may not be done as frequently as needed.
7. Availability of large databases can be hindered because _____ of data may take long amounts of time.
8. Reorganization and recovery can be enhanced by REDUCING/INCREASING the amount of data in a database.
9. Reducing the amount of data in a database, NECESSARILY/DOES NOT NECESSARILY imply less data to be managed by DB2.
10. Logically relating data, while reducing the physical size of any component ENHANCES/HURTS reorganization/recovery needs.
11. Data that is seldom accessed is the first candidate for removal from the production environment. (T/F)
12. Archival data is often _____ from the production environment.
13. Data can be split by _____ range.
14. Key range splits can be done by _____.
15. Splitting of data by key does not affect processes that access ___ rows.
16. Splitting of data by key may have a negative effect on processes that access _____ rows of a database.
17. Not only rows, but _____ entries are a factor in large databases.
18. Using an index to sequence data requires _____ I/Os per index entry.
19. Massive resequencing of a database by means of an index SHOULD/SHOULD NOT be done online.
20. Clustering of data WILL/WILL NOT reduce the number of index entries.
21. One form of denormalization is creating rows with multiple occurrences of data. Multiple occurrences are ALWAYS/ARE FREQUENTLY more tightly packed than in one entry per row existed.
22. Creating rows with multiple occurrences saves space when the occurrences are uniform for every key of the row. (T/F)

Chapter 4 **DB2 Performance 2**

23. Creating rows with multiple occurrences saves space when the occurrences are uniform for every key of the row. (T/F)
24. Creating rows with multiple occurrences wastes space when the occurrences occur randomly for every key of the row. (T/F)
25. Many FEWER/MORE index entries are required when multiple occurrences of data are packed into a row.
26. Total database space is SAVED/LOST by placing multiple occurrences of data in a row.
27. Some of the factors that determine whether multiple occurrences of data in a row is a good design choice are _____.
28. Archival data is data that will never need to be accessed again. (T/F)
29. The future use of archival data is generally KNOWN/UNKNOWN.
30. Generally speaking, archival data is data that MAY/MAY NOT be updated.
31. Name two kinds of archival processing.
32. Generally speaking, there is _____ data in the archival environment.
33. Archival data is stored at the LOWEST/HIGHEST level of detail.
34. Archival data can be placed on a SLOWER/FASTER media.

CHAPTER 5

DB2 Performance 3

VARIABLE-LENGTH FIELDS

One option the database designer has with DB2 is the option of variable-length fields. The proper design and use of variable-length fields is important to performance because the improper use of variable-length fields can lead to unnecessary I/O. In addition, the management of variable-length fields requires a certain amount of CPU overhead. Another cost incurred in the usage of variable-length fields is the overhead of storage required for each variable field. Two bytes of storage are required to identify the existence and length of the variable.

A variable-length field is one that can have different lengths for different occurrences of data. Names and text are common candidates for variable-length fields. As a simple example, suppose the designer has specified NAME as a field in a table. Then the name—JEANNE FRIEDMAN—will require 15 bytes of information for its occurrence as a variable-length field and the name—TF CHANG—will require eight bytes of information for its occurrence as a variable-length field.

There is nothing wrong, per se, with variable-length fields as far as performance is concerned, but instances can arise where variable-length fields can cause much CPU and I/O to be consumed. Consider the following example. The name—JEANNE FRIEDMAN—exists in a table as an occurrence of a variable-length field. Jeanne Friedman marries and decides to take the name of her husband: James Sylvester.

The programmer retrieves the name JEANNE FRIEDMAN and wishes to replace that name with the name JEANNE SYLVESTER. So far, no unnecessary amount of I/O has been expended. But upon trying to replace 16 bytes where there once were 15 presents an opportunity for I/O. I/O is used when the extra byte cannot be accommodated by available free space in the page upon replacement.

If the data is loosely packed (i.e., packed with much free space), there probably is no data management required. But if the data is tightly packed, then, at the very least, the row containing the name for JEANNE SYLVESTER must be replaced within the page. But there may not be room for the new row in the page, and another page must be located where there is available space. Locating that page and adjusting the index does require I/O.

The converse design problem—that of replacing smaller variable-length fields than what was originally retrieved does not cost I/O but does cost space in the database that cannot be easily retrieved. For example, suppose Jeanne Friedman had married Fred Smith and had decided to change her name. To reclaim the space under normal circumstances requires a database reorganization. For all practical purposes, the DB2 page has lost three bytes of data until the next reorganization.

One caution is that variable-length fields can cost I/O or wasted space when, once created, they are allowed to be updated. Of course, if the length of the field is established at the moment of creation of the row and *never* changes, then there is no performance conflict. For example, suppose a title company wishes to list the street address of properties it manages along with other information about the property. Once the street address is written, it is highly unlikely that the address will ever change. But the amount of storage used for one property description and another differs dramatically, so a variable-field definition is in order. The stability of the description is such that the row of data, once created, is very unlikely to change, thus minimizing the problems with I/O or wasted space.

The DB2 physical database design option PCTFREE can be used to alleviate some of the problems of variable length rows. PCTFREE is used in the loading of a table and indicates the amount of free space (in terms of percentages) that is to be left unused after the loading of the first record. If the designer anticipates variable rows with a high degree of volatility, then free space can be left. If, however, the space becomes used or otherwise unavailable, a reorganization of the data must be done to reallocate free space. Note that FREEPAGE, another related DB2 physical database design option, does nothing to alleviate the problems of variable rows flowing beyond the boundary of a single page when the size of a variable-length field changes.

CONTROL DATABASES

While most relational tables contain data that is directly related to an application—such as customer, account, part number data—it is frequently useful to put data that can be considered auxiliary (or utilitarian) in a relational table as well. Such databases can be called *control databases* and typically hold such data as security data, audit data, table data, terminal data, etc. There is nothing wrong, per se, with control databases. But control databases often are candidates for performance bottlenecks.

One of the online features of DB2 is locking of data. Locking prevents two online users from accessing and updating the same data at the same time. Locking in DB2 normally occurs at two levels, the page level and the tablespace level. Furthermore, locking can be done "exclusively" or "shared." When locking is exclusive, no other program can access the data while the data is locked. When locking is shared, read-only access of the data is allowed while the data is locked.

Figure 5-1 shows that user A has accessed and is updating (or at least has the potential for updating) a terminal security table. In the example shown, locking is exclusive and at the page level.

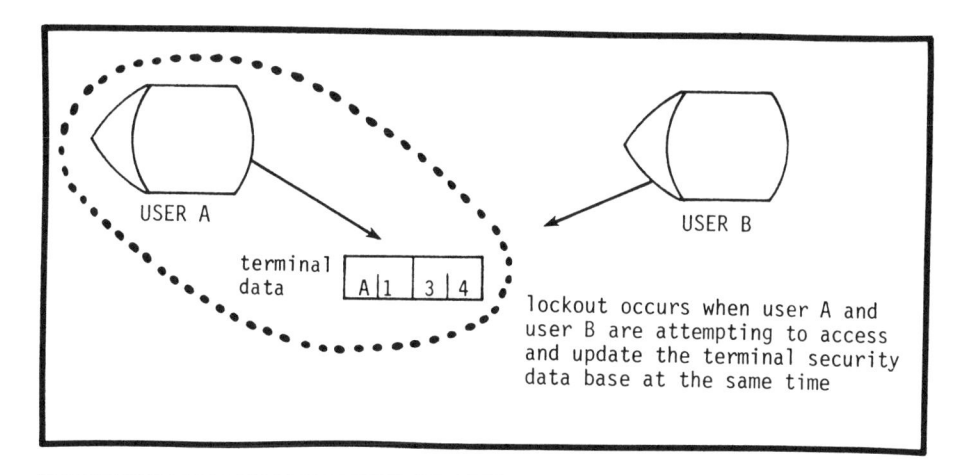

FIGURE 5-1. An example of locked data. Lockout occurs when user A and user B are attempting to access and update the terminal security database at the same time.

While user A is controlling the terminal security database, user B must wait. The two users are in contention for the same data at the same time, and the system is essentially single-threaded. User A must free the terminal security data for user B to be able to continue processing.

There are several solutions to the problems presented by control databases at the design level, depending upon the needs of the application.

One solution is to duplicate the data in the terminal security database, as shown by Figure 5-2. In this case, when user A wishes to access and update the terminal security data, there is no contention with user B because user B is accessing a copy of the data, not the actual data being held by user A. This solution, of course, depends upon the fact that the terminal security data can be duplicated, which is often not the case.

Another option is to subdivide the terminal security data into small units of access and thus physically separate the data (i.e., creating physically separate tables or separating different types of data into separate tables), as shown in Figure 5-3.

In Figure 5-3, there is no contention between users A and B because the users are after different parts of the terminal security database. The design techniques of separation and replication can be used, of course, for noncontrol databases, where contention and locking are potential problems.

It is worth noting that the techniques discussed for the manage-

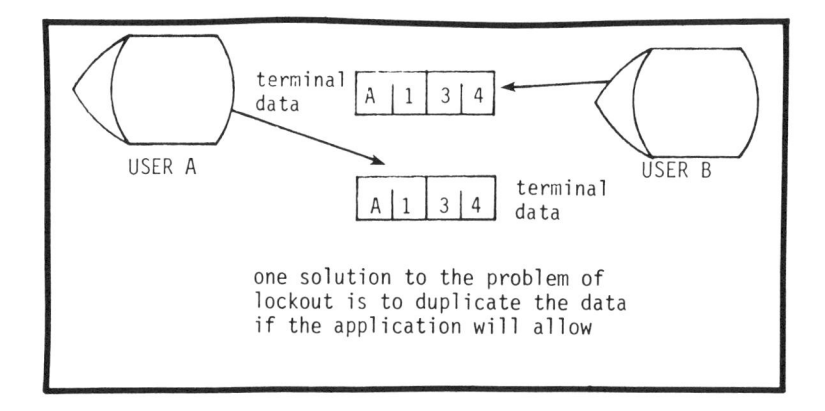

FIGURE 5–2. One solution to the problem of lockout is to duplicate the data if the application will allow.

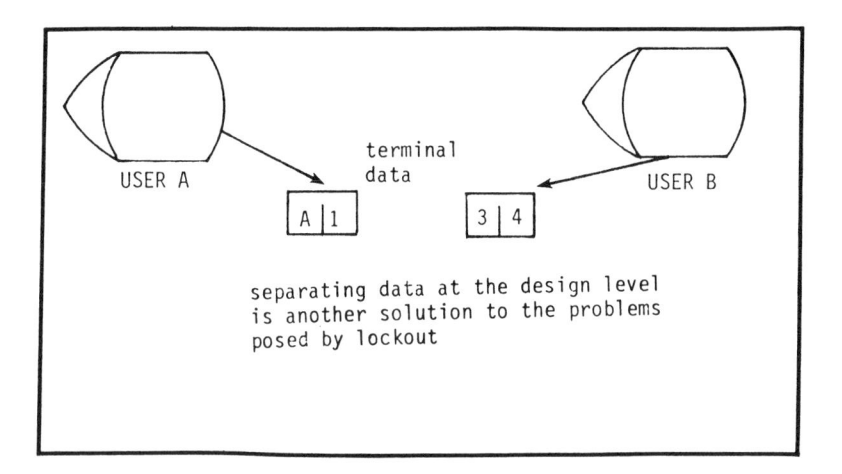

FIGURE 5–3. Separating data at the design level is another solution to the problem of lockout.

ment of control data have their downside. Duplicating data and breaking data down into very fine divisions have implications of integrity, update, program development and maintenance, and so forth.

DATA VIEWS

One feature of DB2 is *data views* (or simply *views*). A view is nothing more than a logical perspective of data, as opposed to a physical perspective of data. Figure 5-4 shows a typical DB2 view of account data and activity.

Views can be useful for creating distinct, easily perceived perspectives of data. But, from a performance standpoint, views can be harmful when the background work done by the system is factored into the view. When a view spans two or more tables, a large amount of I/O may be required to service the view. On one hand, the view appears as a simple structuring of data to the user. On the other hand, the view may require large amounts of I/O to be consumed. As a result, the designer should be careful in the assignment and usage of views. Generally speaking, the designer is safest with presenting data as it is defined in its table.

When views do not span multiple tables, they may actually enhance performance. Consider the table shown in Figure 5-5.

Suppose the fields—account, date opened, and location—were indexed, and the remaining fields in the table were not. The view

```
              Date
Account       Opened        Location      Balance
1456          Jun2374       Burlingame     596.52
1984          Aug1379       San Mateo    11662.45
9721          Jan0181       Sunnyvale       26.62
0112          Jul2086       Palo Alto     1340.91
  :             :             :              :

              Activity
Account       Date          Amount        Form
0112          Oct0186        13.14        EFT
0112          Oct0286        29.36        EFT
0112          Oct0786      1000.00        TJM
0112          Oct0986        78.41        EFT
0112          Oct1586     (2553.53)       EFT
0112          Oct1786        75.00        TJM
  :             :             :            :
```

a view of data -
the account information
and the activity for
October 15 for account
0112. The view spans
two tables

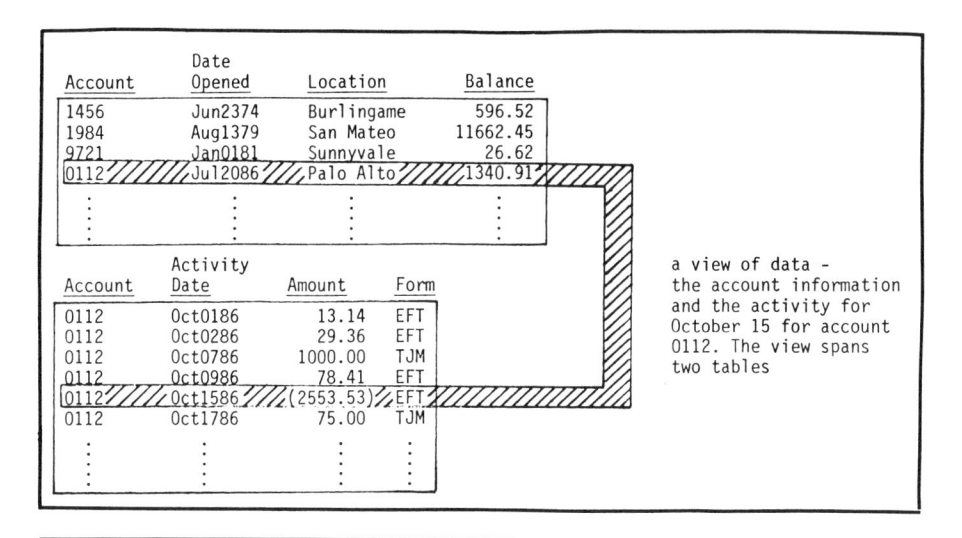

FIGURE 5–4. A view of data: the account information and the activity for October 15 for acount 0112. The view spans two tables.

allows the user to access the table only on fields that are quickly and efficiently retrievable (other than indexing on balance, which is a questionable field for indexing in any case). Because a subset of data is chosen that does not span multiple tables and that does not allow access or retrieval on nonindexed fields, a view may actually enhance performance.

```
                                                       Unique
Account     Opened      Location      Balance   Options  Identification
1456        Jun2374     Burlingame     586.52    AQR       1585
1984        Aug1379     San Mateo    11662.46    ---       JV72
9721        Jan0181     Sunnyvale       26.62    ARM       3081
0112        Jul2086     Palo Alto      137.78    AD        4381
  :           :            :              :       :          :
```

a view of data looking at a subset of
a table

FIGURE 5–5. A view of data looking at a subset of a table.

SEQUENTIALLY ACCESSING DB2 DATA

DB2 data can be accessed either sequentially or randomly. If there is only a small amount of data to be handled, the issue of the basic access path is not terribly important. But in the face of large amounts of data, the designer must carefully choose the basic access path because much I/O can be wasted if the designer fails to make the correct choice.

The first method of organizing DB2 data is in an unclustered fashion, as shown by Figure 5-6.

The index in Figure 5-6 is sequenced and points to data, which is itself randomly organized. Unclustered data is ideal for online transaction processing that must access a single row of data at a time, satisfying such online activity as "what is the quantity on hand of part 20156?"

But if more than one row of data is required (especially if many rows of data are required), then accessing DB2 unclustered data may cost many I/Os, as the satisfaction of one row request through the index to the next may cause an I/O for each row requested.

A second design option is to cluster data, so that as many row requests in one page can be satisfied as possible. In other words, when data is clustered, an I/O is done to retrieve a row. But to retrieve the next row, and the next, and so on, no more I/Os are needed as

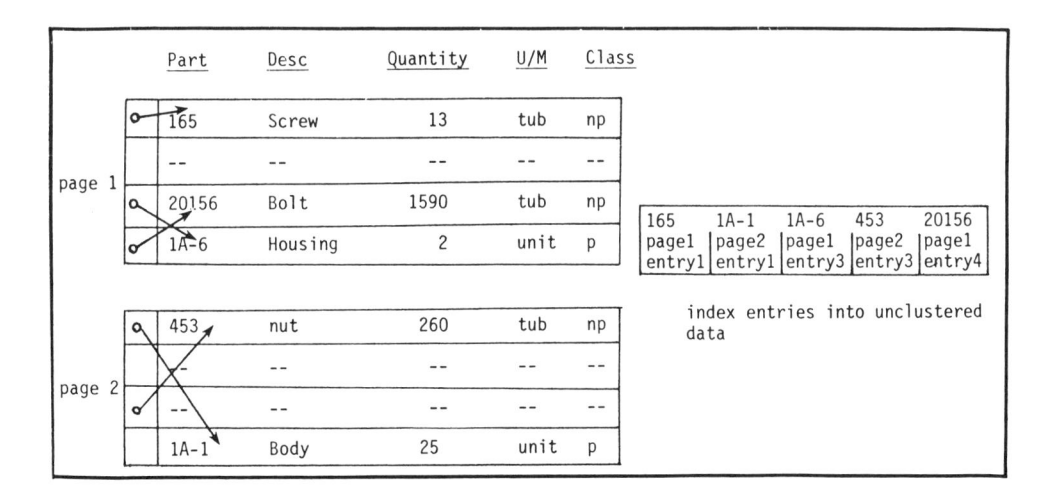

FIGURE 5–6. Index entries into unclustered data.

long as the rows are in the same page and the page is being held in the buffer area. If rows are arranged in a sequence meaningful to the application processing, a minimal amount of I/O is needed. Consider the data in Figure 5-7.

Suppose the application designer desires to go from one part number to the next in sequence. Retrieving part 165 requires an I/O. But no I/O is required for the retrieval of parts 1A-1, 1A-6, and 453 because the page is already resident in the buffer area and doesn't require another I/O. Only when part 20156 is fetched will another I/O be required.

If clustering of data can save I/O upon access, shouldn't all tables, then, be clustered? The answer is no because, upon insertion of data, clustering of data can actually cost I/O. For example, suppose the row for the part number 1A-5 were to be inserted into the small database shown in Figure 5-7. The row must be inserted into the middle of the page, but there is no room for it. As a consequence, part of the data in the page must be moved to other pages and more I/O is required for data management.

But clustering of data has other disadvantages as well.

Consider the I/O required if the part table is to be accessed by means of description. Assume an index is built on DESCRIPTION, as shown by Figure 5-8.

If the parts are accessed in order of description, the effect (in terms of I/O consumed) is the same as if the parts were unclustered.

	Part	Desc	Quantity	U/M	Class
page 1	165	Screw	13	tub	np
	1A-1	Body	25	unit	p
	1A-6	Housing	2	unit	p
	453	Nut	260	tub	np
page 2	20156	Bolt	1590	tub	np
	--	--	--	--	--
	--	--	--	--	--
	--	--	--	--	--

165	1A-1	1A-6	453	21056
page1	page1	page1	page1	page2
entry1	entry2	entry3	entry4	entry1

index entries into clustered data

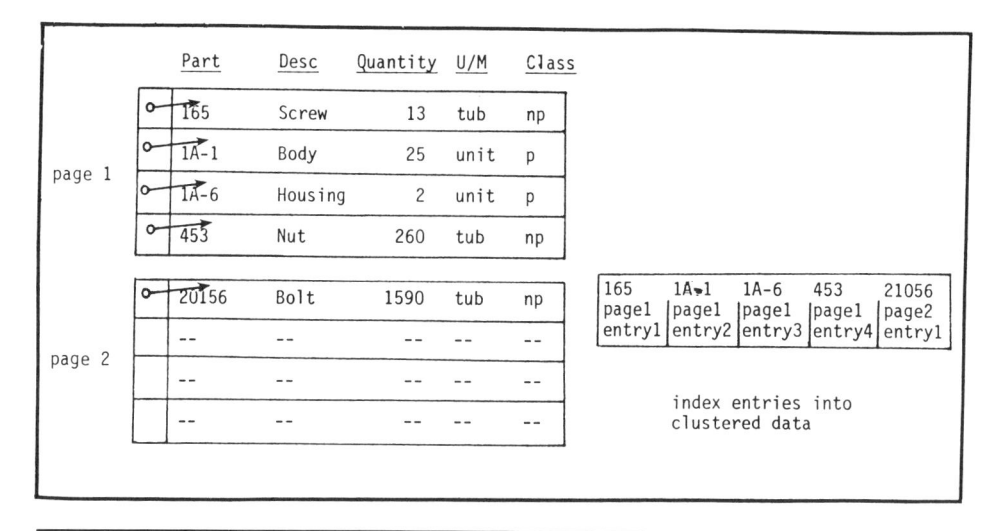

FIGURE 5-7. Index entries into clustered data.

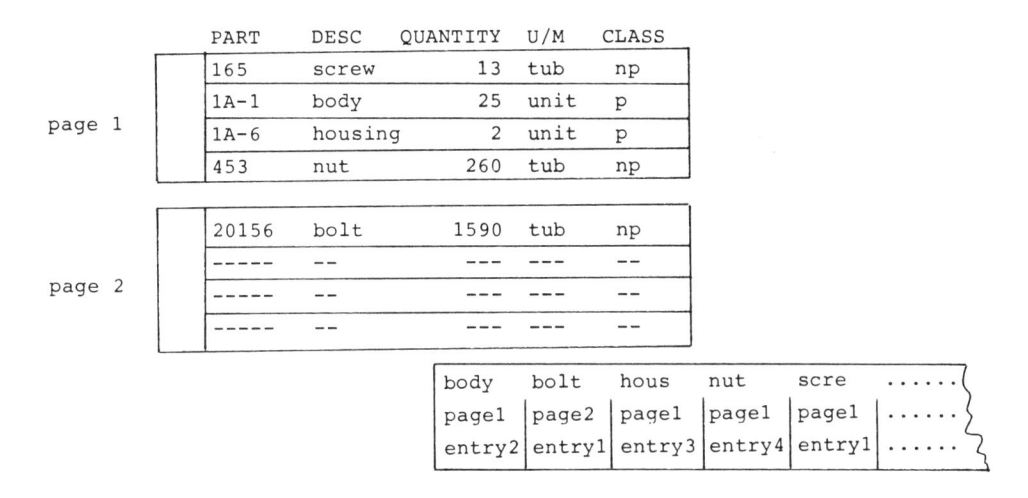

	PART	DESC	QUANTITY	U/M	CLASS
page 1	165	screw	13	tub	np
	1A-1	body	25	unit	p
	1A-6	housing	2	unit	p
	453	nut	260	tub	np

	PART	DESC	QUANTITY	U/M	CLASS
page 2	20156	bolt	1590	tub	np
	-----	--	---	---	--
	-----	--	---	---	--
	-----	--	---	---	--

body	bolt	hous	nut	scre	......
page1	page2	page1	page1	page1	......
entry2	entry1	entry3	entry4	entry1	......

FIGURE 5–8. Index entries into clustered tables on other than a primary key.

Clustering, then, can be used to optimally arrange data in a physical sequence that is propitious for sequential access. But only one physical optimization of data is possible, even though the data may be sequentially accessed any number of ways. It is a temptation to say that an index can be used to sequentially reorder data in a manner other than that used for the clustering of the data.

If ALL the application desires is to see the key values of the index in another order, then an index can, in fact, be used to resequence clustered data. But if more than the key values (or the data that is stored in every index entry) is required to satisfy the query and access of data, then using an index to resequence data is terribly wasteful of I/O, as the I/O required to go from each index entry into the data area can be enormous.

As a consequence, if large amounts of data need to be accessed in a sequence other than in the order in which they are clustered and if there is a need to see more than the mere key value of the data, then it is usually less expensive (in terms of I/O consumed) to enter the data base, strip off appropriate records, sort the records, and create a new table. Figure 5-9 shows two typical stripping techniques.

In Figure 5-9, one algorithm strips the clustered data on part and description data, but does so for all the records. The other algorithm strips all types of data for a certain classification of data. In either case, the resulting data can be sorted and tightly packed so

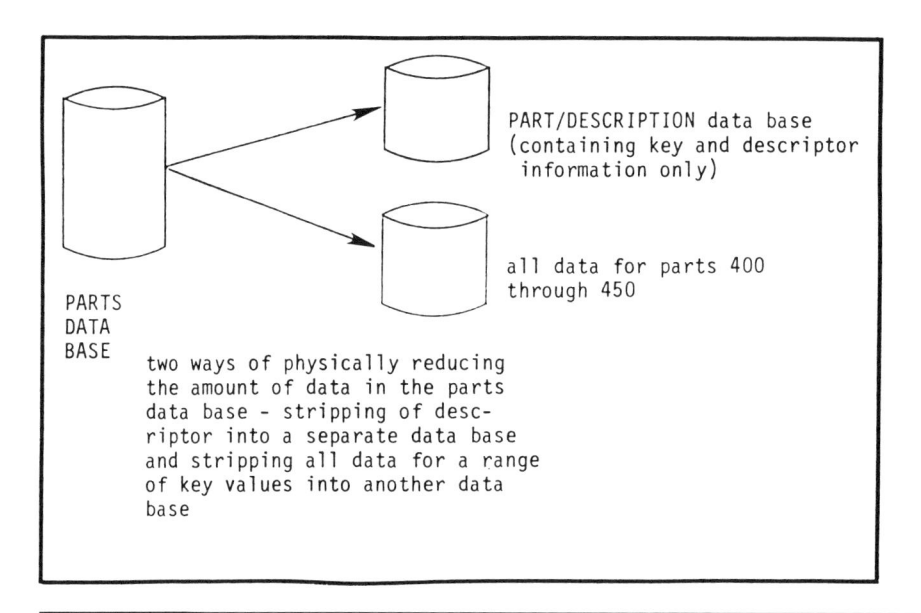

```
┌─────────────────────────────────────────────────────────────┐
│                                                             │
│      ___                 ___                                │
│     /   \              /    \   PART/DESCRIPTION data base  │
│    |     |────────────▶|     |  (containing key and descriptor│
│     \___/        \      \___/   information only)          │
│                   \                                         │
│                    \     ___                               │
│                     \   /    \                              │
│                      ▶ |     |  all data for parts 400     │
│                         \___/   through 450                │
│     PARTS                                                   │
│     DATA                                                    │
│     BASE      two ways of physically reducing               │
│               the amount of data in the parts              │
│               data base - stripping of desc-               │
│               riptor into a separate data base            │
│               and stripping all data for a range          │
│               of key values into another data             │
│               base                                         │
│                                                             │
└─────────────────────────────────────────────────────────────┘
```

FIGURE 5-9. Two ways of physically reducing the amount of data in the parts database.

that efficient access in other than the primary clustered sequence can be efficiently achieved.

QUESTIONS: DATABASE DESIGN

1. Text, names, addresses are often stored in the form of a _____.

2. There ARE/ARE NOT inherent performance difficulties with variable-length data.

3. When variable-length data is accessed at one length and extended to another length, performance may be a problem. (T/F)

4. When variable-length data is created and is not updated, performance IS/IS NOT an issue.

5. When a variable-length field is accessed and is updated with a smaller value, space is usually _____.

6. Variable-length data should always be placed BEFORE/AFTER fixed-length data in a row.

7. Organizing variable-length data that will be updated with a certain amount of free space WILL SOLVE/WILL HELP BUT NOT SOLVE the problems of performance.

Chapter 5 — DB2 Performance 3

8. The DB2 option _____ can be used to alleviate some of the problems of the variable-length data.

9. PCTFREE will reserve free space in every _____ upon loading.

10. A database not directly related to the application but still useful is called a _____ database.

11. Name some typical control databases.

12. Control databases, because of their popularity and frequent usage, are ideal candidates for _____.

13. UPDATE/ACCESS of control databases is the worst offender in the leading to the enqueue condition.

14. Update of data causes the database manager to protect individual records. (T/F)

15. Duplicating of control data is a design option that is (a) never applicable, (b) often applicable, (c) sometimes applicable, (d) always applicable.

16. When there is not much data and the data is not updated in the online environment, then duplication of control data is a viable option. (T/F)

17. Separation of data at the row level, or even at the field level, MAY/PROBABLY WON'T alleviate the problems of control databases.

18. A data view can span _____ or more tables.

19. When a data view spans only one table, it is unlikely that performance will be an issue. (T/F)

20. When a data view spans more than one table, performance (a) is a problem, (b) may be a problem, (c) sometimes might be a problem, (d) is not a problem.

21. The utilities for _____ and _____ form the basis for availability analysis.

22. When a database fails, for whatever reason, it must be _____.

CHAPTER 6

DB Performance 4

PARTITIONING DATABASES

The factors most significant to availability of data are database size and the recovery and reorganization utilities required to support the databases. While a database is being recovered or reorganized, it is unavailable for otherwise normal processing. Therefore, two factors greatly affect the elapsed time required for either utility—database size and complexity. In general, the more data and the more complex the structure (i.e., the interrelationships of structures with other databases), the longer the copy, recovery, and reorganization utilities take to run.

One feature of DB2 is the ability to *partition* databases. A database that is going to contain a large amount of data may be divided into up to 64 separate partitions. The major advantage of a partition is that it can be reorganized or recovered independently of any other partition. If the damage or problem with a database can be localized to a small amount of data, then only a few partitions of data need to be run under the recovery or reorganization utility. Figure 6-1 illustrates the partitioning of data under DB2.

Figure 6-1 shows the difference between a reorganization of a simple tablespace and a partitioned tablespace. The savings in terms of elapsed time required for reorganization is dramatic—from 10 hours to 10 minutes.

Of course, not all reorganizations can be restricted to a small (or

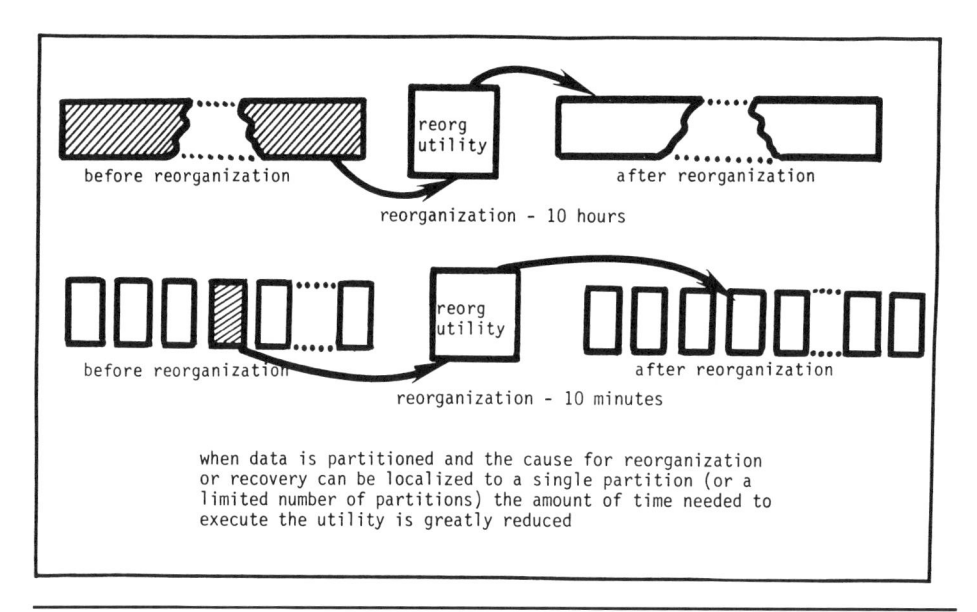

FIGURE 6-1. When data is partitioned and the cause for reorganization or recovery can be localized to a single partition (or a limited number of partitions), the amount of time needed to execute the utility is greatly reduced.

single) number of partitions. In the case where all data must be reorganized (for example, when the structure of the data needs to be redefined), partitioning of data does not reduce the elapsed time needed to reorganize.

The factors that typically lead to a reorganization of data in DB2 include the following:

- The need to reorganize data because of the internal disarray of data. For example, when more updates occur for a table than expected (especially more inserts of rows), then the pages of data and the indexes probably need to be reorganized.
- Changing a nonclustered table to a clustered table. Rows need to be rearranged, and the clustered index must be either built or reconstructed.
- Changing of a field, indexed or otherwise. When the DDL definition of a field changes, the field must be converted to its new size, requiring a reloading into the new format.
- Changing of a field that is indexed. When the DDL definition of a

field changes, the index on that field must be likewise changed and the data reloaded in the new format.
- Addition of columns. If only a small amount of rows will actually have data in the new columns, a reorganization of data may not be necessary. But if large amounts of data are involved in the addition of new columns of data, then a reorganization of the table is probably essential. However, it should be remembered that data cannot be redistributed and partitions cannot be added or deleted.

Databases are connected by a foreign key in DB2, in theory, the connected databases should never be out of synchronization. At the moment of reorganization, it may be prudent and convenient to run a utility that cross-references databases that are connected. Of course, this foreign key utility must be written by the application programmer if the foreign key relationship is built and maintained at the application level.

But partitioning of data can be an asset for reasons other than data availability. Partitioning is for large databases. The data can be broken up into 2 to 64 partitions. Each partition can be placed on a separate physical device. The separation across devices allows the data to be managed asynchronously and independently, thus reducing contention for access. In fact, access can take place in a parallel fashion, thus introducing the possibility of greatly reduced elapsed time in the processing of the access of a set of data. However, the column on which the data is partitioned, once partitioned, cannot be updated at the individual row level (i.e., the row can be added or deleted but not changed, because the column on which partitioning is done serves as the primary key and must maintain its uniqueness).

In addition, when data is partitioned, data that is highly accessed can be placed on high-performance DASD, and data that has a lower probability of access can be placed on slower (or busier!) DASD. In such a manner, the performance of the system can be enhanced.

ENCODING OF DATA

The fewer number of tables, the fewer occasions to have to join relational data. One opportunity the designer has to minimize the number of tables without compromising the design of the system is to avoid encoded data.

A simple example of an encoded value would be the one byte of storage denoting either male or female—M or F. Another form of encoding might be:

1. Headquarters, New York, New York
2. Branch Office, Detroit, Michigan
3. Field Office, El Paso, Texas

When encoded values are used, there may be no need to go from the encoded value to its transformation, and in doing so use I/O.

However, the usage of encoded values is not quite as straightforward as the declaration that they should never be used. The designer should factor in the following considerations:

- Some encoded values are commonly recognizable abbreviations, such as F for female and M for male. When encoded values are self-evident, they can save space and require no I/O.
- Some encoded values are so commonly used within a company that a transformation from the encoded value to the actual value will seldom take place. In this case encoding requires minimal I/O.
- Retrievals requiring translation (i.e., lookup in separate tables) may be a small percentage of total retrievals required in processing the row. For example, a human resources system may encode job class to save space in each row, but only rarely will the printing of the actual job class be required.
- Encoding can save I/O in some cases. Suppose the headquarters of a company is at one location and is encoded as "Hdqtr" throughout the system. When the headquarters is moved from Ithaca, New York, to Buffalo, New York, the change in address need be made in only one place. All encoded references are still valid even though the actual value has changed.
- The length of the encoded transformation may vary widely. This may (or may not) present special data management problems. When the data is encoded, the data management problems are minimized.

From the above discussion it is clear that whether to encode or not is a product of many factors. In general, encoding may cost I/O. But there may exist special circumstances in which encoding offers other benefits that more than compensate for the I/O that might be consumed.

Chapter 6   DB2 Performance 4

SUMMARY

Database design for DB2 assumes that the conceptual foundations for data are in place before the designer attempts to translate the requirements into a physical database design. At the minimum, the conceptual foundation must include the separation of primitive and derived data, the subject orientation of primitive data, and the recognition and consolidation of commonality across disparate functional areas.

Once the conceptual requirements are in place, data elements are normalized, and the denormalization process occurs. Denormalization is done in accordance with the frequency of usage of data.

An issue the physical designer faces is referential integrity, which, in DB2, is either up to the application programmer or managed by DB2. Referential integrity can be an impediment to performance and must be designed with the underlying physical I/Os that are required in mind.

Large databases require special handling for reasons of performance and availability. In general, large collections of data should be broken up into multiple, smaller collections of data.

Variable-length fields have their own performance implications. When a variable-length field is accessed and replaced with more data than was present when the variable field was accessed, then there is potential for I/O needed for data management in the storage of the variable-length field.

Control databases can become a bottleneck to performance when one or more applications are forced to single-thread through a control database, especially where the control database is being updated. Control data can be proliferated or broken into finer units of storage in order to expedite the flow through the database.

Clustering of data, where applicable, can provide a means of minimizing I/O requirements where data is being sequentially accessed.

Encoding of data is a technique that can harm performance if used improperly. Both CPU and I/O resources are used in the encoding and decoding of data.

QUESTIONS: DB2 PERFORMANCE 4

1. It should be assumed that all online data bases, at one time or the other, are going to fail. (T/F)
2. There are a variety of reasons for reorganization of data. Some of them are _____.

3. When a data base is being recovered or reorganized, it is _____ for other processing.

4. The larger the data base, the LONGER/SHORTER the time required for recovery or reorganization.

5. The time required for recovery and reorganization SHOULD BE/CANNOT BE calculated prior to programming and detailed design.

6. The amount of time required for some types of recovery and reorganization can be cut by breaking data into physically fewer units. This technique is called _____ data.

7. Partitioning of data can be done at the _____ or the _____ level.

8. Partitioning will save resources in ALL/SOME cases.

9. For a restructuring of a database, partitioning WILL/WILL NOT save resources.

10. Encoding of data COSTS/MAY COST/SAVES/MAY SAVE I/O.

11. When encoding is done, that data stored in the database is _____ of a larger value.

12. When encoding causes two tables to be physically accessed, then encoding costs I/O. (T/F)

13. When encoding is done, so that tables do not have to be dynamically scanned, then encoding _____ I/O.

14. The decision to encode must be based on all the design factors, such as _____.

CHAPTER 7

DB2 Transaction Design for Performance: Part 1

The first step in the achievement of consistent online performance in the DB2 production environment is the establishment of the appropriate environment. The next step is the proper design of applications. Application design has two components, database design and transaction design. Database design, discussed in chapter 2, centers on arranging data so that a minimum of physical I/O is required in the access and update of data. Transaction design, an equal partner to database design in the achievement of performance, is discussed in this chapter.

DB2 PERFORMANCE IN THE FACE OF "UNDESIGNED" TRANSACTIONS

A "designed" transaction is one that is constructed in a disciplined manner to—

- achieve the user's function, and
- use a minimal amount of resources.

To build and maintain adequate DB2 online performance, all transactions running during the peak online period must be designed.

The importance of designed transactions being mixed in the online workload with undesigned transactions is best illustrated in terms of an example. Suppose a designed transaction, which uses a minimal amount of resources (i.e., I/Os), is represented by a small box or rectangle, analogically representing the usage of a small number of resources. Suppose an undesigned transaction, which uses an indeterminate number of resources—either large or small—is represented analogically by a large box or rectangle, which suggests the consumption of many resources. What happens when these two types of activities—designed and undesigned—are mixed in the same system? Figure 7-1 shows the results.

At 8:00 a.m., when the system is very lightly loaded and a few designed transactions are flowing through the system, system response time is in the 1- to 2-second range. Note that machine utilization is around 10 percent to 15 percent in this time zone.

At 9:00 a.m., the system is fully loaded but is operating only on designed transactions. Response time is in the 4- to 5-second range for all transactions, with machine utilization over 85 percent.

At 10:00 a.m., the system is at its peak usage. In the queue waiting to use the system are many designed transactions. In the

	Processing Queue	Processor	Utilization	Response Time
8 AM			10% - 15%	1-2 Secs
9 AM			85% - 99%	4-5 Secs
10 AM			85% - 99%	2-30 Mins
1 PM			20% - 90%	2 Secs - 15 Mins
7 PM			10% - 95%	overnight batch processing

Processor Utilization in the Relational Environment

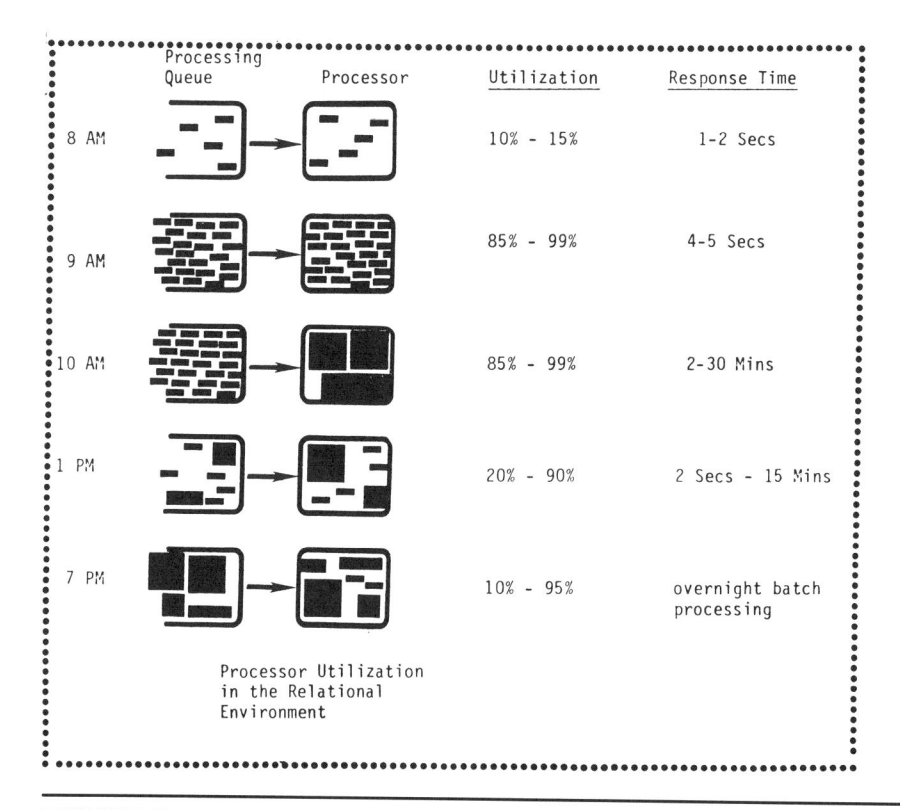

FIGURE 7–1. Processor utilization in the relational environment.

processor are several undesigned transactions that are in execution. The system is running at the speed of the slowest activity in the system, which happens to be undesigned transactions. The speed of the undesigned transactions through the system is indeterminate. Designed transactions that took 2 to 3 seconds at 8:00 a.m. may take 30 to 45 minutes at 10:00 a.m. The designed transactions' speed through the system depends on queue time, which has nothing to do with the resources required by the transaction that is queued, but has everything to do with the resources required by the transactions queued in front of the transaction. (Note: the diagram at 10:00 a.m. is pedagogically designed to show the worst that can happen in online systems.) However, note that machine utilization is high throughout this period.

At 1:00 p.m., in a less fully loaded state, the system exhibits a fluctuating set of characteristics. Some of the time, when there are few undesigned transactions in the system, the system yields good response time; at other times, when there are many undesigned transactions in the system, the system yields spotty response time. Note that system utilization varies widely in this configuration.

DB2 performance, in an unarchitected environment (i.e., where designed and undesigned transactions are freely mixed), is said to fluctuate with the workload. In other words, when the workload has one makeup of transactions, response time is good; when the workload has another makeup of transactions, the response time is bad. The fairly normal state illustrated at 1:00 p.m. in Figure 7-1 reinforces this notion.

Finally, in the evening (in the case of the example, around 7:00 p.m.), the batch window begins and the DB2 environment turns into an exclusively batch environment.

Why do DB2 systems, when fully loaded, exhibit the performance characteristics described by the vignette in Figure 7-1, and what can be done about it?

WHY UNDESIGNED TRANSACTIONS IN DB2 DAMAGE ONLINE PERFORMANCE

In DB2, undesigned transactions damage overall system performance because of the queue time they can cause for other transactions entering the system or executing after the undesigned transactions have gone into execution. In other words, a transaction's largest impediment to overall system performance is the resource utilization of the transactions that are queued in front.

As an illustration of this simple principle, suppose a person wishes to cash a check and goes into a bank where there are two lines—line A and line B—that the person may enter. Both lines are approximately the same length, and both lines are served by competent tellers who operate at roughly the same speed. Which line, then, should the person enter in order to get the best service and to cash a check the quickest?

Suppose that in line A, everyone wants to either cash a check or change a $10 bill, activities that require only a small amount of time. Suppose that in line B, everyone except one person wishes to cash a check. But one person wishes to balance a checkbook and verify every transaction for the last six months with the records of the bank. In this case, line B will be much slower than line A because of the nature of the activities of the people in the queue.

This simple bank-queueing example illustrates the effect of placing an undesigned transaction in a queue with designed transactions. The designed transactions that are queued behind the undesigned transactions run at the speed of the undesigned transactions, which is slow.

WHAT TO DO ABOUT UNDESIGNED TRANSACTIONS

Several options in the management of undesigned transactions are:

1. Recognize undesigned transactions as they enter the system and do not allow them to be queued with designed transactions. This solution makes the assumption that undesigned transactions can be recognized prior to execution and that some queue for the "slow" transactions exists where the undesigned transactions can go where they won't be harmful to performance.

The first assumption—that undesigned transactions can be recognized upon entry into the system—is only very partially true. Many transactions must go into execution before the resources used by the transaction are apparent. But by the time the transaction goes into execution, it is too late to protect online resources.

Furthermore, even if there were a way to recognize undesigned transactions, a considerable amount of resources are required because every transaction, upon entry to the system, must be analyzed to determine whether it is designed or undesigned.

Chapter 7 DB2 Transaction Design for Performance: Part I

The second assumption is that there is a queue in which to send the undesigned transactions to get them out of the way of the designed transactions. If the undesigned queue is one that runs after hours, then there is no problem with online performance. Unfortunately, the problem arises because a user submitting an undesigned transaction must wait until the next day to receive the output from his or her request for processing.

But merely assigning all undesigned transactions their own queue, and then letting the queue operate on online databases in tandem with queues that hold designed transactions opens up other impediments to performance. Shared buffer pools, disk access of data (i.e., arm and head movement), internal integrity mechanisms and facilities, etc. are all shared by online queues of transactions—whether the queue is designed or not. Consequently, performance exposures abound even when undesigned transactions are removed to their own queue and are allowed to access commonly shared data on the same processor as designed transactions.

2. Allow the system to page undesigned transactions out whenever the system reaches the state portrayed by 10:00 a.m. in Figure 7-1. Certainly, when the undesigned transaction is paged out, designed transactions are allowed to flow through the system quickly. But there are some major drawbacks to paging as a solution to performance. The first and most obvious is the resources required for paging.

Paging causes physical I/O just as a regular read or write of a database does. But the problems of paging run deeper. Not all undesigned transactions can be conveniently paged out.

Suppose an undesigned transaction is updating an entire database and is partially through with the update. To maintain integrity of the data, either all of the database updates must be backed out or all data that has been updated and potentially can be updated must be protected against further access or update until the paged program can be reentered into the system. In the case where paging occurs and data is left protected, if one of the transactions that wishes to execute needs to go against the data that has been protected, then deadlock occurs and a real performance bottleneck is created. In the case where a massive backout of database updates occurs, the resource requirements are tremendous. An irony is that once the program is paged back in the updates must be re-applied once again, using even more resources.

Because of the automatic inefficiencies of paging and the problems of database-update integrity, paging is not a popular option.

3. Separation of designed and undesigned transactions by the end user at the moment of entry into the online system. Another option (that, realistically, has limited applicability) is to require the end user to separate designed transactions from undesigned transactions prior to the entry into the online system. Surprisingly, when this option is applicable, it is a very plausible solution. Unfortunately, this option is applicable only infrequently. Requiring end users to separate designed transactions from undesigned transactions requires both a sophisticated and a motivated end user.

Most users lack the background to be able to distinguish an undesigned transaction from a designed transaction. Even the end user who can make this distinction is hard-pressed to say why the separation should be made.

Furthermore, suppressing the submissions of transactions requires a user to sacrifice immediate personal needs for the good of the online community. Most end users do not understand or support such approaches.

Consequently, voluntary separation of end-user requests based on resource consumption is an infrequently chosen option.

4. Creating designed transactions from undesigned transactions at the design level and allowing only designed transactions to run online in the peak processing period is another option. This option, in the long run, easily is the most effective (and ironically the most inexpensive) option.

Furthermore, it is noted that every undesigned transaction can be broken into a series of designed transactions, although at first this transformation capability is not apparent. More importantly, the notion of transforming undesigned transactions into designed transactions fits very closely with the establishment of the production environment, as has been discussed.

CHARACTERISTICS OF DESIGNED AND UNDESIGNED TRANSACTIONS

The preceding discussion explains why online systems are so sensitive to designed and undesigned transactions. In short, under any volume of processing, DB2 cannot tolerate undesigned transactions and sustain good online performance.

What are the characteristics of designed and undesigned transactions in DB2? The primary difference between designed and undesigned transactions is the resource consumption of the transaction, and resource consumption revolves primarily around the I/Os consumed.

In general, a designed transaction will consume no more than 8 to 10 physical I/Os per execution of the transaction. An undesigned transaction may consume an indeterminate number of I/Os—from 15 to 15000+.

DATA-DRIVEN PROCESSES

A word of caution is in order concerning a special class of transactions. Some undesigned transactions consume a small amount of I/O in some cases, and, in other cases, depending upon the data on which they are operating, consume large amounts of I/O. Such transactions are referred to as *data-driven* processes.

For example, suppose a canned query is made where a bank teller can query the monthly activity for an account. John Jones queries his account in 4 I/Os. Mary Smith queries her account in 6 I/Os. And the accounts receivable clerk for IBM queries the IBM account in 15,000 I/Os. The amount of resource consumption of any given transaction depends not as much on the efficiency of the calls of the transaction or the optimization of the efficiency of the path of calls, but on the amount of data on which the transactions operate.

The amount of resource consumption of a data-driven transaction depends on the data on which the transaction operates, not on any superficial analysis by a call optimizer. Data-driven transactions are one of the variables that make distinguishing designed transactions from undesigned transactions prior to execution very difficult.

I/Os

I/Os, then, are the primary resource consumed by transactions that separate designed transactions from undesigned transactions. Why is I/O the most critical factor?

I/Os are the factor that they are because they operate at mechanical speeds—in the millisecond range. Other computer operations operate in the electrical range, at nanosecond speeds. Electronic speeds are about two to three orders of magnitude faster than mechanical speeds. Consequently, the flow of activities in an online environment is constrained by I/O because of the mechanical nature of I/O.

But I/O consumption, as singularly important as it is, is not the only reason why undesigned transactions throttle performance.

DATA CONTENTION

Consider the probability of contention for data in the light of undesigned and designed transactions. A designed transaction accesses a limited amount of data. Because a designed transaction operates on a limited amount of data, the chances are good that the designed transaction will not try to access data that is already locked by another online transaction. Furthermore, the designed transaction will lock up only a small amount of data. And finally, since the designed transaction executes only a small amount of instructions, the designed transaction locks up its data for only a short amount of time.

Now consider undesigned transactions. An undesigned transaction accesses much data. Consequently, the odds are good that the undesigned transaction will attempt to access data that already is locked by another transaction. The differences between designed and undesigned transactions is illustrated by Figure 7-2 and Figure 7-3.

Since the undesigned transaction runs for a long period of time, the odds are good that the data that is locked will be locked for a long period of time. All of these factors increase the probability of contention for data in the online environment.

The solution to contention is obvious. Simply do not allow undesigned transactions to run during the peak period of processing when online response time is critical.

TRANSACTION ISSUES

The DB2 language—SQL—operates on sets of data, not on records of data. To achieve good performance, the designer must structure the usage of SQL so that only very limited sets of data can be retrieved or operated on.

Some of the techniques for minimizing the resources used by a transaction are the following:

- Do not use language structures that will require full or partial database scans such as AVERAGE, SUM, etc.
- Do not use search criteria based on nonindexed fields.
- Fully qualify every SQL query so that the absolute minimum of data is accessed. Ideally, one row will satisfy every SQL call.

Chapter 7 DB2 Transaction Design for Performance: Part I

when each online user requests a limited amount of data, the probability of conflicting with the needs of another user is greatly minimized, thus reducing the number of lock conflicts

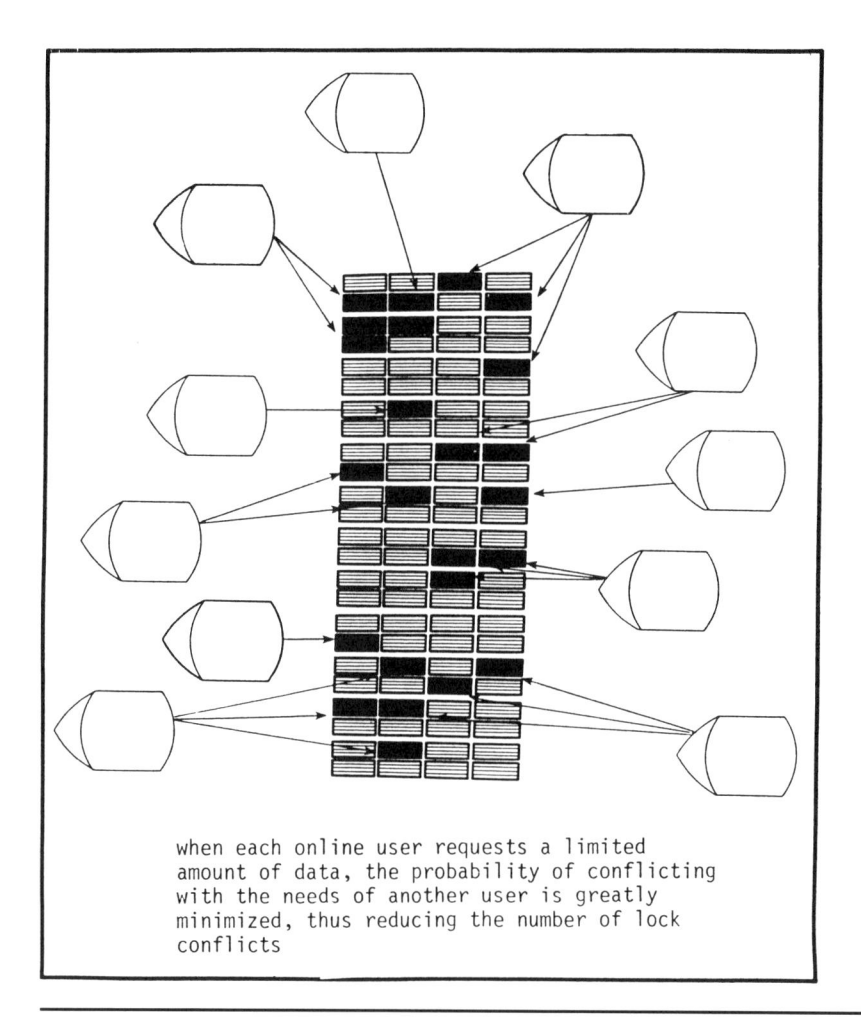

FIGURE 7-2. A designed transaction. When each online user requests a limited amount of data, the probability of conflicting with the needs of another user is greatly minimized, thus reducing the number of lock conflicts.

- When multiple SQL rows are needed, access data as if it were clustered.
- When multiple SQL rows are needed, retrieve no more than 10 rows per execution of the transaction.
- When data must be accessed sequentially on a nonclustered field, access no more than 10 rows for each iteration of the transaction.
- When views are used, do not use views that access data across multiple tables.

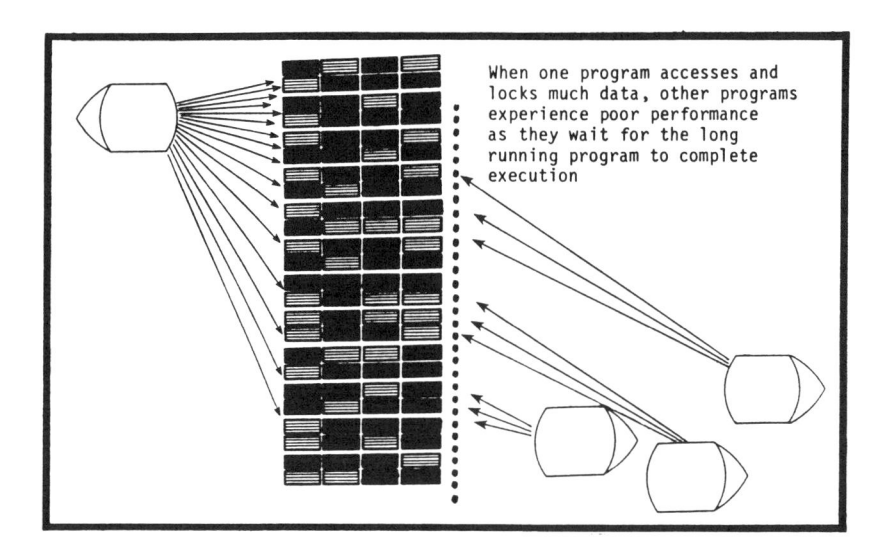

FIGURE 7-3. An undesigned transaction. When one program accesses and locks much data, other programs experience poor performance as they wait for the long-running program to complete execution.

- When foreign keys must be used to relate data, do not use the foreign key relationships more than 10 times in the execution of the transaction.
- Do not access data through QMF; use embedded SQL in COBOL or PL-I only.
- Do not do relational joins or projects during the online peak-period processing.
- Do not do DDL processing during peak-period processing.

EXAMPLES: DESIGNED AND UNDESIGNED TRANSACTIONS

The following illustrates what a designed transaction looks like and how an undesigned transaction may be transformed into a designed transaction. Consider the access of the simple database shown in Figure 7-4.

An example of a designed transaction might be:

```
SELECT PART, QOH, DESCRIPTION
FROM PARTABLE
WHERE PART = '515-9';
```

Chapter 7 DB2 Transaction Design for Performance: Part I

```
Part      Description   U/M    Class   QOH
461-J     Mold          unit   p          45
491-A     Bed           unit   p          13
513-I     Casing        unit   p         186
515-Q     Joint         vat    np      50000
521-T     Brace         box    np        106
521-X     Y-brace       box    np         35
  :          :           :      :          :
  :          :           :      :          :
  :          :           :      :          :

Part number/Inventory table -
primary key - part number,
clustered
```

FIGURE 7–4. Access of a simple database: Part number/Inventory table—primary key—part number, clustered.

The result of the transaction is:

```
'515-q,50000,Joint''
```

From a resource utilization perspective, the question becomes: What amount of I/O was required to process the simple transaction?

Of course, every transaction has a certain amount of overhead I/O—receiving the query from the terminal and sending results back to the terminal represent I/O that is required for every transaction regardless of any other activities. But this ordinary I/O—as long as it is not excessive—is not of great concern to the system developer.

Instead, the system developer addresses himself or herself to the incremental I/O used by a transaction.

In the case of the example, one I/O is required to access the index looking for the key—part number 515-q (assuming the index has not been placed entirely in memory, which is not likely for an index for a large production database). The I/O to the index yields the page number needed, and another I/O is done to find the page that contains the row being sought.

Of course, if, by chance, the page that was being sought was already in the buffer area, no I/O would be needed. In all, a maximum of two database I/Os will be required to service the transaction easily within the bounds of a designed transaction.

As long as all online transactions are within the boundaries of a designed transaction (as far as resource consumption is concerned), DB2 performance will be optimal.

Contrast the simple designed transaction described above with the following data-driven, undesigned transaction. Using the database shown in Figure 7-4 and assuming that there is an index on description, the following SQL request is made:

```
SELECT PART, QOH
FROM PARTABLE
WHERE DESCRIPTION = 'NUT';
```

The amount of I/O needed to satisfy this request is indeterminate and potentially large. If there are 500 parts that satisfy the criteria and if three index pages must be read, then 503 I/Os will need to be done (discounting a few fortuitous hits in the buffer). If there are 10 parts with a description of "NUT," then 10 I/Os plus at least one I/O for the index will be required.

In short, not until the transaction goes into execution will it be known whether the transaction is going to violate the criteria for being designed or undesigned. But certainly 500+ I/Os violates the criteria for being a designed transaction. (Note: This transaction is a classical example of a data-driven transaction and illustrates the difficulty of predetermining designed and undesigned transactions prior to execution).

A third type of transaction is illustrated by the request:

```
SELECT COUNT(*)
FROM PARTABLE
WHERE CLASS = 'P';
```

In this case, the analyst wishes to determine how many parts that have been classified as precious goods (i.e., where class = P) there are in the database. Assume that no index exists on class because it is a commonly occurring value.

The number of I/Os required is the number of pages there are in the database. If the database is large and there are 1,500 pages, then 1,500 I/Os will be required. Unlike the previously discussed transaction, which, depending on the data, may or may not require much I/O, it is predictable that this transaction will be an undesigned transaction for anything but the smallest of tables.

To achieve good, consistent online performance, none of the

undesigned transactions must be allowed to execute during online, peak-period processing.

QUESTIONS: TRANSACTION DESIGN

1. The first step in the achievement of online performance in the DB2 environment is the proper _____ of the environment.
2. Transaction design and database design ARE/ARE NOT important if the online environment has not been properly established.
3. After the online environment has been established, BOTH/EITHER transaction design and database design need to be done.
4. A "designed" transaction MODIFIES/DOES NOT MODIFY user functionality.
5. A "designed" transaction may cause user function to be repackaged. (T/F)
6. Designed and undesigned transactions MAY/MAY NOT be mixed during the online day.
7. Undesigned transactions (a) will never be allowed to run during peak hours, (b) may be allowed, (c) are allowed.
8. When transactions arrive faster than the computer can execute them, the _____ condition has been reached.
9. When the enqueue condition has been reached, response time is a function of two things: how long the transaction takes to execute, and how long the transaction is _____.
10. When a transaction has reached the enqueue condition, queue time is often much LONGER/SHORTER than execution time.
11. Whether a transaction is designed or not depends on the resources used by the transaction. In general, resources used are measured in terms of (a) seconds, (b) I/Os, (c) enqueue time, (d) number of instructions.
12. I/Os are usually the bottleneck because they operate at mechanical speeds and computers operate at _____ speeds.
13. The speed of I/O is measured in _____ seconds.
14. Electronic speeds are measured in terms of _____ seconds.
15. The I/Os a transaction consumes are directly related to the database calls done by the transaction. (T/F)

16. The batch window IS/IS NOT insensitive to the running or separation of designed and undesigned transactions.

17. The interactive environment IS/IS NOT insensitive to the running or separation of designed and undesigned transactions.

18. The online environment IS/IS NOT insensitive to the running or separation of designed and undesigned transactions.

19. If designed and undesigned transactions are separated before entry into the online environment, then performance will not suffer. But separation prior to execution implies that the difference between designed and undesigned transaction can be _____.

20. Once a transaction goes into execution, it is too _____ to recognize that it is undesigned.

21. Even if designed and undesigned transactions can be separated prior to entry to the system, something must be done with undesigned transactions. One solution is to hold the undesigned transactions for processing in the _____ window.

22. But holding undesigned transactions for the batch window implies overnight turnaround. Overnight turnaround is very user FRIENDLY/UNFRIENDLY.

23. Another alternative is to enter undesigned transactions in a separate queue and run them during the day. But separate queues running on the same computer still share resources such as _____.

24. A special kind of undesigned transaction is the _____ driven process.

CHAPTER 8

DB2 Transaction Design for Performance: Part 2

A critical question the developer must ask is whether large batch sequential scans of data should be done during peak-period processing in the first place. Philosophically, what is the business function served by batch sequential scans, and are those scans cost-justified? This question must be thoroughly addressed before proceeding. In general, most sequential processing will be relegated to the off-hours processing window.

But if the user absolutely insists on doing large, batch-oriented database scans online, then, at the very least, those scans must be repackaged to fit within the requirements of the peak-period processing window.

Controlling resource consumption under DB2 is difficult, but not impossible, because SQL does processing of data set-at-a-time. To illustrate the difficulty of the control of resource utilization under normal SQL, consider the following simple SQL program operating against the table found in Figure 7-4.

```
SELECT PART
FROM PARTABLE
WHERE CLASS = 'P' AND PART < '1000';
```

Such an SQL statement would effectively retrieve only parts with a key less than 1,000, where class equals P and probably, depending on the database, would use a modest amount of I/O, however DB2 chose to access the data. Of course, the number of parts retrieved depends upon knowledge of the database. If there are few parts from a key range of 0000 to 1000, then the query will use few resources. If there are many parts between 0000 and 1000, then the selection criteria can be narrowed down to a smaller range, say from 000 to 100. Of course, intelligent range-selection of this type depends on the data being indexed and clustered by part number.

But the program would be a strange one indeed, because, undoubtedly, many other parts exist that satisfy the criteria beyond the key range selected.

In the spirit of using a small amount of resources for each online execution, if the user wished to continue to scan the data, then the user can remember where the last part number was that was accessed, go to that part, and sequentially scan some more parts.

Suppose part 1258-QX were the last part that was retrieved. The following SQL program could then be used to continue the batch scan:

```
SELECT PART
FROM PARTABLE
WHERE CLASS = 'P' AND
PART BETWEEN '01258-QX' AND '02000-ZZ';
```

This process (where the parameters of the set being accessed are reset for every execution) could be iterated for as long as the end user desired, retrieving a small amount of data in each execution of the program and beginning each execution where the previous one left off.

As long as data was being accessed along its clustered field, then the number of parts to be retrieved per iteration may be substantial. Instead, 50 or 60 parts could be retrieved for each iteration because less I/O will be required in going from one clustered part to the next.

But there are some pitfalls to the simple approach described here. One pitfall is that, between executions, the data that is being queried may in fact be updated. For example, suppose, in iteration n, the last part number retrieved was 9409-MZ. Immediately after the nth execution, the part number was deleted by some other transaction. Now, on the n+1th iteration, when the user tries to position the program to part 9409-MZ. Application program logic may be affected by this "disintegrity."

Another assumption the technique of reiterating a large scan of data makes is that the same PLAN will be used for each execution. Under normal conditions, this assumption will be true. But there is no reason why the PLAN may not be changed from one iteration to the next.

The technique described here—that of iterating through a batch sequential scan—has the advantage of requiring only a limited amount of resources and freezing those resources for only a short while. Unfortunately, effective execution of this technique requires a detailed knowledge of the data that is being operated on.

As such, the technique of reiterating a large scan of data is able to transform an undesigned transaction into a designed transaction. But there is a certain amount of overhead associated with the technique. DB2, like all online software, requires a certain amount of initiation and shutdown processing. Each iteration requires this overhead.

Care must be taken with the coding techniques used in the iterating by the end user through a database scan, because DB2 may not yield the desired performance in every case. Consider what would happen if the data were not indexed and clustered. Suppose the very simple SQL query were issued—

```
SELECT PART, UM
FROM PARTABLE
WHERE CLASS = 'P' AND
      UM BETWEEN 'TON' AND 'YARD';
```

In this case, DB2 will scan the entire database for EVERY execution of the query regardless of where the parameters of set delineation are set.

Another approach is to execute only so many instructions and then automatically require the end user to continue processing in off-hours. For example, the (pseudo) SQL program accomplishes this objective:

```
SELECT PART
FROM PARTABLE
WHERE PART < '1000'
   (issue message to continue
   processing offline if more
   parts are desired)
```

Because sets of data are scanned by DB2 and because DB2 has limited facilities for monitoring resources used, controlling resource utilization of nonindexed, nonclustered data is very difficult. But where the designer knows that there is a large amount of unclustered data with like values to be accessed, at the application level, the designer can artificially introduce criteria that will force sets of data to be subdivided. As a simple example, consider a personnel database that has employees classified either as male or female (i.e., the field for SEX contains the values M or F).

Any query against the personnel file using sex as a criterion will result in a large number of rows satisfying the criterion, and the entire database being scanned. But suppose an artificial classification were introduced for an employee (call the artificial field ECLASS for employee class). For the first 50 employees, the value of 1 is assigned as their classification. For the next 50 employees, a value of 2 is assigned, and so forth. Now assume an index is created on SEX and ECLASS. A query can now be done so that SQL does not yield a huge result and a subset of the database can be scanned in an iterative fashion:

```
SELECT EMPNAME, SEX, DOHIRE
FROM EMPTABLE
WHERE SEX = 'M' AND ECLASS = 1;
```

This query will yield all the men with ECLASS = 1, roughly 25 rows on the average, assuming there are about as many women employees as men employees. To retrieve the next set of male employees, ECLASS = 2 is used as the qualifier, and so forth. In such a fashion, an indexed, unclustered table can be iteratively accessed without using a damaging amount of I/O. Note that, without an index on SEX and ECLASS, the entire database must be scanned with each iteration, certainly defeating the purpose of managing online resources.

The update of ECLASS is an issue using the above scheme. Because ECLASS is artificial, the accuracy of the data is not terribly important (i.e., individual inserts and deletes, as long as there are not too many of them, do not affect the usefulness of the field ECLASS). But, on occasion, it will be useful to create a batch program (running during the off-peak hours) that will sequentially scan the database, resetting ECLASS.

In fact, when the selection is based entirely on unindexed fields,

Chapter 8 DB2 Transaction Design for Performance: Part II

the entire database must be scanned. Breaking large scans into a series of smaller scans is practically impossible.

A variation of this same technique is possible if there is an arbitrary division of data that already exists and is indexed and clustered. For example, suppose EMPLNO is an indexed, clustered field and is unique to every employee. The following query effectively separates employees into manageable subsets of data—

```
SELECT EMPNAME, SEX, DOHIRE
FROM EMPTABLE
WHERE SEX = 'M' AND
      EMPNO BETWEEN 000 AND 100;
```

This query could expect to receive about 50 replies and operate on only a subset of the database. As employee number goes from 1 to 100, and so on, a manageable number of I/Os is consumed for each iteration.

Another approach to controlling the I/O done by an SQL program is to break down function very finely. Suppose the functional specifications were issued for an SQL program, as shown in Figure 8-1.

Figure 8-1 shows that the function accomplished by SQL processing has been broken into a series of smaller processes that accomplish the same thing. There are many advantages to the separation of function into small components. The first and most obvious advantage is that performance is greatly enhanced (i.e., all processing during peak period is designed). The resources required by any given program in execution are much less than the resources required by the large conglomeration of requirements taken together. The amount of data held by a PLAN is much less than if all the requirements were conglomerated.

But there are other advantages as well. In the case of the example in Figure 8-1, when there is a problem encountered in the middle of the execution of processing, the entire processing that has already occurred must be backed out. But when functions are broken down into fine units of execution, the problems that occur can be resolved without backing out otherwise validly processed data.

Care must be taken in using iterations of transactions to scan a large database(s) because, in some cases, iterating transactions can cost I/O and actually hurt performance. Suppose the simple database, as depicted in Figure 8-2 is to be scanned.

Functional Specifications for a SQL Program

o Locate Part number
o Update Part number quantity
o Locate Supplier for Part Number
o Get Supplier discount, price, eoq, shipping data
o Issue Purchase order
o Send Invoice data to Accounts Payable
o Update inventory
o Prepare Shipping dock reception

The functional specifications can be broken up
into several SQL programs -

SQL program 1 -
```
o Locate Part number
o Update Part number quantity
```

SQL program 2 -
```
o Locate Supplier for Part number
o Get Supplier discount, price, eoq, shipping data
o Issue Purchase order
```

SQL program 3 -
```
o Send Invoice to Accounts Payable
```

SQL program 4 -
```
o Update Inventory
o Prepare Shipping Dock reception
```

breaking a large amount of function that is accomplished
in a single program into a series of transactions that
collectively accomplish the same thing

FIGURE 8-1. Breaking a large amount of function that is accomplished in a single program into a series of transactions that collectively accomplish the same thing.

The database depicted in Figure 8-2 is a very large database. A query is to be run against the database seeking all activities of the amount $74.32. The first query against the database looks like this:

```
SELECT ACCT, ACTDATE, LOCATION
FROM ACTABLE
WHERE AMT = 74.32 AND
      ACCT BETWEEN 000 AND 100;
```

This first query against the database will access the pages and index for all accounts between 000 and 100—in all the activity of at

Chapter 8 DB2 Transaction Design for Performance: Part II

```
ACCT    ACTDATE       AMT  LOCATION     ID
0129    860103   12308.90  Fremont      IP
0129    860103     300.00  Fremont      TR
0129    860104      74.32  San Jose     UY
0129    860110      25.00  Sunnyvale    --             indexed, clustered
  :        :          :        :        :              on ACCT, ACTDATE
  :        :          :        :        :

0129    861006    2009.08  Fremont      LK
0129    861008      25.00  Sunnyvale    PL
0129    861019     150.00  Fremont      --
0129    861021     209.00  Santa Cruz   LL
  :        :          :        :        :
  :        :          :        :        :
```

FIGURE 8-2. A large database indexed, clustered on ACCT, ACTDATE.

most 100 accounts. Depending upon the density and population of the activities and the accounts (i.e., how many activities per account there are and how many accounts there are), a modest amount of I/O will be used.

Now consider the I/O required for the nth iteration of the scan (for the purpose of this example, m = n + 1).

```
SELECT ACCT, ACTDATE, LOCATION
FROM ACTABLE
WHERE AMT = 74.32 AND
      ACCT BETWEEN n00 AND m00;
```

The number of pages to be accessed is the same as in the first iteration, but the index must be rescanned for each iteration. Each iteration causes DB2 to rescan the index from the beginning of the index. Even with a hierarchical index, the amount of I/O used to scan the index mounts up in the face of a very large database. For small databases and small indexes, this repositioning of the transaction for each iteration of processing presents no problem. But for large amounts of data, such is not the case.

The repositioning of each transaction in the database for iterative processing of the database points out one of the difficulties of managing large databases in DB2. Of course, the database could be broken into a series of smaller databases, and many of the performance problems would be minimized.

Of course, in the example shown, only the index had to be rescanned for each iteration of the transaction. Suppose the designer had used a selection criteria such that the index was not used by DB2. In this case, the entire database (i.e., the pages) must be rescanned from the start for every iteration of the query.

STATIC/DYNAMIC SQL

Another SQL option the designer has is to execute Static or Dynamic SQL statements. Under normal conditions, Static SQL will be executed online, in the fashion associated with standard online transaction processing. Under Static SQL, the embedded SQL is prepared for execution so that, at the moment of execution, very little transaction preparation is required.

Under Dynamic SQL, the syntax of SQL can be either changed or created prior to the execution of the transaction. Upon completion of the modification/entry of the SQL text, a substantial amount of overhead is incurred in preparation for execution. Dynamic SQL is typical of the processing found in the interactive environment, not the online environment. The overhead of preparation for execution for Dynamic SQL is such that only under the most extreme cases/unusual cases should Dynamic SQL be used in the online environment.

EXPLAIN

A standard practice is that of using the EXPLAIN function to determine what access paths and index usage will be done. After the transaction is bound, the programmer runs the EXPLAIN function against the PLAN. The output of the EXPLAIN function is then analyzed to make sure that the strategies the designer has planned in fact are occurring. This simple practice can save large amounts of unnecessary processing. For this reason, all online transactions, as a matter of shop standards, should be scrutinized by the EXPLAIN function prior to execution.

EMBEDDED SQL

All production DB2 processing should be done from embedded SQL. To that end, the developer needs to be familiar with the mechanics of embedded SQL. The following is a brief description of the language mechanics required to use DB2 in the production online environment.

Chapter 8 DB2 Transaction Design for Performance: Part II

Embedded SQL operates (usually) out of a PL-I or COBOL program. The following shows a simple example of the mechanics of how embedded SQL in a PL-I program retrieves a single row of data:

```
PLISQLPG: PROC OPTIONS (MAIN);
DCL PARTNO CHAR(10);
EXEC SQL INCLUDE PARTABLE;
EXEC SQL INCLUDE SQLCA;
      .  .  .  .  .  .
      .  .  .  .  .  .
         .  .  .  .  .  .
    GET LIST (PARTNO);
    EXEC SQL SELECT PARTROW INTO = :PARTROW
            FROM PARTABLE
            WHERE PART = :PARTNO;
    IF SQLCODE=0
         THEN PUT EDIT (PARTROW)
                       (A(25));
    ELSE
         PUT EDIT ('SQL ERROR CODE IS:', SQLCODE)
                  (A(18), F(10));
      .  .  .  .  .  .  .  .  .
      .  .  .  .  .  .  .  .  .
      .  .  .  .  .  .  .  .  .
```

In the program example shown, a single row would be processed by the PL-I program. But what if there were more than one row that might be returned by the SQL program?

The following skeleton program illustrates the technique for executing a program that accesses multiple rows:

```
PLISQLPG:  PROC OPTIONS(MAIN);
DCL PARTNO CHAR(10);
EXEC SQL INCLUDE PARTABLE;
EXEC SQL INCLUDE SQLCA;
EXEC SQL DECLARE A CURSOR FOR
         SELECT *
         FROM PARTABLE
         WHERE PART = :PARTNO;
END-EXEC.
     .  .  .  .  .  .  .
     .  .  .  .  .  .  .
EXEC SQL OPEN A;
ENDE-EXEC.
```

```
         .    .    .    .    .    .    .
      .    .    .    .    .    .    .
         DO WHILE (SQLCODE=0);
EXEC SQL
      FETCH A INTO :PARTABLE;
            .    .    .    .    .;
         .    .    .    .    .;
    . . . . . . . . . . . . . . . . . . . .
    . . . . . . . . . . . . . . . . . . . .
    . . . . . . . . . . . . . . . . . . .
EXEC SQL CLOSE A;
END;
```

The SQLCA is a commonly included reference (that is mandatory) to the SQL communications area. The values returned in the communications area determine the validity or success of the SQL call just completed. A SQLCODE value of 0 indicates a normal completion with a new row returned.

For a complete, more detailed description of all the programming techniques and the meaning of the different statements, refer to the application programming guides (IMS, CICS, etc.) in the bibliography.

RESOURCE FACILITY (Governor)

A useful facility in some cases for the controlling of the resources used by a DB2 SQL call is the Resource Limit Facility or the "Governor." The governor applies only to individual SQL calls and to only the activities inside DB2. In order to limit the total resources used by a given transaction (not a particular call) facilities other than the governor must be used.

The governor is established prior to the execution of a transaction and applies to only dynamic SQL. The governor, once the limit of resources is established, returns control to the programmer, having achieved a partial result. The further set of activities is up to the programmer.

It is recommended that the governor be used only for the accessing of data; not the update, insertion, or deletion of data. The application program logic that is required to repair integrity as the result of an aborted update, insertion, or deletion attempt is such that development is simpler by merely avoiding the governor in the first place.

Chapter 8 DB2 Transaction Design for Performance: Part II

SUMMARY

The second major issue of design for performance is that of transaction design. Transaction design calls for the creation of *designed* transactions. A designed transaction is one that uses a limited amount of resources. Only designed transactions will be allowed to run in the online production environment. The essence of designed transactions is to break large amounts of function into smaller subsets, or to execute long-running transactions in a series of small iterations.

One of the difficulties of DB2 transaction performance is that SQL operates only on sets of records at a time. To achieve good performance, the sets of records must be broken into subsets.

It is assumed that certain resource-intensive commands will not be executed in online processing, such as SORT, SUM, AVG, etc.

QUESTIONS: TRANSACTION DESIGN

1. A data-driven process is one whose resource consumption depends on the data on which it _____.
2. It is (a) impossible, (b) very, very difficult, (c) difficult, (d) no problem to predetermine how many resources a data-driven process will use.
3. The overhead of predetermining how many resources a data-driven process will use is _____.
4. DB2 does set-processing. As long as the sets processed are small, then DB2 transactions can be _____.
5. But when DB2 processes against large or indeterminate sets, then DB2 transactions are _____.
6. The general strategy for DB2 transactions is to operate against sets of _____ size.
7. Every undesigned transaction can be broken into a series of designed transactions. (T/F)
8. One way to reduce the resources consumed by an undesigned transaction is to break the _____ of the undesigned transactions into multiple small steps.
9. If an undesigned transaction has only one function, another way to break the transaction into pieces is to _____ the transaction.
10. In addition to breaking designed transactions up, proper coding technique should be used. The following is a list of coding tech-

niques that can be used in the online DB2 environment: AVERAGE, SUM, SORT. (T/F)

11. Search criteria should be used for indexed fields for online processing. (T/F)
12. All SQL calls should be as fully qualified as possible for online processing. (T/F)
13. No more than 10 rows per iteration of a transaction should be retrieved for online processing. (T/F)
14. Views may span multiple tables for online processing. (T/F)
15. Foreign keys can relate many tables together for many rows for online processing. (T/F)
16. QMF can be used for online processing. (T/F)
17. SQL needs to be embedded and precompiled (in COBOL, DL1, etc.) for online processing. (T/F)
18. Relational joins or projects are not done during the online day for online processing. (T/F)
19. DDL processing is done only during the batch window. (T/F)
20. Only database I/O needs to be considered for online processing. (T/F)
21. Database and index I/O are the primary types of I/O to be considered for online processing. (T/F)

PART III

DB2 Application Design: Part I

Chapter 9 Data Structures and Data Relationships

- Standard Data Structures
- Application-Supported Relationships
- Multikeyed Relationships
- Multikeyed Cross Reference Tables
- Secondary/Sparse Indexes
- Internal Arrays
- Stacks
- Logically Related Tables
- Key-Splitting
- Recursive Structures
- Summary
- Questions: Data Structures and Data Relationships

Chapter 10 Referential Integrity

- Application Responsibility
- Different Forms of Referential Integrity
- Deferred Referential Integrity
- Application Conventions
- Independent Audits
- Frequency of Audit
- Summary
- Questions: Referential Integrity

Chapter 11 The DB2 Batch Environment

- The Batch Window
- What Runs in the Batch Window
- I/Os and Joined Databases
- Parallel Sequential Runs
- Single-Extract Processing

- Sorting Transactions into Primary Processing Sequence
- Ordering Batch Runs
- Consolidation of Update Requirements
- Peak-Period Processing
- Small Databases
- System Considerations
- Summary
- Questions: Batch Processing

Chapter 12   Testing DB2 Production Systems
Section 1—The DB2 Test Environment

- Input to Testing
- Stress Tests
- Stress-Testing and Service Level Agreements
- Measuring the Stress Test
- Driver Programs
- Modularized Programs
- Separate Environments
- "Preliminary," "Full" Test Databases
- Testing Coordination across Projects
- Administering the Test Environments
- Summary
- Questions: The DB2 Test Environment

Section 2—Testing Programs in DB2

- General Transaction/Program Control
- Single-Table Manipulation
- Referential Integrity
- Program Modularization
- Algorithmic Verification
- Data Access
- Recursive Relationships
- Continuous Time Span Rows
- Extract Processing
- Summary
- Questions: Testing Programs in DB2

CHAPTER 9

Data Structures and Data Relationships

This chapter is on data structures and data relationships in DB2. The first part of the chapter describes some simple data relationships and where they might be used. The second part of the chapter describes more complex relationships and their usage. Throughout, the emphasis is on the utility and the performance of data relationships.

STANDARD DATA STRUCTURES

The subject of data structures in DB2 must begin with the standard DB2 structures. DB2 has tables and indexes. Tables can be simple or partitioned. A simple tablespace may be segmented or not segmented. Indexes can exist for single fields or for multiple fields. Indexes can be used for clustered or nonclustered tables. Indexes can be used to force uniqueness in a table. Figure 9-1 shows the standard data structures in DB2.

This short list of the standard DB2 structures belies the richness of structure that can be achieved at the application level.

APPLICATION-SUPPORTED RELATIONSHIPS

The simplest application-supported data relationship in DB2 is from one row in a table to another row in another table. Suppose there are two tables—a part table and a supplier table as shown in Figure 9-2.

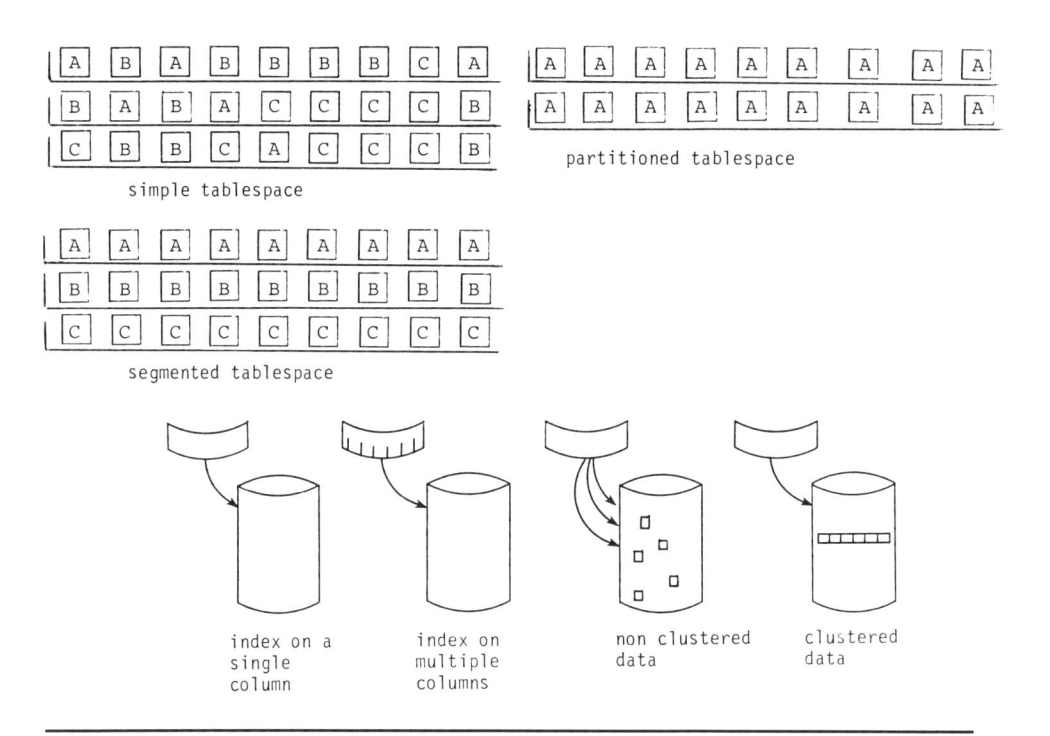

FIGURE 9-1. The standard DB2 data structures.

Each row in the part table has a supplier field. If all the user desires is to see who the supplier of the part is, then there is no need to go beyond the part table, since the supplier is contained in that table. But suppose that, upon having retrieved the part row and having looked at the supplier, further information about the supplier is desired.

The programmer uses the supplier field found in the part table

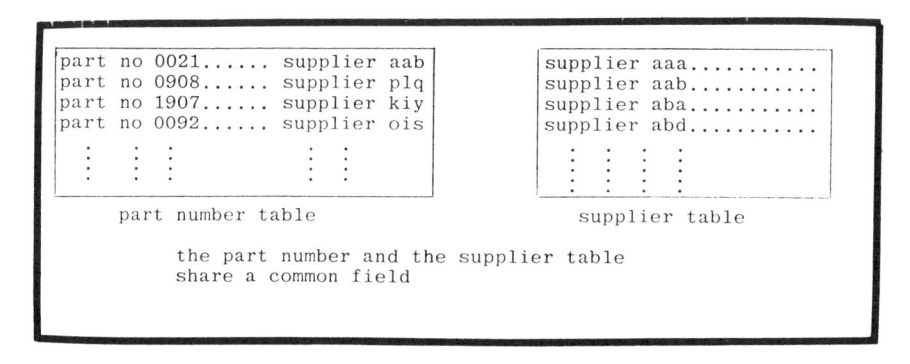

```
part no 0021...... supplier aab      supplier aaa..........
part no 0908...... supplier plq      supplier aab..........
part no 1907...... supplier kiy      supplier aba..........
part no 0092...... supplier ois      supplier abd..........
   :      :            :                 :    :
   :      :            :                 :    :
      part number table                supplier table

         the part number and the supplier table
         share a common field
```

FIGURE 9-2. The part number and the supplier table share a common field.

Chapter 9   Data Structures and Data Relationships

to locate the corresponding row in the supplier table. In the supplier table there is much information about the supplier that is not found in the part table. The SQL program shown retrieves some supplier information—NAME and ADDRESS—from the supplier table as shown:

```
SELECT NAME ADDRESS
FROM SUPPLIER, PART
WHERE SUPPLIER.SUPP = PART.SUPP;
```

Going from part to supplier for a small table is not difficult as long as there are not many suppliers. If, however, there are more than a few suppliers, then creating an index on "supplier" will allow the entry into the supplier table to be made efficiently.

Now suppose the reverse traversal of tables needs to be made. In this case, the programmer is at a supplier row and wishes to see what parts are supplied by the supplier. An SQL request is issued which looks for a parts description:

```
SELECT PART DESCR
FROM PART, SUPPLIER
WHERE PART.SUPP = SUPPLIER.SUPP
```

In this case, many parts are potentially returned as a result of the query. The set of all parts that are supplied is returned. If there are only a few parts, a direct scan of the pages where the parts reside is efficient. But, if there are many parts, an index into the parts database using the field supplier will speed up the access of the data. Of course, if there are many parts, then an index will be mandatory.

While the SQL requests may look very similar, the results are very different. To specifically retrieve a part from a supplier requires that either one of two things be done. One choice is to leave the data the way it is, retrieve all parts supplied, and look back through the set of parts retrieved for the one being sought. The other choice is to restructure the data, as shown in Figure 9-3.

In the figure, a part is shown having a relationship to a supplier in the supplier table. The SQL looking for description and unit of measure call would complete the supplier to part relationship:

```
SELECT PART DESCR UM
FROM PART, SUPPLIER
WHERE PART.PART = SUPPLIER.PART;
```

```
┌─────────────────────────────────────────────────────────────────────┐
│  ┌───────────────────────────────┐  ┌───────────────────────────────┐ │
│  │part no 0021...... supplier aab│  │supplier aaa........ part no 1097│ │
│  │part no 0908...... supplier plq│  │supplier aab........ part no 0802│ │
│  │part no 1907...... supplier kly│  │supplier aba........ part no 0082│ │
│  │part no 0092...... supplier ois│  │supplier abd........ part no 2297│ │
│  │   :      :          :         │  │   :       :           :         │ │
│  │   :      :          :         │  │   :       :           :         │ │
│  │   :      :          :         │  │   :       :           :         │ │
│  └───────────────────────────────┘  └───────────────────────────────┘ │
│         part number table                    supplier table           │
│              the part number and the supplier tables                  │
│              share multiple common fields                             │
└─────────────────────────────────────────────────────────────────────┘
```

FIGURE 9-3. The part number and the supplier tables share multiple common fields.

In this case, only one part will be returned as a result of the SQL call. But only in the oddest of circumstances would a supplier be the source for a single part. Usually, a supplier will be the source for multiple parts. And only under odd circumstances would a part have one and only one supplier. Under normal circumstances, a part would have multiple suppliers. The data structures that have been shown are ill-equipped to handle the more general case of the m:n part/supplier relationship.

Consider a data relationship in which a part can have multiple suppliers and vice versa as shown in Figure 9-4.

There are two "base" tables—a part table and a supplier table. Then there are a cross-reference table from part to supplier and another cross-reference table from supplier to part. A part can have multiple suppliers and vice versa. The SQL call looking for the name and address of a supplier would access the set of suppliers for the part 'xxx . . .' by the call:

```
SELECT SUPP, NAME, ADDRESS
FROM PART.SUPPLIER.XREF
WHERE PART.PART = 'xxx . . .
```

Based on the results of the call, the set of suppliers can be accessed to find the information desired.

The cross-reference tables can be used to relate suppliers to parts. The SQL call that looks for the description of a part shown does exactly that:

Chapter 9   Data Structures and Data Relationships   123

```
SELECT PART, DESCR
FROM PART, SUPP, XREF
WHERE SUPPLIER.SUPP = 'xxx....'
```

While this call will execute, it will be inefficient because the entire index—the entire cross-reference—must be searched. A more efficient means of access—if it is desired to go from supplier to part—is to use the reverse cross-reference table—the supplier/part cross-reference as shown in Figure 9-5.

The contents of the supplier/part cross-reference is the same as the contents of the part/supplier cross-reference. The difference is that the order of the contents is different. The SQL program shown

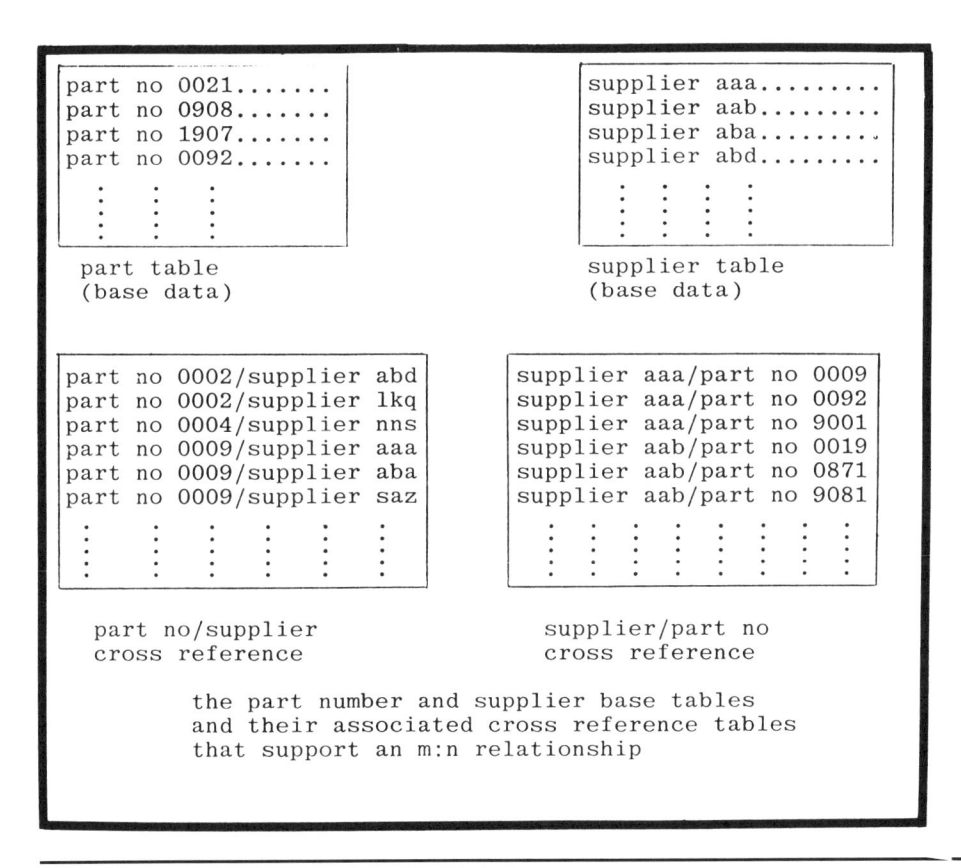

```
part no 0021.......         supplier aaa.........
part no 0908.......         supplier aab.........
part no 1907.......         supplier aba.........
part no 0092.......         supplier abd.........
  .  .  .                     .  .  .  .
  .  .  .                     .  .  .  .
  .  .  .                     .  .  .  .

 part table                 supplier table
 (base data)                (base data)


part no 0002/supplier abd   supplier aaa/part no 0009
part no 0002/supplier lkq   supplier aaa/part no 0092
part no 0004/supplier nns   supplier aaa/part no 9001
part no 0009/supplier aaa   supplier aab/part no 0019
part no 0009/supplier aba   supplier aab/part no 0871
part no 0009/supplier saz   supplier aab/part no 9081
 . . . . . .                 . . . . . .
 . . . . . .                 . . . . . .
 . . . . . .                 . . . . . .

 part no/supplier           supplier/part no
 cross reference            cross reference

       the part number and supplier base tables
       and their associated cross reference tables
       that support an m:n relationship
```

FIGURE 9–4. The part number and the supplier base tables and their associated cross-reference tables that support an m:n relationship.

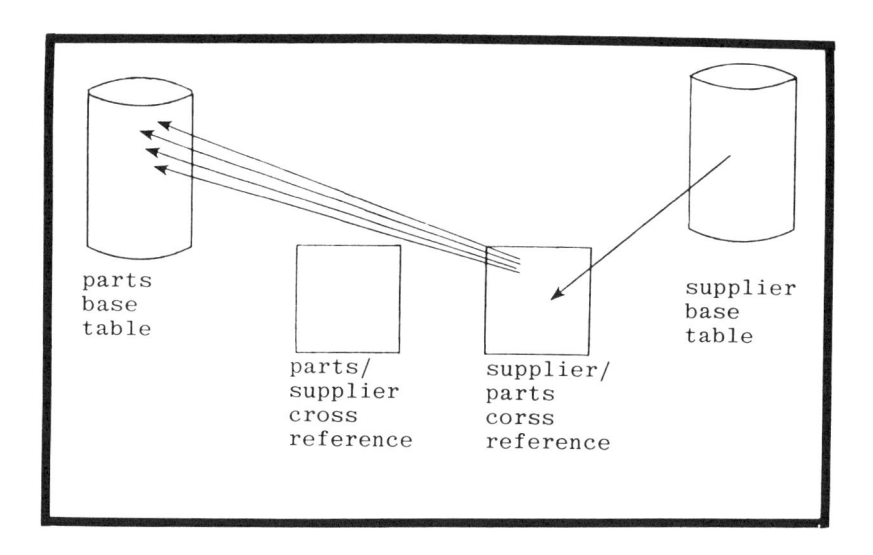

FIGURE 9-5. The supplier/part cross-reference in the reverse cross-reference table.

uses the supplier/parts cross-reference to efficiently access parts from a supplier:

```
SELECT PART NAME DESCR
FROM SUPP.PART.XREF
WHERE SUPPLIER.SUPP = 'xxx . . .'
```

The efficient traversal from parts to supplier and vice versa can be accomplished by the usage of two cross-reference tables. Note, however, that when the update of relationships needs to be done, updates must occur in multiple places. Also note the data is independently organized and can be processed independently (i.e., the cross-reference tables can be processed independently, the parts table can be processed independently, etc.).

Cross-reference tables may simply contain the information pertaining to the relationship being documented, or cross-reference tables may contain other information as well. That information is often called *intersection information*. For example, for a parts/supplier cross-reference table, the field—qty (quantity)—may be added as well as shown in Figure 9-6.

The field qty indicates the number of parts actually furnished by the supplier. If there are multiple cross-reference tables, intersection

Chapter 9   Data Structures and Data Relationships   125

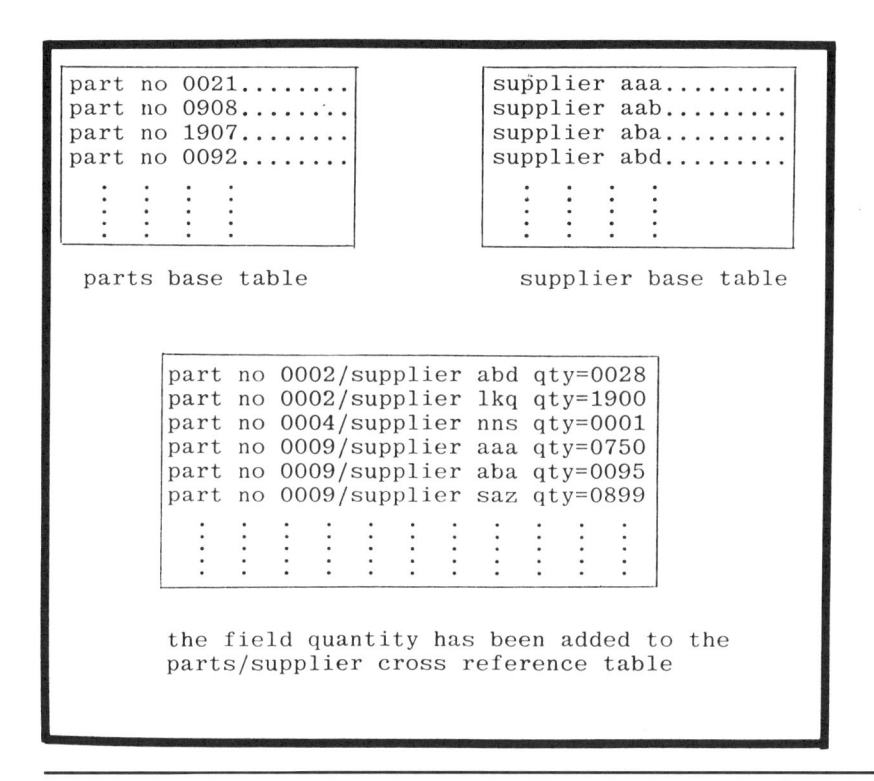

```
part no 0021........          supplier aaa.........
part no 0908........          supplier aab.........
part no 1907........          supplier aba.........
part no 0092........          supplier abd.........
    :  :  :  :                    :  :  :  :
    :  :  :  :                    :  :  :  :
    :  :  :  :                    :  :  :  :
  parts base table              supplier base table


      part no 0002/supplier abd qty=0028
      part no 0002/supplier lkq qty=1900
      part no 0004/supplier nns qty=0001
      part no 0009/supplier aaa qty=0750
      part no 0009/supplier aba qty=0095
      part no 0009/supplier saz qty=0899
       :  :  :  :  :  :  :  :  :  :  :
       :  :  :  :  :  :  :  :  :  :  :
       :  :  :  :  :  :  :  :  :  :  :

      the field quantity has been added to the
      parts/supplier cross reference table
```

FIGURE 9–6. The field quantity added to the parts/supplier cross-reference table.

data will logically fit in more than one place. But, in practice, intersection data is stored only in a single place (for most purposes).

MULTIKEYED RELATIONSHIPS

Data relationships can span more than one table. Suppose not only parts and suppliers exist, but suppose orders for parts from a supplier exist as well as shown in Figure 9-7.

Two tables have to be added. One table shows order number, the supplier to whom the order was made, the date of the orders, and the total amount ordered. The second table that has been added shows order by part, the quantity, and the price. Relationships now exist between part, supplier, and order. With the tables shown, it is easy to go from order to part or from order to supplier (i.e., it is efficient to make such a traversal).

It is not necessarily efficient to make the reverse traversal. For

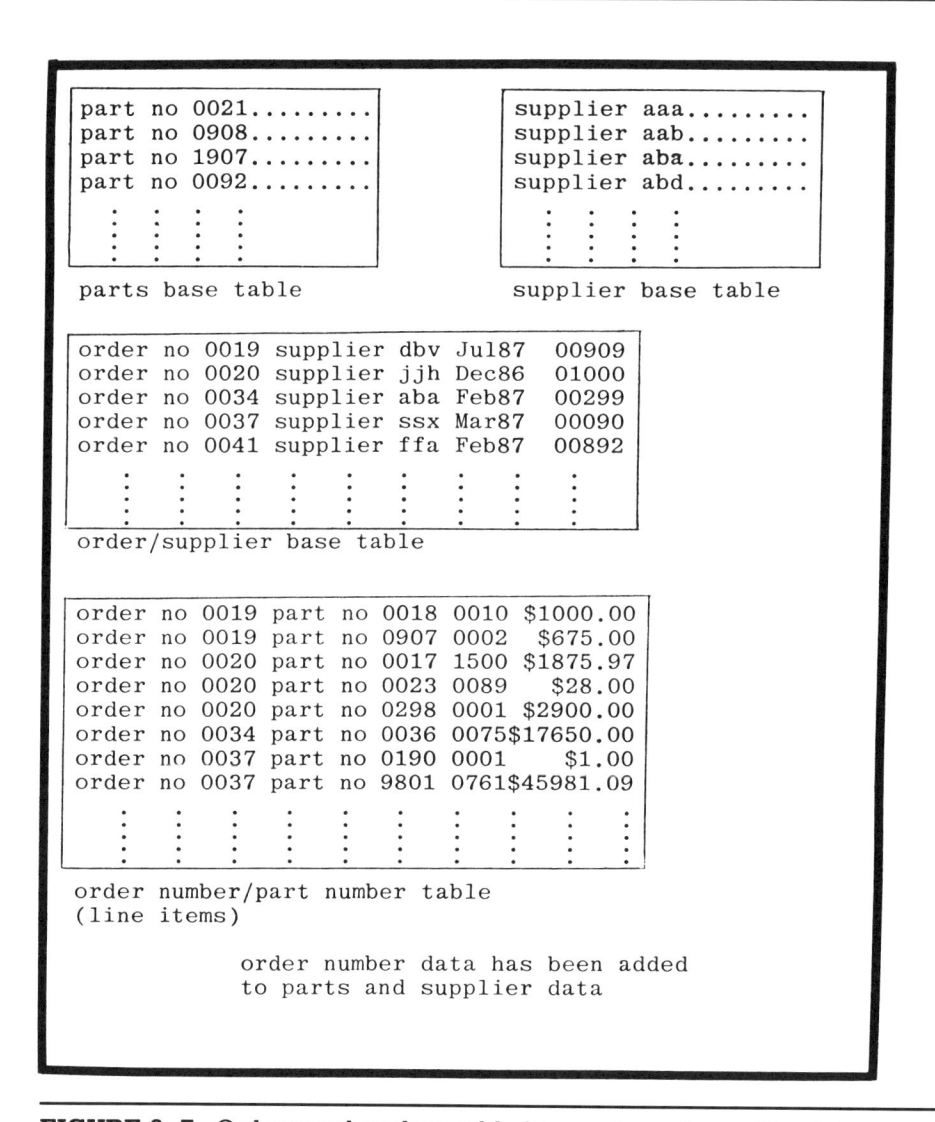

```
part no 0021.........        supplier aaa.........
part no 0908.........        supplier aab.........
part no 1907.........        supplier aba.........
part no 0092.........        supplier abd.........
   . . . .                      . . . .
   . . . .                      . . . .
   . . . .                      . . . .
parts base table             supplier base table

order no 0019 supplier dbv Jul87  00909
order no 0020 supplier jjh Dec86  01000
order no 0034 supplier aba Feb87  00299
order no 0037 supplier ssx Mar87  00090
order no 0041 supplier ffa Feb87  00892
  .    .    .       .    .    .      .
  .    .    .       .    .    .      .
  .    .    .       .    .    .      .
order/supplier base table

order no 0019 part no 0018 0010 $1000.00
order no 0019 part no 0907 0002  $675.00
order no 0020 part no 0017 1500 $1875.97
order no 0020 part no 0023 0089   $28.00
order no 0020 part no 0298 0001 $2900.00
order no 0034 part no 0036 0075$17650.00
order no 0037 part no 0190 0001    $1.00
order no 0037 part no 9801 0761$45981.09
  .    .    .    .    .    .    .    .
  .    .    .    .    .    .    .    .
  .    .    .    .    .    .    .    .
order number/part number table
(line items)

         order number data has been added
         to parts and supplier data
```

FIGURE 9–7. Order number data added to parts and supplier data.

instance, finding all orders for a part requires traversing the entire order/parts table. The use of a cross-reference would make the part-to-order traversal more efficient. Every time new relationships and new cross-references are added, it must be remembered that referential requirements grow, that the complexity of the structures grow, and that the resource requirements for maintenance grow.

MULTIKEYED CROSS REFERENCE TABLES

Cross reference tables can exist for more than just an m:n relationship. For example, for a part, a supplier, and an order, it may be useful to build a table whose key is part, supplier, and order. The table that would result is useful for certain requests, such as:

```
SELECT PART, QTY, ORDERNO
FROM PART,SUPPLIER,ORDER,XREF
WHERE PART = 'xxx . . .' AND
      SUPPLIER = 'yyy . . .';
```

SECONDARY/SPARSE INDEXES

Another useful data structure in DB2 that is built at the application level is that of the *secondary index* or *sparse index.*

When an index is created in DB2, if the table is unclustered or not clustered along the column the index is created for, the index is for all rows. For a large table, there are correspondingly many index entries. If the application developer is willing to build and maintain separate tables, the size of an index can effectively be reduced. For example, suppose an application processes loan payments. A few loan payments each month have a late surcharge made. If the application were to scan each month's loan payments to determine how many charges there were, many resources would be required. Each entry would need to be scanned.

A better choice would be to build an index and scan the index, since an index packs data much more tightly than a row. But the index would still contain many entries, and most entries would indicate no late payment. Even scanning (not to mention building) an index on a large table requires large resources.

A third design option is the sparse index. The sparse index is built and maintained at the application level. The sparse index is a table of ONLY accounts that have a late payment. The table is simple. It consists of account number and possibly the amount and date of the surcharge as shown by Figure 9-8.

For most accounts, there is no entry into the sparse index. But when a late surcharge is made, the application inserts a row into the table.

At a later point in time, processing against the sparse index is

```
acct    date    amt     late
0021    Jul86   167.09  -----
0023    Jul86   209.92  -----
0024    Jul86   187.65  -----
0029    Jul86   175.63  29.78
0031    Jul86    98.80  -----
0034    Jul86   199.00  -----
0036    Jul86   286.98  -----
0037    Jul86   398.73  -----
0038    Jul86   288.39  62.98
0040    Jul86   786.54  -----
0042    Jul86    78.25  -----
0044    Jul86   197.65  -----
0046    Jul86    36.00  -----
0048    Jul86   175.40  -----
0049    Jul86   239.87  43.87

account payment table
```

```
acct    surcharge
0029     29.78
0038     62.98
0040     43.87
0054     17.74
```

a "sparse" index on late paying accounts

FIGURE 9-8. A "sparse" index on late-paying accounts.

very efficient. The table, of course, can be indexed and clustered if desired.

The usage of a sparse index as an application-maintained data structure can save significant resources, especially in the face of large amounts of data.

INTERNAL ARRAYS

The simple data relationships shown are the common type that are encountered on a daily basis in DB2. But they are hardly the only relationships that are possible. Consider the simple array where activity for an account is posted in the same row as account.

Up to n activities can be posted in a row. Each activity is named in the DB2 Data Definition Language (DDL) as a different field. Variable-length rows can be created if the number of activities varies widely from one account to the next. Or a predetermined number of activities can be allocated for each row if the number of activities is constant (or reasonably constant).

The creation of internal tables within a row can save considerable disk space because the key information for the row does not have to be repeated many times. In addition, performance can be enhanced in that only one I/O is needed to retrieve multiple activities for an

Chapter 9 Data Structures and Data Relationships 129

```
acct    date1   amt1    date2   amt2    date3   amt3  ......  daten   amtn
0005    860602  234.98  860604  175.00  860606  188.97         860716  675.75
0078    860607   25.00  860607  199.00  860702   67.00         ------  ------
0086    860604  175.00  ------  ------  ------  ------         ------  ------
0092    860601   25.00  860601   25.00  860603  276.99         860604   25.00
0095    860602  187.65  860603   35.00  860604   50.00         860604  136.92
  :       :       :       :       :       :       :              :       :
  :       :       :       :       :       :       :              :       :

              each row can hold up to n occurrences
              of date and amount activity for an
              account
```

FIGURE 9-9. Each row of an account payment table can hold up to n occurrences of date and amount activity for an account.

account. Were the activities for an account defined separately, then the activities might reside in separate pages, thus requiring I/O as the programmer scanned from one activity to the next.

Of course, a burden of complexity is borne at the application level when the usage of internal arrays is specified.

STACKS

Another type of structure that can be made using standard DB2 tools is the *stack*. A stack is useful for first-in/last-out (FILO) processing. A stack is made with a standard DB2 table and a variable that determines where the top of the stack is. Oftentimes, this variable is called the *pointer* or the *stack pointer*. The key of the stack indicates the order of entry into the stack.

The creation and usage of a stack is illustrated in terms of an example shown in Figure 9-10.

At moment n, the stack is empty and the variable—stack pointer—equals zero. At moment n + 1, an entry in the stack is made. The first allocation of space in the stack is made (i.e., the first row), and the stack pointer is set to one. At moment n + 2, the next entry in the stack is allocated, and the variable—stack pointer—is set to two. At moment n + 3, the most recent entry in the stack is removed. Space previously used is freed and the variable—stack pointer—is set to one. At moment n + 4, the most current entry in the stack (the only entry) is removed, and the variable—stack pointer—is set to zero.

Stacks are useful for recursive processing, such as that found in

```
                                    entry 2
                   entry 1          entry 1         entry 1

moment n          moment n+1       moment n+2      moment n+3
stack             stack            stack           stack
pointer=0         pointer=1        pointer=2       poniter=1
```

```
                        the dynamics of a stack over time
                        as entries are inserted and deleted
                        from the stack
moment n+4
stack
pointer=0
```

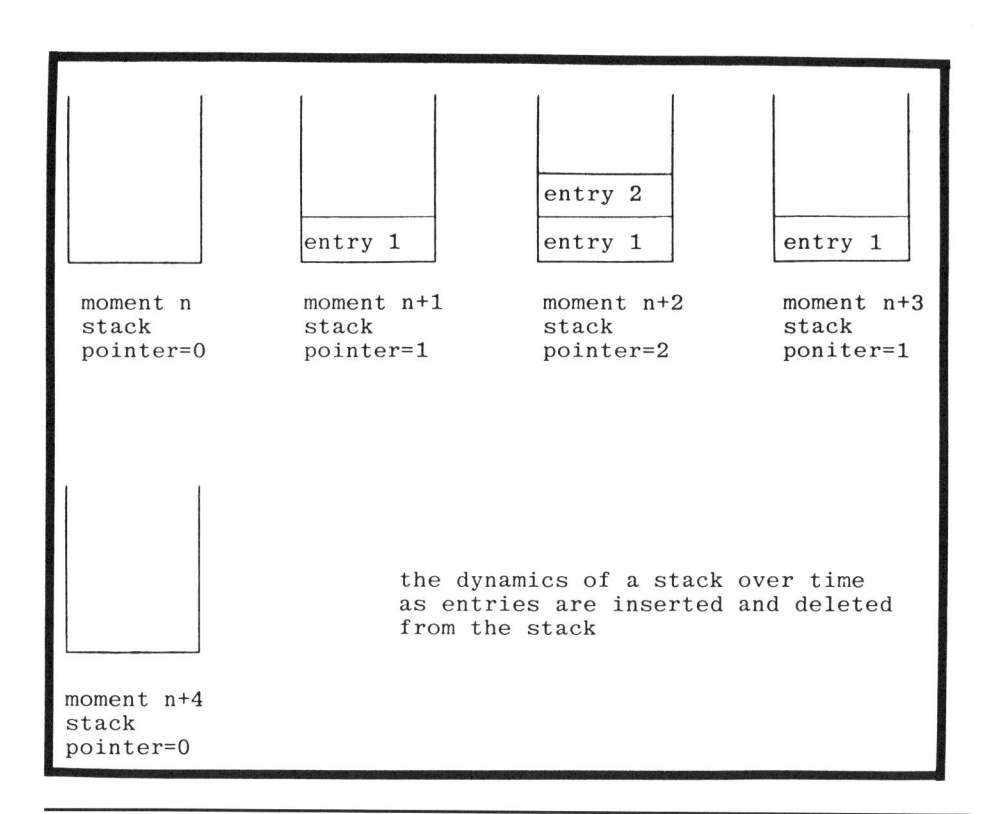

FIGURE 9-10. The dynamics of a stack over time as entries are inserted and deleted from the stack.

the bill-of-materials explosion algorithm. The pointer indicates where the most recent entry into the stack is. When the pointer equals zero, the stack is empty. The stack is normally a table that is defined to DB2 like any other table. The discipline in the usage of the stack is maintained at the application level.

LOGICALLY RELATED TABLES

Another form of data relationship that is possible in DB2 is the creation of logically related data. In DB2, multiple tables can have the same key or partial key. In that sense, tables are logically related by the common key that they share. Of course, in DB2, the tables can be defined as part of a database, but DB2 does not participate in the maintenance of the logical key relationships.

The system may or may not know of the relationship between logically related tables. The example shown in Figure 9-11 for supplier

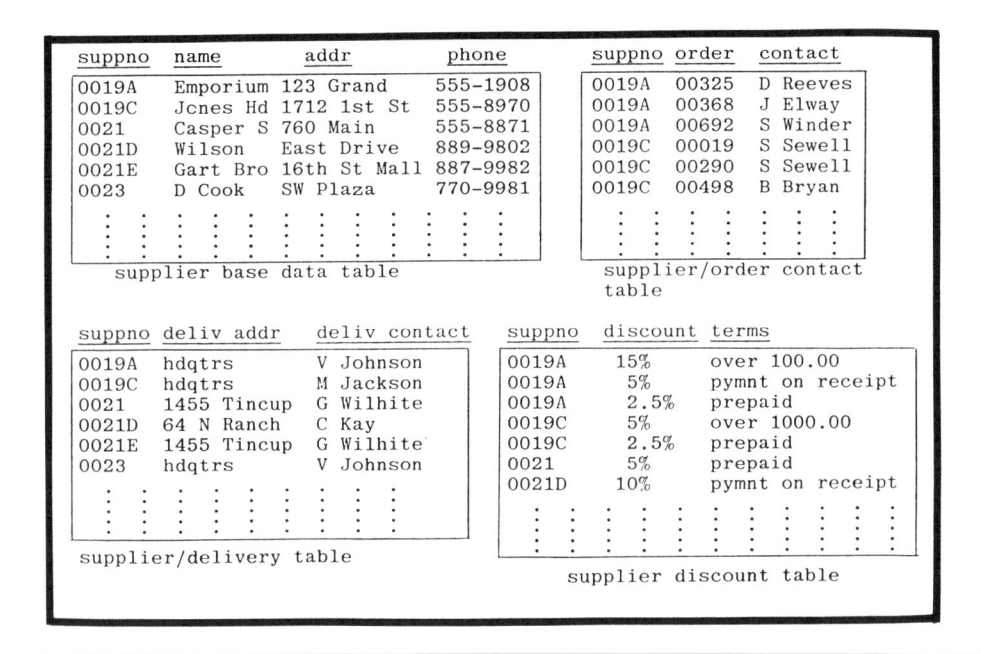

Chapter 9 Data Structures and Data Relationships 131

```
suppno  name      addr            phone       suppno  order   contact
0019A   Emporium  123 Grand       555-1908    0019A   00325   D Reeves
0019C   Jones Hd  1712 1st St     555-8970    0019A   00368   J Elway
0021    Casper S  760 Main        555-8871    0019A   00692   S Winder
0021D   Wilson    East Drive      889-9802    0019C   00019   S Sewell
0021E   Gart Bro  16th St Mall    887-9982    0019C   00290   S Sewell
0023    D Cook    SW Plaza        770-9981    0019C   00498   B Bryan
  :       :         :               :           :       :        :
     supplier base data table                supplier/order contact
                                              table

suppno  deliv addr    deliv contact    suppno  discount  terms
0019A   hdqtrs        V Johnson        0019A   15%       over 100.00
0019C   hdqtrs        M Jackson        0019A   5%        pymnt on receipt
0021    1455 Tincup   G Wilhite        0019A   2.5%      prepaid
0021D   64 N Ranch    C Kay            0019C   5%        over 1000.00
0021E   1455 Tincup   G Wilhite        0019C   2.5%      prepaid
0023    hdqtrs        V Johnson        0021    5%        prepaid
  :       :              :             0021D   10%       pymnt on receipt
                                         :       :         :
supplier/delivery table
                                       supplier discount table
```

FIGURE 9-11. Four logically related tables, each containing normalized data.

contains four logically related tables—a base table where common information about every supplier exists, a supplier/order table where the contact for any order is stored, the supplier/delivery table where specific delivery information is stored, and the supplier/discount table, where the date of discount, percent, location, and total amount of discount are stored.

Each table contains normalized data. Supplier is the primary key of all of the tables, and some of the tables have more than one key, although no two tables have exactly the same key. The tables logically form a database. The system may not be aware of the fact that there is a relationship between the different tables. The coordination of update, insert, delete, and so forth must be done at the application level.

KEY-SPLITTING

The simple data relationships discussed so far are not the only possibilities in DB2. Another common structuring of data is shown in Figure 9-12.

A supplier/order database is shown as n physical tables. The first table contains supplier/order information for suppliers whose keys

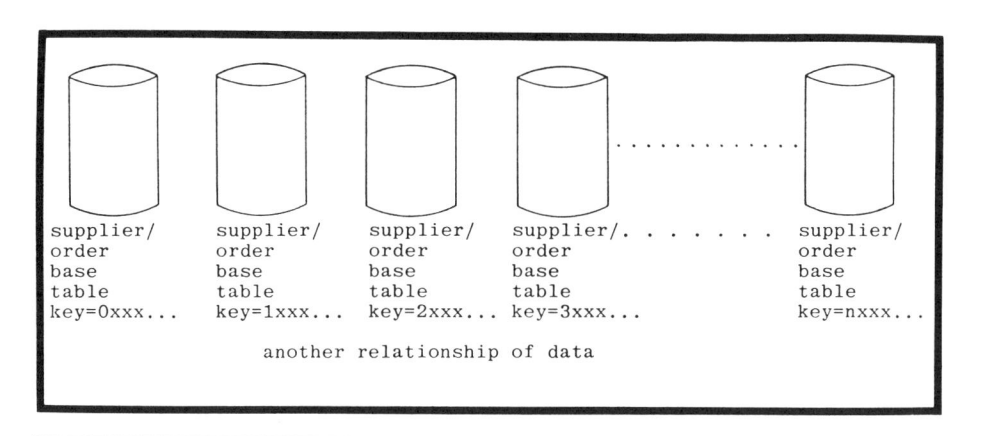

```
┌─────────────────────────────────────────────────────────────────┐
│   ___          ___          ___          ___              ___   │
│  |   |        |   |        |   |        |   |            |   |  │
│  |   |        |   |        |   |        |   |  . . . . . |   |  │
│  |___|        |___|        |___|        |___|            |___|  │
│                                                                 │
│ supplier/    supplier/    supplier/    supplier/.......  supplier/ │
│ order        order        order        order            order   │
│ base         base         base         base             base    │
│ table        table        table        table            table   │
│ key=0xxx...  key=1xxx...  key=2xxx...  key=3xxx...      key=nxxx... │
│              another  relationship  of  data                    │
└─────────────────────────────────────────────────────────────────┘
```

FIGURE 9–12. Data related by key-splitting.

begin with 0. The second table shows supplier/order information for suppliers whose keys begin with 1, and so forth. Each of the tables forms—logically—a single table even though there are in fact n physical tables.

The tables may or may not contain roughly the same amount of data. If table 1 contains 200 suppliers whose key begins with 0 and all other tables contain 75 suppliers in all, then table 1 is likely to have much more data in it than all other tables. Or if table 2 contains one or two suppliers who have received very many orders and the other tables contain information about suppliers who only infrequently receive orders, then table 2 is likely to be proportionately larger than all the other tables.

The simple distribution of data based on key value separation does not necessarily ensure an even split of data, although the key ranges may be divided evenly.

Another aspect of data-splitting by key range is that the definition of the data to the system is identical to each table. Each table contains the same key, the same type of data, the same type of data elements, and so forth. In short, the DDL definition is identical. Only the contents of the tables are different. The splitting of data must be accomplished by programs or by standard DB2 partitioning of data. As will be discussed later, splitting data by key range is useful for enhancing system availability, managing large volumes of data (such as that found in an archival environment), and enhancing the performance of data that must be reorganized frequently.

RECURSIVE STRUCTURES

A useful structure supported by DB2 application code is that of the *recursive structure*. A recursive structure is nothing more than a relationship of a table with itself rather than with another table. The two common forms of recursive structures are hierarchical recursive structures and peer level recursive structures. The two types are explained in terms of an example. Consider a part number bill-of-material structure as shown in Figure 9-13.

A part is shown as having one or more subassemblies. The subassembly has its own subassemblies, and so forth. Two DB2 tables represent this hierarchical recursive structure. One table—the base table—contains part and nonkey information representing all parts. The second table contains two keys—the assembly and the subassembly.

The second kind of recursive relationship represented in an application-supported DB2 relationship is the peer level recursive relationship. In the bill-of-materials example, parts of data are related to each other in a hierarchical manner—where one part was a "parent" of another part. But in a peer level recursive relationship, all nodes or components of the recursive structure are peers. For example, in the manufacturing environment, a part may have one or more substitute parts.

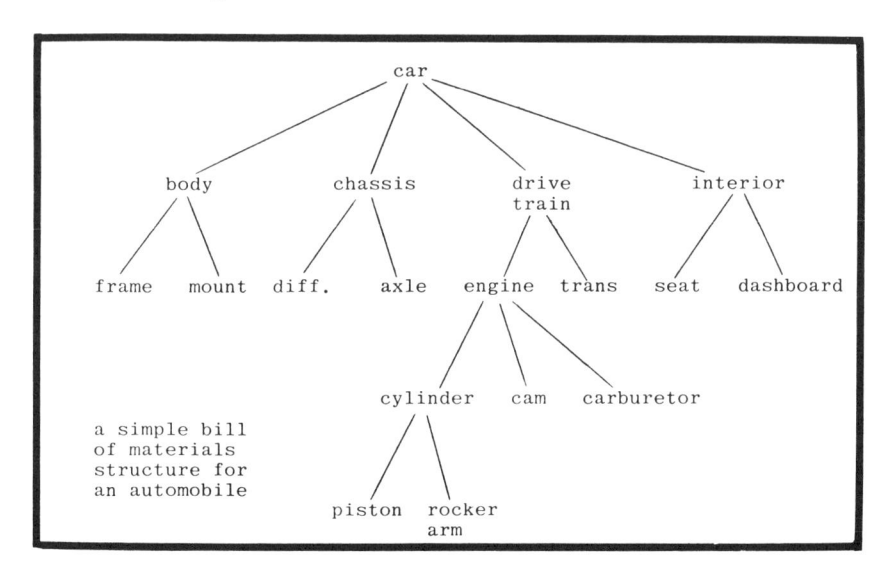

FIGURE 9–13. A simple bill-of-materials structure for an automobile.

```
            part 1053
          / |  \   \
         /  |   \   \
part 5096 part 2007 part 1099 part 8711

substitute parts for part
1053 - a form of peer level
recursion
```

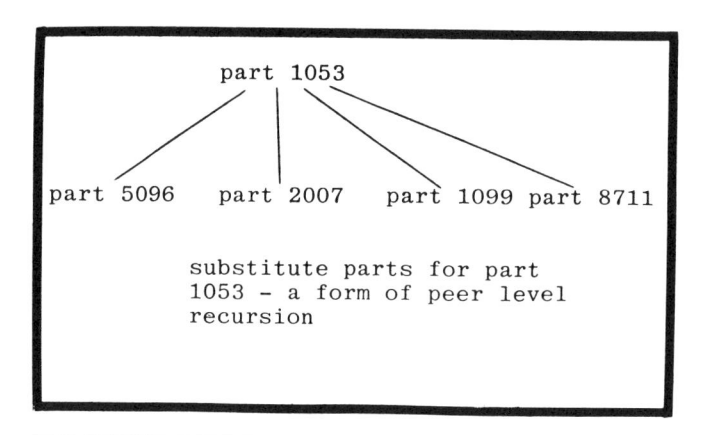

FIGURE 9-14. A form of peer level recursion: substitute parts for part 1053.

Two DB2 tables can be defined to support this peer level relationship. One table is the base table, as previously described. The other table is the substitute part table. The substitute part table contains two keys—the part and its substitute. A chain of substitute parts can be created by going from a part to its substitute, then to its substitute, and so forth. There is no notion of a hierarchy of parts as there was in the bill-of-materials structure.

SUMMARY

This chapter has discussed some simple and some advanced data structures and relationships that can be built in DB2. The structures have been described along with salient points of usage. The simple tables of DB2 can be creatively extended to form elegant structures.

QUESTIONS: DATA STRUCTURES AND DATA RELATIONSHIPS

1. The two basic structures DB2 has are _____.
2. Tables can be _____ or _____.
3. Indexes can be for single fields or _____ fields.
4. Indexes can be for _____ or nonclustered tables.
5. DB2 can support much more than the simple relationships, but the nonstandard relationships have to be supported at the _____ level.
6. Two tables can be joined on a common _____.
7. Joins of tables can extend over one or _____ tables.

Chapter 9   Data Structures and Data Relationships   135

8. Joins are usually done by a _____ program.
9. An _____ on a field prevents the entire database from being searched when a scan of data is done.
10. For a small table, a _____ of the table may be more efficient than the usage of an index.
11. For a large table, seldom if ever will a _____ of data be more efficient than using an index.
12. An m:n relationship between tables is often accomplished by means of a _____ reference table.
13. For an m:n relationship, OFTEN/SELDOM two cross-references are needed.
14. Two cross-references for an m:n relationship allow the relationship to be traversed both directions. (T/F)
15. More than two tables can be referenced by a cross reference table. (T/F)
16. Cross reference tables MAY/MAY NOT contain more information than that pertinent to the relationship.
17. Nonrelationship data (i.e., nonkey data) in a cross-reference table is often called _____ data.
18. A single cross-reference table can be used for traversal in BOTH/ONLY ONE direction(s) of an m:n relationship.
19. However, when a single cross-reference table is used for traversal in both directions, one traversal is necessarily _____.
20. Intersection data often is redundant. This means that when the data needs to be updated, it must be changed in multiple _____.
21. The sparse index IS/IS NOT a standard DB2 data relationship.
22. Sparse indexes are supported at the _____ level.
23. A sparse index is an index that contains entries for ALL/ONLY A FEW rows in a table.
24. When a large table is to be accessed, usage of a sparse index can save much unnecessary processing. (T/F)
25. Another name for a sparse index is a _____ index.
26. Arrays (internal to a row) are suited to MOST/A FEW PATTERNS of data access and organization.
27. Because of normalization, DB2 is unsuited to support arrays internal to a row. (T/F)
28. In DB2, each field in an array must be separately _____.

29. DB2 IS/IS NOT aware that fields with different names are related together in an array.

30. A data structure especially useful for FIRST IN/LAST OUT processing is the _____.

31. Stacks generally are associated with a variable known as the _____.

32. A standard DB2 table CAN/CANNOT easily be used to create a stack.

33. Logically related data contains a common _____.

34. Logically related data is often the result of _____.

35. When a table is physically split, it is often split according to the value of its _____.

36. If a table is split on a key, each partition of data WILL/WILL NOT/MAY NOT have an equal amount of data.

37. When data is split by key, each partition MUST/MAY have the same definition.

38. When data is split at the key level (a) availability, (b) performance, (c) availability and performance are usually enhanced.

39. A recursive structure is one in which one type of data points to _____.

40. Some classical recursive structures are _____.

41. Two forms of recursive structures are the _____ level recursive structure and the _____ recursive structure.

CHAPTER 10

Referential Integrity

Referential integrity is the action taken by the system or the application to ensure that the integrity of data relationships is complete and valid. In previous discussions, data structures and relationships were addressed. Referential integrity is the means by which those data relationships are built and maintained. This chapter identifies the typical forms of referential integrity and how those forms of referential integrity can be implemented.

AN APPLICATION RESPONSIBILITY

Through Release 3 of DB2, referential integrity is the responsibility of the application designer. After Release 3, referential integrity may be accomplished by DB2. Referential integrity in DB2 is implemented only to the extent that the application designer specifies.

Consider the simple relationship between a part and a supplier as shown in Figure 10-1.

A part is provided by a supplier and a supplier provides a part. There may be multiple parts for a supplier or multiple suppliers for a part. The most straightforward way to build the relationship at the application level is by means of an application built and supported cross-reference table. To support the cross-reference relationship, two cross-reference tables exist: a part/supplier cross reference table and a supplier/part cross-reference table. Of course, at the DB2 level the relationship could be built by means of DB2-supported referential

```
┌─────────────────────────────────────────┐
│                                         │
│      ( part )◄──────►( supplier )       │
│                                         │
│      an m:n part supplier               │
│      relationship                       │
│                                         │
└─────────────────────────────────────────┘
```

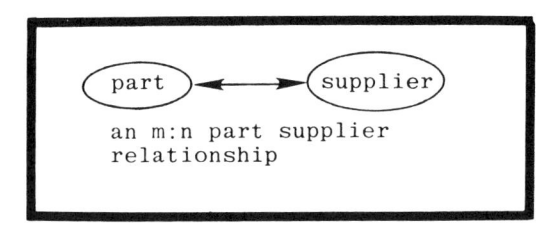

FIGURE 10-1. An m:n part/supplier relationship.

integrity using a parent table and a dependent table. The parts table could be specified as the parent table and the supplier table could be the dependent table. Both tables would contain the column part number. Part number would be the primary key in the parts table, and would be the foreign key in the supplier table, under a DB2 implementation of the relationship.

The content of the two cross-reference tables in the application support case are identical; only the order of the contents is changed. (In other words, any relationship supported in one cross-reference table will be supported in the other cross-reference table.)

The dynamics of the tables are illustrated by an example. On day 1, part A is added to the parts database, and supplier B is added to the supplier database. At this point in time, there is no relationship between the part and the supplier even though the base information is in the system. On day 2, the production control analyst decides that part A can have supplier B as a provider. At that time, two entries are made into the cross-reference tables.

In the part/supplier cross-reference table, a row is inserted with keys—part A, supplier B. In the supplier/part cross-reference table, a row is inserted—supplier B, part A.

At this point in time, a relationship exists between part A and supplier B. Upon termination of the relationship, both entries in the cross-reference tables need to be deleted. Note that the termination of the relationship does not necessarily mean the termination of the base data. Part A can go on existing as well as supplier B. It's just that they no longer have a relationship.

Of course, if part A is deleted or if supplier B is deleted, then, at that moment, the relationship between the two is likewise deleted.

When the relationship is supported under DB2, rather than the application, the design does not have to worry about the dynamics previously discussed. Instead, the designer must take into consideration the rules of referential integrity surrounding the activities of

Chapter 10   Referential Integrity   139

DELETION, INSERTION, and UPDATE. As a simple example of the deletion considerations, suppose a relationship between a part and supplier exists. Now, suppose a particular key—PART ABC—is deleted. Referential integrity may specify that the deletion cannot occur until all occurrences of PART ABC in the supplier table are deleted. This simple example gives rise to the phenomena known as the "cascading delete." The cascading delete is a chain reaction phenomena that can occur using DB2-supported referential integrity.

For example, suppose a deletion of a part causes several suppliers to be deleted. The deletion of one or more suppliers causes many orders to be deleted. The deletion of many orders causes even more inventory records to be deleted, and so forth. With a little imagination it is easy to see a single, innocent deletion setting off a large chain reaction.

DIFFERENT FORMS OF REFERENTIAL INTEGRITY

This simple form of a data relationship supported by referential integrity serves to illustrate the basic interactions. There can be MANY forms of referential integrity over different types of relationships. As

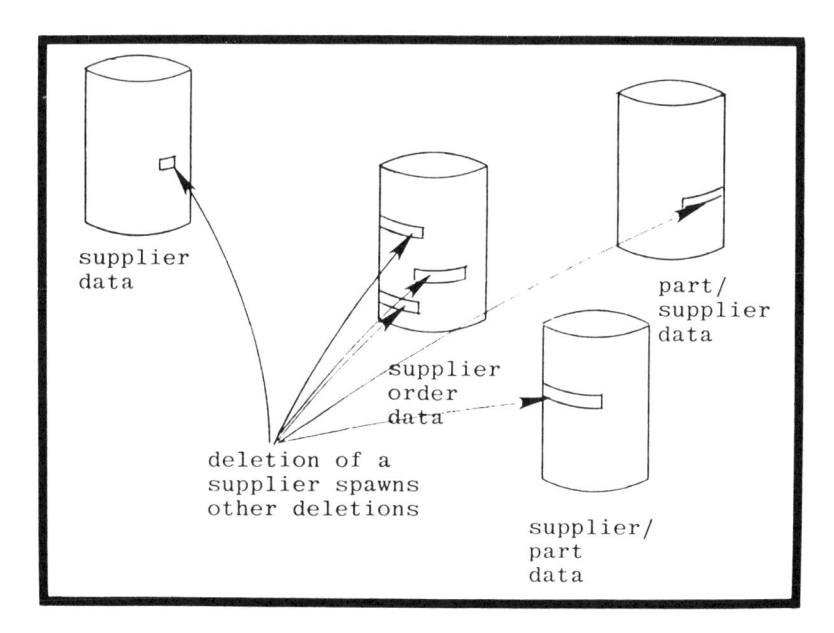

FIGURE 10–2. Referential integrity work resulting from the deletion of a supplier from the database.

an example of a simple form of referential integrity, if employee payroll status equals "a" for active, then employee death date must equal null values. Or, as another simple example of a data relationship, if employee row does not exist, then an employee/dependent row must likewise not exist. The types of referential integrity and data relationships take many forms. The forms taken are patterned after the business rules of an enterprise.

Referential integrity, whether implemented by the application or by DB2, is an application design and implementation issue primarily during the database activities of insertion and deletion of data. As data is inserted and deleted, it must conform to the basic existence dependency rules of the business or enterprise. On occasion, replacement of data (i.e., update of data) will affect the activities of referential integrity.

The amount of overhead done by the system or the application caused by referential integrity can be significant. For example, suppose, in a manufacturing environment, that a supplier is deleted. With the deletion of a supplier comes a deletion of all orders to the supplier, all part/supplier and supplier/part relationships, and so forth as shown in Figure 10-2.

The amount of data accessed and the number of deletions done can be enormous.

One scenario for the maintenance of the relationship using application supported integrity is for maintenance to occur immediately upon changing of the data. For example, in the case of the manufacturing environment, where a supplier is deleted, the deletion of all related supplier information is done in the execution of the same program in which the supplier was deleted. The effect is continuous integrity of the data relationship.

But, oftentimes, maintaining referential integrity is quite expensive in terms of the resources consumed on behalf of integrity. In the case of a deletion of a supplier, many I/Os may be consumed by the subsequent deletion of related supplier data and data relationships.

DEFERRED REFERENTIAL INTEGRITY

Because of the online resources consumed, instantaneous maintenance of referential integrity often is not desirable or even possible. An alternative strategy is to do database updates, deletions, and inserts online and leave the maintenance of relationships for later batch processing. This strategy saves online resources in that heavy maintenance occurs away from the online window.

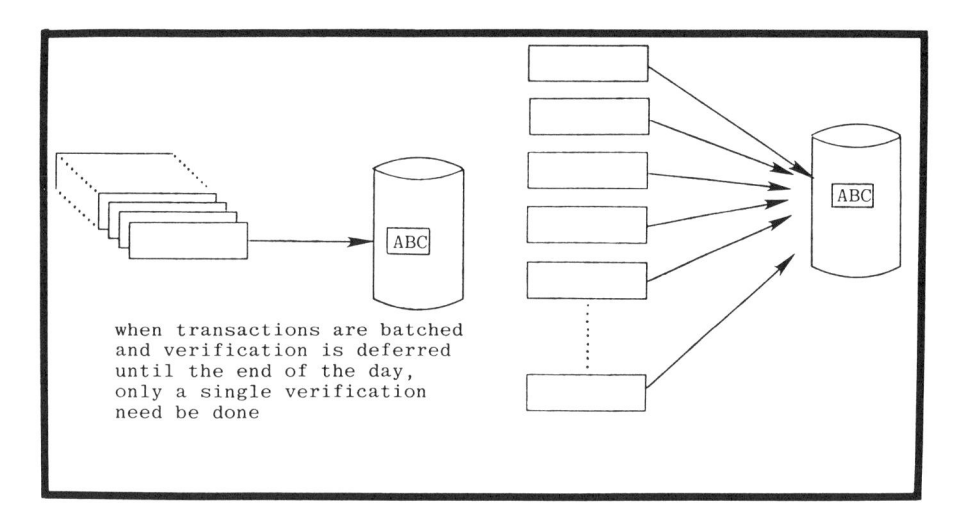

FIGURE 10-3. When transactions are batched and verification is deferred until the end of the day, only a single verification need be done.

But the deferred maintenance approach to referential integrity has an exposure. From the time that the online update is made until the batch maintenance of the relationship is done, the data is logically "impure." In other words, for a period of time, the integrity of the relationship has been violated.

Depending upon the data and the nature of the relationship that is supported by referential integrity, this exposure may or may not be significant. Of course, if the exposure is serious, then a strategy of deferred maintenance will not suffice.

There may be other economies in delaying the maintenance and verification of referential integrity. Consider the example of an order, a part and a supplier. These entities are logically related by the business of the enterprise. Suppose that, during the daytime, the orders are received. Each order normally contains many line items. To verify that an order can be filled during the daytime requires verifying the existence of the supplier and the part, as well as other related items. For the verification of a large order, many I/Os are required.

Suppose orders are stored during the day with no verification. During the evening, all daily orders are batched together and the parts that have been ordered are sorted in part sequence. Now, when the existence of a part must be verified, it will be verified only once, not for each time that it was ordered during the day.

For example, if throughout the day there have been 10 orders for part ABC, then the verification of the existence of part ABC will be done only once in the evening, not 10 times throughout the day as illustrated by Figure 10-3.

The result is that the batching and sorting of post-online activities can be much more efficient than if the same activity were handled individually throughout the day. Of course, an order must wait for overnight verification to determine if it was a valid order, which may not be acceptable to the customer in some cases.

Consider the case when an order appears that contains one or more invalid parts. The part (or line item) is deleted and the order is adjusted. Depending on the customer and the order, the customer may or may not be notified that the part being ordered will not be filled.

APPLICATION CONVENTIONS

Another way that significant savings can be made in the implementation of referential integrity at the application level is in the usage of *application conventions*. An application convention is merely a means of coordinating the needs for referential integrity over an entire application. Application conventions apply where one data relationship is known to be dependent on other relationships.

For example, suppose that there is a delivery made of a part to a customer based on an order. The application programmer only needs to verify that an order for a part has occurred. Referential integrity does not need to confirm the existence of the part itself, based on the assumption that an order for a part could not exist unless earlier application code had made the verification. The total needs for referential integrity can be limited by carefully coordinating the different applications that operate on data.

INDEPENDENT AUDITS

A final concern of referential integrity is the occasional audit that needs to be made, independent of the normal application code that supports updates, deletions, and insertions. In theory, as long as a relationship is designed and programmed correctly, there is no need for independent audit of data relationships. But design and programming flaws do exist, as well as operating flaws. There are a host of reasons why data relationships—under the best of circumstances—sometimes get out of synchronization.

As a result, independent audits created by the application programmer need to be run periodically. Consider the audit of a simple part, supplier, part/supplier cross-reference and supplier/part cross-reference. An audit program can be written to capture all the parts (from the part table) and sort them if necessary. The first step of the audit matches the sorted parts against the part/supplier cross-reference. Every cross-reference entry should have a corresponding part entry, although not every part will necessarily be found in the part/supplier cross-reference. Next, the supplier table is sorted on supplier number (if necessary) and is matched against the supplier/part cross-reference table. Like the part and part/supplier cross-reference, every entry in the supplier/part cross-reference must exist in the sorted supplier table. And a supplier may or may not exist in the supplier/part cross-reference.

Next, one of the cross reference tables is sorted into the sequence of the other one, and the two tables are matched against each other. There will be a one-to-one relationship between the two tables. Any entry existing in one table and not the other will be an error.

FREQUENCY OF AUDIT

The frequency of audit is determined by several factors, such as—

- how sensitive the data is,
- how complex the relationship is,
- how much data is contained in the relationship, etc.

Generally speaking, the volume of data that must be manipulated is such that audits are done on as infrequent a basis as possible.

APPLICATION SUPPORTED OR DB2-SUPPORTED REFERENTIAL INTEGRITY?

A major decision facing the developer is whether to implement referential integrity at the application level or by DB2. If the issues center on control, it is likely that application-supported options give the designer the most choices and the greatest amount of control. If the issue is on simplicity of code, it is likely that DB2-supported relationships are the best choice. In any case, the underlying work done by the system should be accounted for. In addition, if DB2 relationships are chosen, the designer should keep the relationships as simple as possible.

SUMMARY

In summary, this chapter has discussed what referential integrity is, the different levels of complexity of data relationships, and how referential integrity is based on business rules. The issues of when to do referential integrity and what application conventions were discussed next. Finally, the auditing of the relationships was discussed.

QUESTIONS: REFERENTIAL INTEGRITY

1. In DB2, data relationships can be managed at the _____.
2. Data relationships are created and maintained across more than one table by the existence of _____ keys.
3. For multivalued m:n—relationships, relationships are maintained by means of _____ tables.
4. When two tables are related, a deletion of a row in one table CAUSES/MAY CAUSE a deletion in one or more tables.
5. When two tables are related, an insertion of a row in one table CAUSES/MAY CAUSE/IS INCIDENTAL TO insertions to other tables.
6. When two tables are related, only when there is a relationship between two rows will insertion/deletion activity need to be coordinated. (T/F)
7. Updates to data—as opposed to insertion and deletions—have NO/LITTLE/FREQUENT/OCCASIONAL bearing on the work required by referential integrity.
8. There are MANY/FEW/A LIMITED NUMBER of forms of referential integrity.
9. Referential integrity CAN/CANNOT be deferred.
10. Referential integrity CAN/CANNOT be deferred in all cases.
11. When referential integrity is deferred, for a period of time there is an _____ exposure.
12. Online referential integrity that is deferred is usually deferred to the _____ environment.

Chapter 10   Referential Integrity   145

13. In the batch environment, integrity verification can be batched. This MAY/WILL/CANNOT save some processing.

14. Deferring referential integrity processing to the batch environment has the effect of _____ online performance.

15. Another way the resources used by referential integrity can be minimized is to use application_____.

16. Another way to verify referential integrity is through the occasional _____ audit.

17. When systems are designed and programmed correctly, there is no need for an independent audit. (T/F)

18. Referential integrity errors can occur because of _____ and _____ errors.

19. Independent audits need to be run as FREQUENTLY/INFREQUENTLY as possible.

20. Independent audits for a large database consume SMALL/MEDIUM/LARGE amounts of resources.

21. The _____ of the data relationship determines, in part, how many resources the independent audit will take.

CHAPTER 11

The DB2 Batch Environment

The first consideration of the production environment is online performance and availability. When adequate online performance cannot be achieved, the question must be asked, Why do transaction processing at all?

But there is more to the production environment than the online, peak-period processing. The other major production environment is the batch environment, which typically occurs during off-peak-period processing hours. Even though the DB2 set processing orientation is ideal for batch sequential processing, several aspects of the batch environment must be carefully considered.

THE BATCH WINDOW

The peak-period processing time frame usually defines—by default—the batch window. In short, everything that is not peak-period is considered to be the batch window. The *batch window*, then, is that period of time when system resources can be used with no impact on online performance. Typically, long sequential processes are run in the batch window.

It is very important that—

> the batch window be carefully estimated, and
> the batch window time frame be formally defined.

As long as a shop handles a small amount of processing and/or a small amount of data, then the batch window will probably remain adequate for all the batch needs in the foreseeable future. But in the face of large amounts of processing and/or large amounts of data (as is common in the production environment), then the batch window, on occasion, may not be adequate. Over time, the batch window tends to shrink. And when the batch window becomes inadequate, the computer operator is left with Hobson's choice—either run the online environment in a performance-impaired state, or do not do some amount of batch processing. In either case, the end user suffers. Consequently, when the production environment is being planned, more than casual attention should be paid to the batch window.

To determine if all batch processing will fit in the window, a series of crude measurements can be made. The following example illustrates one of these crude measurements.

Suppose a large database must be scanned. Suppose there are 10,000 pages of data in the database. Assume the index will not be used and assume that the data is reasonably well organized.

Assume that no other program will attempt to access the data while the scan is occurring. To calculate the length of the batch run, two times are calculated: initiation/shutdown time and database processing time. (Note that machine time, not elapsed time, is being calculated here.)

Processing time = initiation/shutdown + database processing

Now database processing time must be calculated. In general, each page of data will require around 25 milliseconds for the I/O needed.

Database processing = 10,000 pages × 25/1000 seconds

Now assume that 30 seconds of startup/shutdown time is required.

Processing time = 30 secs + (10,000 × 25/1000) = 280 seconds = 4.66 min.

Many other factors must be considered in the calculation of total batch resources required than just the machine requirements, however.

- Does the database have to be scanned sequentially? If it can be scanned in parallel, then elapsed time may be substantially less than machine time.
- How busy is the machine? Does the machine have to process a heavy workload, and consequently stretch elapsed time significantly longer than machine time?
- What contention will there be for data? If there is a fair amount of contention for data, elapsed time may be significantly longer than machine time.

In short, the simple calculation presented for machine time requirements only gives a relative figure for the rough estimation of the required length of the batch window.

WHAT RUNS IN THE BATCH WINDOW

The sorts of activities that typically run in the batch window include—

- utilities—backup, image copies, space management, data analysis, reorganization of data, data definition, etc.
- application—resorting, merging, summarization, extraction, etc.
- system software—testing, release preparation, etc.

ALL of the processing requirements for the batch window must be factored into total batch window requirements. But many of the processes that are run are only incidental to the application designer. For example, the designer has very little influence over the data analysis utilities that are run by data administration and database administration. However, the designer does have influence over such batch activities as the batch application processing that occurs and the size of the databases. As a consequence, this chapter will focus on those aspects that can be controlled by the designer.

I/O AND JOINED DATABASES

In the online environment, it has been noted, databases that require joins use much I/O and, in doing so, potentially harm performance. But joined databases can be detrimental to the amount of resources used in the batch window as well as the online window. Careless or uninformed usage of joined databases can cause massive amounts of

I/O to be consumed. The tremendous savings of I/O that is possible is illustrated by an example. Consider the data structure found in Figure 11-1.

Figure 11-1 shows three databases—a parts database, a supplier database, and a parts/supplier cross-reference database. The intent of processing for the batch program being considered is to create records for each part/supplier relationship for the two databases—a classical batch sequential processing activity.

A simple approach is to use a relational join of the two databases to be scanned and simply create the intersection of the two databases. The relational join would begin with the parts database and select a part. Then the cross-reference database would be accessed based upon the value of the part, selecting all the suppliers that supply the part. Then the different suppliers would be accessed, completing the join.

This simple programming technique suggested creates a call pattern as shown by Figure 11-2.

Figure 11-2 shows that the parts database is accessed sequentially, and the pattern of access suggested above is followed.

The amount of I/O used to process the simple algorithm is considerable. Indeed, just how much I/O is consumed?

The parts database is scanned sequentially using 250 I/Os (assuming buffer-flushing does not occur). The parts supplier database is likewise scanned sequentially using another 200 I/Os (and likewise assuming buffers are not being rapidly flushed). Then each entry into the supplier database goes into a different page (except for the occasional fortuitous buffer hit) using 30,000 I/Os. (For the sake of

```
PARTNO      DESCR         UM    QOH      PARTNO/SUPP       SUPPLIER      NAME          PHONE
01258-QX    ball bearingbox    900       01258    JONE     JONES Hdware  JP Carson     998-0791
01258-QZ    plate         unit  89       01258    KANS     KANSas SupplyJB Rivers      807-7760
01260       assem 18      crat  125      01258    EMPO     EMPOrium       R D'field    880-8076
01268       assem 980     unit  0        01259    JONE     WILSon SupplyB Hackett      908-5554
   :           :            :    :          :      :           :             :            :
   :           :            :    :          :      :           :             :            :

data base statistics:
   PARTNO Table     -    40 rows/page        250 pages       10000 parts
   PART/SUPP Table  -   150 rows/page        200 pages       30000 part/supp xrefs
   SUPPLIER Table   -    25 rows/page         40 pages        1000 suppliers
```

FIGURE 11–1. Three databases illustrating a classical batch sequential processing activity.

```
call sequence to join the
two data bases -

part1     part1/suppA     supplier A
          part1/suppG     supplier G
          part1/suppL     supplier L
part2     part2/suppB     supplier B
          part2/suppC     supplier C
          part2/suppG     supplier G
          part2/suppM     supplier M
          part2/suppP     supplier P
part3     part3/suppA     supplier A
part4     part4/suppC     supplier C
          part4/suppK     supplier K
          part4/suppL     supplier L
  .          .               .
  .          .               .
  .          .               .
```

FIGURE 11-2. Call sequence to join the two databases.

argument, assume 27,000 actual I/Os are done—at a rate of 10 percent fortuitous buffer hits). The number of I/Os needed to process the simple batch join is—

$$250 + 200 + 27{,}000 = 27450 \text{ I/Os}$$

Now consider a much more complex programming approach. Assume that the part/supplier relationship is sorted and is ordered by supplier order. Next, the sorted part/supplier data is passed against the supplier database, creating a part/supp/supplier intermediate record. Now the part/supp/supplier intermediate records are sorted by part number. Then the parts database is scanned and is matched against the part/supp/supplier intermediate record, creating the desired part/supplier joined data.

Consider the I/O required to support this algorithm:

1. Sort part/supp into supplier order—200 reads, 200 writes, sort I/O

2. Creation of part/supp/supplier intermediate records—200 reads (part/supply sorted data), 40 reads (supplier data), 200 writes (of the intermediate record)—assuming the intermediate record fits into the same number of pages as read out of)

3. Sort intermediate records by part number—200 reads, 200 writes, sort I/O

4. Merging of intermediate record with parts data—250 reads, 200 reads, 400 writes (assuming the joined record created is long enough to require more space)

The I/O required then is—

step 1	400 I/Os	sort I/Os
step 2	440 I/Os	
step 3	400 I/Os	sort I/Os
step 4	850 I/Os	
total	2,090 I/Os	2 sort I/Os

Even if the sorts require as much as 1,000 I/Os (which is probably a high number), the economics of not using the simple relational join greatly favor a less straightforward approach of sorting and merging data.

The order of magnitude of difference in I/Os used is anything but far-fetched. And the I/Os consumed in the batch environment are as important as the I/Os in the online environment when considered collectively for the batch window.

Furthermore, the example shown is for relatively small amounts of data over very simple relationships that use indexed clustered data (i.e., the best of all possible worlds). In something less than the best of all worlds, it is safe to say that the I/O consumed by the first approach would be substantially more.

Consequently, the designer must be very careful in the design and management of joined relationships in the batch environment.

PARALLEL SEQUENTIAL RUNS

An important design strategy in the management of the batch window is the ability to break long batch processes into a series of shorter running processes that can be run in parallel. Consider the two types of runs shown in Figure 11-3.

In Figure 11-3, there are two scenarios. In one scenario, all parts are updated in a single batch run, requiring four hours of processing. In another scenario, each batch run updates one-fourth of the database, and an elapsed time of one hour is required. In addition, there is no reason why the runs cannot be run on separate processors.

Chapter 11   The DB2 Batch Environment   153

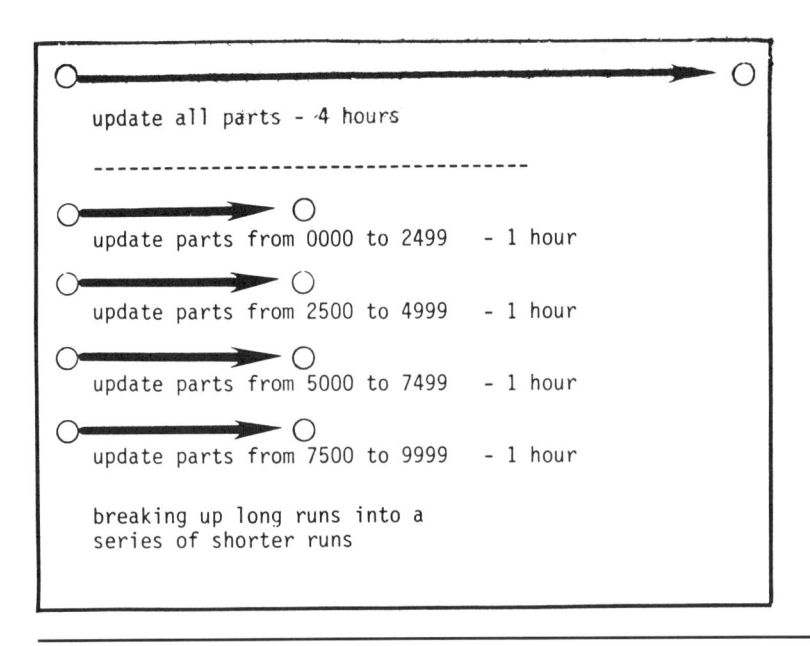

```
○─────────────────────────────────────►○
  update all parts - 4 hours
  -------------------------------------
○──────►○
  update parts from 0000 to 2499    - 1 hour
○──────►○
  update parts from 2500 to 4999    - 1 hour
○──────►○
  update parts from 5000 to 7499    - 1 hour
○──────►○
  update parts from 7500 to 9999    - 1 hour

  breaking up long runs into a
  series of shorter runs
```

FIGURE 11–3. Breaking up long runs into a series of shorter runs.

The ability to break large runs into asynchronously executable shorter runs depends upon many factors, such as—

- the ability to insulate data. If all four shorter runs operated on the same data, then there would be no point in breaking up the runs.
- the ability of the host processor to multiprocess. If only one task can be run at a time, then there is no point in breaking up long batch runs into shorter runs. Often the ability to multiprocess is not a function of the operating system but of the application. Because of the contention for data and the need to run a job serially, classical multiprocessing at the operating system level is not applicable.

The design option that greatly facilitates these goals is the physical separation of data at the application level. When the application divides the data over four physically separate data bases—

- update contention is minimized because the system considers the data bases to be separate and distinct, and
- the ability to spread processing physically over multiple processors is enhanced because data can be processed independently.

Of course, when the designer breaks data into physically smaller and separate databases, then the processing strategy naturally follows. For example, if a database were broken by geographic location, the batch processing would not be broken along the lines of marketing divisions. In other words, the major divisions of data must apply throughout the organization.

SINGLE EXTRACT PROCESSING

It is common during the batch window to do a certain amount of extract processing. In some cases, there is only a small amount to be done; in other cases, a large amount needs to be done. When a large amount of extract processing needs to be done, it makes sense to process against the data being extracted once, not multiple times, as shown in Figure 11-4.

The first savings in the consolidation of extract processing is in the database that is being extracted—the database is passed once, not multiple times. Suppose there are m pages of data in the database being extracted and suppose there are n extracts of the database being made. Then the savings are—

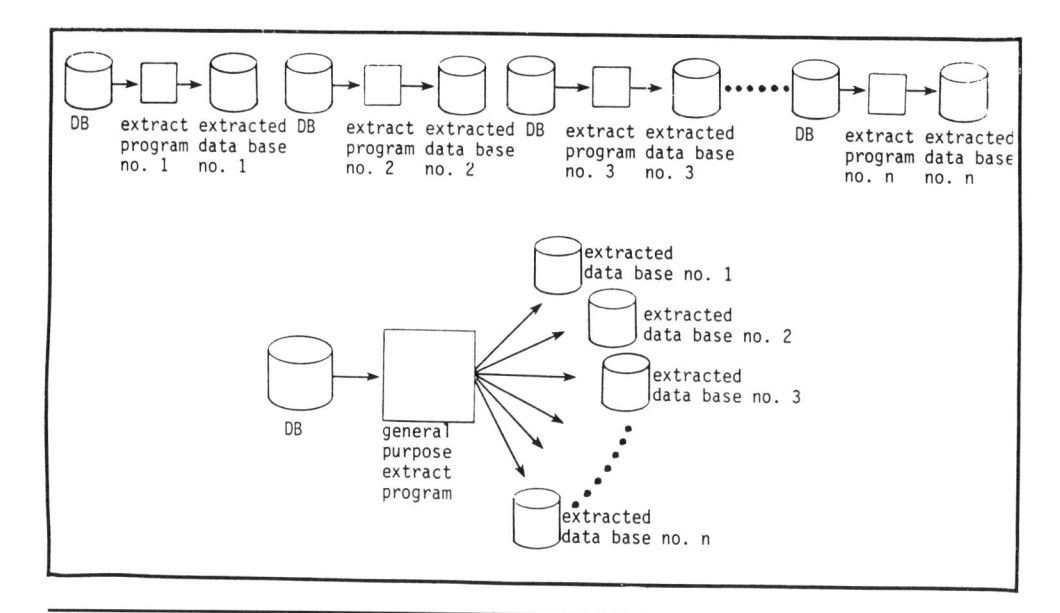

FIGURE 11-4. Single-extract processing.

$$(n-1) \times m = \text{saved I/O}$$

But saved I/O is not the only performance gain. When extracts are done sequentially, the access to the database being extracted can become its own bottleneck. In other words, extrtact n (and all the processes that depend upon extract n being completed) cannot proceed until extracts 1, 2, 3, . . . , n−1 have been completed. But when there is a single extract, extract n does not have to wait on other extracts to be completed.

To this end, the following practices apply:

- Save extracted files until the next extract is run. If unanticipated needs arise, the extracted file may suffice without having to rerun the extract program.
- Extract the full set of information that may possibly be used. Oftentimes, an extract is done, and, after the extract, it is determined that a slightly different set of data is needed. When the extract is done precisely, yielding only the exact amount of data needed, another extract must be done. But when a "superset" of data is extracted originally, there may be no need to go back and re-extract from the original database.

SORTING TRANSACTIONS INTO PRIMARY PROCESSING SEQUENCE

A considerable amount of I/O can be saved by sorting the transactions that will be processed in batch into a sequence compatible with the file against which they will be processed. For example, suppose a parts database is updated nightly in the batch window by transactions collected throughout the day.

Suppose there are 1,000 transactions gathered on the average, and that the transactions must go against 500 pages of parts data. If the transactions are not sorted into parts sequence, then it is likely that each transaction is going to require its own individual I/O into the parts database (ignoring the occasional fortuitous buffer hit). In the case where unsorted transactions are processed, 1,000 I/O will be needed.

Now suppose the transaction file is sorted into a sequence compatible with the parts database. In this case, up to 500 I/Os will be required (plus a few more I/Os where the buffer is flushed and must be reread.) The savings in I/O are obvious.

ORDERING BATCH RUNS

Two factors determine the order in which batch runs are executed in the batch window:

- The mandatory sequence of execution
- The priority of execution when there is no mandatory order

The mandatory sequence of execution is determined when one job cannot execute until another job is finished. For example, suppose job A updates a database and job B writes a report from the database. It does not make sense to run job B until job A has completed. The entire job stream executed in the batch window must be sensitive to this mandatory ordering of jobs.

But not all jobs or job streams are sensitive to a mandatory ordering of processing. When there is no mandatory ordering of jobs, a prioritization of job processing must be made. The sooner in the batch window a job can execute, the less chance the window will close without having executed the job. As a consequence, the most important jobs should be scheduled for execution at the beginning of the batch window.

A normal part of every job (and job stream) is a contingency plan for the job in the event the job fails to execute. In some cases, the job may not run because of an application failure. In other cases, the job may not run because of the abnormal closing of the batch window. In any case, every batch job requires its own contingency plan.

In some cases, a report will not be delivered to the user, with no other impact. In other cases, the impact is more severe. The user may not be able to use the database until the batch processing is done. At the very least, the contingency plan should outline what other batch (and online) processing will be impacted by a failure to execute.

CONSOLIDATION OF UPDATE REQUIREMENTS

Just as extract requirements should be consolidated into a single program, so should batch update requirements be consolidated, as shown by Figure 11-5.

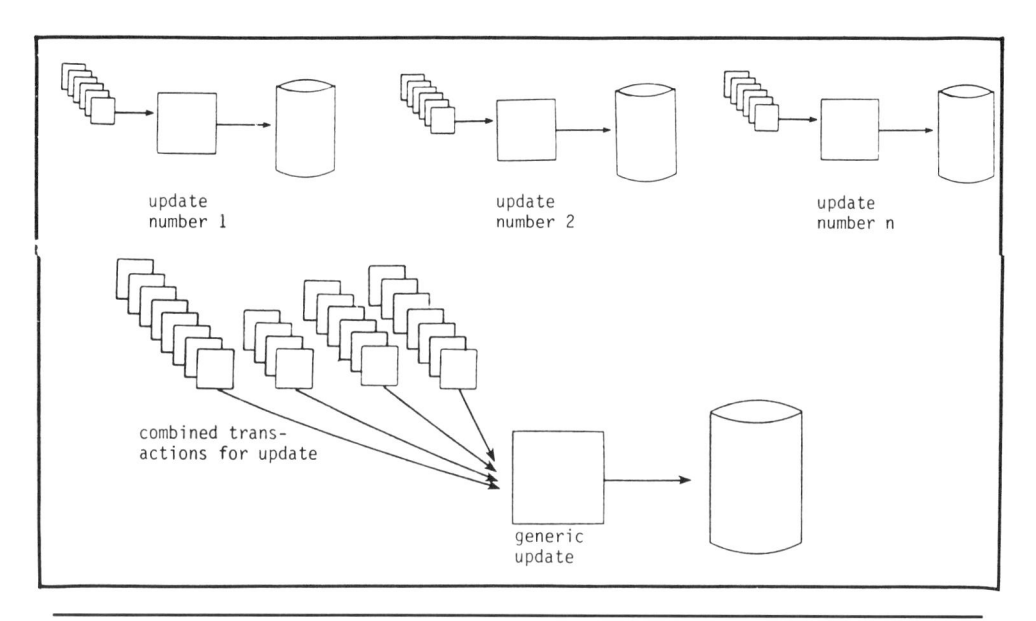

FIGURE 11-5. Consolidation of batch update requirements.

PEAK-PERIOD PROCESSING

The batch window, like the online window, typically has its peak-period processing moments. And the consequences of not anticipating peak-period requirements in the batch window can be as severe as not anticipating them in the online window.

When the batch window must be extended, either the online window does not come up as scheduled or the amount of work done in the batch window is short-changed.

The peak periods for the batch window typically include month-end processing, year-end processing, business cycle peak periods, and so forth. It is worth the DB2 designer's time to anticipate these peak periods.

When peak periods are anticipated, there are several options the designer has:

- Split processing (if possible) across more than one processor
- Reduce peak periods by altering applications. For example, a bank may produce statements for its customers once a month, but may do so in independent cycles so that, on any given working day, only a fraction of the customers have statements produced.

SMALL DATABASES

In many other contexts, the usefulness of small databases has been noted. In the management of the batch window, small databases are likewise quite useful. If there is a generic design practice in DB2 for the management of the batch window, it is that databases be kept as small as possible.

Small databases—

- allow the largest amount of freedom in the structuring of the job stream in the batch window,
- affect (beneficially) not just application batch processing but utilities as well,
- give the operator managing the batch window the most flexibility in ending or extending the batch window,
- reduce the amount of work needed in reprocessing and/or backing out data in a recovery, in the eventuality of a failure,
- automatically reduce the set size that is processed by a DB2 SQL statement,
- provide opportunities for parallel processing on separate processors,
- can be tailored to a specific users needs rather than having to generically fit a large population of users.

In short, the advantages of small databases far outweigh the disadvantages and are strongly advised for the management of the batch window.

SYSTEM CONSIDERATIONS

In the batch environment, certain standard design practices must be followed. For example, internal data integrity resources must be periodically released, as well as buffers, etc. In the DB2/IMS environment, this means that BMPs must be checkpointed frequently. Periodic checkpoints have the effect of streamlining the flow of processing through DB2.

Checkpointing can be done on a basis of elapsed time, number of calls issued, or application logic breaks (or some combination of these).

Chapter 11   The DB2 Batch Environment

SUMMARY

The batch environment for DB2 is as important as the online environment. If batch processing extends into the online processing day, the performance implications are obvious.

Planning for the batch window begins with an estimation of how long the window needs to be open, both on the average and in the worst case. The requirements of the batch window are compared with the business requirements of the online day.

Some techniques for the minimization/streamlining of processing in the batch window are the following:

- Minimizing the need for relational joins. Usually, relational joins require many more resources than simple sort and merges.
- Creating parallel runs. The elapsed time can be significantly shrunk when a long run can be broken into a series of shorter runs that can be run in parallel.
- Do extract processing in a single run.
- Sort transactions in an order compatible with the physical organization of the database against which the transaction will be run.

QUESTIONS: THE DB2 BATCH ENVIRONMENT

1. The production environment has two major divisions—online processing and _____ processing.
2. Long sequential processes are run during the _____ window.
3. The batch window is ALWAYS/SOMETIMES during off peak hours.
4. Online processing is hampered when the batch window extends into the online day. (T/F)
5. If the batch window is not long enough, either it must be extended or batch jobs that are scheduled to run will not be run. (T/F)
6. The length of the batch window varies SUBSTANTIALLY/ONLY SLIGHTLY.

7. The length of the batch window needs to be estimated as part of the design of the APPLICATION/THE ENTIRE BATCH ENVIRONMENT.

8. Estimates of batch processing may take into account buffer "hits" due to sequential processing. (T/F)

9. Batch I/Os are done in the SAME/LESS THAN/MORE THAN time range as online I/Os.

10. Database design is SAME/LESS THAN/MORE THAN level of importance as it is for online systems.

11. Name some typical activities that run during the batch window.

12. Database joins are no problem in the batch environment. (T/F)

13. For a large database, a sort and merge procedure is OFTEN/SELDOM more efficient than a join.

14. Batch updates are run more efficiently if, prior to update, they are _____ in the sequence of the database against which they will be processed.

15. Parallel sequential runs can be executed when the same data IS/IS NOT needed by the two or more runs.

16. Parallel runs have the potential of being run on _____ processors.

17. Most DSS databases are periodically fed by a batch process known as an _____ program.

18. Extracted data is sent to the DSS environment for _____ processing and analysis.

19. There may be great economies of processing if there is much extract processing and if all the extracts against a given database are combined into a _____ extract.

20. Extracting as much data as might be needed, not merely the amount specified by the analyst often saves _____.

21. Saving extract files until the next major extract (a) can save unexpected processing, (b) wastes space, (c) is overly cautious.

22. When batch job A updates a database and batch job B reports from the database, then job A MUST/MIGHT be run before B.

23. There USUALLY/ALWAYS/SOMETIMES is a mandatory sequencing of batch jobs.

24. When there is no mandatory sequence of execution of batch jobs, then the jobs can be _____.

25. Typical periods of peak batch processing come at _____, _____, _____, etc.

26. The analyst must account for peak-period batch processing as well as peak-period processing. (T/F)

CHAPTER 12

Testing DB2 Production Systems

This discussion is divided into two sections. The first section discusses the establishment and usage of the DB2 test environment. It is for the database administrator, the system administrator, or anyone interested in the DB2 testing environment. The second section is on testing individual DB2 programs, primarily for the production environment. This section is for programmers.

THE DB2 TEST ENVIRONMENT

DB2 is a powerful tool that can be used in many different ways. When DB2 is being used in the ad hoc or information center environment, there is a need to test the accuracy of programs so that the proper calculations are done. But when DB2 is used in the production mode, there is a need to do much more rigorous testing because there are more variables that must be accounted for. Not only is the testing of code and algorithms important in the production environment, but the usage of data, the volume of processing, the volume of data, and so forth must be accounted for. By the time an application goes into implementation, it is expensive to try to retrofit characteristics such as performance and availability into the production environment. Properly executed testing, then, is one of the major keys to the achievement of satisfactory production DB2 systems. Of course, testing should be done not only for new development, but for major changes to existing systems as well.

The first step in the proper testing of a DB2 application is the establishment of the DB2 test environment.

There are three major components to the DB2 test environment: the input used to drive the test environment, the databases on which testing is done, and the actual configuration of the teleprocessing monitor and DB2. Each of these components will be discussed at length.

INPUT TO TESTING

Input to the test environment is what is used to stimulate the execution of DB2 transactions and programs. As in any test environment, the input needs to be carefully constructed in order to fully verify the many conditions that may occur once the system is into production. Typically, test input must be carefully coordinated with test data so that nonsensical conditions will not arise. For example, an update of a table where no rows exist serves only to check out exception logic; the test does not check out the actual application update logic. Because of the need to orchestrate input and test data carefully, care should be taken in the design, execution, and ultimate storage of both test input and test data.

Input test data serves at least two purposes: the verification of program logic and the means to "stress" test the system. There are different considerations to both types of testing. The testing of program logic should test all reasonable possible conditions, both legitimate and illegitimate. Of course, illegitimate conditions should trigger error conditions and should be handled without bringing the system down. Legitimate input should exercise the full cycle of data—from creation to deletion. Of course, the interrelationships of DB2 tables should be tested as well.

The testing of programmatic relationships usually requires that each unit of input be created manually in coordination with a known test database. To verify that inserts, deletes, etc. are being done properly requires a foreknowledge of what data is and is not in the test database. Because of the complexity of the conditions that may exist and the need for coordination between data and program, the data for the testing of programmatic relationships is usually small. The test database, of course, must be able to be reinitialized to recreate the test conditions.

STRESS TESTS

Stress tests of a DB2 application are not nearly as sensitive to program logic that is being executed. Indeed, the same activity can often be run repeatedly in a stress test. However, stress tests are sensitive to the amount of data, the amount of activity, and the rate at which the activity arrives for execution that will be executed in the production environment.

As long as the mixture of updates to access is properly maintained, as long as the sequence of transactions is properly constructed, and as long as the job stream being used for testing is representative of the final implemented workload and does not create queues that would not naturally form otherwise, practically any transaction will do for stress-testing of a DB2 application.

For systems that are being converted rather than being written for the first time, a sampling of existing transactions may suffice as input into the stress test. Of course, when existing transactions are used for stress-testing, care must be taken to not update or transact against real data. For new applications, the input for stress testing must be created from scratch.

STRESS-TESTING AND SERVICE-LEVEL AGREEMENTS

In some cases, the maximum number of transactions that must be driven through the online system is known. The stress test must then achieve the same level of throughput to simulate the workload that will be implemented. In the case where the maximum workload is known, it is good practice to drive the system at least 10 percent higher than the maximum known rate to transaction processing. This slight overkill may be useful in identifying "hot spots" in the design and represents some degree of protection if the maximum rate that is targeted is too low. In the case where the maximum transaction rate is not known, it is good practice to estimate as carefully as possible the maximum transaction arrival rate (MTAR), then add at least 25 percent for the purposes of testing.

Of course, the MTAR that is used for stress-testing represents ALL the transactions that will be flowing through the system during peak-period production processing.

In DB2, not only must the MTAR be taken into consideration, but the actual number of I/Os done by the transactions must be accounted for also. Because DB2 does set-at-a-time processing, it is possible to have a wide variation in the resources used by different transactions or even by the same transaction operating on different data. For example, at one point in time, DB2 may be servicing transactions at a rate of 25 per second. But, because the transactions are accessing only very small sets of data, only 100 I/Os per second are being serviced by DB2 at that time.

At a later point in time, DB2 is servicing 15 transactions per second, but the transactions are accessing very large sets of data. At this point in time, DB2 is servicing 200 I/Os per second. In this case, the MTAR is misleading. A better measurement is the total activity being done by DB2, such as the number of pages being accessed per unit of time.

The number of calls issued by DB2 is measured by GETPAGEs, and the number of I/Os issued by DB2 is measured in READPAGEs. The stress test then must measure both the maximum transactions per second and the number of GETPAGEs per second, or the number of READPAGEs if there are a large number of I/O requests that are being satisfied in the buffer.

MEASURING THE STRESS TEST

The result of the stress test is measured in two places: by the DB2 database monitor and by the measurement of the flow through the teleprocessing (TP) monitor.

Monitoring the database helps to locate the databases that were stressed during the test and to locate any bottlenecks or potential bottlenecks. A simple way to monitor the database is through the DISPLAY command that can be issued from the MVS console, DB2I, or from the DSN processor. The DISPLAY command may be used to investigate such things as THREAD usage, DATABASE allocation and usage, or the status of utility programs.

An example of the monitoring that is done is an indicator that tracks lock/latch suspensions in IRLM. Normally, this indicator should be in the range of tenths of a second. However, if the indicator grows significantly larger, then it is an indication that lockouts are occurring.

A more sophisticated database monitor is the DB2 Toolkit, by Innovative Designs. With the DB2 Toolkit, much more detailed information is available about the stress test, such as details about the activity that is occurring against a database are available.

The measurement of activity run through the teleprocessing

monitor gives information about response time, arrival rates, queue lengths, and so forth. Either the Information Management System (IMS), DC monitor or Customer Information Control System (CICS) trace facility will yield the desired results. In the DB2 production environment, information about BOTH database and teleprocessor activities are necessary for evaluating the results of stress-testing.

Another type of stress test that needs to be run for DB2 production systems is the determination of the length of the batch window requirements. Of course, the batch window must be long enough for the entire stream of batch processes to run.

Estimating batch run-time is a fairly straightforward process. The first calculation that is necessary is to determine the ratio of the size of the test database versus the size of the production database. A ratio of 1:5, for example, indicates that the test database is five times as small as the production database.

In general, a ratio of 1:10 or less may produce faulty results because of anomalies that arise with batch startup and shutdown time. As a rule, any database ratio less than 1:10 should not be used for batch stress-testing.

After the ratio is determined, the length of the test run is measured by the reciprocal of the ratio. If the ratio is 1:5 and the length of the batch test run is 3 minutes and 30 seconds (or 210 seconds), then 210 seconds are multiplied by 5:

$$210 \times 5 = 1050 \text{ seconds} = 17.5 \text{ minutes}$$

All batch processing that will be run in the batch window must be accumulated to determine whether the batch window will be adequate.

This rough extrapolation process to determine the length of time required for batch processing serves as a fairly accurate guideline as long as the batch process is not doing many relational joins. If the batch process is doing a fair amount of relational joins, then it is recommended that a ratio of no less than 1:3 be used. The resources required for relational joins oftentimes do not occur in an arithmetic progression and tend to skew a simple extrapolation method as has been described.

DRIVER PROGRAMS

Input used to test program logic is usually run through a driver. A driver program is one that simply reads the input, translates the input into a transaction, then issues the transaction to the teleprocessing monitor.

Oftentimes, when stress testing is done, the driver program is a standard piece of software that feeds transactions to the teleprocessing monitor. Typical software used for stress testing in this fashion is TPNS or SURF.

When DB2 is run under IMS or CICS, testing may occur either in IMS, CICS, or TSO environment. When testing occurs in the IMS or CICS environment, testing usually is done on a separate system running IMS or CICS that is specially designated for testing. When testing is done under TSO, a piece of software that simulates the terminal activity is often used, such as BTS.

MODULARIZED PROGRAMS

On occasion, a program will be modularized so that the teleprocessing activity is separated from the database activity within the application program.

In this case, the database modules may be able to be tested in TSO. Of course, the teleprocessing modules will have to be tested at some point in time, either in BTS or in the native teleprocessing environment.

There may be strong motivation for doing testing in the TSO environment, especially when TSO is used as the development environment as well. Of course, only programmatic verification can be done in the TSO environment when IMS or CICS is the production teleprocessing monitor. Stress testing in TSO for the IMS or CICS environment is difficult to simulate.

SEPARATE ENVIRONMENTS

Only under very unusual circumstances will the test environment actually be the same environment as the production environment. If the organization is embarking on its very first application, ample resources may be available to actually test in the production environment. But once the production environment begins to operate on live data and execute real programs and transactions, computing resources become taxed to the point that testing and production processing cannot coexist gracefully in the same environment.

In addition, when testing is done in the production environment, there is always the possibility that tests will cause errors that will show up in production processing—potentially costing performance and availability.

Another powerful motivation for separating the test and the production environment is to do new software release testing in the test environment without disturbing the production environment. This is especially important when DB2 is being run with CICS or IMS.

"PRELIMINARY," "FULL" TEST DATABASES

In DB2, two types of test databases are required. One test database—the *preliminary* test base (or baseline test database) is used to check program logic. The preliminary test database is small and contains only the minimum data needed to verify that a program is operable. Generally speaking, this DB2 test database will be able to be altered at will by the programmers testing on it. The preliminary test database may be reinitialized as often as necessary. The preliminary test database represents the organization "in miniature."

One of the unique uses of the preliminary test database is its usage as a basis for testing sequences of transactions. Oftentimes, transactions are designed so that they execute in a prescribed sequence. Testing the sequence of execution of the transactions is easy with the preliminary test database because the size of the preliminary test database is small enough so that it can be easily reinitialized each time the sequence of the transactions needs to be repeated.

The second type of database needed in the DB2 environment is the *full* test database. The full test database should be no less than 10 percent of the size of the final implemented production database. The full test database should contain one set of every variety that will be needed to be tested. In addition, the MAXIMUM set size should be included for each set. Under most circumstances, it is not a trivial exercise to accurately create the maximum set size that is needed in the full test database. It is not normal to reinitialize the full test database frequently due to the size of the full test database.

The reason the full test database must contain at least one occurrence of the maximum set size of each set that will be accessed is because of the set processing nature of SQL.

When DB2 testing is done on only small sets of data, the full impact of production data is hard to gauge. In the test environment, where a test operates on small sets of data, a transaction may appear to consume few resources. But when the same transaction—using the same programming logic—runs in the production environment, it consumes many more resources because it operates on much larger databases that contain much larger sets of data. A program in the test environment that runs in 2 to 3 seconds may execute in 35 to 45 seconds in the production environment. The difference in the execution of the program in the test and the production environment is in the set size on which the program operates. And the set size dissimilarities make a HUGE difference in the amount of resources used in execution.

If there is going to be a problem with large variations in set sizes between the test and the production environment, the problem needs to be discovered in testing. The only way that the problem can be uncovered is to create maximum set sizes in the full test database. As a consequence, the full test DB2 environment must be created carefully.

The difference between the full test database environment and the preliminary test environment is in day-to-day usage. The preliminary test database is merely a database for simple, quick tests. As a programmer creates new modules, iterative tests are run against the preliminary test database. Mistakes and errors arise very frequently in the preliminary environment and are expected. However, the size and general usage of the preliminary test data are such that errors are tolerated. The preliminary test database is much like a scratch pad or a work area database.

The full test database environment is used much less frequently than the preliminary test environment. After a program has been shaken out and the first iterations of testing against the preliminary database have been completed, testing against the full test database can commence.

TESTING COORDINATION ACROSS PROJECTS

One of the knotty issues of testing DB2 applications is the coordination of testing across the different parties involved in development. In a large project, the issues of coordination of testing can be very complex. One solution is to give each project its own small test database. Upon completion of tests against the small project database, the project then tests against a larger community database.

This approach has the advantage of keeping people from stepping on each others' toes at the inception of the project. But the approach requires the establishment of MANY test databases, which can be a burdensome task. In addition, once the project begins to maintain and alter its own project data, there tends to be very little coordination of test results with other projects.

Another approach is to establish community preliminary and community full test databases. This approach is simpler and requires fewer resources, but requires greater coordination between projects as first one project and then another accesses and manipulates the community data.

One technique for the interproject coordination between databases is to create a test log, identifying changes to a database made by a given test. The log contains the date of the test, who conducted the test, and what data was altered. The log is updated each time a test is made.

The log can be kept externally with a simple pad of paper, or it can be formalized as an actual part of the test database and is actually updated as part of the test. Logging of alterations of the database can be done at the row or even the field level if necessary. The log is useful in determining exactly what tests have been done and when the tests were done. For example, if a programmer looks today for data that was there yesterday and does not find it, the programmer can look to the log to explain why unexpected results occur.

ADMINISTERING THE TEST ENVIRONMENT

The DB2 test environment must be administered just like any other database environment. It usually falls to the database administrator to manage the test environment. The database administrator has such tasks as—

- creating tables,
- granting, revoking authority,
- creating, restoring utilities,
- monitoring size and content of test databases,
- moving table definitions from test to production,
- monitoring, administering, naming conventions, and so forth.

Generally speaking, the test environment requires much less attention than the production environment. Only during peak periods of testing will the test environment consume the attention of the database administrator.

The tools the database administrator works with are typified by the following DB2 commands/utilities:

- CREATE
- DBEDIT
- COPY
- DROP
- SAVE
- LOAD

One of the important issues of administering the test environment is who is in charge of creating/altering test databases. Unlike the production environment, where database alterations are done infrequently and under careful control, data structures change in the test environment frequently.

Where very tight database administration controls are enforced in the test environment, the database administrator may become a roadblock for progress. While there are no concrete rules that apply to determine where the database administrator should and should not have control, the following guidelines may be used:

DBA control

- Large projects
- Projects requiring control over different development groups
- Projects involving large databases
- Projects where reinitialization of test databases is done frequently
- Projects where development will occur over a long period of time
- Projects for operational systems
- Projects built under a data architecture

Application control

- Small projects
- Projects with a very tight deadline
- Decision support projects
- Departmental projects

- Projects independent of other development groups
- Projects that have no future development planned
- Projects that do not involve high performance
- Projects dealing with summarized data
- Projects dealing with subsets of data

Whatever the stance taken by the organization, it should be clear at the outset of the project who will be controlling the database creation and manipulation. It is a mistake to take a "laissez faire" approach and let the ambiguities of control be resolved by default.

SUMMARY

This section has discussed the importance of the test environment. Three aspects of the test environment that are essential are the input to testing, the databases on which testing is done, and the actual physical environment itself.

There are two types of test to be done for the production environment—programmatic tests that verify program logic, and stress tests that verify that the volume of data and processing which will be run in production will not overwhelm the resources available. Two types of databases are recommended: a "preliminary" test database and a "full" database.

The results of the stress test can be measured in several ways: by the teleprocessing monitor, by a database monitor, or programmatically.

Driver programs are a necessary part of the test environment. Driver programs may be written at the application level or may be a standard piece of software.

Separate environments are necessary for a variety of reasons, such as the resources consumed by the production environment, the chance that the production environment may actually be modified by testing, and so forth.

QUESTIONS: THE DB2 TEST ENVIRONMENT

1. Testing IS/IS NOT important in the information center environment.
2. Testing is of MORE/LESS/THE SAME importance in the op-

erational environment than in the ad hoc or information center environment.

3. In the production environment, the two aspects of the design that must be tested are _____ and _____.

4. Even though an application has gone into production, tuning can be done to achieve online performance. (T/F)

5. Testing should be done for both _____ systems and changes to _____ systems.

6. The three components of the test environment are _____, _____, and _____.

7. Test input MUST/SHOULD BE/MIGHT BE/SOMETIMES IS coordinated with test data in order to produce a meaningful test.

8. Input test data serves to verify program logic and to _____ the system.

9. ALL/SOME/MOST program logic conditions should be tested.

10. An illegitimate condition should be detected without _____ the system down.

11. Table _____ should be tested in addition to program logic.

12. Testing programmatic relationships is done against LARGE/SMALL databases.

13. When testing of programmatic relationships is done, the test database is usually _____ to ensure the status of the data.

14. Stress tests ARE/ARE NOT sensitive to program logic as a rule.

15. Stress tests are sensitive to (pick all that apply)—
    a. the rate of arrival of transactions
    b. the volume of data run against the database during the test
    c. the language the program is written in
    d. the structure of the data run against
    e. the amount of processing done by the programmer

16. For conversions, existing transactions MAY/MAY NOT be used for input into the stress test.

17. When existing transactions are used for stress testing, care must be taken not to _____.

18. For new applications, test input must be _____.

19. When the number of transactions to flow through the system is

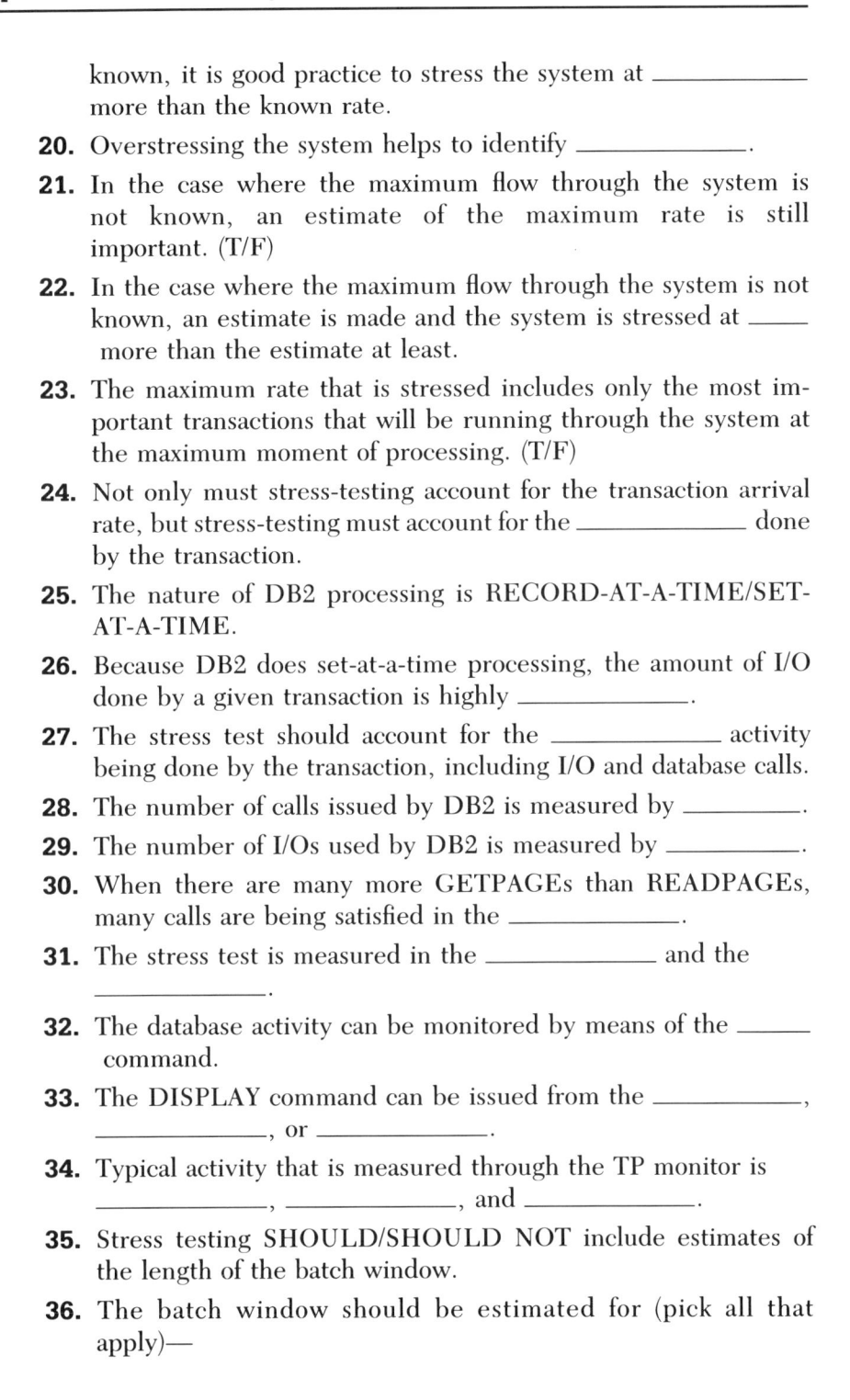

known, it is good practice to stress the system at _____ more than the known rate.

20. Overstressing the system helps to identify _____.
21. In the case where the maximum flow through the system is not known, an estimate of the maximum rate is still important. (T/F)
22. In the case where the maximum flow through the system is not known, an estimate is made and the system is stressed at _____ more than the estimate at least.
23. The maximum rate that is stressed includes only the most important transactions that will be running through the system at the maximum moment of processing. (T/F)
24. Not only must stress-testing account for the transaction arrival rate, but stress-testing must account for the _____ done by the transaction.
25. The nature of DB2 processing is RECORD-AT-A-TIME/SET-AT-A-TIME.
26. Because DB2 does set-at-a-time processing, the amount of I/O done by a given transaction is highly _____.
27. The stress test should account for the _____ activity being done by the transaction, including I/O and database calls.
28. The number of calls issued by DB2 is measured by _____.
29. The number of I/Os used by DB2 is measured by _____.
30. When there are many more GETPAGEs than READPAGEs, many calls are being satisfied in the _____.
31. The stress test is measured in the _____ and the _____.
32. The database activity can be monitored by means of the _____ command.
33. The DISPLAY command can be issued from the _____, _____, or _____.
34. Typical activity that is measured through the TP monitor is _____, _____, and _____.
35. Stress testing SHOULD/SHOULD NOT include estimates of the length of the batch window.
36. The batch window should be estimated for (pick all that apply)—

a. the peak period
b. the average day
c. a slack day
d. end-of-year processing
e. end-of-month processing

37. The test database should be no less than _____ of the production database.

38. Raw extrapolation of test to production runs based on database size MAY/PROBABLY WILL NOT/WILL PROBABLY produce anomalies.

39. Raw extrapolation most likely will fail to account for initiation and _____ times.

40. Batch testing in the face of many or large relational _____ must be done very carefully.

41. The resources used for relational joins do not progress _____, therefore, extrapolations must be done carefully.

42. A driver program's prime purpose is to _____ transactions.

43. The driver program is often a standard piece of software such as _____ or _____.

44. When testing is done for DB2 under IMS or CICS, testing can be done in IMS, CICS, or _____.

45. Terminal activity in TSO is simulated by _____.

46. When TSO is the development environment, it is USEFUL/HARMFUL to do testing in TSO.

47. Under USUAL/UNUSUAL conditions, testing can actually be done in the production environment.

48. When testing is done in the production environment, there is always the possibility of _____ live data and transactions.

49. _____ types of databases are required for testing in DB2.

50. One type of database is the "full" database; the other is the _____ test database.

51. The preliminary test database is used to test _____.

52. Because of its size, the preliminary test database can be _____.

53. The full test database should be no smaller than _____ of the production database.

Chapter 12   Testing DB2 Production Systems   177

54. The full test database should contain at least _____ of every variety that will be encountered in the production database.

55. It IS/IS NOT an easy exercise to properly create the full test database environment.

56. Because of its size, the full test database MAY/MAY NOT be easily reinitialized.

57. Because of the _____ processing nature of SQL, the full test database must contain one full set of every variety that will be encountered.

58. Because of the set-processing nature of SQL, a transaction that runs in 2-3 seconds in the test environment may run in _____ seconds in the production environment.

59. The problems in the variation of processing from the test to the production environment SHOULD/DO NOT NEED TO be discovered during testing.

60. The way to discover wide variations between testing and production processing is to create _____ set sizes in the test environment.

61. The _____ test database environment is like a scratch pad or a work area database.

62. In a large project, each development group may have its own test database. (T/F)

63. After doing preliminary testing against the "local" test database, the project then does testing against the _____ test database.

64. Giving each development group its own test database in a large project ultimately means that _____ test databases must be created.

65. A means of coordinating testing is through a _____.

66. The test log contains such information as _____, _____, and _____.

67. List five tasks that are in the domain of the database administrator.

TESTING PROGRAMS IN DB2

The first step in program testing in DB2 is the verification of the validity of program logic. If program logic is not correct, then very little else matters. To verify program logic in DB2 requires test tables on which to exercise the logic of the program. The contents of the test tables directly affect the success or validity of the test. The programmer must carefully predetermine what data is or is not present in the test database prior to the test.

Because of the need to closely coordinate programming-testing with the contents of the test database, the programmer often must reinitialize the test database prior to execution. Reinitialization ensures that, if other tests have been executed against the test database, the contents of the test database are in a known state. Standard reinitialization routines are available to reset the test database. The database administrator or the project manager will be able to point out what these routines are.

After the test database has been reinitialized, the program test may commence. The test may be run in TSO, IMS/DC, or CICS, depending on which environment testing is done in. Sometimes program tests consist of running a single program. Other times, a test requires that several transactions or programs be run in sequence. When one transaction alters a table and another transaction enters the table and accesses the data that has been altered, then the transactions must be sequenced together.

Actual transactions may be fed to the test system in sequence, or parameters are consecutively passed to a driver program that, in turn, uses the parameters for the creation of transactions. After the driver program has created the transaction, the transaction is fed to the test system for execution.

On occasion, it may be necessary to put special instructions in the test version of a program to aid in debugging the program. These special instructions help trace the logic and the sequence of execution of the program. Upon completion of testing, these special instructions are removed.

After the execution of the transaction or transactions, the results of the test are verified through a variety of channels such as BTS traces, through dumps of the test database, through screen transmissions, through reports, or through dumps. The programmatic conditions that should be checked include the following:

GENERAL TRANSACTION/PROGRAM CONTROL

- Input all parameters that are valid
- Input combinations of valid and invalid parameters
- Input less than all parameters needed
- Input more than valid parameters (if possible)
- Identify and cause to execute ALL abnormal ending conditions
  - repair from dump, if dump occurs
  - repair database, if database goes down
  - repair transaction definition to TP monitor, if damaged
- Determine whether cursor stability or repeatable read has been specified; verify program logic appropriately

SINGLE-TABLE MANIPULATION

- Insert against a row that already exists
- Insert against a row that does not exist
- Delete a row that does not exist
- Delete a row that does exist
- Update a row that does exist
- Update a row that does not exist
- Insert a row so that default values are created
- Insert a row so that null values are created
- Insert a row with values in range of edits
- Insert a row with values out of edit range
- Update a row with values in range of edits
- Update a row with values out of edit range
- Where there is a relationship between two or more fields in the same row
  - create a change in row A; observe the effect on other variables,
  - create a change in row A which is invalid; observe the effect on other related variables.

REFERENTIAL INTEGRITY

- Where row B can exist only when row A exists
  - attempt to create row B when row A does not exist,
  - attempt to create row B where row A does exist.

- Where row B is deleted when row A is deleted
  - attempt to delete row A and not delete row B,
  - attempt to delete row A and delete row B as well.
- Where row A and row B may exist independently but where there may be a relationship between the two
  - create row A and row B independently,
  - create a relationship between row A and row B where both exist,
  - attempt to create a relationship between row A and row B where row A does not exist,
  - attempt to create a relationship between row A and row B where row B does not exist,
  - attempt to delete row A where a relationship has been already established,
  - attempt to delete row B where a relationship has already been established,
  - delete the relationship between row A and row B,
  - change the relationship between row A and row B to a relationship between row A and row C,
  - in the case where separate relationships between row A and row B and row B and row A are kept (i.e., A/B and B/A are maintained)
    - change A/B and observe the effect on B/A,
    - delete A/B and observe the effect on B/A,
    - insert A/B and observe the effect on B/A.

PROGRAM MODULARIZATION

- Determine what parameters are passed to each module
  - pass more parameters than are necessary,
  - pass less parameters than are necessary,
  - pass invalid parameters,
  - pass parameters in an invalid order.
- Determine what range any given parameter should have
  - pass a value in the valid range,
  - pass a parameter out of the valid range.
- When an error condition is encountered in the called module, how does the calling module react?
- Create parameters that will cause each path of logic to be executed.
- What return codes from DB2 are possible? Will program logic handle all possible return codes?
  - create conditions that will simulate each DB2 return code that is possible.

- Is there a standard module for the handling of errors?
- Is there a standard module for the handling of calls to the database (i.e., an I/O module)?
  - will the I/O module handle all needed conditions?

ALGORITHMIC VERIFICATION

- Create input to exercise all algorithms
  - verify the results of the calculation.

DATA ACCESS

- Access and display a row of data that is known to exist
- Access and display a row of data that does not exist
- Access a set of data that is known to exist
- Access a set of data that does not exist
- Access a set of data through all VIEWS that have been defined

Recursive Relationships

- When row A and row B are involved in a recursive relationship and row A exists in a superior relationship to row B
  - insert row B without making row B subordinate to row A,
  - insert row B making row B subordinate to row A,
  - when row A and row B exist
    - attempt to delete row A without deleting the relationship to row B,
    - delete row A and delete the relationship to row B,
    - attempt to delete row B without deleting the relationship to row B,
    - delete row B and the relationship to row A,
    - insert row C as a subordinate of row A.
- For an explosion of the recursive relationship
  - attempt to create an infinite relationship by creating the rows and relationships—row A → row B → row A → row B,
  - verify from program logic that the infinite loop has been detected.
- For dependents of a superior row where the dependents must be sequenced
  - attempt to delete the first dependent row,
  - insert a dependent row at the last of the sequence,

- attempt to insert a row in the middle of a consecutively ordered sequence of dependent rows.

CONTINUOUS TIME-SPAN ROWS
(where rows are logically grouped to form continuous definition of a variable)

- Insert a row at the start of the time span
- Insert a row at the end of the time span
- Update the variable for an amount of time completely contained within a single time span
- Update the variable for an amount of time spanning more than one time span
- Attempt to delete the variable for a period of time within the range of continuity
- Delete all related time-span rows
- Determine if two or more consecutive time spans can hold the same values for the variable; if so, why aren't the spans collapsed into a single row?

EXTRACT PROCESSING

- For the running of an extract program
  - verify that all data that should be selected in fact was selected,
  - verify that no data that should not be selected in fact was not selected.
- For data that is accumulated, aggregated, etc. during extract
  - verify that all data that should be aggregated in fact is aggregated,
  - verify that no data that should not be aggregated is in fact not aggregated.
- Verify that the time and/or conditions of extract processing are able to be determined for each extract

After programmatic testing is done, the next phase of testing is stress testing.

When errors occur, there are a variety of sources to turn to for information for the resolution of the errors. The source that is most appropriate is dependent on where the error was detected. A standard list of the source for error detection and diagnosis includes—

- output from the precompiler, if a precompiler was used,
- output from the compiler or assembler,
- linkage editor output,
- BIND process information,
- source listings of the program,
- JCL used during execution,
- application program output,
- system dumps,
- database or teleprocessing monitor of activity during execution,
- BTS (if applicable).

Stress-testing begins with identification of the "'full'" test database. Generally, this database will be a different database than the one under which the programmatic tests are run. The full test database is a large database that contains samples of the production database that is to be built.

The point of testing against the full test database is to determine how many resources are used by each of the processes that will be run.

The stress tests that are run should use the EXPLAIN function. The EXPLAIN function indicates such things as the access paths that were chosen by DB2 and whether an index was used. The EXPLAIN function can be invoked interactively through SPUFI or QMF, or EXPLAIN can be invoked at the moment of BIND. In general, it is better to specify the EXPLAIN function at the moment of BIND or REBIND because, if EXPLAIN is included in code, it is easy to forget to remove it. In addition, the EXPLAIN function is useful in determining such things as method of joins, the number of columns where a matching index will be used, the name of the access path, and so forth.

When the stress test is run, the programmer looks for how many resources were used by each process. For transactions that will run in the online environment, as long as each process uses under 20 GETPAGEs or 15 READPAGEs in total, there is no problem. But when a transaction exceeds that number, then the designer must reconsider how to reprogram or redesign the transaction.

Another simple way the resources used in execution against the full test database may be measured is by using a host variable to count each of the rows returned. The counter is initialized to zero.

Then, as each cursor positioning occurs, the host variable is incremented by one.

The results of the calculation may be displayed along with other data. When the host variable indicates that more than 75 total rows are accessed (Note: This number is subject to variation if clustered data is being accessed), then the designer may want to consider alternate programming techniques. Of course, the display of the host variable is disabled upon going into production. The test and calculation of resources used against the full database is especially important where relational joins are specified because of the potential resources that may be consumed by the join.

The final step in the stress test is the analysis of the arrival rate of the transactions. The anticipated arrival rate—at peak-period processing—is estimated. Next, the transaction to be tested is aggregated with all other transactions that will be running during peak period and a test run is executed. Usually, the final stress test is administered by the database administrator or the project manager who has overall project responsibility.

SUMMARY

The first step in testing is to select the database that will be tested against. There is usually a prepared database that contains data that can be tested against. The test database usually needs to be reinitialized before each test to ensure that tests run since last initialization have not altered the content of the data.

The first tests that are run address the algorithmic content of programs: Is the program logic written correctly? Algorithmic verification is done in the following areas:

- General transaction/program control
- Single-table manipulation
- Referential integrity
- Program modularization
- Algorithmic/calculation verification
- Data access
- Recursive relationships
- Continuous time span creation/manipulation
- Extract processing

After programmatic testing is done, the next step is stress-testing. Stress-testing is done against a database specially designed just for stress tests. The first part of stress-testing determines how much data any given SQL call requires. If too much data is needed by a transaction, then the program must be broken into smaller pieces.

The final phase of testing is the transaction arrival rate testing, where all transactions that will be run during peak period are run together, simulating the processing that will occur during peak-period processing.

QUESTIONS: TESTING PROGRAMS IN DB2

1. The content of test databases AFFECTS/DOES NOT AFFECT the validity of a test.
2. The programmer must _____ what data is or is not present in the test database prior to the test.
3. It is normal practice to _____ a database prior to testing.
4. The _____ is able to point out what reinitialization routines are available.
5. Some tests require that a single program be run; other tests require the running of _____ programs in sequence.
6. Actual transactions or transactions from a _____ program may be used for the test.
7. Special debugging instruction MAY/MAY NOT be put into a program for testing.
8. The programmer must remember to _____ the special debugging instructions before going into production.
9. Special debugging statements help to trace the _____ of logic.
10. List five ways the results of the test can be verified.
11. Transaction/program control testing ensures the _____ of logic are correct.
12. All possible paths should be tested. (T/F)
13. Invalid data SHOULD/SHOULD NOT be used for transaction/program control testing.
14. ALL combinations of parameters, internal and external, should be tested. (T/F)

15. The programmer needs to _____ the system to create abnormal return codes in SQLCA.
16. Testing recovery routines is not important since the test database can easily be reinitialized. (T/F)
17. Using cursor stability or _____ has a potentially large impact on transaction performance.
18. Single-table manipulation requires that an insert, a _____, an _____ and an access be done against a row.
19. Activity should be done against rows that exist and rows that do not exist, even though error conditions will be triggered. (T/F)
20. Insertion and updates of values in and out of _____ should be done against single rows as well.
21. Where rows are related by means of a foreign key, the relationship is termed _____.
22. Where row B exists only when row A exists, test logic should insert row B both when row A exists and when row A does not exist. (T/F)
23. Where row B is deleted, row B should be inserted before row A. (T/F)
24. Where there is an m:n relationship between row A and row B, _____ existence of the rows and the relationship should be verified during testing.
25. Program modularization is NO MORE THAN/NO LESS THAN/THE SAME AS the issue in DB2 as in regular systems.
26. Centralization of access to the data base is often done by means of an _____.
27. Much code can be saved and responses can be standardized for incorrect conditions by means of an _____.
28. Each error condition that can exist must be created by test conditions or by _____.
29. All set sizes and all _____ relationships must be verified by the I/O module.
30. A relationship of one type of data with itself is called a _____ relationship.
31. Where row A is subordinate to row B, row B CANNOT/CAN/MAY BE ABLE TO exist when row A does not exist.
32. The testing done for an infinite loop in a recursive relationship

MAY/MAY NOT be removed from the program once the system is debugged.

33. Testing for data-fracturing may be removed once continuous time updates and inserts are debugged. (T/F)

34. List five common sources where debugging information can be found.

35. After program logic is tested, then _____ testing must be done.

36. Stress testing is run against the _____ test database.

37. The test administrator is usually responsible for coordinating the stress test of _____ programs.

38. The purpose of the stress test is not to verify logic; instead, the purpose of the stress test is to determine _____ by the program.

39. The _____ function describes what indexes a program will use.

40. Host variables may be used to count how many resources are used. Host variables must be _____ by the program.

41. Relational _____ cause special concern in testing because of the potential for using resources.

PART IV

DB2 Application Design: Part II

Chapter 13   Bill of Materials Processing

- The Bill of Materials
- Recursive Relationships
- Continuity of the Level Count Field
- A Second Level Count Field
- The Generalized Recursive Structure
- A Simple Explosion
- Bill of Materials Explosion
- Implosions
- A Recursive Infinite Loop
- Other Bill of Materials Processing
- Algorithmic Differences
- Other Recursive Structures
- Differences between Levels
- Online/Batch Bill of Materials Processing
- Summary
- Questions: Bill of Materials Processing

Chapter 14   Denormalization

- Normalization of Data
- Internal Arrays
- Interleaving Data
- Other Options
- Summary
- Questions: Denormalization

Chapter 15 High Availability

- Importance of Design
- Recovery/Reorganization
- Phases of Recovery
- Reorganization—An Unload/Reload Process
- Estimating Downtime
- Probability of Downtime
- Reducing the Volume of Data
- Referential Integrity and High Availability
- Summary
- Questions: High Availability

Chapter 16 Extract Processing

- Extract Logic
- Designing the Extract Process
- Using the Extracted Data
- Granularity of Data
- The Right Level of Detail
- Less Extracted Detail
- The Hardware Environment
- The Piggyback Approach
- Incremental Changes
- Indexes and Extracted Data
- Periodic Loading
- Compacting Data
- Other Options
- A Final Note
- Questions: Extract Processing in DB2

CHAPTER 13

Bill of Materials Processing

A *bill of material* is a recursive structure, where one node or component of the structure relates to another node or component of the structure. Bill of materials processing is important because it occurs so commonly and because recursive processing and data structures, when not designed properly, can become very complex. Several alternative processing and design approaches are discussed, in addition to the standard techniques.

THE BILL OF MATERIALS

A bill of materials is a special kind of data relationship in which one occurrence of data relates to another occurrence of data. The data relationship is made unique by the fact that the relationship is between data occurrences of the same type and that the relationship is m:n. For example, in a manufacturing environment, the parts that are to be manufactured are related to each other by the manufacturing process. The final assembly is made up of subassemblies. Each major subassembly is made up of its own subassemblies. The assembly process is broken down into finer levels of detail until a subassembly is made up of raw goods. Figure 13-1 shows a simple bill of material. These simple data relationships form what is known as a bill of materials. A bill of materials describes the manufacturing process from raw goods to final assembly.

At first glance, there seems to be substantive differences between

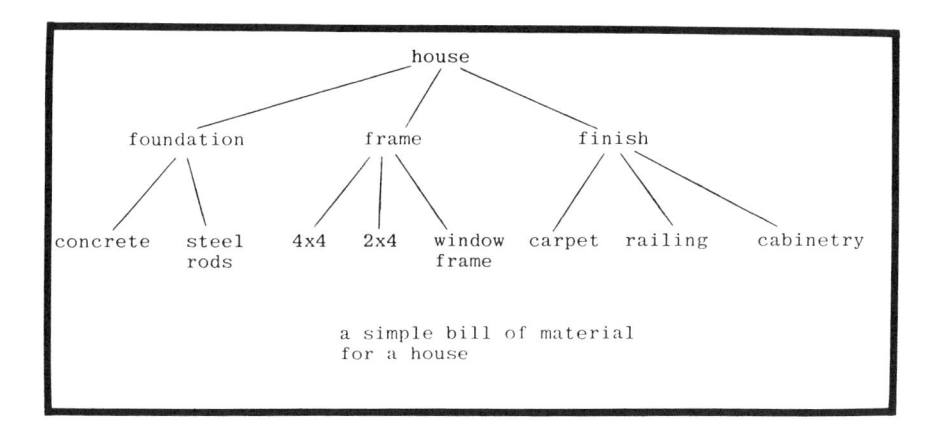

```
                              house
                   /            |          \
            foundation        frame         finish
             /     \         / | \         /  |   \
        concrete  steel    4x4 2x4 window carpet railing cabinetry
                  rods              frame

                    a simple bill of material
                         for a house
```

FIGURE 13-1. A simple bill of material for a house.

finished goods, assemblies, and raw goods. But each type of part—sometimes called a "node" in the bill of material—contains common information such as description, unit of measure, quantity, and so forth. Whether a part is finished, assembled, or raw, it is still a part. The only fundamental difference from one part to the next is the relationship between the parts.

RECURSIVE RELATIONSHIPS

The type of relationship where a part of one type relates to another part of the same type is called a *recursive relationship*. Recursive relationships appear in many places, not just the manufacturing environment. The family tree where a parent relates to a child is a form of recursion. In the case of the family tree, both a parent and a child are forms of a human. The typical organization chart is another classical form of recursion. Each node in the organization chart is a form of an organizational unit, with one or more relationships to other organizational units. Recursive relationships are very common although they are classically associated with the manufacturing environment.

At first glance, nothing is terribly difficult about recursive relationships. But processing recursive relationships with relational tables requires special techniques to keep the design from becoming very complex.

The logical structure used to show recursion is a node pointing into itself, such as a part pointing to itself in a bill of materials or a person pointing to another as a member of a family tree as in Figure 13-2.

At the level of physical design—at the DB2 table level—recursive structures are shown in terms of a base table and one or two pointer tables. The base table contains information that applies to every part, such as key, description, unit of measure, and so forth. One part table contains the "downward" pointer, and the other pointer table contains the "upward" pointer. The downward pointer—sometimes called the "where from" pointer—contains two fields: the part being pointed at and the part that is doing the pointing. A typical bill of materials structure is shown in Figure 13-3.

In the case of a bill of materials, every finished good would have one or more downward pointers indicating what subassemblies it was made of. A car would have a downward pointer for the drive train, for the chassis, for the body, and so forth. Raw goods, on the other hand, would have no downward pointers, since they are at the lowest level of assembly and nothing goes into raw goods. Of course, subassemblies would have downward pointers showing what subassemblies they are made of.

The other type of pointer (that may or may not exist, as will be discussed later) is the upward pointer—sometimes called the "into" pointer. There are two key fields in an upward pointer: the part being pointed at and the part that is doing the pointing. The part that is being pointed at is the lower part of the assembly. For example, a car—an example of finished goods—would have no upward pointers since the car is not assembled into anything else. But raw goods would have many upward pointers since raw goods form the basis for manufacturing.

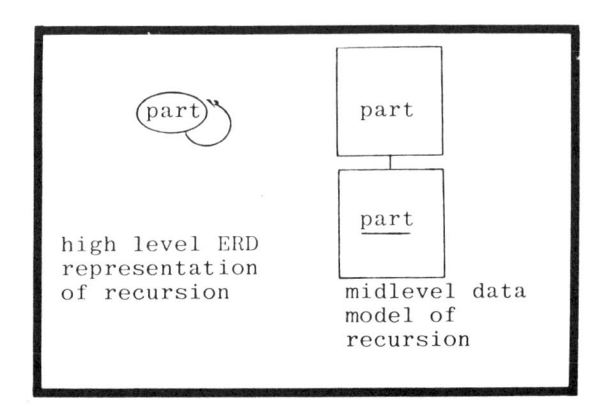

FIGURE 13–2. High-level ERD representation of recursion.

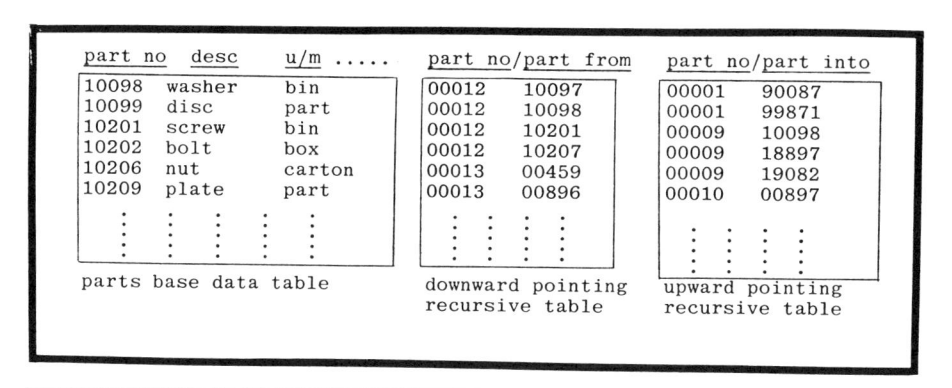

```
part no  desc    u/m  .....   part no/part from    part no/part into
10098    washer  bin          00012    10097       00001    90087
10099    disc    part         00012    10098       00001    99871
10201    screw   bin          00012    10201       00009    10098
10202    bolt    box          00012    10207       00009    18897
10206    nut     carton       00013    00459       00009    19082
10209    plate   part         00013    00896       00010    00897
  :       :      :              :        :           :        :
  :       :      :              :        :           :        :
  :       :      :              :        :           :        :
parts base data table         downward pointing    upward pointing
                              recursive table      recursive table
```

FIGURE 13-3. Typical bill of materials structure.

On occasion, the upward pointer contains a nonkey field—quantity. In this case, the field—quantity—indicates the number of subassemblies that go into the next level of assembly. For example, the upward pointer for an engine might contain the value of six for pistons going into an engine, if the engine were a six-cylinder vehicle.

The upward pointer and the downward pointer do not represent different relationships; they are the logical equivalent of each other. But the upward and downward pointers are used in very different ways. The upward pointer is used to traverse the bill of materials structure upward—from raw goods to final product. Conversely, the downward pointer is used to traverse the bill of materials structure from the top to the bottom—from the finished product to the raw goods.

If there is never to be a traversal in one direction, then the corresponding set of pointers does not need to be created and maintained. The existence of one set of pointers or the other is a function of the usage of the bill of materials structure.

For some bills of materials, it is necessary to keep track of the order of subassemblies beneath the assembly. In particular, in DB2 bill of materials processing this sequencing of subassemblies comes in very handy. To achieve this subsequencing, another field needs to be added to the downward pointing table—the *level count* field. Level count is nothing more than the enumeration of the subassemblies of a part at any level. For example, suppose the part "1053" has four parts as its immediate subassembly. The four parts are "5096," "0012," "1463" and "2007." Part 5096 will have a level count of one, part 0012 will have a level count of two, part 1463 will have a level

Chapter 13 Bill of Materials Processing 195

count of three, and part 2007 will have a level count of four, as shown by Figure 13-4.

When a new part is added as a subassembly for part "1053," it will have a level count of five. Each new part added as a subassembly will have a level count of one greater than the previous one added.

CONTINUITY OF THE LEVEL COUNT FIELD

When a level count is deleted, the level count sequence must remain intact and continuous. For example, suppose for part 1053 that part 0012 is deleted as a subassembly. When part 0012 is deleted, level count 2 is not present and the sequence of level counts is broken. There are several options to repair level count. One option is to set the level count of 9001, the part that was most recently added, to 2, thus resequencing level counts. However, using the last level count to "fill in" the level count that was deleted has the effect of resequencing the chain of level counts. The other option that keeps the level counts in sequence and maintains the continuity of the level counts is to resequence all level counts when a deletion is done. If level count n is deleted, then level count n + 1, n + 2, etc., have their level counts reduced by one. In the case of the deletion of part 1053, when subassembly 0012 is deleted, then the level count for 1463 is set to two and the level count for 2007 is set to three.

In any case, maintaining the continuity of the sequence is the

part no	part from	level count
1053	5096	1
1053	0012	2
1053	1463	3
1053	2007	4

the logical representation of the data structure

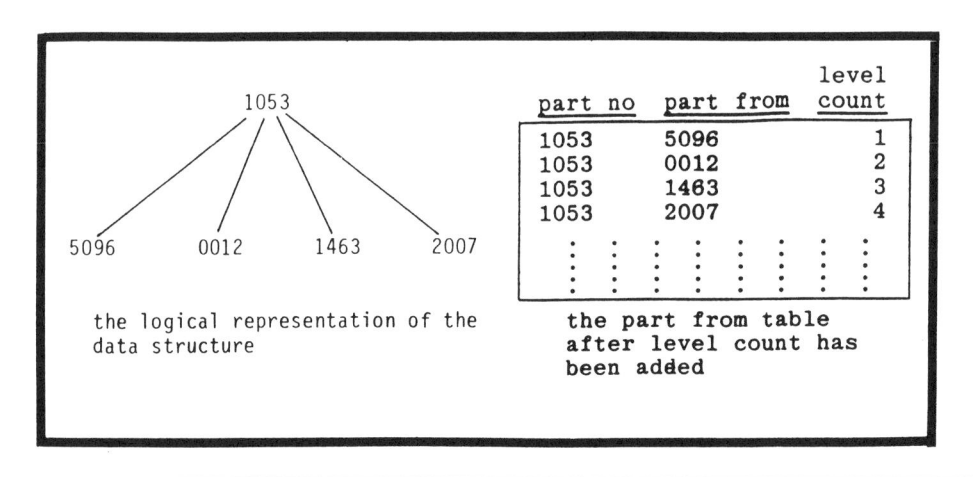

the part from table after level count has been added

FIGURE 13-4. The logical representation of the data structure.

most important factor. Only under unusual circumstances will there be a need to maintain the order of subcomponents of an assembly. In that case, it will be necessary to preserve the order through the wholesale resequencing of the level count field when the sequence is interrupted by an insertion or a deletion. In normal cases, mixing the order of the subassemblies causes no problem.

A SECOND LEVEL COUNT FIELD

Where there are many updates to a bill of materials and where the parts that are subassemblies do not have to maintain their original sequence of entry, then it may be worthwhile to store the number of subassemblies at the assembly level. For example, the part 1053 would have a total level count that equalled five, indicating that it had five subassemblies.

When the total number of subassemblies is stored at the assembly, there are two level counts. One level count indicates how many subassemblies the assembly has, and the other level count indicates the position of the part with its peers.

The management of level counts is unquestionably burdensome and awkward for many bill of materials operations. Unfortunately, many bill of materials operations depend on the uniqueness forced by level count in the face of set-only processing.

THE GENERALIZED RECURSIVE STRUCTURE

The base table and the one or two sets of pointers constitute what is termed the *generalized* form of recursion. The generalized form of recursion—

- provides a generic representation of the key and nonkey data applicable to all nodes in the bill of materials structure,
- can be used to represent n levels of recursion where n is a variable number,
- has no restrictions as to what type of node can be placed where in the logically derived bill of materials structure.

Each of the salient aspects of the generalized bill of material structure will be explored.

The definition of every node is identical. A finished good has associated with it a description, unit of measure, quantity, and so forth. All other levels of nodes in the structure have the same nonkey data associated with them. The type of data that is applicable does not change from one node to the next. Of course, the contents of the data vary from one node to the next, but not the form.

There is no limit to the number of levels of recursion that can be represented. To create another level simply requires the formation of a new relationship, which the generalized structure is equipped to do, ad infinitum. To create a new level merely requires creating a new node with the lowest level pointing into the existing structure.

There are no structural implications of the different levels. For example, a common bolt may be a raw good. But the bolt can go into the bill of materials assembly in any number of places—into the body of the car or into the engine of the car.

A SIMPLE EXPLOSION

As a simple example of processing against the base tables and the upward and downward pointers, suppose an engineer wished to see the subassemblies for part 1053. The execution of the SQL program produces the desired parts.

```
SELECT PARTFROM DESC
FROM TABLE.DOWN
WHERE PART = '1053'
```

The results of the execution of this SQL program would be all the downward parts (that go down one level) and their descriptions. If all that is required is simple recursive processing, as shown, then there is no problem and practically any structuring of recursive data would suffice. But recursive processing can become complicated very quickly where more than one level of recursion is required. For example, suppose the engineer wished to take a part down to its raw goods. Then each part would in turn need its own recursive processing. At this point program logic becomes very complex.

BILL OF MATERIALS EXPLOSION

A standard process associated with bill of materials processing is known as the *explosion*. An explosion is the level-by-level expansion of a part into all of its subassemblies, down to the point of raw goods. The SQL program that has been discussed goes down one level of recursion. What is required for an explosion is a similar traversal of the structure down n levels.

To manage the complexity of processing in DB2, a special data structure is required, known as a *stack*. The stack can be built as a regular DB2 table or can be built in working storage. In the example that is being developed, the stack is built in memory but could just as well have been built as a DB2 table. A stack is a table that is equipped to do first in, last out (FILO) processing, as has been discussed in the chapter on data structures. To accomplish this type of processing requires the use of a variable, often called the pointer or stack pointer.

The dynamics of a stack are described in chapter 9.

Each entry into the stack contains two pieces of information: the part that is the subassembly—STACK.CURR—for the level previously accessed, and the associated level count—STACK.SUB. For example, for the simple bill of materials that has been discussed, if the part 1053 is being exploded, then the part 5096 would be put on the stack with the level count of one. (Level count equals one since 5096 is the first subassembly of part 1053.) The stack then contains a map of the path down the bill of materials that is being processed at any moment in time.

The algorithm used to process a bill of materials explosion is illustrated by—

```
EXPLODE = 'Y'
POINTER = 0
ACTIVE = 'xxx...'
NEXT = 1
DO WHILE EXPLODE = 'Y'
 SELECT PARTPTR
 FROM TABLE.DOWN
 WHERE PART.DOWN = ACTIVE AND NEXT = PART.LEVEL.COUNT
 IF PARTPTR FOUND THEN DO
 OUTPUT ACTIVE
 POINTER = POINTER + 1
 STACK.CURR(POINTER) = ACTIVE
 STACK.SUB (POINTER) = NEXT + 1
 ACTIVE = PARTPTR
 NEXT = 1
 END
IF PARTPTR NOT FOUND THEN DO
   IF POINTER = 0 THEN EXPLODE = 'N'
   IF POINTER > 0 THEN DO
```

```
            OUTPUT ACTIVE
            ACTIVE = STACK.CURR(POINTER)
            NEXT = STACK.SUB(POINTER)
            POINTER = POINTER - 1
                  END
            END
END
```

In the algorithm, the part to be exploded is loaded into the field ACTIVE. The control variable NEXT is set to 1. NEXT will control the level count for each new level of explosion that is required. The control variable EXPLODE determines when the explosion has finished. And the control variable POINTER controls which level of the stack is being operated on. The stack contains two fields: CURR and SUB.CURR indicate the part that is being worked on, and SUB contains the level count.

The algorithm retrieves one part after the next, beginning with the part to be exploded. The order of retrieval is based on the logical structure of the bill of materials. When a PARTPTR is found, it is exploded and its position is recursively "remembered." After it is exploded, processing continues with the next part at the same level (whose level count is one greater than the part that has been exploded).

Note that the downward table does not have to be indexed. It can be randomly sequenced and unindexed, although for a large bill of materials, an index on the keys of the downward table will improve performance by not requiring a full table scan each time a part is sought.

IMPLOSIONS

The algorithm has shown the activities for a downward explosion of a bill of materials. An upward explosion is possible using the upward table, although, in practice, an upward explosion often does not make sense. When an upward explosion is done, it is called an *implosion*. The processing logic required for an implosion is almost identical to the logic required for an explosion.

A RECURSIVE INFINITE LOOP

One of the anomalies of the algorithm for explosion is the possibility of an infinite loop being encountered in the structure of the bill of materials. If a part ever appears as its own subassembly, even several levels removed, the bill of materials is logically in an infinite loop. There is no technical reason why an infinite loop cannot be created by an unaware production control analyst. As a consequence, the programmer needs to verify that an infinite loop does not exist in the bill of materials structure.

Fortunately, checking for an infinite loop using the explosion algorithm is easy to do. The data stored in the stack of the algorithm represents the active leg of the structure that is under analysis. If any part is repeated in the stack, then there is an infinite loop in the structure. Code can be written to check the contents of the stack every time a new entry is about to be placed on the stack.

```
    .
    .
    .
CHECKER = POINTER
LOOP = 'N'
DO WHILE CHECKER > 0
     IF STACK.CURR(CHECKER) = PARTPTR
     THEN LOOP = 'Y'
       CHECKER = CHECKER - 1
END
IF LOOP = 'Y' THEN . . .
    .
    .
    .
```

The simple subroutine merely verifies that the new PARTPTR encountered is not already on the STACK. If the part is already on the STACK, then the variable LOOP will equal "Y" and an infinite loop will have been detected. Upon detection, appropriate action can be taken.

OTHER BILL OF MATERIALS PROCESSING

The bill of materials processing that has been discussed is made complex by the fact that a level count is required for every part. Building and maintaining the level count field is artificial and awkward, although, for some processes, it is necessary. Other design alternatives may apply in special cases.

In the case where level count is part of the data structure, the bill of materials could be large or small; the processing of the algorithm is indifferent to the size of the bill of materials. But suppose the bill of materials to be exploded is not large or that there is plenty of main memory in which to do stack processing. Then the complexity introduced by the level count in the first explosion process discussed is not necessary. Level count can be discarded and the explosion can be done somewhat differently.

Suppose the parts databases are designed as described but with no level count field. Then the following algorithm can be used to process the bill of materials explosions:

```
EXPLODE = 'Y'
POINTER = 0
ACTIVE = 'xxx....'
DO WHILE EXPLODE = 'Y'
    SELECT PARTPTR
    FROM TABLE.DOWN
    WHERE PART.DOWN = ACTIVE
    IF PARTPTR FOUND THEN DO
        OUTPUT ACTIVE
        LOOP = 'Y'
        DO WHILE LOOP = 'Y'
            POINTER = POINTER + 1
            FETCH PARTPTR INTO STACK.CURR(POINTER)
            IF SQLCODE = 100 THEN LOOP = 'N'
        END
        ACTIVE = STACK.CURR(POINTER)
        POINTER = POINTER - 1
    END
    IF PARTPTR NOT FOUND THEN DO
        IF POINTER = 0 THEN EXPLODE = 'N'
        IF POINTER > 0 THEN DO
            OUTPUT ACTIVE
            ACTIVE = STACK.CURR(POINTER)
            POINTER = POINTER - 1
        END
    END
END
```

ALGORITHMIC DIFFERENCES

The first algorithm for bill of materials explosion-processing that was discussed can be termed a *level count* algorithm, in which individual subassemblies were processed one at a time, using the field level count to individually sequence the parts. The second bill of materials explosion algorithm that was discussed did not require the level count field and processed subassemblies set-at-a-time.

There are several differences between the previously discussed level count explosion and the set processing explosion. One difference is that sets of data are processed by the *set processing* algorithm. The set processing algorithm will require a stack substantially larger than the level count algorithm. While the set processing algorithm requires more storage, it also is simpler and requires a simpler data structure.

OTHER RECURSIVE STRUCTURES

The structure of the bill of materials that has been discussed is called the *generalized bill of materials structure*. While the generalized structure is flexible and suits most needs for bill of materials processing, it is hardly the only structuring possible. The logical structure of a bill of materials can be turned into an identical physical structure. For example, for a three-level bill of materials structure, three levels of information may actually be stored in a single row. Or a separate table may be constructed for each level. As long as the bill of materials structure is very rigid and as long as there are not too many levels, then there may not be too many problems.

But, in general, defining a bill of materials structure in other than the generalized form leads to complexities that are not easily solved.

Another way that recursion is often designed is by building recursion into the key structure of data. For example, a key of ABCD indicates that A is the finished product, that B is an assembly of A, that C is a subassembly of B, and that D is a raw good. Embedding recursion in a key structure, in all but the most unusual of cases, is a poor practice. Inevitably, the structure is inflexible. Furthermore, the embedded key structure is wrapped up in the code of the system, and when changes need to be made, the result is massive disruption of code.

DIFFERENCES BETWEEN LEVELS

The question can be legitimately raised, For a generalized recursive structure, isn't it possible to have differences from one level to the next? The single definition of data in a generalized structure does not easily accommodate the unique differences between levels. For example, suppose a generalized bill of materials structure has been built for an organizational structure. Each node in the organization structure has its own manager, its own budget, its own overhead, and so forth. The generalized definition applies as easily to the headquarters as to the departments of a division.

But suppose at the headquarters there were some special needs. A manager at the headquarters level is allocated special funds for research and development that are not applicable at other levels of the organization. A special table can be created—away from the bill of materials—for these special needs that apply to only part of the organization.

ONLINE/BATCH BILL OF MATERIALS PROCESSING

A final issue relating to bill of materials processing is what kinds of processing need to be done in batch and what kinds of processing can be done online. The same principles of division of processing apply to bill of materials processing as apply elsewhere. Long-running programs are not run in the online environment. Long-running programs are run in batch. The nature of bill of materials explosion or implosion processing is such that it is doubtful if those processes would ever be run in the online environment.

SUMMARY

In summary, this chapter has focused on what a bill of materials is, how it needs to be structured, and how that structure is manipulated. Two processes have been identified as complex to execute: an explosion and an implosion. One danger of bill of materials processing is the existence of an infinite loop. The infinite loop can be uncovered by verification in the stack.

QUESTIONS: BILL OF MATERIALS PROCESSING

1. In a manufacturing environment, the relationship of assemblies to subassemblies is called a _____.
2. In a bill of materials, one part _____ to another part.
3. When one part relates to another part, the relationship is called a _____ relationship.

4. Recursive relationships are found in other than the manufacturing environment. Name two other common forms of recursive relationships.

5. The components or parts in a bill of materials are sometimes called _____.

6. The bill of materials recursive relationship is a HIERARCHICAL/PEER LEVEL relationship.

7. There MAY BE/MUST BE/CANNOT BE two sets of pointers representing the recursive relationship.

8. One set of pointers is called the upward pointer. The other set of pointers is called the _____ pointer.

9. Another name for the upward pointer is the _____ pointer.

10. Another name for the downward pointer is the _____ pointer.

11. When only one set of pointers is used, the structure can be efficiently traversed in ONE/TWO directions.

12. The two sets of pointers along with the base data is called the _____ recursive structure.

13. _____ levels of recursion can be represented in a generalized recursive structure.

14. The field level count is used to indicate how many _____ an assembly has.

15. Each subassembly has its own _____ number.

16. Taken collectively, the level counts for the subassemblies of an assembly are _____ in sequence.

17. Going from a part to all of its raw goods is called a bill of materials _____.

18. Explosions generally use a data structure called a _____.

19. A stack can be created in working storage or can be a _____.

20. The top of the stack is located by means of the _____.

21. Stacks manage data in a FIRST IN/FIRST OUT/FIRST IN/LAST OUT manner.

22. The reverse of an explosion is an _____.

23. Implosions ARE/ARE NOT as common as explosions.

24. When a part is being exploded and the explosion leads to the same part, an _____ has been created.

Chapter 13 — Bill of Materials Processing

25. There IS/IS NOT a technical reason why an infinite loop may be created.

26. The existence of an infinite loop can be detected during an explosion by examining the contents of the _____.

27. Explosions CAN/CANNOT be done in DB2 without the use of the level count.

28. Explosions done without the use of a level count require _____.

29. A recursive structure can be represented in other than the _____ recursive structure.

30. Other recursive representations, for large recursive structures, often are very _____.

31. A recursive structure can be created in an embedded _____ structure.

32. In nearly all circumstances embedding a recursive structure in a key is a _____.

33. When there are legitimate differences between one level of recursion and the next, separate _____ may be created.

34. Bill of materials processing (especially explosions) normally occur in the BATCH/ONLINE environment.

35. Because of the special nature of bill of materials processing, there is no need to limit the resources used by a transaction in the online environment. (T/F)

CHAPTER 14

Denormalization

The performance of relational systems can be enhanced through the physical placement of data in an optimal fashion. The result of normalization is usually many small tables of data. When data must be dynamically joined, the result is the consumption of much I/O. There may be significant performance gains to be made by *denormalizing* the data immediately prior to physical database design.

Denormalization, then, is the design process of taking normalized data and producing a physical design in which normalized data is rearranged so that optimal access and manipulation of data can be achieved.

NORMALIZATION OF DATA

The process of normalization (which is one of the foundations of relational technology), requires that data be organized into individual tables. Each table is distinct from other tables and has its own unique key. All of the nonkey data in a table logically depends on the full key of the table for its existence. For example, in a table representing an employee, the key of the employee may be employee number, and the nonkey information may include information such as date of hire, location of hire, starting position, and so forth. If an employee did not exist, there would be no date of hire or location of hire. The nonkey data depends on the key data for its existence. Figure 14-1 shows a simple normalized table.

```
employee no   date of hire   location of hire   conditions
   0012          850312         Tucson Az        finish degree
   0015          701215         El Paso Tx       -------------
   0018          750730         Tempe Az         -------------
   0020          761116         Dallas Tx        -------------
   0022          771215         Houston          no part time work
   0024          821217         Waco Tx          complete CPA
   0025          791010         Pecos Tx         -------------
   0028          810801         Las Cruces NM    -------------
    :             :               :   :            :   :
    :             :               :   :            :   :

     a simple normalized table - each nonkey field
     depends on the key for its existence
```

FIGURE 14–1. A simple normalized table. Each nonkey field depends on the key for its existence.

Prior to physical database design, all data is normalized into relational tables. One result of normalization is that the tables defined tend to have few data elements in each table, and there tend to be many tables. There is nothing inherently wrong with this very fine division of data. But if a high volume of processing is to be done and if the processing requires frequent reference from one table to the next, then the result is the consumption of much I/O. And when much I/O is consumed, the result is poor performance. Figure 14-2 illustrates the dynamic joining of several relational tables.

Note that, if the high volume processing goes against only data in a single table, then the techniques of denormalization do not apply. When high-performance processing goes against a single table, then combining tables (i.e, denormalizing tables) has little or no effect on performance and the I/O consumed. It is only when processing frequently must jump from one table to the next that denormalization will enhance performance. Denormalization will also enhance performance of the offline environment if there is a heavy amount of processing occurring in batch and if the batch processing frequently jumps from one table to the next.

Denormalization, then, is the process of taking many small tables and combining them into fewer, larger tables, so that less I/O is required. Figure 14-3 shows a table that has been denormalized.

The data elements in the same row in Figure 14-3 have different existence criteria and, as such, are not normalized.

Chapter 14 Denormalization

```
SELECT ......
FROM SUPP.TABLE,
     SUPP.ORDER.TABLE,
     SUPP.DELIV. TABLE
WHERE SUPPNO = '1053'
```

a SQL program executes and dynamically forms a new table based on the values found in existing tables

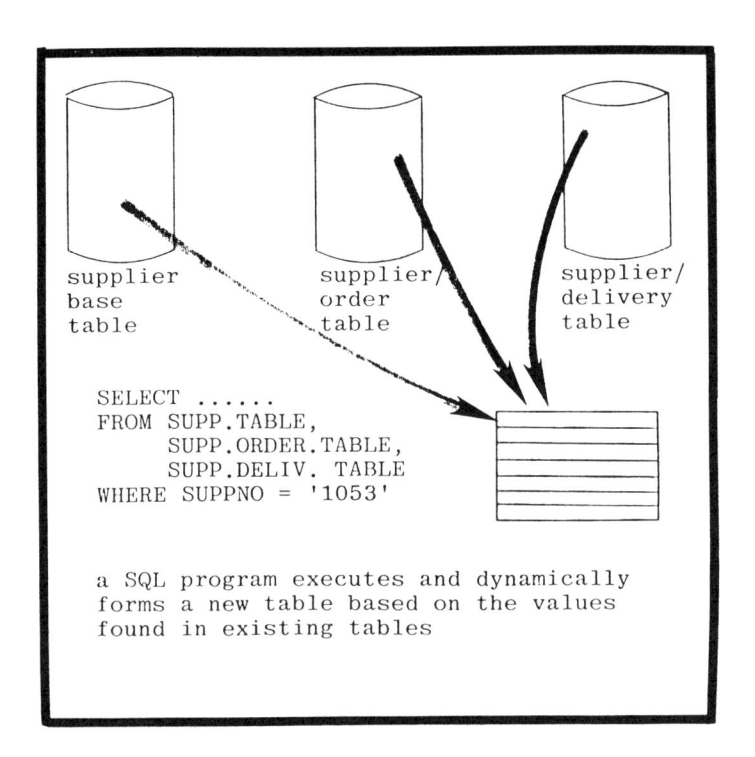

FIGURE 14–2. An SQL program executes and dynamically forms a new table based on the values found in existing tables.

employee number	name	address	age	manager	office phone	school	degree
00013	G Frey	123 Main	39	B Bach	555-1234	Yale	MBA
00016	D Henley	1689 1st St	42	B Bach	555-2298	Harvard	MS
00019	T Schmit	134 Grand	43	C B Sag	778-9981	UCLA	BS
00021	J Walsh	990 Teton	45	B Bach	887-3397	USC	BA
00201	D Felder	1455 Tincup	39	W Nelson	889-9972	Stanford	--
00202	S Nicks	220 Pine	41	T Wynett	998-2208	U Texas	BS
00204	M Fleet	220 Pine	45	G Jones	555-6692	U Conn	--
:	:	:	:	:	:	:	:

an unnormalized table

FIGURE 14–3. An unnormalized table.

THE USAGE MATRIX

The first step in the denormalization of data is to determine what processes represent the heaviest volume and what tables those processes are operating on. A convenient aid in this analysis is to create a matrix, matching process against tables. Going down the left-hand side of the matrix are the tables that are being analysed. Going across the page are the processes that are being analysed. Figure 14-4 shows an example of a usage matrix.

Each cell in the matrix then, represents the access of the table by the process.

After the matrix is created, the first (rather raw) analysis is to determine how many times the process will be executed, usually for a 24-hour period. (Note: Some period of time must be chosen as a baseline for the building of the table/process matrix.) Then the number of times the process will operate against the table is calculated for every table. For example, if process A accesses tables 2, 5, and 6, and if process A executes 100 times a day, then the cell representing the intersection of process A and tables 2, 5, and 6 will contain the value 100, and other cells where the table was not accessed will contain a value of zero.

In addition to the mere access of data, the analyst may wish to use the usage matrix to keep track of update and access information.

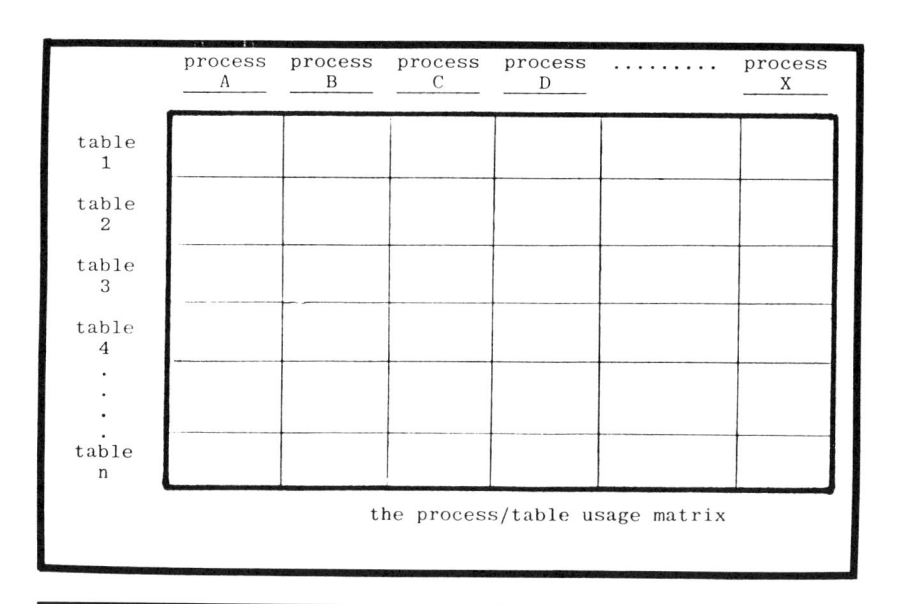

FIGURE 14-4. The process/table usage matrix.

In other words, it may be useful to distinguish between access and update for some types of processes.

The estimate of the number of executions for a process can become complex because of several factors. In some cases, a process has never been run before, and the number of times the process will be executed is purely a guess. In other cases, the process will execute 100 times on one day and 1,000 times on another day, in a random pattern. And, in other cases, a process will require high performance while other processes will not need the same level of performance. Still another factor is that a transaction will show an execution frequency of 1,000 and a batch process will show a frequency of execution of 1 or 2 for the same 24-hour period.

THE PROCESSING FREQUENCY ANOMALIES

ALL of the processing frequency anomalies need to be taken into account if the denormalization process is to be effective. In the case where the number of times a process is to execute is not known, generally speaking, the highest reasonable estimate should be used. The estimate may come from empirically derived data or the estimate may be analytically derived. In any case, to err slightly too high is acceptable; to err too low is not acceptable.

In the case where there is a substantial difference between one day's processing activities and another day's activities, the high-water mark should be used.

In the case where there is a substantial difference between the priorities of different transactions, the transactions with the higher priorities should be weighted in favor of the more important transactions. The weighting is done by multiplying the number of transactions run per day by a factor of 2 or 3.

All differences have been accounted for with the exception of the difference between batch processing and online processing. For example, the frequency of execution of an online process may be 400 times a day, while the frequency of execution of a batch process may be 2 times a day.

ESTIMATING ROW ACCESS FREQUENCY

After the number of executions have been placed in the appropriate cell in the matrix, the next step is to determine how many rows of the table will be needed by each execution. In other words, when a process accesses a table, how many rows will it normally access?

For example, the value in a cell may be 150, indicating that a process will access a table 150 times throughout the day. The next cell has a value of 200. The analysis now requires that the number of accesses be multiplied by the number of rows per access. The first process accesses one row per access, and the next process accesses 25 rows per access. Factoring in the number of rows per execution leaves values of 150 and 5,000 in the two cells. The values in the cells are now more representative of the true processing needs of the system.

The number of accesses per execution in some cases is a very straightforward number, and, in other cases, it is not. For example, suppose a process accesses 5 and only 5 rows per execution. Then it is clear that the process frequency for the cell needs to be multiplied by 5. For another cell, suppose that the average number of rows accessed is 10, with a standard deviation of .5. This means that most executions will use 10 rows. The cell is multiplied by 10. But suppose the average number of rows accessed per execution is 15 with a standard deviation of 12.5. In this case, there is a wide variance between the number rows accessed per execution. As a rule, one-half of the standard deviation should be added to the mean as the factor to be applied to the frequency of execution. In the example being discussed, one-half of 12.5 is 6.25. Thus, 6.25 is added to 15, yielding 21.25, which is the factor that should be used.

At this point, batch processing is factored in. A batch process may show only one execution per day, but, in executing, the batch process accesses 40,000 rows.

HEURISTIC AND ITERATIVE ANALYSIS

The next analytical step is to determine two things: which tables should be combined and which tables should be clustered. The analysis to follow is heuristic and iterative, and does not follow any prescriptive path.

The first pass at denormalization is an attempt to combine the most heavily used tables. The total row/table usage may be calculated from the table by adding each line to the right. In other words, the total number of rows needed for all processing is the sum of all row accesses going across the page. Based upon the total numbers of usage, the analyst asks the question, Which two or more rows can be merged so that data used together is placed in the same row?

Generally speaking, the rows that can be combined share part of a common key. For example, an employee base table, an employee education table, and an employee job history table may be able to be combined. But an employee table and a parts usage table would not be candidates for tables that could be combined. The first cut at analysis is to identify heavily used tables that are logical candidates for combination. Key commonality is the first clue to the successful combination of data.

However, not all commonly shared keys can be successfully combined. Consider the simple case of a bank balance table and a bank activity table, where activities add up to the current balance. Certainly, these tables share a common key, and, certainly, these tables are used together, but the distribution of keys is so dissimilar that the pieces of data are combined only with difficulty. For example, activity may be incorporated into the balance table, but activity is frequently updated and occurs a variable number of times. Figure 14-5 illustrates the difficulties of combining balance and activity rows.

Admittedly, some savings can be effected, but at a cost of complexity that is most likely undesirable.

After the candidates that can be merged together are merged, the savings analysis is done. In the perfect case, table A is accessed 1,000 times and table B is accessed 5,000 times per day. By combining the tables, all accesses to B will be combined with accesses to A. The total number of accesses to the combined A/B is 1,000 in the optimal case.

The advantage of the usage matrix is that it allows different combinations of data to be merged and allows the different economies of consolidation to be measured quantitatively.

Of course, the analyst should carefully consider the full range of design criteria when combining two tables. Such issues as the ability to split the data at a later point in time or the creation of very large tables should be considered along with the performance considerations.

CLUSTERING ANALYSIS

Considered in combination with the consolidation of tables is the issue of whether data should be clustered or not. When the total number of table accesses was calculated, no considerations were given

```
account  balance  activity  date
10089    100.00   +25.00    1215
10089     75.00   -25.00    1216
10089    150.00   +50.00    1216
10089    189.36   +39.36    1217
10089     60.36   -120.00   1218
10089   1060.36  +1000.00   1218
  :        :        :        :
```

the table that results when balance is superimposed on activity. A new balance is created every time there is an activity, and there is much duplication of key data

```
                   activity 1        activity 2              activity n
account  balance   date   amount     date   amount   .....  date   amount
10089    1060.36   1215   +25.00     1216   -25.00          1218   +1000.00
10091    1078.98   1218   -1000.00   1219   +35.00          ----   --------
10092   10908.72   1215  +15000.00   1221   -10.00          1221  +12000.00
10092-1  -------   1222  -12000.00   1224  +2798.76         1224  +35997.19
10092-2  -------   1226   +200.00    1226   -566.98         ----   --------
10094     187.56   ----   --------   ----   --------        ----   --------
  :         :       :        :        :        :             :        :
```

the table that results when activity is superimposed on balance. There are a widely varying number of activities for each account for the same period of time. Some accounts have no activity - such as account 10094 and other accounts have so much activity that more than one row must be used. When more than one row is used - as in the case of account 10092 - application convention is that the active balance is stored in the first occurrence of the account.

two tables that show that even when data is related that combining the data into the same row can be difficult and may not be advisable

FIGURE 14-5. Two tables that show that, even when data is related, combining the data into the same row can be difficult and may not be advisable.

to whether the access was direct or sequential. A direct access is one where a single row and only a single row is accessed. A sequential access is one where one row after another is accessed in rapid succession. When data is clustered and much sequential processing occurs, then it may be assumed that multiple rows may be read in a single I/O (i.e., as many rows as exist in a page). In the analysis of which rows need to be combined, the issue of clustering can be factored in. When it is assumed that a row is clustered, the total number of sequential accesses is adjusted to reflect the lessened need for I/O.

AUTOMATED TOOLS

The combination of consolidation of data and clustering that reduces the *total* number of accesses to the data in the system is the optimal plan for denormalization and clustering of data. Because of the number of tables and because of the combinations that are possible, this phase of denormalization analysis is heuristic and iterative. It often makes sense to use a spreadsheet tool such as LOTUS 1-2-3 as an aid in this phase of analysis. In using an automated tool, not only can different options be documented, but new options can be calculated rapidly.

As an example of a successful table denormalization, suppose a supplier/order table and an order/supplier line item table have been specified by the data analysis and normalization process. The supplier/order table contains information about who the supplier of an order is, the supplier contact, name, and phone number, as well as conditions of the order. The order/supplier line item table contains information about the line items of an order, the amount of each item ordered, the price, and so forth. Most processes that access one table access the other. Creating a single table allows access to be done in a single I/O, since consolidation forces the data into the same row. Figure 14-6 shows the effect of consolidation.

REDUNDANCY

After the analysis is done, another variable is to be considered: the deliberate introduction of redundancy into the system. To this point, it has been assumed that the data in the system was nonredundant. The nonredundancy of data optimizes update of data at the expense of access of data. The issue of denormalization now must address the question, Will the deliberate introduction of redundancy into the system significantly reduce the total amount of accesses that the system makes?

This analysis is addressed heuristically and iteratively, like the previous analysis. The first clue as to which data elements are candidates for redundant existence comes from the frequency matrix that has been developed. Those tables that are being frequently accessed and are not being frequently updated may contain data that, when positioned redundantly in more than one table, reduces total access needs. Of course, the analyst must keep in mind that the proliferation of data may reduce access needs but increases update needs when

				item 1			item 2		
supplier	contact	phone	conditions	part	amount	price	part	amount	price	......
10098	P McCartney	555-8891	FOB	110-a	9000	100.00	1998	800	977.00
10100	R Starr	669-2298	COD	1187		16000.00	----	----	----
10100	G Harrison	778-2209	---	1187		15500.00	1998i	10	67.98
10100	J Lennon	550-8873	FOB	22098	20	998.45	----	----	----
10102	M Jagger	887-3398	FOB	110-s	20	776.00	1109	50	998.21
10103	H Nillson	665-9981	COD	1187		16000.00	----	----	----
......	......	......	......	......	......	......	......	......	......

the consolidation of two tables into a single denormalized row

FIGURE 14-6. The consolidation of two tables into a single denormalized row.

the data values change. Generally speaking, only limited amounts of data are deliberately proliferated.

As an example of the selective use of redundancy, suppose there is a parts table, a supplier table, and a cross-reference table. The cross-reference table contains only the key values—part and supplier. It is found that, when the cross-reference table is used in going from part to supplier, in most cases, only the supplier name and address are needed. Other information contained in the supplier table is accessed only infrequently. The analyst places supplier name and address in the parts/supplier cross reference table as nonkey data as shown by Figure 14-7.

Supplier name and address are not placed in the supplier/parts cross-reference table. Now, when cross-reference needs to be made to the supplier, only the part/supplier cross-reference table must be accessed, saving an access to the supplier table. The analyst must factor into the savings the work required by the system to keep the supplier name and address current in the cross-reference table. The cross-reference table must be updated—potentially in many places —when supplier name and address change. Fortunately, the fields that have been made redundant are stable fields and do not require frequent maintenance.

After the redundancy analysis is done, the analyst adjusts the matrix to reflect the new pattern of access and update of tables.

part	supplier	supplier name	supplier address
1009	10098	Emporium	123 Grand
1009	10199	Grand Auto	17th Street
1009	19087	Wilson Hd	16 N Ranch
1009	20098	Jones Dry	16th St Mall
1010	10098	Emporium	123 Grand
1011	10099	Denver DG	16th St Mall
1011	10200	Denver DG	SW Plaza

a cross reference table with name and address added

FIGURE 14-7. A cross-reference table with name and address added.

INTERNAL ARRAYS

Another technique of denormalization available to the analyst is the specification of internal arrays of data in a row. If a row contains a small number of nonkey data elements, if the data elements are frequently accessed in a sequential manner, if the pattern of access is stable, and if the number of occurrences of nonkey data can be reliably calculated for the key values of a table, then the analyst should consider violating the first form of normalization by placing the elements of data into an array. In an array, a row contains multiple occurrences of nonkey data. When the conditions are met, a substantial savings in resources consumed is possible.

As an example of the usage of an array within a row, consider a payroll history file. The logical design specifies that the twice-monthly paycheck be stored individually. But there is no reason why an annual payroll history table cannot be created. The annual table contains 24 occurrences—one for each twice-monthly paycheck. The order of insertion of the occurrences of data, the number of occurrences for each employee, the access of the occurrences is very stable. The violation of the first form of normalization yields many performance dividends, not to mention the savings of space in the reduced need for key data. Figure 14-8 shows this form of denormalization.

INTERLEAVING DATA

A final option appropriate to DB2 that is applicable in a few cases is the *interleaving* of data. Interleaving occurs where two tables are

employee number	pay Jan 15	pay Jan 30	pay Feb 15	pay Feb 28	pay Mar 15	....
0021	1500.00	1500.00	1500.00	1475.00	1500.00	
0023	1789.00	1775.00	1789.00	1775.00	1789.00	
0024	1050.89	1100.00	1050.89	1100.00	1050.89	
0026	998.78	998.78	998.78	996.35	998.78	
0029	767.90	767.90	767.90	659.89	767.90	
0031	1976.98	1976.98	2060.76	2100.00	2060.76	

a payhistory data with individual pay amounts organized into an array

FIGURE 14-8. A pay-history data with individual pay amounts organized into an array.

stored in the same page(s) of data. Interleaving is not an option for partitioned data. When the probability of access is high, there may be some performance gains by interleaving data. For example, suppose an account balance table and an account activity table are often accessed together, and the designer does not wish to combine the two tables into a single row. Then the analyst may sort the data together to combine the two tables into the same page based on like key values.

Upon loading the databases, the data is loaded in a sequence so that like keys from different tables are stored in the same page. The effect is that one I/O services multiple requests for data from different tables.

There are several problems with interleaving. Interleaving cannot be used with partitioned data. Interleaving must be done as databases are loaded. Once an interleaved database is updated, there is no guarantee that the data will be properly placed. And finally, a reorganization of data will not restore the proper order of data after update. Instead, interleaved data must be resorted and reloaded.

As an example of the usefulness of interleaving, consider an account balance and account activity data. Sorting the tables by account and then loading like tables into the same page have the effect of placing unlike tables with like data in the same physical proximity. Of course it is recognized that update of the data destroys the effect of interleaving. Figure 14-9 shows the interleaved data.

OTHER OPTIONS

The design techniques for denormalization to this point have merged data into the same row so that a minimum of I/O is used once the row is accessed. But merging unlike data together is not the only denormalization technique. Suppose a bank account table is to be

acct balance	acct activity	acct activity	acct activity	acct balance	acct activity	....
10029 $45.02	860612 +12.78	860614 -36.90	860615 +100.00	10031 $100.00	860201 +90.56	....

data that has been interleaved in a DB2 page

FIGURE 14–9. Data that has been interleaved in a DB2 page.

created. The key of the table is the account, and nonkey elements include bank balance, domicile, date account opened, and other similar elements. The key—account number—is 16 bytes in length and the nonkey data is 64 bytes in length. Total row space is 80 bytes.

To enhance performance, the table is split into two tables. One table contains the account key and balance. A row in this table is 22 bytes in length. The other table contains the key and all the nonkey data elements other than balance. The length of a row in this table is 74 bytes.

An analysis of the accounts table shows that the frequency of access of the balance data is heavy. Every time an activity against an account is transacted, the balance table is accessed and updated. The remaining account data—domicile, date account opened, etc.—is accessed very infrequently.

By splitting the data into separate tables, the probability of a fortuitous hit in the buffer is raised. In the original design, a row was 80 bytes in length. In a fully packed 4k buffer, about 50 rows would fit. In the new design, for the balance table, about 180 rows will fit in the buffer. The odds of a fortuitous buffer hit are raised by shrinking the size of the row with the most activity and packing the highly accessed data together so that there is a greater chance of a buffer hit.

This technique of denormalization, then, is a radical departure from other techniques of denormalization that rely on the consolidation of data.

SUMMARY

In summary, this chapter has focused on what denormalization is and why it can enhance performance. The building of a usage matrix to determine the effectiveness of denormalization was discussed, as well as the heuristic and iterative analysis that centers on the matrix. It is suggested that an automated tool, such as a spreadsheet, be used to create and maintain the matrix. Finally, the deliberate introduction of redundancy into the system was suggested.

QUESTIONS: DENORMALIZATION

1. Normalization of data is one of the foundations of _____ theory.
2. In a normalized table, each _____ field depends on the _____ field for its existence.

Chapter 14   Denormalization   221

3. The result of normalization is that data is separated into MANY/FEW tables.

4. When data is separated into many tables and those tables are turned into physical databases, data is widely _____.

5. The dispersion of data costs I/O when those tables must be _____ joined by an application program.

6. The performance implications of normalization APPLY/APPLY PRIMARILY/DO NOT APPLY to the batch environment.

7. The performance implications of normalization IMPLY/DO NOT IMPLY that normalization should not be done.

8. Denormalization is the process of arranging _____ in other than its normalized form.

9. Normally denormalization requires that data be combined into a single _____.

10. When data is combined into a single row, it can ALWAYS/USUALLY/SOMETIMES be accessed with a single I/O.

11. For data to be combined in a single row, it usually contains a _____ key.

12. Furthermore, for data to be combined in a single row, the _____ frequency must be similar or the same.

13. Combining data into a single row has NO/SOME/A LARGE effect on performance unless many processes access all the data in a single execution.

14. The data that is denormalized should be sensitive to the frequency of execution of the processes. (T/F)

15. Another form of denormalization is the splitting of data into very small fields, which maximizes the probability of a fortuitous _____ hit.

16. Concentrating on buffer hits is an issue only for HIGH/LOW performance data.

17. A usage matrix table suggests what rows should be combined and what rows should be indexed and/or _____.

18. A row that is heavily used and is accessed in a sequential manner is an ideal candidate for _____.

19. A row can SOMETIMES/NEVER UNDER ANY CONDITIONS/EASILY be clustered more than once.

20. A partitioned data base MUST/MAY be clustered.

21. Another form of denormalization that may reduce the total accesses required is the deliberate introduction of _____.
22. Redundancy maximizes access of data at the expense of _____ of data.
23. Usually data that is VOLATILE/STABLE is a candidate for redundancy.
24. The designer may reduce the number of accesses required by the introduction of redundancy, but the designer must factor in the accesses required to update the data when the data _____.
25. When multiple occurrences of data are placed in a single row, the _____ level of normalization is violated.
26. Arrays of data in a row can save I/O in that, in SOME/MOST/EVERY case, only one I/O will be needed to access all data in the array.
27. Whether to place data in an array in a row DEPENDS ON/DOES NOT DEPEND ON how often and in what pattern the data is to be used and updated.
28. Arrays of data in a row can also save SOME/MUCH space in that the repetition of keys is not necessary.
29. When data from two different tables is loaded into a page of a simple tablespace so that there is a relationship between the keys of the two tables, _____ of data has occurred.
30. Interleaving IS/IS NOT an option for partitioned data.
31. When data is updated, the page in which the data is placed can be controlled so as not to interrupt the effect of interleaving. (T/F)
32. Reorganizing interleaved data RESTORES/DOES NOT RESTORE the order of the data.
33. The only way to restore the order of interleaved data is to sort it and _____ it.

CHAPTER 15

High Availability

This chapter discusses the problems associated with achieving a high degree of system *availability* in DB2. The issues of online availability center on the number of times the online system goes down and the amount of time required to bring the system back online. The two principal activities that occur during database down time are database recovery and database reorganization. Techniques for minimizing the resources used for reorganization and recovery are discussed.

IMPORTANCE OF DESIGN

There are two essential facets to the online environment: online performance and online availability. Performance is designed into the transactions and databases of the system; performance is not tuned into the system after the fact. Availability is likewise designed into the system—primarily into the databases of the system.

Database availability is primarily a function of the downtime of the system. Some aspects of availability, such as power supply stability, machine failure, and acts of nature are all beyond the scope of control of the database designer. Fortunately, most system outages are not caused by uncontrollable factors. Most occur at the application or operational level, and, in fact, are very much influenced by the analyst.

RECOVERY/REORGANIZATION

The two primary reasons for system unavailability are the activities of *recovery* and *reorganization*. Recovery occurs when there is a system failure and the data and transactions of the system need to be restored. Recovery is an unscheduled event, unlike database reorganization, which is scheduled. Whenever recovery or reorganization are occurring, the database is unavailable for other processing. The strategy for high availability is to minimize the time required for recovery and reorganization.

PHASES OF RECOVERY

There are three phases to the recovery process. The first phase is the discovery of the error. Database size is seldom a factor in the discovery phase. The second phase is the analysis required to understand why the error occurred and what to do about the error. Database size is very much a factor in this phase of recovery. Large databases often require many resources for diagnostic analysis.

The smaller the databases, the faster diagnostics can be run. In fact, large database size may prevent iterative analysis after a failure. And massive amounts of data often mask pertinent information that otherwise would be obvious, or at least easy to get to. Exaggerating the effect of database size is the fact that the second phase of recovery analysis is often the lengthiest phase. Anything that can be done to shorten this phase is beneficial.

The third phase of recovery is the prescriptive phase, in which action is taken as a result of the analysis made in the second phase. Depending on the error and the fix, database size may play a part in this phase. On occasions, a fix can be implemented immediately with no significant data manipulation. In this case, database size is not a factor. In other cases where databases must be manipulated, database size is a factor.

The three phases of recovery are shown by Figure 15-1.

To minimize the work done in phase 2 or phase 3 of recovery requires that the units of data on which analysis is being done and on which recovery measures are being taken be minimized. Strictly speaking, the size of the physical unit on which analysis and recovery is done is what needs to be minimized.

```
     phase1           phase2                    phase3
/-------/ /--------------------------/ /------------------------/
  error        diagnosis and formulation    prescriptive measures
  detection
                    the three phases of recovery
```

FIGURE 15–1. The three phases of recovery.

REORGANIZATION—AN UNLOAD/RELOAD PROCESS

Reorganization occurs for a plethora of reasons. The most common reason for reorganization is the internal disorganization of data either at the table and/or at the index level. A reorganization of data has the effect of reconciling the logical and the physical order of data. Disorganized data is physically placed so that the system requires unnecessary I/O to access the data. The degree of organization (or disorganization!) is determined by utilities that monitor the physical placement and access of data.

During a reorganization, data is read in its old state, sorted or modified if necessary, and reloaded in its new state. Once reloaded in its new state, the logical and the physical sequence of the data are synchronized and the system can access the data efficiently. Because of its functional simplicity, a reorganization is sometimes called an *unload/reload program*.

Figure 15-2 shows the mechanics of a reorganization.

When a table is reorganized, its indexes are normally reorganized as well.

But internal disorganization (i.e., unoptimal physical placement of data) is not the only reason for reorganization of data. When the structure of data undergoes radical redefinition, the data probably needs to be reorganized. The difference between a reorganization for internal cleanliness of data and for radical redefinition of data is important.

Reorganization for internal cleanliness of data may be done for (and may actually affect) relatively few rows of data. But reorganization for structure redefinition is done because of a need to modify every row.

The smaller the database (down to a point!), the faster the re-

```
┌─────────────────────────────────────────────────────────────────┐
│   ___                                                      ___  │
│  |   |     ┌──────┐      ___       ┌──────┐              |   | │
│  |   |──▶  │      │──▶  (   )──▶   │      │──▶           |   | │
│  |___|     └──────┘      ‾‾‾       └──────┘              |___| │
│                                                                 │
│  disorganized  unload    temporary      reload     reorganized │
│  data          step      storage;       step       data        │
│                          sort, modify                           │
│                          if necessary                           │
│                                                                 │
│            the mechanics of data reorganization                │
└─────────────────────────────────────────────────────────────────┘
```

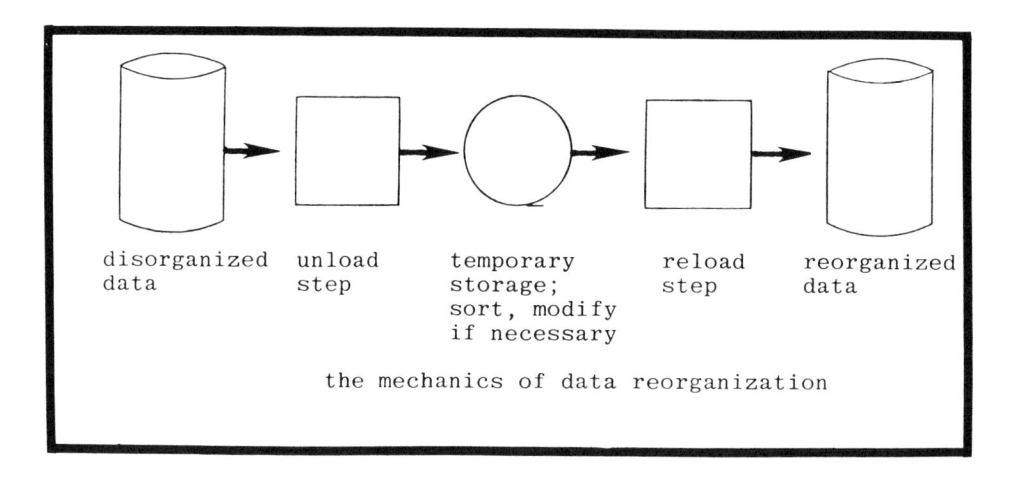

FIGURE 15–2. The mechanics of data reorganization.

covery and reorganization. The faster recovery and reorganization can be done, the higher the system availability.

ESTIMATING DOWNTIME

The analyst knows a database is too large by estimating the time required for recovery and reorganization. To estimate the time needed for the execution of these utilities, the size of the database must be estimated. Database size is estimated by calculating the amount of data in the row, the overhead in the row, the number of rows, the freespace in the page and the number of free pages, and the space required for an index.

All indexes should be taken into account and all three levels of index space must be factored in. In addition, database size as the database goes into full production must be estimated, not just the size of the database immediately after implementation.

After the size of the database is estimated, recovery and reorganization time must be calculated. There are several approaches to this calculation. One approach is to compare the recovery needs with a similar table that is already in existence. As long as there are the same number of indexes and as long as row size and the number of occurrences of rows are approximately the same, the comparison is valid, at least in gross terms.

Another approach is to prototype the recovery and reorganization needs. Usually, a small amount of data is used in the prototype and an extrapolation is done. If there is any question as to the recovery and reorganization requirements for a database, a prototype should be done.

Generally speaking, a prototype is done using either 10 percent of the data that will actually exist or, for large databases, one spindle's worth of data. In addition, the prototype must be sure to include one occurrence of each foreign key relationship that will exist. Another consideration is the representative population of tables, especially tables that are often accessed and have multiple foreign keys.

One factor that cannot be prototyped is the phase 2 recovery time: the time spent in analysis. The time estimations for phase 2 must be added to the estimated or prototyped recovery time—which is really phase 3 time.

PROBABILITY OF DOWNTIME

After the estimates for downtime are created, the probability of downtime must be calculated. Generally speaking, the downtime pattern of a shop is constant—some shops experience very few outages, and other shops experience frequent outages. The frequency of outages is due to several factors—design, implementation, operations, etc. The track record of a shop should be the guiding factor in the estimation of the frequency of outages. As a result, it does not matter whether the probability of outage is being calculated for a new system or the rewrite or enhancement of an older system.

The probability of an outage should be considered along with the length of the outage to determine if system availability goals will be met. It is assumed that availability goals have formally and in a quantified manner been established. If system availability goals have not been established, then there can be no objective measurement against the goals.

REDUCING THE VOLUME OF DATA

The following analysis should be done for every database that is large and requires a significant amount of uptime.

To reduce the volume of data, the first (very basic) question to be asked is whether all the data is necessary and whether the data will be used. Figure 15-3 shows a database of which only a small portion will ever be accessed.

In Figure 15-3, only a portion of the data will ever be accessed.

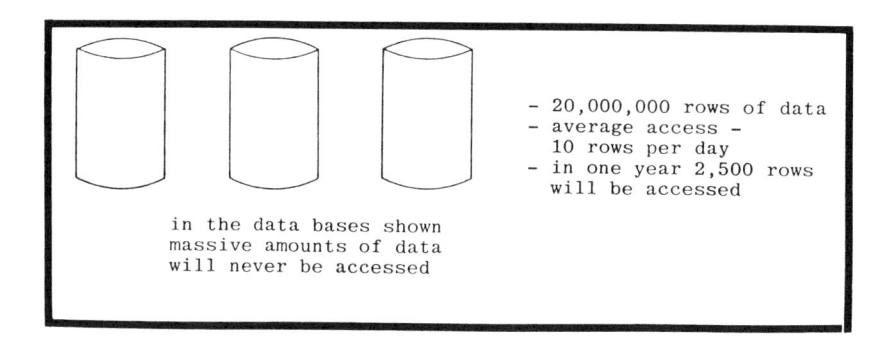

```
┌─────────────────────────────────────────────────────────────┐
│   ___       ___       ___                                    │
│  /   \     /   \     /   \      - 20,000,000 rows of data   │
│ |     |   |     |   |     |     - average access -          │
│ |     |   |     |   |     |       10 rows per day           │
│ |     |   |     |   |     |     - in one year 2,500 rows    │
│  \___/     \___/     \___/        will be accessed          │
│                                                              │
│       in the data bases shown                                │
│       massive amounts of data                                │
│       will never be accessed                                 │
│                                                              │
└─────────────────────────────────────────────────────────────┘
```

FIGURE 15-3. In the databases shown, massive amounts of data will never be accessed.

The data that will not be accessed still is expensive to maintain in an automated form.

Analysis should be done to determine what data can be culled from the database. Typical criteria for culling data include the age of the data, the size of the account that is being represented, the size of the customer whose data is kept, active data versus inactive data, and so forth. There are probably an infinite number of criteria for the culling of data. Each of the criteria serves to separate the data with a high probability of access from the data with a low probability of access.

If there are large volumes of data that will never or very infrequently be accessed, then clearly some reduction of data is in order.

On occasion, the system requirements will specify that data is needed but that only very infrequently will some of the data be accessed. At this point, the economics of user requirements enter the picture. What is the cost of storing and maintaining data online when it will seldom be needed?

Most likely a more cost effective alternative is to store the data offline, on magnetic tape or another medium. Offline storage does not mean that the data cannot be accessed, but that access to the data will be slower than online access. But the cost of offline storage and the cost of offline access are much lower than the corresponding online costs.

The utility of fast access and slower access must be measured against the associated costs.

The first level of availability analysis questions whether the data is cost-justified in the first place. The second level of analysis follows directly from the first. Has there been a conscious and deliberate split of primitive and derived data? (For an in-depth discussion of primitive and derived data refer to *Information Engineering for the Practitioner*, Yourdon Press, 1987.)

Generally speaking, primitive data is stored online and derived data is moved offline or closer to the end-user community. One criterion to determine whether data is primitive or derived is that primitive data is vulnerable to update and derived data is not. This criterion fits very nicely with the movement of derived data to offline storage and processing.

The third level of analysis calls for the split of administrative and operational data. The split of the data does not reduce database size. Instead, it ensures that data is as untangled as possible. Operational data is that data which is directly concerned with the day-to-day operations of the enterprise. Administrative data is that which is related to the administration of the enterprise. For example, in a banking environment, customer and account data are operational. By the same token, employee payroll, insurance processing, and salary administration data are administrative.

The splitting of administrative and operational data does not imply that neither one should be online (as was the implication of the split of primitive and derived data). Instead, the separation of administrative and operational data allows the data and the accompanying processes to be moved to separate systems if need be, or to recover or reorganize one set of data independent of the other. A failure in the operational world will have no effect on the administrative world and vice versa.

The fourth level of analysis calls for the separation and segregation of one application from the next. Unlike the split between administrative and operational data, the split of applications into their own distinct units is not easily accomplished after the system has been designed. If this split is to be done, it is most effective to split the data prior to the building of actual databases.

However, like the split of operational and administrative data, no data is purged from the online environment. Data is separated into small units so that recovery and reorganization can be done quickly and independently on each unit. The failure of one unit has no effect on other units, further enhancing the availability posture.

The fifth level of analysis occurs for single applications that are large and still have an availability exposure. For a single application, consideration must be given to the splitting of the application according to the key values of the databases. The total amount of data is not reduced; instead, the data is spread over distinct units, each of which is smaller than the collective database.

There are two ways to reduce the unit of recoverability in DB2 when data is split within the application. One way is at the system level—by the partitioning of data. DB2 allows a database to be partitioned in up to 64 partitions. Each partition has the same physical definition (i.e., the same physical database design). The difference between one partition and the next is the content of data.

In DB2, data is partitioned on one and only one key. A partition can be recovered or reorganized independently in most cases. There are two drawbacks to the partitioning of data. One drawback is that, if a reorganization is being done to restructure data, all partitions must be reorganized. In this case, partitioning does not reduce the unit of recovery. The second case where partitioning will not enhance availability is the case where one or more partitions need to be transferred to another processor and/or another copy of DB2. In this case, partitioning of data is not an advantage.

Another technique for the splitting of data across units of recovery is in the physical definition of multiple databases. One database contains all keys whose first digit is 0. Another database contains all keys whose first digit is 1, and so forth. This technique is sometimes called placing data in "like" data bases or in "like" partitions.

Figure 15-4 illustrates the two options for the splitting of data.

For partitions that are managed at the system level, there is no difference among the definition of the different like partitions. The only difference from one partition to the next is in the content of the data. One disadvantage of specifying like partitions of data is in the number of control blocks generated. If there are many like partitions, then many control blocks will be generated.

The second disadvantage of building like partitions is that the system is totally unaware of the relationship between any two partitions. In the case of system-managed partitions, the system was aware of the relationship between any two partitions. In the eventuality that ALL the like partitions need to be recovered or reorganized, the system is not aware of any need for coordination.

A major advantage of like partitions of data is that each like database can be reorganized and recovered independently. The unit of reorganization and recovery has been reduced to a minimum for all cases. Another advantage of like partitions is that one partition can be moved to another processor and/or copy of DB2 with no concern of the effect on other like partitions. Unlike system-partitioned data that needs to be controlled in its entirety, like data can be managed

Chapter 15 High Availability

```
partitioned                 split of data at the
data - the                  application level - the
different                   split of data and the
partitions                  management of data is
are known                   known at the application
to and are                  level
managed by
DB2

          the two ways an application's
          data can be split and managed
          in DB2
```

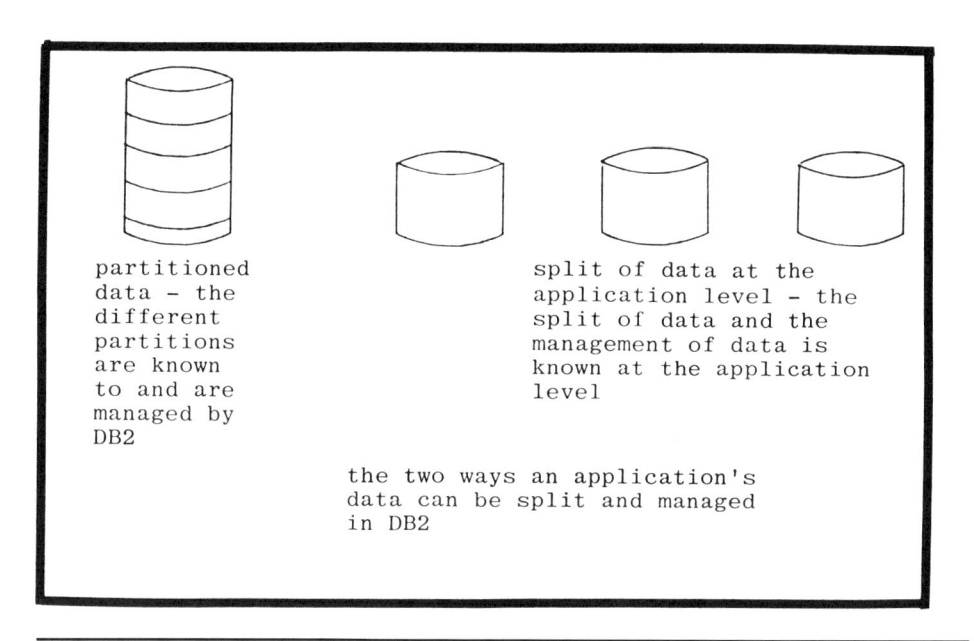

FIGURE 15–4. The two ways an application's data can be split and managed in DB2.

independently. Not only does the ability to move data across processors enhance availability, but it can enhance performance as well.

Splitting data across an application has many ramifications, each of which must be considered by the analyst. One consideration is the interface with other applications. If one application has a key split by line of business and another application has a key split by marketing division, then interfacing the two systems may be complex. Furthermore, splitting both of them onto separate processors may prove difficult if there is any amount of interaction between the systems at all.

A second consideration of splitting data is in the effectiveness of the split. If a database is split into 10 like partitions, but 90 percent of the data resides in a single partition, then the split has not been effective. Figure 15-5 shows such an occurrence.

And the analyst must consider not just today's data and distribution of data, but also must factor in tomorrow's trends.

One of the significant advantages of splitting data—at the system or the application level—is that the impact of failure is limited. Not only does recovery occur more quickly, but the data that is impacted by the failure is significantly less. Consider a large database that is not split. Suppose the database experiences a failure. Because of its

```
key=0xxx    key=1xxx    key=2xxx      key=3xxx           key=9xxx
250 rows    100 rows    250000 rows   280 rows           75 rows
```

even though the keys appear to be evenly split, the distribution of data does not follow in an even manner

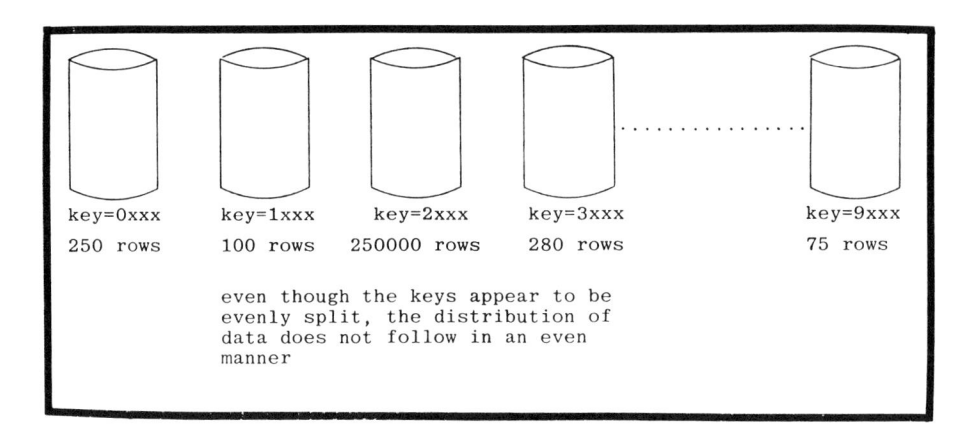

FIGURE 15-5 Even though the keys appear to be evenly split, the distribution of data does not follow in an even manner.

size, recovery takes a long time and much data is made unavailable as the recovery is effected.

REFERENTIAL INTEGRITY AND HIGH AVAILABILITY

One of the advantages of application support of referential integrity is that no data relationships are supported by direct pointers. A data relationship supported by application code goes through an index as one table points to another. There are no hard-coded addresses between one table and the other. The implication is that one table can be recovered independently of another table, which reduces the time required for reorganization.

SUMMARY

In summary, this chapter has discussed the issues of availability from the perspective of the options that are available to the designer. The reduction of the raw amount of data was the first step the designer could take. Next, the designer could separate derived data from primitive data. Next, the separation of administrative and operational data, as well as the separation of data by application, was considered. Finally, the splitting of databases within the same application allowed the designer to reduce the data into as fine a unit of recovery and reorganization as desired.

QUESTIONS: HIGH AVAILABILITY

1. There are two factors to availability: the _____ of time the computer stays down when it goes down, and the _____ of outages.
2. Before a design can be undertaken, a _____ goal of availability needs to be set.
3. Two common activities that cause system outages are _____ and _____.
4. Reorganization IS/IS NOT a planned activity.
5. Recovery IS/IS NOT a planned activity.
6. The general strategy to minimize the length of time required for recovery or reorganization is to _____ the amount of data in a database.
7. A reorganization is often called an _____ process.
8. There are _____ phases to recovery.
9. The first phase of recovery is the _____ of an error.
10. The first phase of recovery IS/IS NOT generally sensitive to database size.
11. The second phase of recovery is the _____ phase.
12. In the diagnostic phase, the reason the error occurred is addressed. (T/F)
13. The second part of the diagnostic phase, a plan is _____ for correcting the error.
14. Data base size IS/IS NOT a factor in the second phase of recovery.
15. Large databases often hide relevant diagnostic information. (T/F)
16. Diagnostics usually require more time to execute in the face of _____ databases.
17. The third phase of recovery is the _____ phase.
18. The prescriptive phase usually IS/IS NOT sensitive to database size.
19. Which two phases of recovery are sensitive to database size?
20. Which two phases of recovery usually take the most time?
21. Which phases of recovery require an indeterminate number of resources?

22. Reorganization of data is done to reorder the _____ structure of data and to _____ data when the entire data structure needs to be changed.

23. The time required for reorganization is directly proportional to the amount of data to be reorganized. (T/F)

24. The number of indexes to be reorganized IS/IS NOT of minor importance.

25. Comparing databases of equivalent _____ and _____ is a good way to estimate downtime needs.

26. Estimation of database size includes _____.

27. All _____ of indexes must be estimated in calculating database size.

28. Variable length fields need to be estimated at their MINIMUM/AVERAGE/MAXIMUM space required.

29. Database size at full growth is the _____ goal for the estimation target.

30. If comparisons to existing databases cannot be made to calculate downtime, another approach is to _____ data.

31. The results of an estimation or a prototype should be shielded from the user, especially if the results show the user's downtime needs will not be met. (T/F)

32. After the length of recovery time is estimated, the _____ of downtime must likewise be estimated.

33. A shop's past _____ is the best indication of the probability of an outage.

34. The first analytical step taken to reduce the amount of data to be recovered is to question whether all the data that will be stored online is _____.

35. Online storage of data is _____.

36. Online storage of data that never will be used is especially _____.

37. Offline storage of data MEANS/DOES NOT MEAN that data cannot be accessed.

38. Offline access and storage of data is less _____ than online storage and access of data.

39. Offline access of data is SLOWER/FASTER than online access of data.

Chapter 15 High Availability 235

40. _____ data is usually stored online; _____ data is stored in a medium convenient to the end user.

41. When primitive data is mixed with derived data, the result is the storage of _____ amounts of data.

42. Operational data should be separated from _____ data.

43. When operational and administrative data are separated, there IS/IS NOT a net loss of data.

44. The segregation of administrative and operational data has the effect of breaking data into small, finely separated groups of data. (T/F)

45. Separating unlike _____ has the same effect as segregating administrative and operational data.

46. The final option to reduce database size is to separate data at the _____ level.

47. Key splits MUST BE/MAY BE/OUGHT TO BE designed into the application at the inception of design.

48. Key splits allow applications to be run on separate _____.

49. If a key split can be done once, generally it can be done _____ times.

50. In DB2, key splits can be done by _____ or _____.

51. When partitioning is done (by the system), processing CAN/CANNOT be split over more than one processor.

52. When partitioning of data is done, a reorganization for the purpose of restructuring data can be done for individual partitions. (T/F)

53. When partitioning of data is done, a reorganization for the purpose of reordering a partition of data can be done _____ of other partitions.

54. When partitioning is done, the system knows when all partitions need to be recovered. (T/F)

55. When data is split at the application level, processing MAY/MAY NOT be split over more than one processor.

56. When data is split at the application level, the system WILL/WILL NOT know about the relationship among different databases that are logically related.

CHAPTER 16

Extract Processing in DB2

Extract processing is an integral part of the DB2 environment. Extract processing is necessary to unlock the flexibility that can be achieved in DB2. There is nothing terribly difficult about extract processing from the standpoint of the programmer. The logic required for most extract processing is simple.

But extract processing soon becomes an issue in the face of the volume of data that must pass through the extract programs. In short order, the amount of time required for extract processing begins to exceed the amount of time that is available. And the total amount of data that is being extracted soon overflows the DASD that is available. If not carefully thought out and carefully constructed, extract processing soon becomes a large issue in the running of a DB2 environment.

Extract processing in DB2 may be done in a variety of manners, such as—

- using the DXT utility,
- using application program logic, or
- using other utilities such as the DB2 ToolKit by Innovative Designs.

EXTRACT LOGIC

The logic required for extract processing is simple. The extract program is fed some parameters. The parameters shape the logic that will be used to determine what data will be selected. Usually, the selection of data is from a production or operational database or databases.

Next, the extract program accesses the original production database(s) that serves as the source of data. The scan through the original database may be sequential from one row to the next, or may be by an index where the program logic is used to select values based on the contents of the index.

After data is selected by the extract program, it is transported to the output file. The output file may be in the same order as the original data, or the output file may be summarized, merged, or otherwise altered.

After the extract program has executed and the extracted output file is created, the analyst uses the extracted data as a basis for reports or decision support analysis, for the creation of trend analysis files, or for other purposes.

The immediate challenge posed by extract processing is that it can consume a large amount of machine resources, principally in the usage of I/O. In addition, much DASD may be used for extracted files.

DESIGNING THE EXTRACT PROCESS

The first step in managing the extract process is not to do extracts in a random, disorganized manner. The extract of data from one environment to another represents a fundamental transformation of data with many implications in the usage, credibility, and efficiency of processing of the data. For an in-depth discussion of these issues refer to *Information Engineering for the Practitioner: From Theory into Practice*, Yourdon Press, 1988, chapter 13. The designer is well advised to carefully consider all the implications of extracts. In short, extract processing should not be an after-the-fact consideration in the design of the production and decision support DB2 environment.

USING THE EXTRACTED DATA

In some cases, the ultimate use and disposition of the extracted data is well known. When the requirements are well established, the designer can design the content and occurrences of the extracted environment with precision. No wasted data should be the goal in this case, as each occurrence of extracted data requires storage and handling.

But, in other instances, the usage and disposition of the extracted data is not known. In these cases, the designer can only guess as to what data will be required. Even where there are unknown requirements for extracted data, it is worth the designer's while to try to anticipate requirements.

In the case of unknown requirements, if there is a lot of data to be managed, the designer will want to sort data into two categories: data that probably will be needed and data that probably will not be needed. The data that will be needed will be extracted and managed in the normal manner. But the data that probably will not be needed should be stored on a bulk archival medium. If the designer has guessed incorrectly, at a later point in time, at least the data that has not been extracted will still be available. The problem is that restoring data from a bulk archival medium is awkward, slow, and expensive.

Of course the designer can adopt the stance that ALL data needs to be extracted, regardless of the probability of access. Then the designer must pay the costs for unneeded storage and unneeded extract processing of data.

The designer should carefully consider the trade-off between storing too little data and having to restore data from an awkward medium, and storing too much data and constantly paying the overhead for data that is never used.

GRANULARITY OF DATA

One of the most important issues the designer faces is the *granularity* of data as data is extracted. Data in the original (i.e., the unextracted state) is as granular as the data is ever going to be. The designer may want to preserve the same level of granularity as the data in its unextracted state, or the designer may want to summarize or otherwise consolidate the data. By consolidating the data upon extract, less I/O will be used for the loading of the extracted file and less DASD will be needed.

As an example of the considerations of the granularity of extracted data, consider a designer in a manufacturing environment who wants to extract data from the daily usage record for a parts file. Each withdrawal or replenishment of a part is recorded throughout the day in a production database. One option for extract processing is simply to select each entry of data—each withdrawal and each replenishment—for the extract file. The extracted file can then be used to answer a host of questions:

- What was the largest withdrawal during the day?
- What part had the most activities against it?
- At what time did the most withdrawals occur? (and so forth)

While these questions may be of interest, they require that data be stored in the extract file at the lowest level of granularity. Each withdrawal and each replenishment must be captured and transported to the extract file. The number of records to be loaded and the amount of DASD required may be significant.

The designer could reduce the level of granularity in the extract file by storing cumulative withdrawal and replenishment activity by part. All daily withdrawals would be added with all daily replenishments for each part. Then the net activity for the day would be stored in the extract file. There would be no savings in the access of the original data, but much I/O would be saved in the writing out of the extract file. In addition, the output file would require much less DASD.

Of course, the analyst could not look at detailed transactions in the extract file. But the analyst still could do much decision support analysis, such as looking at trends of parts usage, for example.

THE RIGHT LEVEL OF DETAIL

There is no right or wrong answer as to what level of detail is appropriate for the extracted file. In general, the designer should choose the highest level of detail (i.e., the most summarized level) that suffices for the queries that will be made against the data. The trade-off is between the type of query that can be made and the cost of extracting and storing detailed data.

The granularity of extracted data and the processing that will be done against the extracted data, then, are the very first two issues that must be addressed by the designer.

LESS EXTRACTED DETAIL

Not only is the granularity of data an issue in the extraction of data, but the level of detail that is extracted is an issue as well. While there may be cases where entire original records are shipped to an extracted environment, the designer should always assume that not all data elements are candidates for extraction.

For example, suppose a bank has a production database where account activities are kept. A typical record in the production database contains the following data elements:

- Account identification
- Date, time of activity
- Amount of activity
- Location of activity
- Personal identification
- Teller window balance at time of activity
- Electronic identification
- Check number
- "Posting" requested?
- Payroll activity?

All of these data elements are required for operational processing and rightfully reside in the production database. But it is unlikely that most of these data elements belong in the extracted file. It is hard to imagine any sort of analytic processing of the extracted file that would require (or even find useful!) data elements such as check number or personal identification. The list of data elements in the original database may be divided into two categories—those data elements needed for extracted processing and those not needed:

- Account identification   [needed]
- Date, time of activity   [needed]
- Amount of activity   [needed]
- Location of activity   [needed]
- Personal identification   [not needed]
- Teller window balance at time of activity   [not needed]
- Electronic identification   [not needed]
- Check number   [not needed]
- "Posting" requested?   [not needed]
- Payroll activity?   [not needed]

The amount of data shipped to the extract file, then, is only a subset of the original data insofar as the type of data elements that are shipped is concerned. Of course, this weeding out of data does not make the scanning of the original data any more efficient. But weeding out data does make the loading of data (and its subsequent access!) more efficient in that less data needs to be loaded. Loading less data implies that the data can be loaded more compactly. The tighter the data that can be loaded, the fewer resources required in the loading and access of the data, and the more quickly the load can be accomplished.

The granularity of the occurrences of data and the details that are shipped to the extract file, then, are two issues the designer must come to grips with.

THE HARDWARE ENVIRONMENT

Another consideration the designer has is the hardware environment where the extract processing will be done. There are two possibilities:

- Both the original and the extracted data will reside on the same processor.
- The original database will reside on one processor and the extracted database will reside on another processor.

As long as there is only a modest amount of data and as long as there is only a small amount of processing being done, there is no reason why both the original database and the extracted database cannot reside on the same machine. But in the face of much data and/or much processing, it makes sense to split the data across separate machines.

In general, the original data will come from the operational, production environment. The extracted data will form the foundation for decision support processing. The generic patterns of processing are very different. Production processing usually entails a fairly static usage of machine resources. Decision support processing entails a dynamic, unpredictable usage of machine resources. Separating the two patterns of machine utilization in the face of volumes of processing makes sense.

When the original database resides on a separate machine from the extracted data, there can be a beneficial separation of processing. The extract process is broken into two distinct operations: a selection and extract process (from the original file) and a load process (into the extracted file). The actual selection and extract processing takes place on the production machine. The data is then transferred to the machine where the extracted data will reside, and the load process is done there. In such a manner, the CPU cycles from two machines share the workload. In addition, if there is a need for summarization or other refinement of data, the machine on which the extracted data resides can be used.

Separating extracted and original data over multiple machines has another beneficial effect. When the extract process is separated over two machines there is a clarity of processing that otherwise may become blurred if all extract processing is done on a single machine. When extract processing is done on a single machine, the code that supports the extract process may become entangled with regular application code. Once code that supports the extract process becomes enmeshed with regular code, it is difficult to address the problems of extract processing independent of the application.

For example, consider a database has been designed for an oil company to keep track of shipments of oil. The database keeps track of oil shipments on a daily basis as the shipments arrive. Billing, refinery, and allocation is done based on the values in the database. In addition, an archiving of shipments is stored in the same database. After today's shipment is processed, the record of activity is kept in the same database. The current record is simply written into an archival portion of the database. The archival of shipment records is used for decision support analysis, looking at historical trends, and so forth.

Over time, the shipment database grows, and the volume of processing overwhelms the machine. Attempting to remove the shipment archival processing from the application is a very disruptive thing to do.

Had the application been designed so that current value shipment data would not be archived off into the same database, then managing the problems of volume at a later moment in time would have been much simpler. In the original design of the application, if there had been a separate extract program that periodically examined shipment records for inclusion in a separate archival file, then the problems of volumes of data and consumption of I/O could have been dealt with separately. But trying to separate extract processing at a later point in time is awkward.

THE PIGGYBACK APPROACH

In truth, extract processing usually grows in an undisciplined fashion. But for those organizations that are facing a large amount of extract processing, a disciplined approach is in order.

Consider an undisciplined extract environment. On day 1, an extract program is designed to look at a personnel file selecting all male employees. On day 2, another extract program is written to look at employees who make more than $50,000 annually. On day 3, a third extract is written to look at employees who have advanced college degrees. While none of the extracts consumes too many resources by itself, collectively, the extracts consume a fair amount of resources.

The scan portion of the extract could be streamlined in that only one scan of the personnel database needs to be done, looking for data that fits one or more of the criteria that are being considered. The logic of the scan program determines if the record being examined is a male, makes more than $50,000 annually, or has an advanced college degree. The record is written to as many extract files as there are criteria that are satisfied. There is a wholesale waste of I/O in the scanning of the same personnel data base three times.

The discipline required for the "piggyback" approach mandates that not only current extract requirements must be consolidated, but all future requirements must be consolidated as well. In other words, whenever a new extract requirement has been identified, the first step the designer takes is to determine what extracts already exist that can be used. The only time the designer specifies a new extract be written is if the extract is against a database that has no extracts already going against it.

The savings in combining criteria to achieve a single scan of data shows up in the I/O needed for the first part of the extract process. Of course, multipurpose scans probably look at data on a record by record basis, rather than accessing data through the index.

There is a point at which scanning an entire database rather than looking at data through the index becomes more efficient. When there are many rows of data that satisfy the search criteria, it is faster to sequentially scan the table than it is to access data through an index. When there are only a few rows that satisfy the selection criteria, it is more efficient to search tables through the index. Each row is most likely in a different page than the last row that satisfied the search criteria. If there are many pages that satisfy the search criteria, then many pages will need to be brought into memory.

INCREMENTAL CHANGES

Some extract processing consists of a blind copy of all data into the extracted format. In this case, the extract appears to be a "snapshot" of data as of some moment in time. There may be a large savings in this type of extract processing if only occurrences of data that have had changes since the last extract are selected for the transportation across the barrier to the extracted file.

As an example, suppose that in an Army personnel database, every six months all officers have their active files extracted into an archived format. This extract (that occurs two times a year) selects all Army officers. The extract takes a long time because there are many officers.

Another approach to the extract is to select only officers who have undergone a change in status in the previous six months. In such a manner, significantly fewer officers could be selected for the extract. For example, if any of the following criteria were met, then the officer would be selected for the extract:

- If marital status changed
- If rank changed
- If an advanced degree were obtained
- If there were a change in dependents
- If the officer had received training in a new subject

The selection of only a subset of data based on incremental activity saves processing in both the scan and the load portions of the extract process. Unfortunately, such an approach probably will require logic in the loading of the extracted data that otherwise would not have been needed. However, the additional logic and complexity are usually worth the savings in processing.

INDEXES AND EXTRACTED DATA

The amount of time required to load extracted data can quickly grow to unreasonable levels if there is a lot of data to be loaded and if the data to be loaded requires that one or more indexes be loaded at the same time. The designer should be VERY CAREFUL of large extracted files with multiple indexes.

The designer should not take for granted that an index is needed for extracted data. Each index should be individually justified.

Certainly, clustering the extracted data can reduce the time and DASD required to load one index. But tables can be clustered only once. Clustering an extracted file, then, has only limited applicability.

Another approach to managing large extracts of data and their corresponding large indexes is to break the extracted data into multiple, separate tables. For example, suppose an insurance company annually extracts the history of claims that have been settled and/or received by the company. Each year, the company receives a large number of claims.

One approach to the extract process is simply to load the extracted data into a table and create indexes. But, quickly, the insurance company discovers that the load and index-building process takes an inordinate amount of time.

The designer decides to break the claims table up into 12 categories. There will be a claims table not for the entire year's worth of claims, but for each month in the year. In other words, depending on when the claim was made, there will be a January claims table, a February claims table, a March claims table, and so forth. The resulting tables take roughly 1/12th the time to load the tables and their associated indexes. Of course, the load process still takes as long in toto to execute. But the load process is broken up into units that are much more amenable to normal operations. And there is the possibility of being able to execute the load processes in parallel.

Even though there is no real savings in the division of a table and its associated indexes into small components, there are real gains in the operability and usability of such data.

It is fair to question what the splitting of a table does to program logic that is required to access the table. Consider the request against the single large table of insurance claims:

```
SELECT DATE, AMOUNT, FROMNAME
FROM CLAIMS
WHERE CLAIMANT = 'Jackson, Bob';
```

When the table is divided, the same request must be run multiple times, as in the following:

```
SELECT DATE, AMOUNT, FROMNAME
FROM CLAIMJAN
WHERE CLAIMANT = 'Jackson, Bob';
```

```
SELECT DATE, AMOUNT, FROMNAME
FROM CLAIMFEB
WHERE CLAIMANT = 'Jackson, Bob';

SELECT DATE, AMOUNT, FROMNAME
FROM CLAIMMAR
WHERE CLAIMANT = 'Jackson, Bob'

SELECT DATE AMOUNT FROMNAME
FROM CLAIMAPR
WHERE CLAIMANT = 'Jackson, Bob'
```

At first glance, the amount of work—both for development and maintenance—required of the programmer appears to have taken an enormous leap. But the requests that are done are repetitious and can easily be generated or otherwise controlled automatically. In addition, there may well be some very important performance gains in the accessing of the tables that have been built, because each request of the claims data does not have to access the entire table.

When dealing with large tables where there are known requirements to access subsets of the data, it may make sense to create *sparse indexes*. A sparse index in DB2 is a construct that is created and supported entirely at the application level. The sparse index most likely is created as the extracted data is loaded.

As an example of the usage of a sparse index in conjunction with extracted data, consider a home mortgage financial institution with a database that tracks payment activities. Once a month, the payment activities are extracted and put in an archival database.

Most payments are made on time, and there is little to say about them. But occasionally a payment is late, and a penalty is added. The decision support analyst has a need to track how many loans are late, whether the same loans are chronically late, and what the trend of late payments looks like over a five-year period.

One approach is to create an index for all loans that is loaded at the moment the extract data is loaded. Most loans have a penalty payment value of $0.00. But every loan has a late-payment record each month. In short, a lot of index space is wasted, and a lot of time loading the index has gone for naught.

The designer could have specified a separate table—a late payments table—to be loaded each month at the same time the extract data is loaded. The late payments table contains the identification of the loan that was late and the amount of the penalty. There would be (relatively speaking!) only a few loans in the late payments table, and an index could easily be created for the table. Processing could go against the table for analysis of late payments. And, on those occasions when there was a need, the individual late loans could be accessed using information from the late payments table.

The late payments table then serves as a separate adjunct to the regular monthly payments table.

The creation of a sparse index does not speed up the extract process. However, it does create the opportunity for efficient usage of extract data and possibly precludes the need for the loading of one or more indexes against a large table.

PERIODIC LOADING

Normally, extract processing is thought of as an activity that is run overnight or in a batch window. In normal circumstances, there is no opportunity to run extract processing during the online day.

But, on occasion, an extract process can be broken up into fine components and run in the middle of the online day. When those occasions arise, it may make sense to do extract processing during the middle of the online day. In a sense, the extract processing becomes a "background" type of processing. Note that this option must be considered carefully and does not fit the general case for extract processing.

When an extract can be broken into fine pieces and when there are slack moments of online processing during the production day, then there may be an opportunity to schedule some of the extract processing when there is spare time.

Some of the conditions that permit this type of processing are where—

- the extract program can "remember" where it last left off,
- no update activity will occur that will destroy the integrity of the extract,
- the extract program can be selectively scheduled,

- the extract program can be stopped and restarted gracefully, and
- a production workload with a great deal of variability in the amount of processing power is used.

The ability to run extract processing during the online day does not shorten or lengthen the total amount of resources spent for extract processing. Instead, the capability spreads the demand for resources over a wider time frame.

COMPACTING DATA

A very useful design technique for the minimization of resources in the load portion of the extract process is the physical compaction of data. When data can be compacted, less data is used (saving DASD) and less processor capacity is required to retrieve data.

One of the best techniques for the compacting of data is the creation of arrays of data inside a row. This form of denormalization cannot be used as a general solution.

As an example of the proper usage of the creation of an array within a row, consider a payroll history file. In this example, employees are paid twice a month. Periodically, the past few months of payroll activity are extracted and put onto a payroll history file. The data elements that are extracted include the following:

- employee number	char(19)
- social security number	char(9)
- paydate—yrmoda	char(6)
- gross amount	dec fixed(11,2)
- net amount	dec fixed(11,2)
- FICA	dec fixed(9,2)
- state tax	dec fixed(9,2)
- federal tax	dec fixed(9,2)
- insurance	dec fixed(9,2)
- other deductions	dec fixed(9,2)

. . . .

71 bytes

Each pay period is defined to be another occurrence in the extracted history table for payroll. The data is defined to be in an array so that repeating groups are combined under a single employee, as shown:

- employee number   char(19)
- social security number   char(9)
- paydate—yr   char(2)
- gross amount(1)   dec fixed(11,2)
- net amount(1)   dec fixed(11,2)
- FICA(1)   dec fixed(9,2)
- state tax(1)   dec fixed(9,2)
- federal tax(1)   dec fixed(9,2)
- insurance(1)   dec fixed(9,2)
- other deductions(1)   dec fixed(9,2)
- gross amount(2)   dec fixed(11,2)
- net amount(2)   dec fixed(11,2)
- FICA(2)   dec fixed(9,2)
- state tax(2)   dec fixed(9,2)
- federal tax(2)   dec fixed(9,2)
- insurance(2)   dec fixed(9,2)
- other deductions(2)   dec fixed(9,2)
- gross amount(3)   dec fixed(11,2)
- net amount(3)   dec fixed(11,2)
- FICA(3)   dec fixed(9,2)
- state tax(3)   dec fixed(9,2)
- federal tax(3)   dec fixed(9,2)
- insurance(3)   dec fixed(9,2)
- other deductions(3)   dec fixed(9,2)
- gross amount(4)   dec fixed(11,2)
- net amount(4)   dec fixed(11,2)
- FICA(4)   dec fixed(9,2)
- state tax(4)   dec fixed(9,2)
- federal tax(4)   dec fixed(9,2)
- insurance(4)   dec fixed(9,2)
- other deductions(4)   dec fixed(9,2)

. . . .

- gross amount(24)   dec fixed(11,2)
- net amount(24)   dec fixed(11,2)
- FICA(24)   dec fixed(9,2)

- state tax(24)   dec fixed(9,2)
- federal tax(24)   dec fixed(9,2)
- insurance(24)   dec fixed(9,2)
- other deductions(24)   dec fixed(9,2)

. . . .

938 bytes

By storing the payroll history data together in an array where the twice-monthly pay information can be stored for an employee, there is a savings both in space and in processing. Space is saved in that there is less total data in the table and that there is 1/24th the amount of space needed for the index. Processing is saved in that one I/O is all that is needed to gather the annual payroll history for an employee. In the case where each payroll entry is its own row, as much as 24 times the I/O is required.

The practice of blocking data at the application level when applicable saves considerable processing not only for extract loads but for extract scans as well. If a designer is faced with an extract scan that promises to consume huge amounts of resources, the designer is advised to look into the blocking of data in the production database.

OTHER OPTIONS

A simple (and surprisingly often overlooked) option for minimizing the resources required for extract processing is the possibility of doing extracts on a less frequent basis. This practice does not shorten the length of time required for the extract, but lessens the total amount of resources that must be dedicated to this kind of processing.

Another simple option that often is overlooked is the usage of log tapes as a basis for gathering transactions. The advantages of using log tapes is that the tape can be taken to another processor and processed independently of the online processor.

The disadvantages of using the log tape are—

- only transactions can be captured,
- many computer operations will not allow the log tape to be used for anything other than backup processing,
- the logic of what gets on a log tape may or may not coincide with the needs of the designer, and
- log tapes often contain much extraneous information.

A FINAL NOTE

Even though the following comment does not directly relate to the efficiency of the extract process, it is tangentially relevant. It is good practice to time stamp each extract. The time stamp can often be used to clarify exactly what data has and has not been extracted. By virtue of the fact that a well designed time-stamping scenario for each extract of data may save much unnecessary processing, time-stamping is a sound design practice.

QUESTIONS: EXTRACT PROCESSING IN DB2

1. Extract processing logic is SIMPLE/COMPLEX.
2. The primary problem posed by extract processing lies in
    a. the volume of data that must be processed
    b. the maintenance of code
    c. the machine resources used
    d. the flexibility of the extract process
    e. the volume of data and the machine resources used
3. Extract processing grows in a manner best described as
    a. orderly
    b. undisciplined
    c. sequenced
    d. random
    e. application-oriented
4. In addition to the amount of machine resources required, extract processing also consumes much _____.
5. Extract processing in DB2 can be done in three ways. List them.
6. Extract processing knows what data to select because of the _____ that are passed to it.
7. Extract processing usually selects data from _____ source(s)?
8. Extract processing may proceed sequentially through a database or may make use of an _____.
9. After data is selected by the extract program, it is transported to the _____.
10. The output file may be in the same order as the original data, or the output file may be _____ , _____ , or otherwise altered.

Chapter 16   Extract Processing in DB2   253

11. List three uses of the extract file.
12. The extract of data represents a major _____ of data.
13. In some cases, the ultimate use and disposition of extracted data is well known. (T/F)
14. When the requirements for extracted data are well known, there SHOULD/SHOULD NOT be any data extracted that will not be used.
15. When the requirements for extracted data are not well known, there SHOULD/SHOULD NOT be any data extracted that will not be used.
16. Anticipating requirements even where requirements are ambiguous IS/IS NOT a worthwhile practice.
17. Data that will not be needed should be stored on a _____ medium.
18. Restoring data from a bulk medium is _____.
19. Storing more data than is needed in the face of unknown requirements is _____.
20. Granularity of data refers to the level of _____ of the rows of data.
21. The most granular data in the system is always located at the file that is being _____.
22. Upon extraction, rows of data may be _____.
23. The _____ level of detail that satisfies the usage of the extracted data should be chosen.
24. The data elements chosen for extraction depend upon the ultimate _____ of the elements.
25. The weeding out of data elements DOES/DOES NOT save scan processing.
26. The weeding out of data elements DOES/DOES NOT save load processing.
27. The extracted data and the original data may reside on the same machine if there is _____ of data.
28. When there is a lot of data, it is a good design practice to _____ the data off onto two or more processors.
29. The extract process can be broken into two distinct sets of activities: a _____ process and a _____ process.
30. When the extract process is split over two processors, the _____ cycles are divided.

31. One way to minimize scan time is to _____ search criteria into a single program so that one pass of data is required.
32. All new extract requirements should first be analyzed to determine whether they can be "piggybacked" onto an existing extract. (T/F)
33. Piggyback scans of data that service multiple search criteria, of necessity, must _____ search each row.
34. All data can be extracted at once or only data that has _____ since the last extract may be extracted.
35. It is almost always MORE/LESS efficient to extract only data that has changed since the last extract.
36. It is almost always MORE/LESS complicated to extract only data that has changed since the last extract.
37. Indexing extracted data is AN IMPORTANT/A TRIVIAL issue.
38. Extracted data requires _____ in order to be processed efficiently.
39. Each index requires _____ and _____ at the time of loading.
40. The size of the tables being loaded may be broken into finer levels at the _____ or the _____ level.
41. Breaking data into partitions DOES/DOES NOT reduce the time required for an individual load program.
43. Breaking data into partitions simplifies the job of the programmer. (T/F)
44. A sparse index is created at the _____ level.
45. A sparse index can greatly REDUCE/INCREASE the size of the index into a large extracted table.
46. A sparse index INCREASES/DECREASES the total amount of DASD required.
47. Extract processing is always done overnight or during the batch window. (T/F)
48. Extract processing may be able to be done during the online day. (T/F)
49. When extract processing is done during the day, it is run as a _____ process.
50. When extract processing is done during the online day, it is done in a series of _____ bursts.

Chapter 16 — Extract Processing in DB2

51. Compacting data reduces loadtime in that less _____ is required to load data.

52. Creating arrays of data in a row is a common form of compaction. This design technique can be done only under stringent conditions. (T/F)

53. Creating arrays of data HAS NO EFFECT ON/REDUCES DRAMATICALLY the index space required.

54. Creating arrays of data IMPLIES/DOES NOT IMPLY that individual occurrences of data can be accessed directly.

55. When there are a variable number of occurrences of data per row, creating internal arrays of data SHOULD/SHOULD NOT be done.

56. The frequency of extract processing IS/IS NOT a variable at which the designer should look.

PART V

DB2 Technician's Part

Chapter 17   Detailed Design and Tuning

- Using an Index
- Indexing Variable-Length Columns
- Defining Variable-Length Fields
- Decimal Data Definition
- Index Space Considerations
- Updating Variable-Length Fields
- Nonstandard Indexes
- Edit Routines
- Row Size Greater Than 4KB
- Questions: Detailed Design and Tuning

Chapter 18   An Introduction to Data Locking in DB2

- The Components of Data Locking
- Lock Components
- Locking Management
- A Typical Locking Sequence
- The Options for Locking Data
- The States of the Options
- The Unit of Recovery
- Some Rules of Thumb
- Cursor Stability/Repeatable Read
- Deadlock
- Summary
- Questions: Data Locking

Chapter 19 Archival Processing

- Criteria for Success
- Archival Media
- Primitive Archival Data
- Subject Orientation
- The Living Sample Environment
- Some Design Considerations—Time-Stamping Data
- Efficient Access of Archival Data
- Integrity and Access of Archival Data
- Foreign Keys in the Archival Environment
- Summary

Chapter 20 Strategic Positioning of DB2—High-Performance Systems

- High-Performance Levels
- The Banking Environment
- Hardware Configuration
- System of Record
- Peak-Period Processing Rates
- The Banking Life Cycle
- Extensibility of the Environment
- Key Structures
- Denormalization of High Performance Data
- Summary

CHAPTER 17

Detailed Design and Tuning

The performance of DB2 is sensitive to the detailed operations of the computer, executing the instructions issued by DB2. The database designer must be aware of the underlying activities that occur as a result of processing DB2. The following are some of the finer points the designer should be aware of.

USING AN INDEX

DB2 elects when to use or not use an index. The choice is not controlled by the programmer. And whether an index is used or not makes a big difference to system performance in terms of I/O consumption. The following discussion outlines some of the instances when DB2 may not use an index. The prudent designer avoids the following instances:

- Comparing different columns within the same row, as illustrated by Figure 17-1

    In the example shown in Figure 17-1, even if the columns PARTNO and DESCR are indexed, a row-by-row search will be done.

- Comparing different character columns where the columns have different lengths, as illustrated in Figure 17-2

```
PART     DESCR          QTY    U/M
01258    Ball bearing   1900   box
21340-A  Housing mold     17   unit      SELECT PARTNO
00897-B  Rear End Assem  891   unit      FROM PARTABLE
98005-A  Idler Arm        67   unit      WHERE PARTNO = DESCR
  :        :              :     :
  :        :              :     :
```

FIGURE 17-1. Example of an instance where an index is not used: Comparing different columns within the same row.

In the example shown in Figure 17-2, two tables are being compared. But the field over which they are being compared is character and has a different length. Consequently, an index comparison will not be made even if the index exists.

- For indexes over multiple columns, the highest order column must be qualified by "=" as shown in Figure 17-3

Figure 17-3 shows a table that will be searched row by row.

- The precision and scale of a decimal field affects whether or not an index will be used. Figure 17-4 illustrates the possibilities.

```
PARTINV TABLE         PARTBOM
PARTNO   QTY          PARTRAW  EXPEDITE    DESCR

01258-QX  90          99020    J Jones     Ball bearing
08797-A  179          99801-Y  S Smith     Camshaft
990-AQ14  16          00198-S  J Wilson    Differential
00178-UT   3          9980-G   J Jones     Throwbolt
  :        :            :        :           :
  :        :            :        :           :

8 bytes               7 bytes

         SELECT PARTNO QTY EXPEDITE DESCR
         FROM PARTINV, PARTBOM
         WHERE PARTNO = PARTRAW
```

FIGURE 17-2. Example of an instance where an index is not used: Comparing two tables over a character field that has a different length.

Chapter 17   Detailed Design and Tuning   261

```
YR* Mon* DAY* ACCOUNT   LOCATION    AMOUNT   TYPE   ID   TELLER
86   12   28   001567   San Mateo   189.87   Nor    JG   ------
86   12   26   001567   Burlngame    90.25   Nor    KY   0067
86   11   17   001789   Oakland    1000.00   --     LP   0081
86   11   13   000019   Palo Alto    75.00   Nor    PE   ------
86   09   27   100989   Fremont     750.00   --     GF   0081
 :    :    :      :         :          :       :     :      :
 :    :    :      :         :          :       :     :      :

              SELECT YR MON DAY ACCOUNT ID AMOUNT
              FROM BANK.ACTIVITY
              WHERE MONTH > 01 AND DAY = 20
```

*- index on these columns in the order shown

FIGURE 17–3. Example of an instance where an index is not used: A table of multiple columns.

```
PARTNO      DESCR         QOM      EOQ       MOQ
001258-QX   Ball bearing   789   125.98    130.00
887001-I    Housing mold    19    23.75     26.79
001670-YR   Drive train   1009  1897.08   1908.96
00002       Camshaft         9     6.90      6.78
   :           :             :       :         :
   :           :             :       :         :

char        char         decimal  decimal  decimal
 15          15           (6,0)    (6,2)    (7,2)


SELECT PARTNO DESCR QOM
FROM PARTINV                      (will not use index)
WHERE EOQ<= 15

SELECT PARTNO DESCR QOM
FROM PARTINV                      (may use index)
ORDER BY QOM

SELECT PARTNO DESCR QOM
FROM PARTINV                      (will not use index)
WHERE QOM = 15

SELECT PARTNO DESCR QOM
FROM PARTINV                      (may use index)
WHERE MOQ <= 25
```

FIGURE 17–4. Examples of instances where an index may or may not be used: Decimal fields of differing precision and scale.

When odd precision is specified as in MOQ, an index may be used. When even precision is specified, an index will not be used except where precision is zero and ORDERED BY is specified. In the latter case, the index may be used.

- If a literal or variable is being compared to a column and the literal or variable is greater than the column in length, then an index will not be used, as specified in Figure 17-5.

In Figure 17-5, the variable being compared to a column is greater than 10 bytes and the column length is 10 bytes. As a result, an index will not be used in the comparison.

- If numeric fields are being compared and the precision of the literal or host variable is greater than that of the column key being compared, then an index will not be used, as shown in Figure 17-6.

Figure 17-6 shows a literal of 10.5 being compared to a column of decimal (7,0). An index will not be used in this case.

- If comparison is done on an expression, an index (or indexes) will not be used, as shown in Figure 17-7.
- If the potential for update exists, the query will not use an index. Figure 17-8 shows the packaging of functions together (including some updating functions) such that all functions packaged together will be unable to use an index.

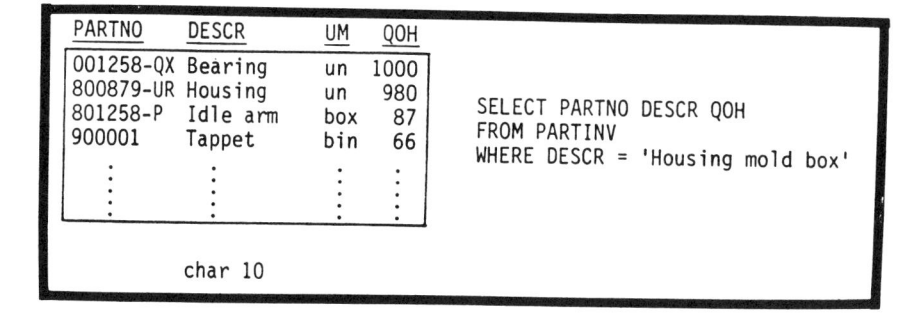

PARTNO	DESCR	UM	QOH
001258-QX	Bearing	un	1000
800879-UR	Housing	un	980
801258-P	Idle arm	box	87
900001	Tappet	bin	66

char 10

```
SELECT PARTNO DESCR QOH
FROM PARTINV
WHERE DESCR = 'Housing mold box'
```

FIGURE 17-5. Example of an instance where an index is not used: Comparing a literal or variable to a column when the literal or variable is greater than the column.

Chapter 17 Detailed Design and Tuning 263

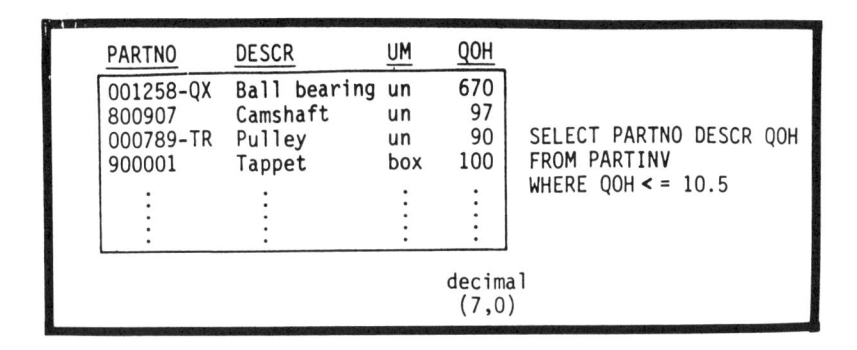

```
PARTNO      DESCR        UM    QOH
001258-QX   Ball bearing un    670
800907      Camshaft     un     97      SELECT PARTNO DESCR QOH
000789-TR   Pulley       un     90      FROM PARTINV
900001      Tappet       box   100      WHERE QOH <= 10.5
   :           :          :     :
   :           :          :     :
                                decimal
                                (7,0)
```

FIGURE 17-6. Example of an instance where an index is not used: Comparing numeric fields when the precision of the literal or host variable is greater than that of the column key being compared.

When the functions shown in Figure 17-8 are broken into smaller packages, the effect of not being able to use an index is spread over a smaller amount of data.

The reader is alerted to the fact that not all the instances of index usage have been covered in this section. Furthermore, unlike basic concepts that are not release-dependent, the treatment of indexes by DB2 is highly release-dependent. The reader is referred to the section on index utilization in the IBM Manual *Application Design and Tuning Guide*, GG24-3004.

```
PARTNO     QOH   DESCR        UM    QINSTORE   QDEL   QISSUED
001258-QX  13    ball bearing un         500     67       130
800906     120   carburetor   un          70      0         0
800070-TW   7    rocker arm   box          3      1         0
900001      0    manifold     kit         28      3         0
009075-PY  16    piston ring  kit        108      0        15
   :        :       :          :           :      :         :

           SELECT PARTNO DESCR
           FROM PARTINV                                   (index not used)
           WHERE QOH = QINSTORE + QDEL - QISSUED
```

FIGURE 17-7. Example of an instance where an index is not used: Comparing an expression.

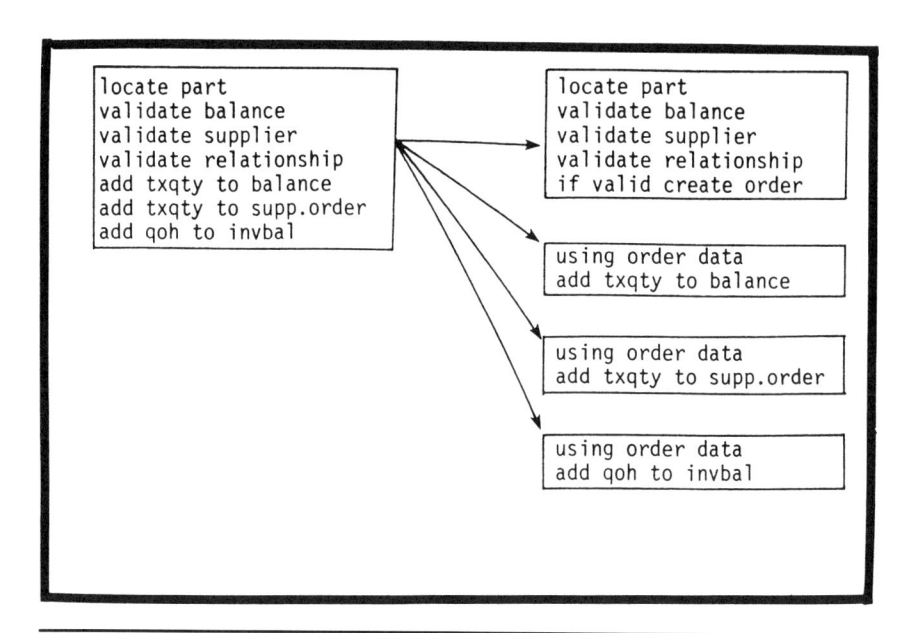

```
┌─────────────────────────────────────────────────────────────┐
│  ┌──────────────────────────┐   ┌──────────────────────────┐│
│  │ locate part              │   │ locate part              ││
│  │ validate balance         │   │ validate balance         ││
│  │ validate supplier        │──▶│ validate supplier        ││
│  │ validate relationship    │   │ validate relationship    ││
│  │ add txqty to balance     │   │ if valid create order    ││
│  │ add txqty to supp.order  │   └──────────────────────────┘│
│  │ add qoh to invbal        │                               │
│  └──────────────────────────┘   ┌──────────────────────────┐│
│                                 │ using order data         ││
│                             ───▶│ add txqty to balance     ││
│                                 └──────────────────────────┘│
│                                 ┌──────────────────────────┐│
│                             ───▶│ using order data         ││
│                                 │ add txqty to supp.order  ││
│                                 └──────────────────────────┘│
│                                 ┌──────────────────────────┐│
│                             ───▶│ using order data         ││
│                                 │ add qoh to invbal        ││
│                                 └──────────────────────────┘│
└─────────────────────────────────────────────────────────────┘
```

FIGURE 17-8. Packaging functions into smaller packages causes the system to function much more efficiently, including allowing indexes to be used where they otherwise would not have been used.

INDEXING VARIABLE-LENGTH COLUMNS

When an index is created for variable-length columns, the index is "filled out," (i.e., padded) so that all index entries are of the maximum length, as shown in Figure 17-9.

Figure 17-9 shows the index entries as they exist in the index and as they exist in the database.

Because of the padding effect, if the maximum length is long, an index on variable-length columns is questionable. A viable option is to break the variable-length column into two or more columns and to index only one of the columns, which has the effect of creating a smaller index.

DEFINING VARIABLE-LENGTH FIELDS

All variable-length fields should be defined at the end of the row after fixed-length fields, as shown in Figure 17-10.

When variable-length fields are defined at the end of a row, less

Chapter 17   Detailed Design and Tuning   265

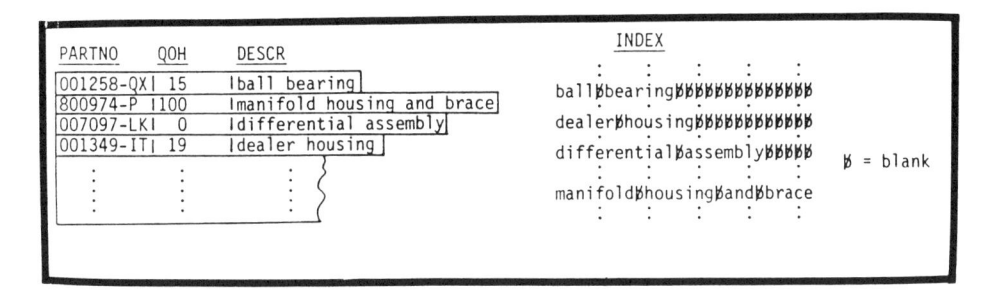

```
PARTNO        QOH   DESCR                               INDEX
001258-QX|    15    |ball bearing|
800974-P     |100   |manifold housing and brace|        ball♭bearing♭♭♭♭♭♭♭♭♭♭♭
007097-LK|    0    |differential assembly|              dealer♭housing♭♭♭♭♭♭♭♭♭♭
001349-IT|   19    |dealer housing|                     differential♭assembly♭♭♭♭♭    ♭ = blank

                                                        manifold♭housing♭and♭♭brace
```

FIGURE 17–9. Index entries as they exist in the index and in the database.

system resources are required in accessing fixed-length fields than if the variable-length fields were defined at the first of the row.

DECIMAL DATA DEFINITION

Decimal data should be defined in odd precision only, because storage requirements will be the same even if the precision is defined with even precision, and because of index utilization of odd-precision decimal data. Figure 17-11 illustrates the storage required for odd and even decimal utilization.

INDEX SPACE CONSIDERATIONS

The amount of space required for an index must be factored into the total system requirements in several ways. For example, consider the two tables shown in Figure 17-12.

One index—on accounts—requires only a nominal amount of

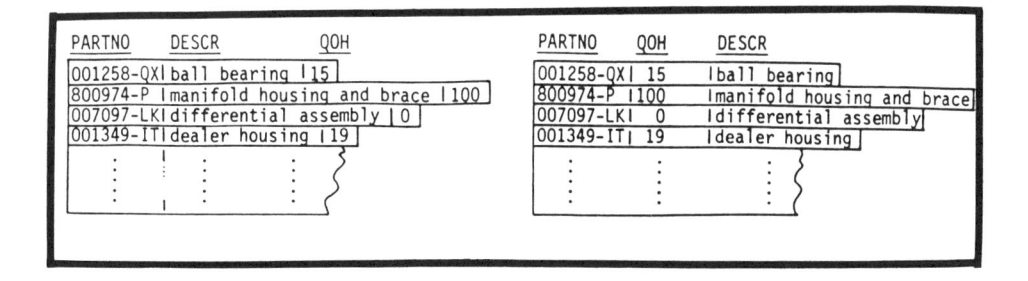

```
PARTNO    DESCR              QOH              PARTNO        QOH   DESCR
001258-QX|ball bearing       |15|             001258-QX|    15    |ball bearing|
800974-P |manifold housing and brace |100|    800974-P     |100   |manifold housing and brace|
007097-LK|differential assembly |0|           007097-LK|    0     |differential assembly|
001349-IT|dealer housing |19|                 001349-IT|   19     |dealer housing|
```

FIGURE 17–10. Variable-length fields defined at the end of the row after fixed-length fields.

```
storage of the number 146583

    decimal (6,0)              decimal (7,0)
   ┌───┬───┬───┐              ┌───┬───┬───┐
   │ ± │ 1 │ 6 │ 8 │          │ ± │ 1 │ 6 │ 8 │
   ├───┼───┼───┤              ├───┼───┼───┤
   │ 0 │ 4 │ 5 │ 3 │          │ 0 │ 4 │ 5 │ 3 │
   └───┴───┴───┘              └───┴───┴───┘

data stored on the left has a specification
of decimal (6,0) and data stored on the right
has a specification of decimal (7,0), but
both specifications require the same amount
of space, as shown in the figure
```

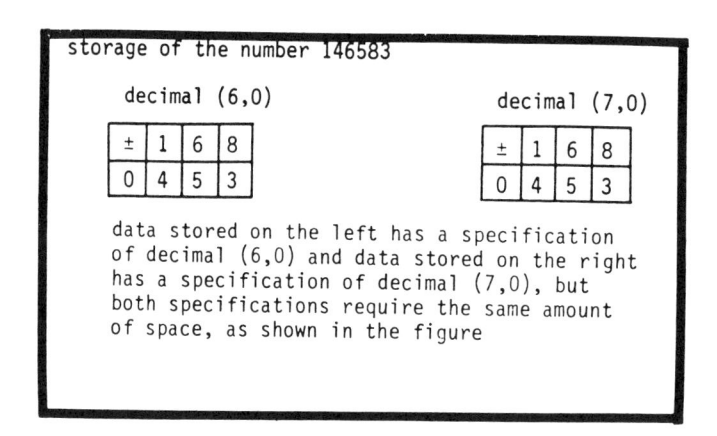

FIGURE 17–11. Data stored on the left has a specification of decimal (6, 0) and data stored on the right has a specification of decimal (7, 0), but both specifications require the same amount of space, as shown.

```
ACCOUNT NUMBER INDEX              PRESIDENTIAL INDEX

ACCOUNT                           NAME
0000101  page12  entry02          ADAMSbJOHNbbbbbbbb    page02  entry02
0000103  page45  entry16          ADAMSbJOHNbQUINCYbb   page19  entry19
0000104  page08  entry20          ARTHURbCHESTERbALAN  page97  entry02
0000109  page29  entry23          CARTERbJAMESbEARLbb   page29  entry13
                                  BUCHANANbJAMESbbbbb   page43  entry04
   ⋮       ⋮       ⋮                 ⋮       ⋮       ⋮       ⋮       ⋮
```

FIGURE 17–12. When an index is built, the amount of data required for the field on which the index is built must be factored into the space requirements. If the field is a large field, then much space will be required just for the index alone.

space. The other index—on name—requires much space because of the length of the field.

UPDATING VARIABLE-LENGTH FIELDS

When variable-length fields are updated and the variable field takes up more space than it did prior to update, then the row may be placed in another page if not enough space exists to fully replace the row in the original page, as shown in Figure 17-13.

In Figure 17-13, the index for part 1250 is page 45, entry 13. But the inventory control clerk decides to add more information to the description field, changing the description to "pipe fitting tee joint." Unfortunately, there is not enough space in row 45 to allow the row to be replaced, so available space is sought elsewhere, and is located in page 59. The row is placed in page 59, and a pointer from page 45 to page 59 is created. But the index entry points to page 45. Now two I/Os (three counting index access) are required to access part 1250.

```
                           Data Before Update
INDEX                 PARTNO   QOH   UM   DESCRIPTION
 :       :       :     :       :     :     :
part1250 page45 entry13 1247    4501  kit  ball joint
 :       :       :     1250     100  bin  pipe fitting    page45
                       1253      69  box  tail assembly   entry13
                        :        :    :    :

                           Data After Update
INDEX                 PARTNO   QOH   UM   DESCRIPTION
 :       :       :     :       :     :     :
part1250 page45 entry13 1247    4501  kit  ball joint
 :       :       :     page59 entry26                    page45
                       1253      69  box  tail assembly  entry13
                        :        :    :    :

                      PARTNO   QOH   UM   DESCRIPTION
                       :        :    :    :
                       1250    100  bin  pipe fitting tee joint   page59
                        :        :    :    :                      entry26
```

FIGURE 17–13. When variable-length fields are updated and the variable field takes up more space than it did prior to update, then the row may be placed in another page.

NONSTANDARD INDEXES

In the case where there are not many pages of data in a database (which is seldom the case in the production environment), the usage and existence of an index is questionable. It may be more efficient to simply access the small database in toto each time it is desired to access any data in the database than it is to create, maintain, and use indexes on the small database. Figure 17-14 illustrates the trade-offs associated with a small database and indexing.

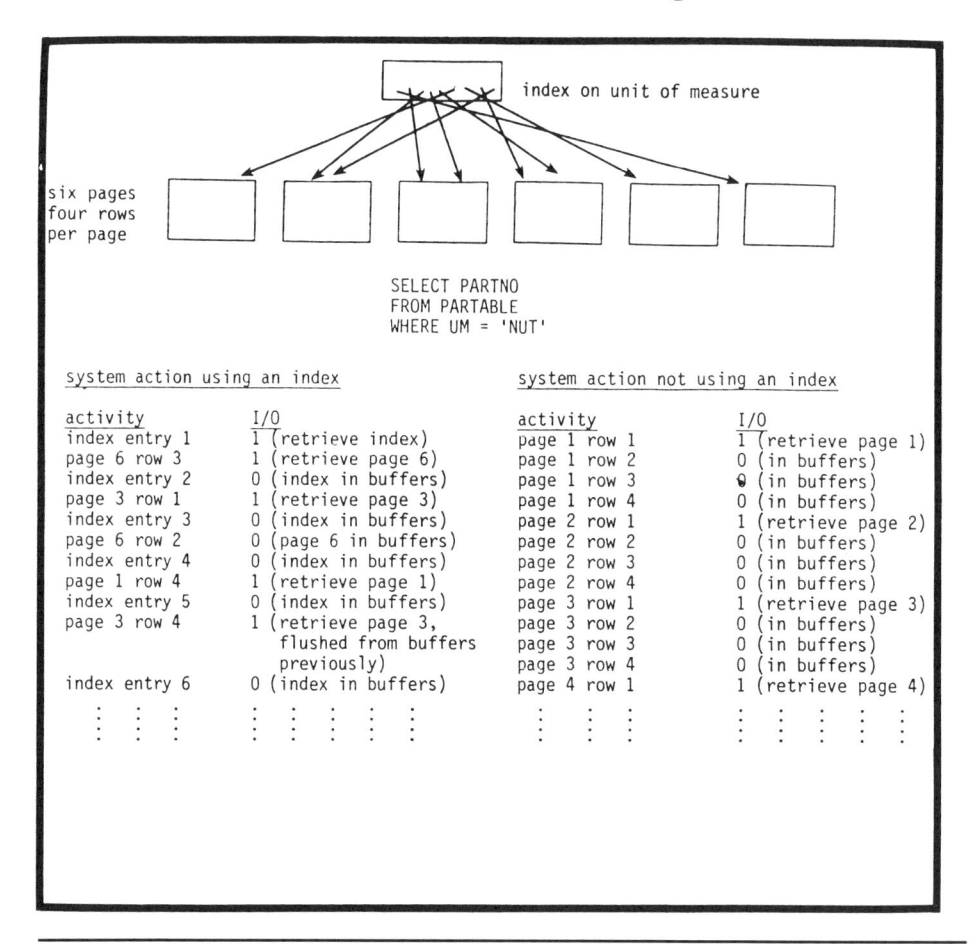

```
                          index on unit of measure

six pages
four rows
per page

                    SELECT PARTNO
                    FROM PARTABLE
                    WHERE UM = 'NUT'

system action using an index              system action not using an index

activity        I/O                       activity        I/O
index entry 1   1 (retrieve index)        page 1 row 1    1 (retrieve page 1)
page 6 row 3    1 (retrieve page 6)       page 1 row 2    0 (in buffers)
index entry 2   0 (index in buffers)      page 1 row 3    0 (in buffers)
page 3 row 1    1 (retrieve page 3)       page 1 row 4    0 (in buffers)
index entry 3   0 (index in buffers)      page 2 row 1    1 (retrieve page 2)
page 6 row 2    0 (page 6 in buffers)     page 2 row 2    0 (in buffers)
index entry 4   0 (index in buffers)      page 2 row 3    0 (in buffers)
page 1 row 4    1 (retrieve page 1)       page 2 row 4    0 (in buffers)
index entry 5   0 (index in buffers)      page 3 row 1    1 (retrieve page 3)
page 3 row 4    1 (retrieve page 3,       page 3 row 2    0 (in buffers)
                   flushed from buffers   page 3 row 3    0 (in buffers)
                   previously)            page 3 row 4    0 (in buffers)
index entry 6   0 (index in buffers)      page 4 row 1    1 (retrieve page 4)
   ⋮  ⋮  ⋮        ⋮  ⋮  ⋮  ⋮  ⋮             ⋮  ⋮  ⋮        ⋮  ⋮  ⋮  ⋮  ⋮
```

FIGURE 17–14. The activities of the processor as an indexed and a nonindexed database are being read. The activities are being requested by the database management system in response to the programs being executed. Adjacent to the activity are the physical I/O events stimulated by the execution of the activity.

Figure 17-14 shows a small database with six pages and four rows per page. An index is shown pointing into the database. The index is on "unit of measure," which is not a field the database is clustered on.

Two series of activities against the database are shown: one series of activities using an index and another series of activities not using an index. In the activities using the index, it is seen that I/Os are done to bring the index into the buffer area, and that each entry in the index requires another I/O unless, of course, the page being sought happens to already be in the buffer.

The probability of a page already being in the buffer area is the result of a combination of factors—the number of buffers that are available, the usage of those buffers, the amount of time a page has already been in the buffer area, the algorithms used to determine buffer management, and so on.

In general, under a normally (or fully!) loaded system, a high degree of random buffer hits cannot be anticipated. Consequently, the I/Os required to service a database query using an index is fairly high.

Now consider system activities not using an index. The mathematics are fairly straightforward. One I/O is required for every page of data. As long as there are not many pages of data, it may be more efficient to simply access every page.

But when there are many pages of data and when only a few occurrences of data satisfy the search criteria, then it is more efficient to use an index.

EDIT ROUTINES

An option the designer has is to use edit routines for such things as data compression, data encoding, data encryption, etc. While these routines can be useful and, in some cases, save much space (and generally don't cost I/O), the designer must keep in mind that every access of data, update of data, and so forth incurs the penalty of CPU overhead. Figure 17-15 illustrates the difference between using edit routines and not using them.

As long as there are a minimal number of edit routines in use, the overhead may not be a major consideration. But when edit routines are used frequently, the CPU overhead can mount.

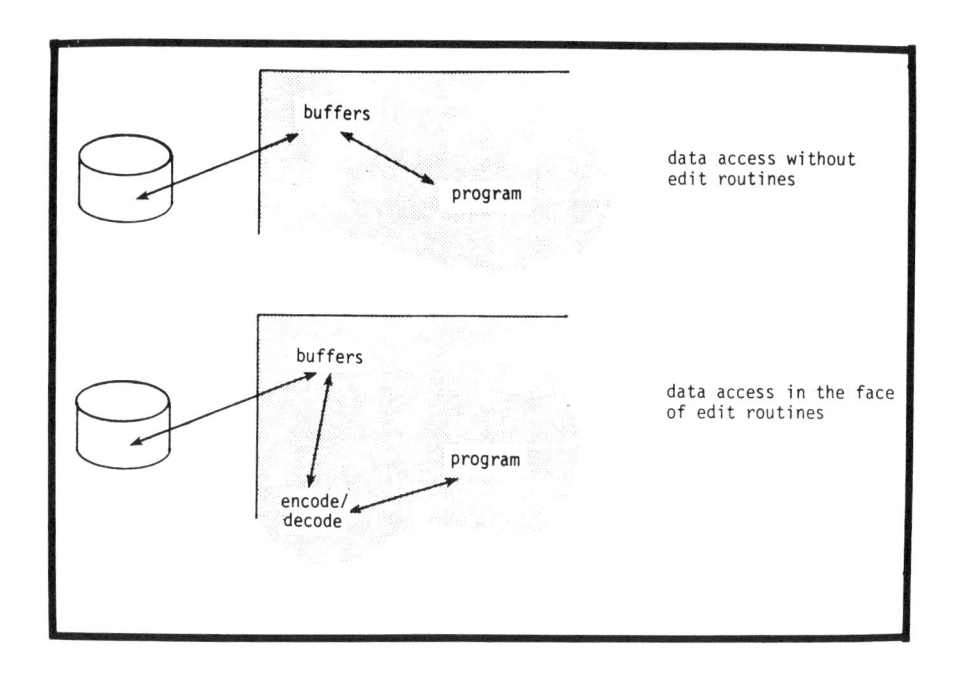

FIGURE 17-15. An illustration of accessing data using and not using edit routines.

ROW SIZE GREATER THAN 4Kb

The defined length of a row, if greater than 4Kb will cause the table to be processed in the 32Kb buffer area, damaging performance, as shown in Figure 17-16.

The defined length of a fixed-length row is simply the bytes used by the columns (collectively) plus overhead bytes. The defined length of a variable-length row (i.e., a row that contains one or more variable columns) is the maximum length of the variable columns plus the fixed-length columns' overhead.

In actuality, a variable-length row may never occupy all its defined space, but the DB2 space management algorithm manages the data as if every row used the maximum amount of data.

As new releases of DB2 occur, the database designer needs to keep abreast of the changes, as future changes and improvements at the detailed level will have a major impact on performance.

Chapter 17   Detailed Design and Tuning   271

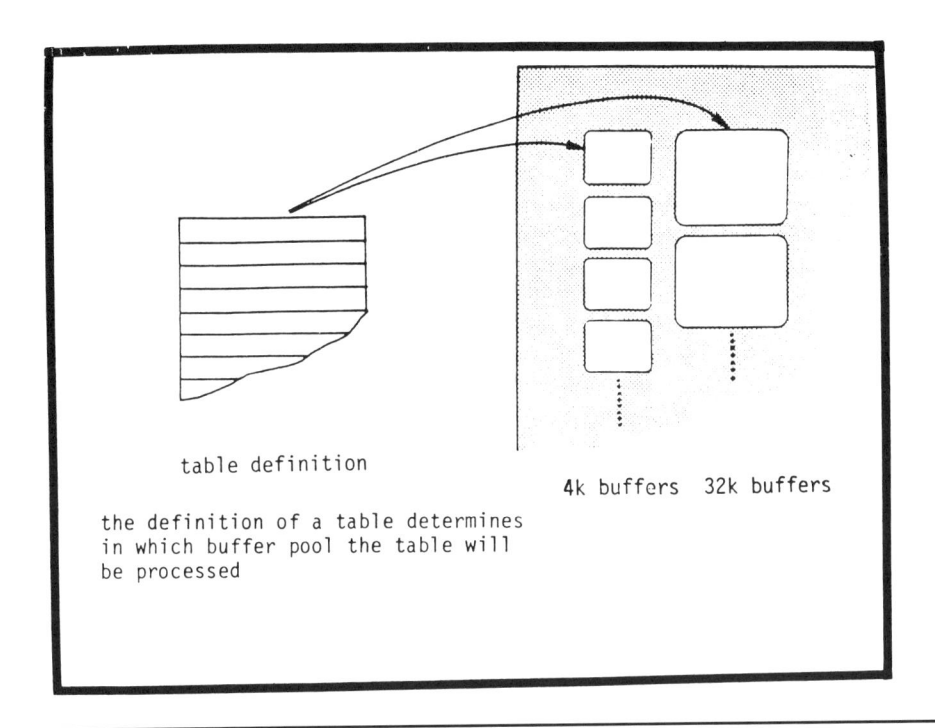

FIGURE 17-16. The definition of a table determines in which buffer pool the table will be processed.

QUESTIONS: DETAILED DESIGN AND TUNING

1. Index utilization (for large databases) can SAVE/COST much I/O.
2. The programmer CONTROLS/DOES NOT CONTROL when an index will be used in DB2.
3. Careful design and programming can enhance the chances of DB2 using an _____.
4. A table has columns A,B, and C. The programmer compares column A to column C. Will an index be used?
5. Table A has column A, Character (15). Table B has column B, character (10). Column A is compared to column B. Will an index be used?
6. If column A were character (10), would an index be used?
7. Table A has columns A, B, and C, and they are indexed in that

order. The qualification for the request is WHERE B = "BOX" and C = 1000. Will an index be used?

8. Table A has columns A, B, and C, and they are indexed in that order. The qualification is WHERE A = 1000, B = "BOX", AND C = 1500. Will an index be used?

9. A table has a field EOQ, decimal (6,2). A query is made WHERE EOQ < = 15. Will an index be used?

10. A table has a field QOM, decimal (6,0). A query is made and is ordered by QOM. Will an index be used?

11. A table has a field QOM, decimal (6,0). A query is made WHERE QOM = 15. Will an index be used?

12. A table has a field MOQ, decimal (7,2). A query is made WHERE MOQ< = 25. Will an index be used?

13. A table has a field DATE, character (6). A query is made WHERE DATE = JULY1986. Will an index be used?

14. A table has a field QUANTITY, decimal fixed (7,2). A query is made WHERE QUANTITY>156,390. Will an index be used?

15. A table has a field A, decimal fixed (5,2). A query is made WHERE A = B + C. Will an index be used?

16. Index utilization rules are very release-DEPENDENT/INDEPENDENT.

17. Table A contains a variable field—NAME—that can contain up to 10 characters. One entry is for JOE MOHR. What does the entry for Joe Mohr look like in the index?

18. When calculating index space for variable fields, it is assumed that every entry in the index is the (a). minimum, (b). maximum, (c). normal length?

19. All variable-length fields should be defined at the (a). middle, (b). beginning, (c). end of the row?

20. A fixed-length field is defined after a variable field in a row. To access the fixed-length field requires that the access of every row use CPU time to go through the variable-field to access the fixed-length field. (T/F)

21. Decimal data with odd precision of n uses the same space as decimal data with even precision of n-1. (T/F)

22. An index may be large simply because of the number of entries it has. Clustering the data will REDUCE/INCREASE the size of the index.

Chapter 17   Detailed Design and Tuning   273

23. For small databases, direct access (rather than access through an index) may be MORE/LESS efficient?
24. Name some uses of edit routines.
25. Do edit routines generally cost I/O?
26. What do edit routines cost?
27. If a single row contains more than 4Kb, then it is sure that the row will be processed in the _____ buffer.
28. If a row is variable-length and 95 percent of the rows are less than 4Kb, then it is sure that the rows will be processed in the _____ buffer.
29. In determining row size, the analyst must consider fixed-length fields, the maximum size of full-length fields, and _____ data.

CHAPTER 18

An Introduction to Data Locking in DB2

The internal protection of data integrity in DB2—the locking of data—is one of the most important aspects of DB2 because the locking mechanism determines who can access data, when data can be accessed, and significantly affects system throughput. *Data locking*, then, is an important subject that the database designer must be aware of in building production DB2 systems. Data locking is especially important for the developer who is building DB2 systems that will be used for high-performance, online transaction processing.

It is incumbent on the DB2 designer to understand the locking that is occurring for his or her design and to select the appropriate options for his or her application that will influence DB2 to choose the proper locking. This discussion will focus on the different states of data locking and the options the designer has to influence those states. The implications of each of the states will be discussed as well as the dynamics of the options.

The importance of understanding data locking and the relationship of data locking to performance is outlined by the following simple example: Suppose user A wishes to access and/or update table ABC. In this example, user A has caused DB2 to choose full table locking. User A sets his or her programs into execution. Because of the data locking that DB2 has elected, the data in table ABC is "frozen," awaiting usage by user A. As long as user A is executing and has control of the data, other users that need to use table ABC in their execution cannot get at the data.

For example, users B and C attempt to run their programs at the same time that user A has control of table ABC. As part of user B's and user C's execution, there is a need to access table ABC. Users B and C cannot run their programs as long as user A controls the data in table ABC. Only after user A finishes with table ABC will DB2 release the lock on the table and allow users B and C to run their programs. Even then, user B may grab table ABC and lock out user C. The speed with which user B and user C may proceed through the system is no faster than the speed of user A, since users B and C must wait for the execution of their program until the completion of user A. Users A, B, and C are, in essence, single-threaded through the system because of their common access and locking of table ABC.

This simplistic example of the relationship between system performance and the locking of data points out how seemingly unrelated activities—the programs of users A, B, and C—in fact are tightly related in that they share the same data and the locking of data by DB2 causes the programs to operate serially with each other.

Fortunately, many states in the locking of data by DB2 can alleviate the degree with which two or more users conflict in the usage of data. The DB2 database designer must be aware of what the options of design are and the implications of the options if locking is not to cause performance difficulties in DB2.

THE COMPONENTS OF DATA LOCKING

The lowest level of data access in DB2 is the row. Rows are physically contained in pages. Each page contains one or more rows, and no row may exist on more than one page. Rows are logically organized into tables. Tables are defined into tablespaces, and tablespaces are combined into one or more databases.

Rows are accessed by programs. A program can access data, update data, insert data, or delete data. A program can run in the TSO, IMS/DC, or the CICS environment. The processing done by a program can be divided up into one or more units of recovery. A program may explicitly cause a unit of recovery to be created, or the commencement of a program will automatically create a unit of recovery.

A *unit of recovery* is all the updates, inserts, and deletions committed to the database by a program. Prior to the creation of a given unit of recovery, any processing done by the program will be part of a different unit of recovery. For example, suppose program A goes into execution. The first thing program A does is to insert a row for a new customer. Next, the balance in the row is updated. But, in further processing in the same program, it is discovered that the customer who has just been inserted is on a list of undesirables who have had bad dealings with the bank on previous occasions. Even though the previous processing had inserted the row, a ROLLBACK is done and the net effect is that no activity against the database has occurred. In other words, the insertion and update of the row was negated because of the ROLLBACK within the same unit of recovery.

Another important component of data locking in DB2 is the *results table*. When a program executes a SELECT statement, a results table is created. The results table is where a copy of the rows that have satisfied the SELECT statement are placed. The results table belongs only to the program that has executed the query. The results table should not be mistaken for the data in the database; it is only a copy of the data.

The *cursor* is another component of DB2 that is of importance to data locking. Oftentimes, it is necessary to examine or access the rows in the results table one at a time. The cursor is merely a marker that indicates which row in the results table is being examined by the program. The cursor can be used for access or update of data. Cursors are opened or closed prior to usage or at the close of usage.

LOCK COMPONENTS

DB2 locks have four basic components:

- Objects—the actual component that is being locked, such as a tablespace or an index
- Duration of the lock—the length of time the lock is held
- Mode of locking—the type of access that is or is not permitted while the object is being locked
- Size—the amount of data that is locked

Each of these components will be briefly discussed.

Objects

DB2 locks tablespaces and indexes at different levels. Tablespaces can be locked, pages within tablespaces can be locked, and subpages within index pages can be locked. When tablespaces are locked, all tables within the tablespace are locked. Of course, when a tablespace holds only a single table, then only that single table is locked.

Duration of the Lock

The duration of the lock is the length of time the lock is held. Locks can be acquired when the application PLAN is allocated (i.e., when the program goes into execution) or when the program first executes SQL calls (i.e., upon first usage of the data). Locks can be released upon deallocation of the application PLAN or can be released by the program at selected times during the execution of the program.

Mode of Locking

The mode of a lock determines the type of access permitted (or not permitted) to concurrent users of the locked object. Some of the modes are SHARE, EXCLUSIVE, UPDATE, and so forth. The mode of locking chosen by DB2 depends upon what type of processing is to be done by the program in execution and how the database locking has been defined to DB2.

Size

The size of the lock refers to the amount of data—tablespaces, pages, etc.—that is locked.

LOCKING MANAGEMENT

Locks are managed internally and dynamically by DB2. The levels of locking that are held at any moment are decided by DB2 as a function of the activity that is occurring in DB2 and by the definition of the data to DB2. As such, the designer only passively influences data locking. Some of the design options the designer has to influence data locking in DB2 are the following:

- At the moment of tablespace creation, the designer specifies whether page locking, tablespace locking, or both can be done. This specification affects the objects that are locked.

- Specification of cursor stability or repeatable read at the moment of BIND for those programs that will be doing page locking. This is one of the few options the designer may proactively choose to influence the levels of locking.

- Update, creation, access of data at the SQL level. The nature of the activity done in the program has a major influence on the levels of locking that are done. A design technique to keep the levels of locking at the lowest level for the longest amount of time is to separate activity that merely accesses data from activity that alters the content of data. By separating processes into different programs according to different types of activity, the designer keeps the mode of locking at the lowest level for the most amount of processing.
- Minimization of the TOTAL amount of activity done by any given transaction. By keeping the amount of work done by any given transaction to a minimum, the duration of the lock held is minimized as well as the size of the lock.
- Electing whether to do locking explicitly (i.e., by actual calls to SQL) or by letting default program options to be taken. This design option applies to tablespace processing and affects the duration of the lock.
- Choosing whether/how frequently to do checkpoints. This option affects the duration of the lock as well as the size of the lock.

These design options, then, can be used to influence how lock management occurs, even though the designer has very little direct control over DB2 locking.

A TYPICAL LOCKING SEQUENCE

To illustrate the components of DB2 locking, consider a typical, simple sequence of DB2 locking from the perspective of the data being locked. Row A in page B in table C prior to the moment of locking is not being used by any program. Soon, a program wishes to access row A. First, the program acquires a read-only lock on the tablespace in which table C resides. Upon the reading of the row by the program, an S (shared) lock is acquired on page B, the page in which row A resides. Row A is placed in the results table. At this point in time, other applications can retrieve a row other than row A from page B, but cannot delete or update row A until the S lock is released.

After a period of time, the program determines it needs to update row A. The S lock is escalated to an X (exclusive) lock. Now row A can be updated by the owning program, but no other rows in page B can be accessed. An X lock is placed on the page.

Of course, while page locks are placed on page B in table C, all other pages in table C are able to be accessed or updated (assuming that they are not already locked by some other program, of course).

Now program A executes sufficient SQL calls to acquire enough page locks in table C to escalate the locking to the tablespace level. If no other page locks are owned by other programs on the page in table C, then the tablespace in which table C resides is locked with an X lock. If, however, at the moment of escalation, there are page locks in table C that are held by programs other than the program that is causing the escalation, then the escalation of the tablespace lock to exclusive level must wait until the locks are freed.

Finally, when all "foreign" page locks are freed in table C, the level of tablespace locking is escalated to exclusive. At this time, ALL tables in the tablespace are locked, not just table C.

Table C may be locked in one of two modes—shared mode or exclusive mode. In the example being described, the mode of locking would be exclusive, since update of data is occurring.

After all processing is done, a commit point is reached, the unit of recovery is completed, and the tablespace lock is freed. Data in table C is now free to be accessed and locked by other programs.

THE OPTIONS FOR LOCKING DATA

Three diagrams can be used to describe the options for locking in DB2. At any moment in time, the different options for locking are described by the different states of the diagrams. The diagrams shown in Figure 18-1 are—

- the locking level diagram,
- the locking mode diagram,
- the locking acquisition/release diagram.

The locking-level diagram shows that there are two levels of locking: at the page level and at the tablespace level. Of course, the same unit of data can be locked at both levels.

Pages are locked with two options: cursor stability and repeatable read. Tablespaces are locked, or, if there is a single table in the tablespace, then a single table is locked when the tablespace is locked.

The locking-mode diagram shows that pages can be locked by sharing data, by updating data, or by exclusively controlling data. Tablespaces can be locked at five levels: the shared intent level, the

Chapter 18 An Introduction to Data-Locking in DB2

Locking Levels

- page
  - cursor stability
  - repeatable read
- tablespace
  - table
  - tablespace

Locking Mode

- page
  - share
  - update
  - exclusive
- tablespace
  - share intent
  - share
  - exclusive intent
  - sahred intent exclusive
  - exclusive

Locking Acquisition/Release

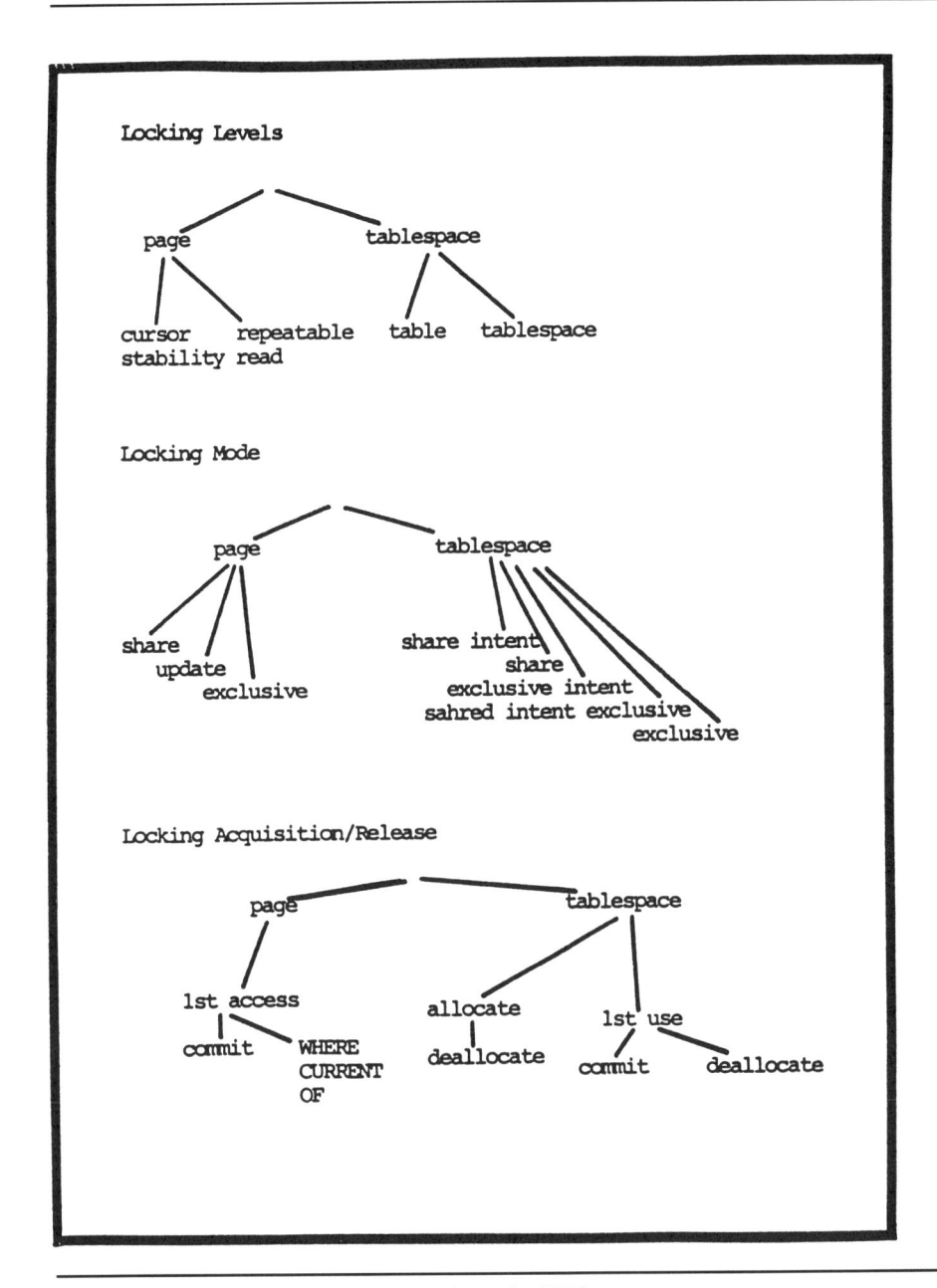

- page
  - 1st access
    - commit
    - WHERE CURRENT OF
- tablespace
  - allocate / deallocate
  - 1st use
    - commit
    - deallocate

FIGURE 18–1. Data locking options in DB2.

shared level, the exclusive intent level, the shared exclusive intent level, and the exclusive level.

The locking acquisition/release diagram shows that pages may be acquired upon first access and are released at a commit point. Another option for pages is to be acquired at first access when cursor stability is specified, WHERE CURRENT OF is specified, and where the data is not updated. Then the page is released when cursor positioning passes beyond the rows in the page that have been locked.

For tablespaces, there are three possibilities for acquisition/release—tablespaces can be locked when the application plan is allocated and released upon deallocation of the application plan; tablespaces can be locked upon first use and released upon commit; or tablespaces can be allocated upon first use and released upon deallocation of the application plan.

THE STATES OF THE OPTIONS

The three diagrams shown in Figure 18-1 taken together represent the combinations of states that DB2 locking may be in. For example, when cursor stability is chosen for page locking, the locking mode at the page level may be exclusive, the locking level at the tablespace level may be exclusive, and the duration of the lock may be from first access to a commit point. Or if tablespace locking is chosen where there is one table in the tablespace, then exclusive intent where allocation is made on usage and released on commit can be elected with no page-level locking.

The first decision to be made by the designer is whether to use page locking. In general, page locking is used for online, transaction processing, or short-running processes that access a limited amount of data. Tablespace locking is used for batch, sequentially oriented processing that accesses much data.

Each of the options has its own advantages and disadvantages. The database designer needs to be aware of the locking options and the corresponding implications. The following is a brief description of each of the options.

Page Locking—Cursor Stability

Cursor stability is the option that allows the finest granularity of data, and, as a result, the highest degree of concurrency. The pages that are locked are locked by an SQL call with as low a level of locking as possible. As processing continues, the level of locking escalates, depending on the action taken by the programs operating on the data. As long as the level of locking has not been escalated, locked pages can be accessed by other programs. Upon reaching a commit point, the data is released. Page locking—cursor stability—is the option usually taken for online, transaction processing.

Page Locking—Repeatable Read

When pages are locked with repeatable read, the data that is locked is not accessible to other programs from the moment the data is allocated until the data is released at a commit point. With repeatable read, data is locked at the highest level of locking required at the outset of execution of the program. Repeatable reads are used for programs or online transactions where access and alteration of data by programs other than the lock owner are not allowed from the moment the program goes into execution until the data is committed.

Tablespace Locking—Tablespaces

When a tablespace is locked, all tables defined within the tablespace are simultaneously locked. This option applies best to small, nonpartitioned tables that are accessed by batch or sequentially oriented programs.

Tablespace Locking—Single Tables

When a tablespace contains a single table and tablespace locking is specified, then only the table defined within the tablespace is locked. This option applies to tables the size of which are normally found in the production environment, i.e., medium to large tables. Tablespace locking for tablespaces with a single table is best for batch or sequentially oriented programs.

Page Locking—Shared Mode

Where page locking is specified in a shared mode, then the lock owner and other programs can access but not alter the locked page. The shared mode is useful for the system to determine which programs are using which data should there be a need to escalate the level of locking to exclusive. This option is for read-only processing by transactions. This is the lowest level of page locking (i.e., the least constraining level of locking with the fewest options for the program holding the lock).

Page Locking—Update

With page locking—update, the lock owner signals the intent to alter data. Only one update lock at a time for a page can be issued. Note that even though one row on a page may be selected by an application program, all rows in the page are locked. When the actual update of data occurs, the system waits until there are no more shared locks, then changes the status of the lock to an exclusive status. This option is for transaction processing that sometimes changes a row based on program logic.

Page Locking—Exclusive

With exclusive page locking, the lock owner may read or change the data as desired, with no interference from other programs. This option is for transaction processing that is going to change, insert, or delete a row once the row is selected. This is the highest level of page locking (i.e., the most constraining level of locking with the most options for the program holding the lock).

Tablespace Locking—Intent Share

When tablespace locking—intent share is specified, the lock owner may read but not update data. Other programs may read and change the data. The intent share option merely serves to indicate to the system what data is accessed should an escalation of locks be needed. This option is for batch programs that need to access data in a "read-only" mode, where the data may concurrently be changed. This is the lowest level of tablelocking.

Tablespace Locking—Share

Tablespace locking—share allows the concurrent owner and other concurrent programs to read but not alter data in the table. The share option is an escalation of the intent share option. This option is for batch processing where the data is accessed in a read-only mode where the data cannot be concurrently changed.

Tablespace Locking—Intent Exclusive

The lock owner and concurrent programs may read data in the table space. When data needs to be altered, the level of locking is changed to exclusive. This option is for batch or sequential processing where data can be read and optionally changed. The program is, in essence, in a read-only state until the data can be changed. Upon changing the data—if, in fact, the data is ever altered—the locking status of the data is changed to exclusive. Only concurrent users of the data may alter the data.

Tablespace Locking—Share With Intent Exclusive

The lock owner may read and change data in the tablespace. Concurrent programs may read data but not alter the data. When the lock owner reads data, a shared lock is acquired. When the lock owner alters the data, an exclusive page lock is acquired as well. This option is the same as the previous option except that concurrent users may not alter the data.

Tablespace Locking—Exclusive

The lock owner at the highest level of table locking may read or alter all the data in the tablespace. This option allows the lock owner to access/alter the data at any time. All other concurrent users are locked out at this level.

Page Locking—First Access-Commit

When page locking—first access-commit acquisition/release is selected, the page is acquired upon first usage of the data and is released upon committing to the data. This option for page locking is used where transactions may update the data being accessed. This option is for dynamic SQL or static SQL where locking control is explicitly executed.

Page Locking—First Access-Where Current of (Cursor Stability)

When page locking—first access—WHERE-CURRENT-OF acquisition/release is chosen, cursor stability must be specified. In this case, the pages of data are locked upon first usage and are released after the cursor has positioned itself beyond the row of data, if the data has not been altered. This option is used for transaction processing where data is accessed but not updated.

Tablespace Locking—Allocate/Deallocate

Tablespace locking—allocate/deallocate acquisition/release is chosen when the tablespace is locked at the moment the application PLAN is allocated and is unlocked when the application PLAN is deallocated. This option is useful for batch processing or sequentially oriented programs that access databases that are infrequently used or when no concurrency is required.

Tablespace Locking—First Use/Deallocate

When tablespace locking first use/deallocate is chosen, the tablespace is locked upon first usage and is unlocked when the application plan is freed. This option is for batch or sequentially oriented programs that access/update tablespaces that are frequently used.

Tablespace Locking—First Use/Commit

When tablespace locking first use/commit is chosen, the tablespace is locked upon first usage and is unlocked upon commitment to DB2. This option is useful for popular tablespaces that are accessed in batch or by large sequential processes.

THE UNIT OF RECOVERY

An important component of DB2 locking is the unit of recovery. The unit of recovery is the period of time during which all activity that occurs in a program is committed or is backed out. The parameters that determine the unit of recovery vary from IMS/DC to TSO to CICS.

In IMS, the unit of recovery starts when the IMS transaction goes into execution or after the execution of a CHKP, ROLL, SYNC, or ROLB has completed. For single mode transactions, the unit of recovery starts when a GU is issued to the I/O PCB.

In TSO, the unit of recovery is delimited when a program goes into execution, when a COMMIT is issued, or by an SQL ROLLBACK statement. The unit of recovery ends upon termination of the program or under the same set of delimiters.

In CICS, the unit of recovery is implicitly delimited by the end of a transaction, signaled by a CICS RETURN command, explicitly signaled by a CICS SYNCPOINT command issued by the application programmer, implicitly issued through a DL-1 PSB termination, or implicitly signaled when a batch DL-1 program issues a DL-1 checkpoint call.

All database activity that has transpired from the time the unit of recovery starts until the unit of recovery ends is committed to the database.

At the completion of the unit of recovery, the locks that are held by the system are released once the data is successfully written to the database. In addition, DB2 closes any cursors that are open at the time of the commit point if the cursor has not explicitly been closed in the program. The implication is that cursors should be closed before the commit point, if they are to be explicitly closed at all. They should be reopened after the commit point. Committing data and then doing an explicit close of a cursor will cause an incorrect programmatic condition.

One of the major trade-offs in DB2 is between the amount of resources used for data locking and the level of concurrency of processing that can be achieved. On the one hand, the system uses a minimal amount of resources for table locking, but the degree of concurrency that can be achieved is minimal. On the other hand, with page locking, the system requires considerable resources for locking pages; each time a page needs to be locked, the system needs to go through its locking routines. But with page locking, the greatest amount of concurrency can be achieved because data is locked at a finer level of granularity.

It goes without saying that, when performance is an issue, where the designer is dealing with large databases as found in the production environment, such simple practices as accessing data through an index should be followed. A full scan of each row in a large table where there is no index to otherwise access the data is as wasteful in data locking as in any other circumstance because of the need to access each row in the table.

In the same vein, resources are tied up when there is no index and when repeatable read is specified. The tablespace is locked even if page locking has been specified.

SOME RULES OF THUMB

The following rules of thumb should be applied to data locking:

- Table locking is for all long-running, batch, sequentially oriented processing

- Page locking is for all online, transaction-oriented processing
- The number of pages locked within a unit of recovery should adhere to the standard work unit established for the online environment.

Although choosing the proper level of locking is important to the achievement of good performance, adherence to the standard work unit is even more important. Having DB2 choose the right level of locking is only of passing importance when the calling transaction is issuing hundreds of calls to retrieve data, for example.

In DB2, at the moment of creating or altering a table, a parameter is to be specified known as LOCKSIZE. LOCKSIZE may be specified as TABLESPACE, PAGE, or ANY. The TABLESPACE option indicates the table is to be locked at the table level. The PAGE option indicates the data is to be locked at the page level. And the ANY option means DB2 may choose whatever locking it wishes. The preferred option is ANY.

When the ANY option is chosen and DB2 locks data at the page level, then, after a certain number of pages are selected and locked by a given DB2 thread, the lock is escalated to the table level. At this moment in time, all page locks are released. The number of page locks that trigger the page to table escalation are parametrically determined by—

- NUMLKTS, and
- NUMLKUS.

NUMLKTS indicates the threshold number of pages that can be locked by any thread in any one tablespace, and NUMLKUS indicates the threshold number of pages that can be held by any one thread in all tablespaces. When NUMLKUS is reached, an SQL error code of 904 is returned, and the transaction is rolled back. These two parameters are specified in the DSNZPARM start-up member. These two parameters determine when page locking escalates to tablespace locking.

Previously, it was stated that tablespace locks could be acquired at the time of PLAN allocation or upon first usage of the data. There are some subtle differences between the two options that the designer should be aware of. In general—

- if the program has SQL processing that is only infrequently used, then the ACQUIRE(USE) option will only allocate data as needed.

This increases the concurrency of processing but also increases the chances of deadlock;

- if the program does SQL calls on the same data in practically every case, then the ACQUIRE(ALLOCATE) option reduces the chances of deadlock;
- if the processing is against data that is frequently used, then the ACQUIRE(USE) option reduces the time the data is frozen;
- if data is commonly accessed but only rarely updated, then the ACQUIRE(USE) parameter will lock data at the lowest level possible, whereas the ACQUIRE(ALLOCATE) option will allocate the data at the highest level necessary;
- if a batch program is to do checkpointing, the ACQUIRE(USE) option will free as much data as possible for as long as possible.

CURSOR STABILITY/REPEATABLE READ

When page locking is selected, there are two suboptions: cursor stability or repeatable read. Under most circumstances, the designer will choose cursor stability because it offers the greatest amount of concurrency. However, there are a few occasions when repeatable read is the appropriate option.

The differences between the two options are best illustrated in terms of the dynamics of the options. Consider how cursor stability operates. Program A has its application PLAN allocated. At that moment in time, no pages are locked. Next, program A executes the following SQL call:

```
SELECT NAME SSNO
FROM EMPLOYEE,TABLE
WHERE SCHOOL = 'STANFORD' AND
      MAJOR = 'EE'
```

The results table contains, as a consequence of the call, the following information:

```
J Jones, 445-71-1981
T Hall,  336-71-7011
```

Progam A continues to execute, and no unit of recovery is signaled.

Next, program B executes the following SQL call:

```
DELETE
FROM EMPLOYEE.TABLE
WHERE SSNO = '336-71-7011'
```

And program C executes as well, issuing the following SQL call:

```
INSERT
INTO EMPLOYEE.TABLE
(NAME, .......)
   VALUES ('W Pickett, ...........)
```

Now still within the original unit of recovery, program A reissues the original SQL statement:

```
SELECT NAME SSNO
FROM EMPLOYEE.TABLE
WHERE SCHOOL = 'STANFORD' AND
      MAJOR = 'EE'
```

Program A's result table looks like:

```
J Jones, 445-71-1981
W Pickett, 392-14-1002
```

Within the same unit of recovery, the data has changed using cursor stability. Of course, if program A had chosen to change the data itself, a different level of locking would have been placed on the data and the data would not have changed. But as long as program A has chosen to only access the data, the data has the capability of changing during the unit of recovery.

Of course, for many types of processing, there is no need to re-retrieve the same data. Or, if the same data is somehow re-retrieved, then there may be no need for tight synchronization with previous results. In the cases where re-retrieval of data is not done, then cursor stability is the appropriate option. However, for some processing, there is a need to re-retrieve the same data and have the results remain the same. In this case, repeatable reads are required.

The difference between cursor stability and repeatable reads is that repeatable reads lock the data accessed for the unit of recovery even if the data is not updated.

Suppose repeatable read processing had been specified in the example previously discussed. Program B and program C simply would not have been allowed to execute while program A was still in the same unit of recovery. The results of both the first and the second SQL calls would have been:

```
J Jones, 445-71-1981
T Hall,  336-71-7011
```

The consistency of data within the same unit of recovery is bought at a price, however. The data accessed under repeatable read is locked for a larger period of time and under a higher level of locking than under cursor stability. Consequently, repeatable reads reduce the concurrency of data that is possible.

DEADLOCK

One of the important subjects related to the locking of data is deadlock. Deadlock occurs when the system must back out one transaction to let another transaction complete processing. As a simple example of deadlock, user A has accessed and has locked table A, and user B has accessed and has locked table B. Now user A needs to access table B to complete processing and, at the same time, user B needs to access table A to complete processing. As long as the system remains in this state, neither user A nor user B may complete their processing. The users are in a logical bind that cannot be addressed at the design or tuning level.

The length of time the system tolerates a deadlock is determined by parameters set at installation time. DB2 breaks the deadlock, once detected, and issues a 911 SQL error code to the user that is interrupted. All the work that was done by the user that is interrupted is backed out to the start of the unit of recovery. After one user is backed out, processing continues for the other user.

The best way to achieve the highest degree of concurrency in DB2 is to do page locking. Failing the opportunity to do page-level-locking, the next strategy is to do table locking from USAGE to COMMIT. Not only is the data tied up for a short amount of time with this option, but the data is locked at the lowest level possible. The options continue to escalate, until exclusive table locking from allocation to deallocation is specified. At this point, deadlock is minimized, but concurrency is minimized as well.

It is noted that the system will automatically detect and remedy deadlock when it occurs. There is nothing the designer need do except prepare to receive a 911 return code. However, the automatic handling of deadlock does not mean the designer should not be aware of and do as much as possible to avoid deadlocks through the judicious selection of locking options and through the design and programming of transactions and batch programs.

SUMMARY

Data locking is a feature of DB2 that profoundly affects the degree of concurrency of users and the integrity of data as well. Locking in DB2 is managed by DB2. But there are several design practices that can be adopted to achieve the degree of locking desired.

The designer must first decide whether page or table locking is desired. These options are set when the tables are defined. The designer must determine whether update processing should be mixed with access-only processing. And finally, the designer must always be aware of the amount of data that is being processed.

While there are other design practices that affect locking, these fundamental parameters greatly affect the level of locking, the object that is being locked, the mode of locking, and the duration of the lock.

QUESTIONS: DATA LOCKING IN DB2

1. The internal protection of data in DB2 is called _____.

2. Data locking determines who can access data, when data can be accessed, and how much _____ is possible.

3. For builders of _____ DB2 systems, data locking is of special interest.

4. Data locking is directly controlled by _____, not the programmer or the application program.

5. The designer and the programmer can select _____, which influence the way DB2 controls data locking.

6. The locking of data goes from one _____ to the next, depending on the amount of data locked, whether update is occurring, and so forth.

7. Programs A, B, and C all update the same table. Even though

Chapter 18   An Introduction to Data-Locking in DB2   293

programs A, B, and C are from unrelated applications, they still affect the rate at which each can process. (T/F)

8. The lowest level of data access in DB2 is the _____.
9. Rows are contained in _____.
10. A row MAY/MAY NOT span more than one page.
11. A _____ contains all rows of the same type.
12. A _____ is made up of one or more tables.
13. A _____ contains one or more tablespace.
14. A _____ is all the updates, inserts, and deletions committed by a program.
15. All activity in the unit of recovery may be cancelled before the end of the unit of recovery by execution of a _____.
16. The data selected by an SQL statement is placed in the _____.
17. Actual data in a DB2 table MAY/MAY NOT be in the results table.
18. The _____ is used to look at rows in the results table row at a time.
19. The cursor can be used for access only of data in the results table. (T/F)
20. An example of an object that is locked is a _____ or an _____.
21. The duration of the lock is the length of _____ the object is locked.
22. The _____ of access refers to the type of access allowed while data is under control of the lock manager.
23. The size of the lock refers to the _____ of data that is locked.
24. When a table space is locked, all tables in the tablespace are locked. (T/F)
25. Locks can only be acquired when the application plan is allocated. (T/F)
26. When a program first executes SQL calls, locks may be allocated. (T/F)
27. Locks CAN/CANNOT be released upon deallocation of the application plan.

28. Locks can be released selectively by the application plan at _____ time, during the execution of the program.

29. Some modes of locking are _____.

30. The mode of locking is directly controlled by _____.

31. The designer ACTIVELY/PASSIVELY controls locking.

32. At the moment of tablespace creation, the designer specifies whether the table can have page locking, tablespace locking, or both. This specification controls the _____ that are locked.

33. Specification of cursor stability or repeatable read is done by the programmer. This option affects the _____ of locking.

34. Update, creation, and access of data by the programmer affects the _____ of locking done by DB2.

35. Separating update from access allows DB2 to use the LOWEST/HIGHEST levels of locking possible.

36. The programmer can control the total amount of activity done by the program. This affects the _____ of the lock as well as the size of the lock.

37. The designer may elect to do locking explicitly or may let default option apply. This affects the _____ of the lock.

38. The programmer may do checkpoints. This affects both the _____ of the lock and the _____ of the lock.

39. Upon going into execution a program automatically issues a table lock even if page level locking is specified. (T/F)

40. During the execution of a program, page-level and table-level locking MAY/MAY NOT be specified for a table at the same time.

41. There are two levels of locking—locking at the _____ level and locking at the _____ level.

42. Pages are locked under two options— _____ and _____.

43. The modes that a page can be locked in are SHARE, UPDATE, and _____.

44. Tablespaces can be locked at five levels. List them.

45. In terms of acquisition/release, pages may be acquired on first access and released at a commit point. Another option is for tables to be acquired on first access where cursor stability is specified, when WHERE CURRENT OF is specified and where data is

Chapter 18 An Introduction to Data-Locking in DB2   295

not updated. Then the page is released when the _____ passes beyond the rows in the page that have been locked.

46. The finest degree of granularity of data allows the highest level of _____.

47. The unit of recovery is the period of time during which all _____ that occurs in a program is committed or is backed out.

48. The parameters that delimit the unit of recovery are the same in IMS/DC, TSO, and CICS. (T/F)

49. In IMS/DC, the unit of recovery starts when the IMS transaction goes into execution or after the execution of a _____, _____, _____, or _____ call.

50. In TSO, the unit of recovery is delimited when a program goes into _____, when a _____ is issued, or when an SQL _____ statement is executed.

51. In CICS, the unit of recovery is implicitly delimited by the end of the _____, signalled by a CICS _____ command, explicitly signalled by a CICS _____ command issued by the application programmer, implicitly issued through a DL-1 _____ termination, or implicitly signaled when a batch DL-1 program issues a DL-1 _____ call.

52. At the completion of the unit of recovery, ALL LOCKS/ONLY THOSE LOCKS HELD BY THE PROGRAM TERMINATING are released.

53. Any cursor left open will automatically be closed at the time of the commit point. (T/F)

54. Table locking requires MANY/FEW/AN INDETERMINATE resources from DB2.

55. The degree of concurrency achieved with table locking is MAXIMUM/MINIMAL/INDETERMINATE.

56. Page locking, under normal circumstances, requires considerably MORE/LESS resources from DB2 than tablespace locking.

57. Page locking ALWAYS/SOMETIMES/NEVER achieves the highest degree of concurrency.

58. Where performance is an issue, the designer must select options that will achieve the HIGHEST/LOWEST degree of concurrency.

59. Table locking is for long running, batch, sequentially oriented processing. (T/F)
60. Because of the overhead of locking pages, page locking is too expensive for online processing. (T/F)
61. Row A and B are in page 1. Row A is updated and its program requires that it be locked. Is row B also locked at the same time?
62. Controlling the total number of rows accessed by a program in the online environment is the single most important thing the designer can do to influence good performance. (T/F)
63. If 50 percent of the applications a shop has are designed carefully, then it is a good bet that the organization will experience good performance. (T/F)
64. LOCKSIZE is specified upon the definition/creation of a _____.
65. The three options that may be chosen when specifying LOCKSIZE are _____, _____, and _____.
66. When ANY option is chosen, the table may be locked at the _____ or the _____ level.
67. Lock escalation occurs when a threshold number of _____ are locked.
68. The threshold is determined by two parameters, _____ and _____.
69. Which offers the greatest concurrency—cursor stability or repeatable read?
70. If a program requires that the value of data remain constant throughout the entire period of execution, _____ should be specified.
71. If a program only needs to know the value of the data it accesses once during the period of execution, then _____ should be specified.
72. Deadlock occurs when programs and data are interlocked. One program must be _____.
73. When DB2 detects deadlock, a _____ error code is issued.

CHAPTER 19

Archival Processing

Archival processing of data is that processing that is done on aged data, usually looking for one or two records of data or looking at a large amount of data to determine trends that have occurred over time. In almost every case, archival processing is done irregularly. Archival processing is seldom scheduled, and usually is done heuristically and iteratively (sharing many common characteristics with classical decision support processing).

Strictly speaking, archival processing is not done in a production data processing environment in most companies. (Of course, in a few organizations, archival processing forms the backbone of the work of the company.) But even when archival processing is not done in the mainstream production processing, it usually enhances and complements production processing. Separating work and data into the archival environment frees resources for higher priority production processing.

CRITERIA FOR SUCCESS

The criteria for success of the archival environment is very different from the criteria for success in other environments. High performance, high availability over long periods of time, rapid system development, and so forth are normally not high priority criteria in the archival environment, as they are in other environments. Only the management of large amounts of data are common criteria of success that are shared by the archival environments and the typical production environment.

In the archival environment, there usually are massive amounts of data—even larger volumes of data than those found in the largest production environment. The management of very large amounts of data is perhaps the single most important criterion of success in the archival environment.

The nature of archival processing is the storage of data for future, unknown needs. Traditionally, analysis of archival data has been done in a heuristic manner. There are, essentially, two types of archival processing, processing to find a few records out of many or processing massive amounts of data. For example, the archival analyst may search a company's files and records to locate all sales made in New Mexico where state tax has been calculated at 3.5 percent between the first of May, 1962, and the sixth of July, 1962. Only a few records would satisfy these criteria, and the search would be like looking for the needle in a haystack.

The other type of archival analysis is the search and manipulation of massive amounts of data. For example, the archival analyst might wish to determine the average length of time between purchases for those customers making multiple purchases between 1981 and 1985. The satisfaction of this analysis requires much manipulation of data.

ARCHIVAL MEDIA

The media on which archival data is stored has a profound influence on the archival analysis that can be done. The primary division of archival storage media is between two categories, electronic reproducible or nonelectronic reproducible media. Examples of an electronic reproducible media are magnetic tape or standard DASD.

An example of nonelectronic reproducible media is microfiche. Once data is put off onto microfiche, searches for single records can be done fairly efficiently if the key of the record desired is known, but massive access and manipulation of data is expensive and awkward in microfiche. Data on electronic nonreproducible media is inexpensive to store and is relatively secure from damage.

When data is placed on an electronic reproducible media, massive manipulation of the data can be done (as well as searches for single records). The cost of storage on electronic reproducible media is relatively expensive, and, on occasion, whole volumes of data become damaged and are not easily replaced or restored.

Based upon the type of archival analysis that needs to be done, the media that is appropriate must be selected. If massive manipulation of archival data is to be done, then an electronical reproducible media should be selected.

Far and above all other issues, the management of massive volumes of data is the overriding issue of archival processing. Not only is there much archival data, but at its typical rate of growth, the volumes of data mount rapidly.

PRIMITIVE ARCHIVAL DATA

The most effective storage of archival data is at the primitive level. Since archival data is stored for unknown usage, the most basic, most detailed data needs to be stored. If a unit of data is not stored for future archival needs, then it is permanently lost, i.e., when any primitive unit of data in the production environment is deleted from the production environment, if the unit is not archived, it is permanently lost. Derived data can be stored in the archival environment as well. Once detailed, primitive data is archived, the data forms the basis for reconciliation of DSS processing and other archival analysis at a later point in time.

Archival data should be stored with a definition that is as "universal" as possible. In other words, the physical layout (i.e., the definition) of archival data should be stored in a manner that will facilitate future retrieval. A simple character definition of a field may waste some space, but will simplify the job of future analysts who are trying to use the data. In addition, the physical format should be in as popular and widely used form as possible. It is a good bet that a simple VSAM layout will present less of a barrier to future usage than will a format from some less popular software or access method.

In addition to the content of data being archived, the format of data should be archived as well. The format should contain the field name, the data characteristics, and any pertinent information about the field that will help future archival analysts understand the meaning and content of the archival data that is available. In addition, any tables that are referenced or any encoding/decoding of archived data that has been done should likewise be referenced and stored.

In general, data relationships in archival files are kept to a minimum if they are kept at all.

SUBJECT ORIENTATION

The orientation of archival data is toward the major subjects of the organization, as are the standard operational databases derived from the business of the enterprise. For example, customer information should be stored with other, related customer information. In the same vein, activity information should be stored with other activity information. Separating and storing archival data according to the major subjects of the enterprise prepares the information for future usage in that there is not a confused intermingling of different types of data with each other.

Over time, detailed, process-oriented aspects of the major subjects of the enterprise are sure to change, but the major subjects of the enterprise—customers, activities, accounts, the enterprise—are slow to change. The orientation of the archival databases to the major subjects of the organization (which is the same orientation as the operational databases) provides a straightforward basis for the flow of data from the operational to the archival environment.

The applicability of DB2 to archival data, at first glance, is severely limited. The volume of data, the infrequency of access, and the inability to predict the usage of the data all present special problems to the DB2 archival analyst. For example, the sheer volume of archival data normally precludes the indexing of ANY of the data, a severe limitation to the usefulness of the DB2 software. Another problem is that the masses of data stored before DB2 became widely available may not be able to be conveniently translated into a format known to DB2. Even if a conversion from an existing format to a DB2 format can be done, the overhead entailed is potentially very large. As a consequence, DB2 is not applicable to the standard archival environment.

THE LIVING SAMPLE ENVIRONMENT

There is one archival environment to which DB2 is peculiarly applicable. The environment is called the "living sample" environment, and DB2 is truly an ideal tool for that environment.

The living sample environment is best described in terms of some examples. Suppose an archival analyst were to analyze 10 years of historical data. The analyst determines that the average sale over the 10-year period was $105.36, that the busiest time of the year was December 16, and that 87 percent of sales were conducted with credit cards. To arrive at those conclusions, the archival analyst went through 750,000 individual transactions that occurred from 1976 to 1986.

Now, suppose another analyst is operating from a living sample archival database. A living sample database is made up of representative samples of data, and is periodically refreshed (thus the term "living sample"). There are 10,000 representative transactions in the living sample database. The archival analyst operating against the living sample database determines that the average sale is $104.96, that the busiest time of the year is December 17, and that 85.6 percent of business is conducted through credit cards.

There is no doubt that the first archival analyst has a more accurate answer than the living sample analyst. But there is likewise no doubt that the cost of processing actual archival data is VERY expensive. The worth of the accuracy of the analysis of the archival data is questionable. The living sample archival analyst has arrived at very close to the same conclusion as the archival analyst, but the living sample analyst has processed 1/75 of the records. Unless there is an unusual need for a high degree of accuracy, the second analyst, using living sample data, has arrived at satisfactory conclusions much more efficiently than the analyst using classical archival data.

DB2 is an ideal tool for the living sample environment. There is not so much data in the living sample environment that it cannot be managed by DB2. Indexes can be created as data is periodically refreshed. The living sample DSS analyst in DB2 has the full gamut of DB2 options with which to analyze data.

Furthermore, many of the constraints of the production environment, such as using "designed" transactions, are not necessary in the living sample environment.

SOME DESIGN CONSIDERATIONS—
TIME-STAMPING DATA

Practically all of the data in the living sample environment will be *time-stamped*. A time stamp is merely an appendage of the key indicating the value or status of a key as of some moment in time. For example, an account may be archived periodically. In September 1986, account 3650 contained $1,584.00. The domicile of the account is the Market Street branch, and the date the account was opened was May 1979. The key of the record would be account/year/month. On the first of October, a "snapshot" of the September data is taken and is archived.

There are two ways that archived data is time-stamped: with a *discrete* time value and with a *continuous* time value. A discrete time value represents the values of data elements as of a single point in time. As an example of discrete data, the balance in account 3650 as of 10:00 a.m. was $500 when the owner of the account wrote a check for $250. Each of the pieces of data about the transaction are examples of discrete data.

A continuous time value has a beginning and an ending time value and represents data as having the values contained for the entire length of time measured by the continuous dates. For example, the bank pays 5.5 percent interest on passbook accounts from January 1985 to July 1987. A continuous time-stamp record would contain a key—the type of account, the beginning date the rate was paid, the ending date the rate was paid—and the rate itself.

Continuous time-stamping is most appropriate to small numbers of data elements that change infrequently. Every time a variable changes values, a new continuous record must be created. The history of the passbook rate is an example of continuous time-stamped data.

Continuous data normally maintains a simple continuity: The ending date of the earlier record is one unit of time less than the beginning date of the later continuous record. But simple continuity is not the only choice. On occasion, discontinuous or overlapping records may need to be kept.

Another consideration is the beginning date of the first continuous time span record and the ending date of the last continuous time span record. These dates may have an actual value or they may be open-ended. For example, if the ending data for the last continuous time span record equals infinity, then the time span information is valid indefinitely, until further update can occur. But if the ending date has a value, then the set of continuous records has a finite ending.

Discrete snapshot data is applicable to large amounts of data that rapidly change (as opposed to continuous time span data). A major concern of discrete time-variant data is the frequency of snapshots. Snapshots taken too frequently will be voluminous and may actually mask long-term trends. Snapshots taken not frequently enough will lose important fluctuations of data.

An issue applicable to both discrete and continuously measured data is that of the unit of measurement. For example, a measurement of a checking account balance by year does not make sense, and the measurement of the Dow Jones Industrial Average by the minute does not make sense. The unit of time used to measure time-variant data must be appropriate to the data.

Chapter 19 Archival Processing

One of the disciplines of the creation of the living sample environment is in the preservation of the complete data needs of the environment. Very often, archival data is made up of the "refuse" of the operational environment. Only those data elements that are being purged from the operational environment are sent to the archival environment.

While newly purged data may well belong in the archival environment, other data that may not be purged ought to be in the archival environment in order to present a clear picture for archival processing. Establishing and using the living sample environment brings to light the complete set of needs of the archival analyst. Another advantage of DB2 in the living sample environment is the orientation of DB2 towards set processing. The time-stamping that occurs arranges data conveniently into sets.

As an example of how DB2 tables might be processed as time-variant tables, consider the following examples.

Two tables are defined to DB2 containing archival data. One table, the account table, contains account identification, the balance of the account as of the 15th of the month, and an identification of the type of loan associated with the account. Figure 19-1 shows the layout of the data for the account table.

The table in Figure 19-1 is recognized as discrete time-variant data. The loan table contains continuous time-variant data. The loan table contains a key of loan type and the beginning date and ending date of the loan, as well as the effective rate during the time span. The loan rows are arranged so that they continuously define all the days of the year. In other words, the beginning date of row n + 1 is one day less than the ending date of row n.

Figure 19-2 shows the table layout for the loan table.

Several other variables are needed. *Cumulative rate* is simply

```
data layout for the account/balance table

ACCT                char(10)    /*key*/
ACCT.DATE
ACCT.DATE.MONTH     pic'99'     /*key*/
ACCT.DATE.DAY       pic'99'     /*key*/
ACCT.TYPE           char(1)
ACCT.BALANCE        dec fixed(9,2)
```

FIGURE 19-1. Data layout for the account/balance table.

```
LOAN.TYPE                 char(1)         /*key*/
LOAN.BEG.DATE
LOAN.BEG.DATE.MONTH       pic'99'         /*key*/
LOAN.BEG.DATE.DAY         pic'99'         /*key*/
LOAN.END.DATE
LOAN.END.DATE.MONTH       pic'99'         /*key*/
LOAN.END.DATE.DAY         pic'99'         /*key*/
LOAN.RATE                 dec fixed(5,4)
```

FIGURE 19-2. Table layout for discrete time-variant data.

the variable used to store values that will be calculated. The variable "calc.date" is used to control the iterations of the algorithm. Figure 19-3 shows the definitions of the variables.

Some sample occurrences of the account and the rate table are shown by Figure 19-4.

The account table and the loan table are relationally defined, but they cannot be joined in the normal sense. Even though the date fields enjoy a logical intersection of data, the actual physical join is more difficult to implement.

Consider a simple logical join. Suppose the interest paid for an account for a year is to be calculated. The balance in one table is to be multiplied by the applicable rate in the other table.

The algorithm shown in Figure 19-5 merges the two tables based on the intersection of dates.

Twelve calculations are made for an account for a year. The rate that is applicable as of the 15th of the month is multiplied by the balance and is divided by 12 (there are 12 accumulations made per year).

The value accumulated in CUMRATE roughly approximates the interest paid by an account for a year.

But a finer calculation may be required. The simple calculation

```
CALC.DATE
CALC.MONTH       pic'99'
CALC.DAY         pic'99'

CUMRATE          dec fixed(11,3)
```

FIGURE 19-3. Definitions of variables for discrete time-variant data.

```
sample occurrences of the account and rate tables -

ACCT=0056              ACCT=0056              ACCT=0056              ......
date=Jan15             date=Feb15             date=Mar15             ......
balance=100051.32      balance=99997.61       balance=99926.31       ......


RATE='L'               RATE='L'               RATE='L'               .......
begdate=Jan1           begdate=Jan6           begdate=Jan16          .......
enddate=Jan5           enddate=Jan15          enddate=Feb3           .......
rate=.053              rate=.057              rate=.059              .......
```

FIGURE 19–4. Sample occurrences of the account and rate tables with discrete time-variant data.

made for each month assumes that the interest rate is constant from the 15th of the month being calculated to the 15th of the next month. But such is not the case. The rate is variable and may change many times throughout the month.

A finer, more precise calculation, done on a day-by-day basis, is shown by Figure 19-6.

In Figure 19-6, each day's interest is calculated. If rates change, then a new SQL call is made to retrieve the new daily rate.

The example shows how two time-variant files can be "joined"

```
CUMRATE=0
CALC.MONTH=1
CALC.DAY=15
DO WHILE CALC.MONTH < 13
    SELECT ACCT.BALANCE ACCT.TYPE
    FROM ACCT.TABLE
    WHERE ACCT='xxx...' AND ACCT.DATE=CALC.DATE
    SELECT LOAN.RATE
    FROM RATE.TABLE
    WHERE LOAN.TYPE=ACCT.TYPE AND
        LOAN.BEG.DATE = < CALC.DATE AND LOAN.END.DATE >= CALC.DATE
    CUMRATE=CUMRATE+((LOAN.RATExACCT.BALANCE)/12)
    CALC.MONTH=CALC.MONTH+1
END
```

FIGURE 19–5. Algorithm for merging two tables based on intersection of dates.

```
CUMRATE=0
CALC.MONTH=1
CALC.DAY=15
DO WHILE CALC.MONTH < 13
   SELECT ACCT.BALANCE ACCT.TYPE
   FROM ACCT.TABLE
   WHERE ACCT='xxx...' AND ACCT.DATE=CALC.DATE
   SELECT LOAN.RATE
   FROM RATE.TABLE
   WHERE ACCT.TYPE=LOAN.TYPE AND
       LOAN.BEG.DATE =< CALC.DATE AND LOAN.END.DATE >= CALC.DATE
   DAYPROC='N'
   DO WHILE DAYPROC='N'
      CUMRATE=CUMRATE+((ACCT.BALANCExLOAN.RATE)/365)
      CALC.DAY=CALC.DAY+1
      IF CALC.DAY=32 AND IF CALC.MONTH=2 THEN DO
         CALC.MONTH=2
         CALC.DAY=1
         END
      IF CALC.DAY=29 THEN IF CALC.MONTH=2 THEN DO
         CALC.MONTH=3
         CALC.DAY=1
         END
         .   .   .   .   .   .   .   .
         .   .   .   .   .   .   .   .
      IF CALC.DAY > LOAN.END.DATE THEN DO
         SELECT LOAN.RATE
         FROM RATE.TABLE
         WHERE LOAN.TYPE=ACCT.TYPE AND
             LOAN.BEG.DATE =< CALC.DATE AND LOAN.END.DATE >= CALC.DATE
         END
      IF CALC.DAY=15 THEN DAYCALC='Y'
END
```

FIGURE 19-6. A precise calculation, done on a day-by-day basis, of an account.

logically even though a physical join is not possible. The balance file is time-stamped with discrete data, and the rate file is time-stamped with continuous data. And they are logically merged based on matching key values and logically intersecting data values.

But logical joins are not the only challenge facing the archival analyst.

EFFICIENT ACCESS OF ARCHIVAL DATA

Some problems are endemic to the archival environment. Although the problems will be illustrated within the context of DB2 processing, it is noted that ANY data management software would experience the same problems.

One problem facing the archival analyst is the arrangement of data so that efficient access can be made. This is the same problem facing the analyst in other circumstances, except that, in the case of archival data, the massive amounts of data and the way the data is collected and accessed presents some peculiar problems.

As an example, suppose on each 15th of the month, account balance information is stripped from production files. The bulk of the data will be loaded into an archival file. If the data is unclustered in the archival file (which is extremely likely, because there normally is so much data that no indexes can be built), the data will be loaded in a sequential fashion. Assuming that the data is loaded sequentially (i.e., loaded in the same sequence as collected) Figure 19-7 shows how a physical page might look after being loaded from the January strip.

Nothing is inherently wrong with the approach of simply loading data from an archival file as stripped and time-stamped. But consider the result of this process as it places data over several pages, as shown by Figure 19-8.

Consider the work done by the system to analyze the balance of a given account over several months or years. The system must go to a new page for every month's activity. Twelve I/Os will be needed to access 12 month's data for an account even if DB2 knows in which pages the data reside.

If it appears that single-account analysis will be a normal archival analytical activity (i.e., an analytical activity that occurs on a fairly frequent basis), then a different organization of data is required.

The data needs to be clustered on an index based on account/data. But merely clustering the data (assuming that the data CAN be clustered!) may not be adequate. Unless MUCH free space is left in the page when the first entry is inserted, the clustering of data

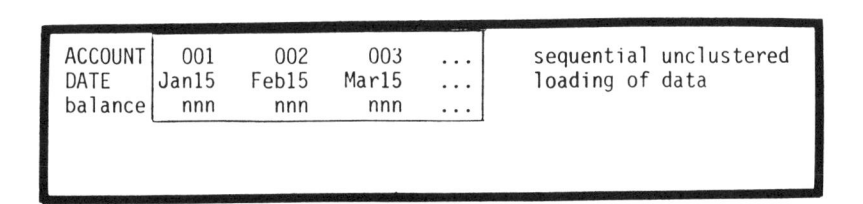

```
ACCOUNT   001     002     003    ...   sequential unclustered
DATE      Jan15   Feb15   Mar15  ...   loading of data
balance   nnn     nnn     nnn    ...
```

FIGURE 19-7. Sequential, unclustered loading of data.

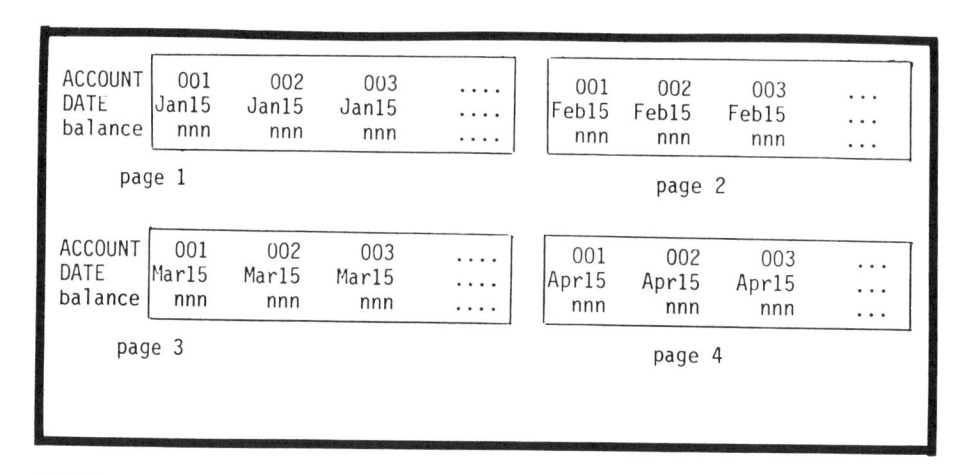

```
┌─────────────────────────────────────────────────────────────────────┐
│  ┌──────┬─────────────────────────────────┐  ┌─────────────────────┐│
│  │ACCOUNT│ 001    002    003    ....      │  │ 001    002    003   ││
│  │DATE   │ Jan15  Jan15  Jan15   ....     │  │ Feb15  Feb15  Feb15 ││
│  │balance│ nnn    nnn    nnn     ....     │  │ nnn    nnn    nnn   ││
│  └──────┴─────────────────────────────────┘  └─────────────────────┘│
│              page 1                                    page 2       │
│  ┌──────┬─────────────────────────────────┐  ┌─────────────────────┐│
│  │ACCOUNT│ 001    002    003    ....      │  │ 001    002    003   ││
│  │DATE   │ Mar15  Mar15  Mar15   ....     │  │ Apr15  Apr15  Apr15 ││
│  │balance│ nnn    nnn    nnn     ....     │  │ nnn    nnn    nnn   ││
│  └──────┴─────────────────────────────────┘  └─────────────────────┘│
│              page 3                                    page 4       │
└─────────────────────────────────────────────────────────────────────┘
```

FIGURE 19-8. Loading data as stripped and time-stamped.

can lead to horrendous data management problems as later inserts are made.

In addition to the clustering of data, the data can be loaded in the following manner: On the January load (assuming the archival databases are created in January), the data for the month of January is entered. At the same time, dummy entries are inserted for February, March, and so forth. The dummy entries contain key values and null values for nonkey data. Figure 19-9 shows a few pages after the January load.

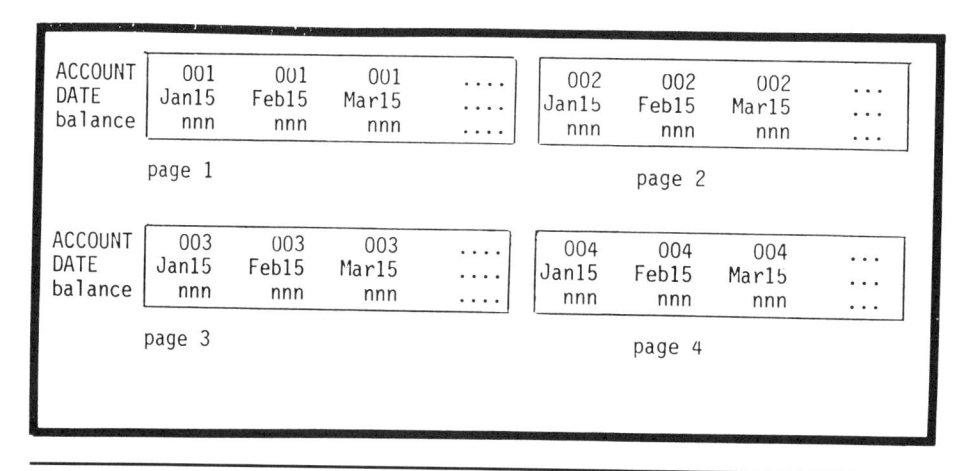

```
┌─────────────────────────────────────────────────────────────────────┐
│  ┌──────┬─────────────────────────────────┐  ┌─────────────────────┐│
│  │ACCOUNT│ 001    001    001    ....      │  │ 002    002    002   ││
│  │DATE   │ Jan15  Feb15  Mar15   ....     │  │ Jan15  Feb15  Mar15 ││
│  │balance│ nnn    nnn    nnn     ....     │  │ nnn    nnn    nnn   ││
│  └──────┴─────────────────────────────────┘  └─────────────────────┘│
│              page 1                                    page 2       │
│  ┌──────┬─────────────────────────────────┐  ┌─────────────────────┐│
│  │ACCOUNT│ 003    003    003    ....      │  │ 004    004    004   ││
│  │DATE   │ Jan15  Feb15  Mar15   ....     │  │ Jan15  Feb15  Mar15 ││
│  │balance│ nnn    nnn    nnn     ....     │  │ nnn    nnn    nnn   ││
│  └──────┴─────────────────────────────────┘  └─────────────────────┘│
│              page 3                                    page 4       │
└─────────────────────────────────────────────────────────────────────┘
```

FIGURE 19-9. Data loaded monthly, with dummy entries inserted.

In February (and in subsequent months), data is replaced, not inserted. With the resulting organization of data, a single account's activity can be accessed in 1 I/O, not 12.

Storage and management of data that occurs or is measured at predictable intervals is relatively simple. Data that occurs or is measured randomly presents entirely different challenges to the archival analyst and designer.

For example, suppose an archival analyst wishes to store information about the checks written by banking customers. Some customers write many more checks than other customers. And the number of checks written in one month may vary significantly from those in another month for a single customer.

One approach is simply to store, by month, all the checks written by all customers. All the checks written are gathered into a monthly file. The gathering of the information is easy and natural, but the utilization of the files can present fearsome problems. To retrieve information, the first qualifications must be on date (or at least month). For some types of processing, this division of data may not be much of a problem. But consider the work the analyst must do in tracking the customer's running balance from one month to the next.

A second option is to reserve as much space as is normally needed for a customer for a year. Each month, the checking activities are loaded into the space reserved for them by individual customer account. But there are some problems with this approach. Suppose 35 "slots" are allocated each month for each customer's checking activity. One month, a customer has used only 15 slots. What happens to the unused slots? Another month a customer uses (or needs) 60 slots. Where do the extra slots come from?

These questions can certainly be answered, but the complexity and management challenges can be severe.

INTEGRITY AND ACCURACY OF ARCHIVAL DATA

Another typical problem facing the designer is that of maintaining integrity and accuracy of data. For example, consider the problems of the programmer in the maintenance of continuous time span data. Updates or creations of data can cause very complex problems when one or more rows of data participates in a continuous definition of a time span.

For example, Figure 19-10 shows some continuous time span rows.

```
rate type='L'      rate type='L'      rate type='L'
dates=Jan1-Jan6    dates=Jan7-Feb14   dates=Feb15-Feb28   .....
rate=.053          rate=.058          rate=.061           .....
limit=1000         limit=1000         limit=1000          .....
                                                          .....
```

FIGURE 19-10. Continuous time span rows.

In the data shown in Figure 19-10, rate type = 'L', loan limit = 1000, and the rate varies from day to day. Each of the rows begins one unit beyond where the previous row ends. In other words, the first row's logical end is on January 6. The next beginning date must be January 7, otherwise, there would be a discontinuity of the data. Note, too, that there is no overlap of data defined by two or more rows. In other words, for any given point in time defined by the continuous time span, there is one and only one set of values that is applicable.

Now suppose the following transaction were entered: Change the limit value of loans to 1500 for the dates of January 4 to January 20. In this case, transaction variables are TX.BEG = Jan4, TX.END = Jan20, and TX.LIMIT = 1500. TX.RATE = 0 (or null values), indicating that rate is not affected by the transaction.

The data after the update has been applied to the continuous time span shown in Figure 19-10 is shown in Figure 19-11.

Several new rows have been created and some existing rows have been updated. The continuity of the data remains the same.

The data was updated by means of the following algorithm: Suppose the transaction has a beginning and ending date of TX.BEG and TX.END. If a nonkey field is to be updated—in this case, LIMIT and RATE—the field to be updated has a value greater than zero. If a nonkey field is not to be updated, it has a null value.

```
rate type='L'      rate type='L'      rate type='L'       rate type='L'       rate type='L'
dates=Jan1-Jan3    dates=Jan4-Jan6    dates=Jan7-Jan20    dates=Jan21-Feb14   dates=Feb15-Feb28   ...
rate=.053          rate=.053          rate=.058           rate=.058           rate=.061           ...
limit=1000         limit=1500         limit=1500          limit=1000          limit=1000          ...
                                                                                                  ...
```

FIGURE 19-11. Data after update has been applied to continuous time span shown in Figure 19-10.

Suppose the DB2 table has (for the data portion of the key) the field DB.BEG. For the purposes of the algorithm to be discussed, assume that the RATE.TYPE of the key has been satisfied (in other words, assume that only the continuous dates must be matched between the transaction and the database.)

The continuous time span database is indexed and clustered, with a data layout shown by Figure 19-12.

Note that the key of the database is the beginning date, not the beginning and ending date. Ending date is not needed for uniqueness.

The algorithm needed to service the continuous time span data structure is shown in ALGO (ALGO is shown at the end of the chapter in four pages because of its size).

FOREIGN KEYS IN THE ARCHIVAL ENVIRONMENT

Foreign key relationships are complicated by the volume of data over which the keys interrelate data and the appendage of data onto the key structure of otherwise normal, straightforward relationships. The volume of data and the infrequency of access under normal circumstances—

- preclude the usage of an index, and
- preclude the usage of a cross-reference table

The remaining choice for relating tables together—dynamically creating the relationship by scanning volumes of data—is likewise unpopular in the face of very large volumes of data. Furthermore, the appendage of data with time stamps—either discrete or continuous—on each key creates logical intersections of data that cannot be joined in the normal manner.

```
TX.BEG      dec fixed (5,0)   /*key*/
TX.END      dec fixed (5,0)
TX.RATE     dec fixed (5,0)
TX.LIMIT    dec fixed (11,2)
```

FIGURE 19–12. Data layout of continuous time span database indexed and clustered.

Clearly, special design techniques are required to manage foreign keys in the face of the DB2 archival environment.

Some design techniques that can be used separately or in tandem with each other are—

- sectioning DB2 data into smaller databases so that standard foreign key relationships can be implemented.
- creating "selective" cross-reference tables, joining selected parts or subsets of tables, not all rows. The selectivity criteria may be on high-dollar items, selected "special" or trouble accounts, etc.
- creating time-dependent-cross-reference tables (as opposed to general purpose cross-references). For example, for the year 1986, one cross-reference can be created. Another cross-reference can be created for 1987, and so forth.
- creating selective intersection copies of data that require no further joins. Instead of creating cross-references, data is duplicated and actual intersection tables are created. It must be kept in mind that, when data is duplicated (especially archived data), the data must conform to the architectural rules for the management of atomic data.

SUMMARY

DB2 is applicable to the archival environment when "living sample" processing of archival data is done. In other cases, the volume of data prevents the usage of many DB2 features, such as indexing.

Archival data is normally time-stamped. Time-variant data that is time-stamped requires special handling. For example, the standard joins of DB2 cannot be done with the time-stamped data in the normal manner. Special algorithms are required to logically actuate the join.

Time-stamped data is either continuous or discrete. The volatility of the data, the number of data elements, the usage of the data, etc. all contribute to the decision of how to manage time-variant data.

ALGO: CONTINUOUS TIMESPAN UPDATE ALGORITHM

```
START:  SELECT DB.BEG DB.END DB. BALANCE DB.LIMIT
        FROM RATE.TABLE
        WHERE DB.BEG <=: TX.BEG AND DB.END >=: TX.BEG
```

```
IF TX.BEG < DB.BEG AND IF TX.END < DB.END THEN DO
     NEWRATE = TX.RATE
     NEWLIMIT = TX.LIMIT
     INSERT INTO RATE.TABLE
     VALUES (TX.BEG, DB.BEG-1, NEWRATE, NEWLIMIT)
     ROWBEG = DB.BEG
     NEWRATE = DB.RATE
     IF TX.RATE > 0 THEN NEWRATE = TX.RATE
     NEWLIMIT = DB.LIMIT
     IF TX.LIMIT > 0 THEN NEW LIMIT = DB.LIMIT
     UPDATE RATETABLE
     SET DB.END =: TX.END
         DB.RATE =: NEWRATE
         DB.LIMIT =: NEWLIMIT
         WHERE DB.BEG = : ROWBEG
     INSERT INTO RATE.TABLE
     VALUES (TX.END+1, DB.END, DB.RATE, DB.LIMIT)
     END
IF TX.BEG < DB.BEG AND IF TX.END = DB.END THEN DO
     NEWRATE = TX.RATE
     NEWLIMIT = TX.LIMIT
     INSERT INTO RATE.TABLE
     VALUES (TX.BEG, DB.BEG-1, NEWRATE, NEWLIMIT)
     ROWBEG = DB.BEG
     NEWRATE = DB.RATE
     IF TX.RATE > 0 THEN NEWRATE = TX.RATE
     NEWLIMIT = DB.LIMIT
     IF TX.LIMIT > 0 THEN NEWRATE = TX.RATE
     UPDATE RATE.TABLE
     SET DB.END =: TX.END
         DB.RATE =: NEWRATE
         DB.LIMIT =: NEWLIMIT
         WHERE DB.BEG =: ROWBEG
     END
IF TX.BEG < DB.BEG AND IF TX.END > DB.END THEN DO
     NEWRATE = TX.RATE
     NEWLIMIT = TX.LIMIT
     INSERT INTO RATE.TABLE
     VALUES (TX. BEG, DB.BEG-1, NEWRATE, NEW.LIMIT)
     ROWBEG = DB.BEG
     NEWRATE = DB.RATE
     NEWLIMIT = DB.LIMIT
     IF TX.RATE > 0 THEN NEWRATE = TX.RATE
     IF TX.LIMIT > 0 THEN NEWLIMIT = TX.LIMIT
```

```
            UPDATE RATE.TABLE
            SET DB.RATE =: NEWRATE
                DB.LIMIT =: NEWLIMIT
                WHERE DB.BEG =: ROWBEG
            TXBEG = DB.END+1
            GO TO START
            END
    IF TX.BEG = DB.BEG AND IF TX.END < DB.END
            NEWRATE = DB.RATE
            NEWLIMIT = DB.LIMIT
            IF TX.RATE > 0 THEN NEWRATE = TX.RATE
            IF TX.LIMIT > 0 THEN NEWLIMIT = TX.LIMIT
            UPDATE RATE.TABLE
            SET DB.END =: TX.END
                DB.LIMIT =: NEWLIMIT
                DB.RATE =: NEWRATE
                WHERE DB.BEG =: TX.BEG
            INSERT INTO RATE.TABLE
            VALUES (TX.END+1, DB.END, DB.RATE, DB.LIMIT)
            END
    IF TX.BEG = DB.BEG AND IF TX.END = DB.END THEN DO
            NEWRATE = DB.RATE
            NEWLIMIT = DB.LIMIT
            IF TX.RATE > 0 THEN NEWRATE = TX.RATE
            IF TX.LIMIT > 0 THEN NEWLIMIT = TX.LIMIT
            UPDATE RATE.TABLE
            SET DB.RATE =: NEWRATE
                DB.LIMIT =: NEWLIMIT
                WHERE DB.BEG =: TX.BEG
            END
    IF TX.BEG = DB.BEG AND IF TX.END > DB.END THEN DO;
            NEWRATE = DB.RATE
            NEWLIMIT = DB.LIMIT
            IF TX.RATE > 0 THEN NEWRATE = TX.RATE
            IF TX.LIMIT > 0 THEN NEWLIMIT = TX.LIMIT
            UPDATE RATE.TABLE
            SET DB.RATE =: NEWRATE
                DB.LIMIT =: NEWLIMIT
                WHERE DB.BEG =: TX.BEG
            TX.BEG = DB.END+1
            GO TO START
            END
    IF TX.BEG > DB.BEG THEN IF TX.END < DB.END THEN DO
            ROWBEG = DB.BEG
            UPDATE RATE.TABLE
```

```
            SET DB.END =: TX.BEG-1
            WHERE DB.BEG =: ROWBEG
            NEWRATE = DB.RATE
            NEWLIMIT = DB.LIMIT
            IF TX.RATE > 0 THEN NEWRATE = TX.RATE
            IF TX.LIMIT > 0 THEN NEWLIMIT = TX.LIMIT
            INSERT INTO RATE.TABLE
            VALUES (TX.BEG, TX.END, NEWRATE, NEWLIMIT)
            INSERT INTO RATE.TABLE
            VALUES (TX.END+1, DB.END, DB.RATE, DB.LIMIT)
            END
    IF TX BEG > DB.BEG THEN IF TX.END = DB.END THEN DO
            ROWBEG = DB.BEG
            UPDATE RATE.TABLE
            SET DB.END =: TX.BEG-1
            WHERE DB.END =: ROWBEG
            NEWRATE = DB.RATE
            NEWLIMIT = DB.LIMIT
            IF TX.RATE > 0 THEN NEWRATE = TX.RATE
            IF TX.LIMIT > 0 THEN NEWLIMIT = TX.LIMIT
            INSERT INTO RATE.TABLE
            VALUES (TX.BEG, TX.END, NEWRATE, NEWLIMIT)
            END
    IF TX.BEG > DB.BEG THEN IF TX.END > DB.END THEN DO
            ROWBEG = DB.BEG
            UPDATE RATE.TABLE
            SET DB.END =: TX.BEG-1
            WHERE DB.END =: ROWBEG
            NEWRATE = DB.RATE
            NEWLIMIT = DB.LIMIT
            IF TX.RATE > 0 THEN NEWRATE = TX.RATE
            IF TX.LIMIT > 0 THEN NEWLIMIT = TX.LIMIT
            INSERT INTO RATE.TABLE
            VALUES (TX.BEG, DB.END, NEWRATE, NEWLIMIT)
            TX.BEG = DB.END+1
            GO TO START
            END
```

CHAPTER 20

Strategic Positioning of DB2— High-Performance Systems

DB2 can be used in the high-performance environment (such as that found in banking and financial institutions). Institutions that depend on the ability of a DBMS to process large amounts of data and achieve good, consistent response time can use DB2. However, DB2 MUST be used in the right place and in the right way (as further outlined by this chapter). Failure to use DB2 properly will result in inadequate performance that cannot be addressed by tuning or adding larger, more powerful processors.

HIGH-PERFORMANCE LEVELS

In the banking environment (and, in general, in the high-performance environment), care must be taken in the strategic usage of DB2 (or for any piece of software sensitive to online performance and throughput). If a piece of software running on a powerful processor is asked to exceed its throughput capabilities, all of the choices available to the system manager are painful.

A larger processor can be purchased if one is available that can produce more throughput. But hardware upgrades are expensive and give only a marginal performance boost. Furthermore, if a large, powerful processor is already being used, then no upgrade of processors may be available.

The next option to achieve higher levels of performance is to break the workload onto multiple processors. This is easy to do if

DB2 is processing many different types of applications, such as payroll, inventory control, personnel, bill of materials, etc. But if a single application is being run and is exceeding the capability of the hardware and software, then this option is not applicable.

A third option is to split data running under a single application onto multiple processors. This split can be done only if the applications have prepared for such a split from the outset. Furthermore, certain applications require the processing of a single database—not discrete parts of a database—all at once, and cannot allow data to be split across multiple processors. Fortunately, most banking (and other high-performance applications) do not fall into this classification.

A final option is to scrap the application and the DBMS and move to a more powerful DBMS. The latter choice always involves significant costs and disruptions. It is never a popular choice. As a consequence, the designer must carefully design the system so that the normal processing capabilities of DB2 are not exceeded or, if the normal processing capabilities of DB2 for a single processor are exceeded, then the application can be split over multiple processors into separate workloads.

The normal measurement of software speed running online transactions is in terms of transactions per second. In designing the high-performance environment, careful and constant attention must be paid to the maximum transaction arrival rate (MTAR) that the software will be expected to handle. Once the arrival rate of transactions entering the system begins to exceed the MTAR, the system reaches the "enqueue" position, where transactions are waiting on other transactions to enter the system.

THE BANKING ENVIRONMENT

The data-base designer has completed the conceptual model for the bank and has determined that three subject areas form the backbone of operational processing: an account, customer, and activity subject areas, as shown by the ERD in Figure 20-1.

From the high-level subjects, detailed design follows and tables are created. The key of an account is 20 bytes, the key of a customer is 15 bytes, and the key of an activity is account number concatenated with date and time, where date (Julian date) and time are fixed bin (31,0) and fixed bin (15,0) respectively. Figure 20-2 shows the physical key structure.

The first two digits of account indicate the "region" and "cycle"

Chapter 20   Strategic Positioning of DB2   319

```
        ( CUSTOMER )
( ACTIVITY )————————( ACCOUNT )

    a partial ERD for the
    banking environment
```

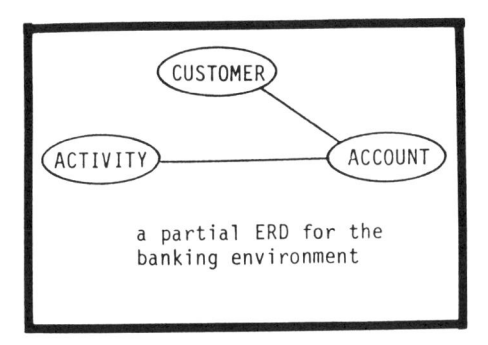

FIGURE 20-1. A partial ERD for the banking environment.

of an account. A region is a geographic locale. Currently, the state being served by the bank is divided into a northern and a southern region (hence, region currently has a maximum value of 2). But, as the number of customers grows and as the bank prepares to expand beyond the geographical boundaries of a single state, it is anticipated that there may be as many as 15 regions (in the largest or maximum growth scenario). The second digit of the key indicates the cycle in which an account is placed. Every account is placed into a cycle as the account is opened. There are 20 cycles indicating when a customer's account will have its statement issued. There are currently, then, 40 separate units into which an account may be placed (i.e., 20 cycles in two regions).

The 20 cycles correspond to the standard statement cycles of the bank. Every cycle/working day (i.e., 20 times per month), the bank processes and sends out the statements for a cycle. In such a fashion, the bank avoids a massive month-end effort for the issuing of statements.

The bank currently has two processing centers, the Northern Center and the Southern Center. The accounts (and, in fact, all data)

```
            KEY STRUCTURES
Account       -    CHAR (20)
Customer      -    CHAR (15)
Activity/Date/Time - CHAR (20)/Bin Fixed (31,0)/Bin Fixed (15,0)
```

FIGURE 20-2. Physical key structure of an account for the banking environment.

are about equally divided over the two centers. All data is domiciled in one or the other center, but not both (i.e., an account is either a Northern or a Southern Center account). The vast preponderance of data and processing is for activities and accounts. Figure 20-3 shows a typical processing profile for a month, in terms of percentage.

HARDWARE CONFIGURATION

The processing configuration of the hardware is shown by Figure 20-4.

ATM (Automated Teller Machines) and teller processing are organized by region (i.e., there are Northern ATM and teller machines and Southern ATM and teller machines). The ATM and teller machines are networked to a centralized processor running IMS Fast Path and IMS Full Function. IMS Fast Path is used for direct teller and ATM processing, while IMS Full Function is used for general purpose processing.

IMS processors in the north and south are interconnected by Multiple Systems Coupling (MSC) link. The MSC link is only used for a very small percentage of activities. Typically less than 1 percent of processing flows over the MSC link. Only when an account holder that is domiciled in the north attempts to process activity in the south is the MSC link used (or vice versa). As the activity enters the system, the key of the account is used to determine if the activity should be processed in another center.

As long as there are only two centers for processing, traffic across the MSC is not burdensome. It is anticipated that, as the bank expands—especially nationally—traffic over the MSC link will expand.

```
Processing Profile
Activities                58%
Accounts -
   Statementing           20%
   Other                  12%
Customer                   8%
Other                      2%
                         100%
```

FIGURE 20–3. Typical processing profile for one month of an account in the banking environment.

```
ATM
ATM
teller ──┐    ┌─ IMS Fast Path/ ─────── DB2
teller ──┘    │  Full Function                Northern Processing
  :   :       │                               Center
              │
              MSC
ATM           │
ATM           │
teller ──┐    │  IMS Fast Path/ ─────── DB2
teller ──┘    └─ Full Function                Southern Processing
ATM                                           Center
  :   :

                    the processing configuration
                    of the high performance banking
                    environment
```

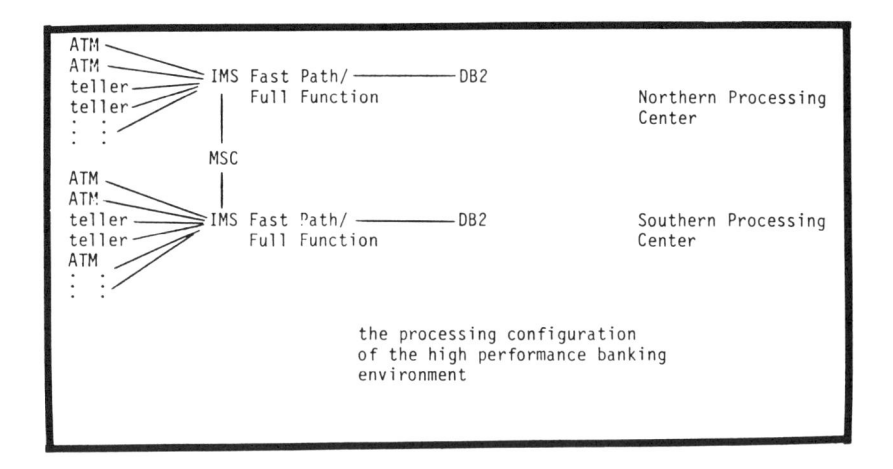

FIGURE 20-4. The processing configuration of the high-performance banking environment.

SYSTEM OF RECORD

Data is organized according to a *system of record* concept. DB2 manages data that is the system of record. The system of record is where the actual customer balance is stored nonredundantly. If there ever is any question as to the accuracy of data, reference can be made to the system of record. When balanced, the system of record contains the accurate value of data, by definition.

In addition to account balance, other data is stored at the DB2 system of record level as well, such as detailed account activity for the last two months, customer data—name, address, age, credit rating and so forth. There is a sparse amount of data stored at the Fast Path level. Only the bare information necessary is stored, and it is refreshed nightly from the system of record after balancing has occurred. Data found at the Fast Path level typically includes: account, balance, related accounts, special posting requirements, and any special handling options that might be applicable.

There is no resident data at the ATM level. ATM requests are serviced directly from the Fast Path processor.

The actual database design at the DB2 level is simple. Tables are connected by foreign keys. The tables are directly derived from the conceptual model. Processing is organized so that any process operates on only a few databases.

Database design for Fast Path is likewise simple. All Fast Path data is stored in a single database segment. Once the I/O is done to retrieve a Fast Path record, the designer is guaranteed that no more I/O need be done. The design and organization of data in the Fast Path environment—not surprisingly—is optimized for performance. In the interest of high performance, data elements that are not necessarily logically related are grouped together.

The denormalization of data in Fast Path for performance overrides the normal database practices associated with normalization. Note, however, that, at the Fast Path level, not many different types of data are affected, and that Fast Path merely holds data in abeyance for rapid access, not data in the system of record.

The IMS processors feed data to DB2, where the system of record resides. DB2 manages the data for accounts, customers, and activities. There are 20 physically separate databases managed by DB2 for activities and accounts, depending upon what cycle an account for an activity is in, as shown by Figure 20-5.

PEAK-PERIOD PROCESSING RATES

Of special interest are the peak-period processing rates for the different components of the system, as shown by Figure 20-6.

Two rates are of interest, rate 1—the ATM to FP rate, and rate 2—the FP to DB2 rate. While there is more than activity processing occurring on a system-wide basis (i.e., customers are opening and closing accounts, customers are changing their place of residence, etc.), the focus in terms of performance centers on activity processing. The normal activity processing includes cashing checks, determining balances, receiving checks, and so forth.

There are two major sources of banking activities: ATMs and tellers. (In the background, run as a steady stream throughout the

```
Northern DB2 databases
Account cycle 1        Activity cycle 1      Customers
Account cycle 2        Activity cycle 2
Account cycle 3        Activity cycle 3
    ⋮                      ⋮
Account cycle 20       Activity cycle 20
```

FIGURE 20–5. Physically separate databases managed by DB2 in the high-performance banking environment.

Chapter 20 Strategic Positioning of DB2 323

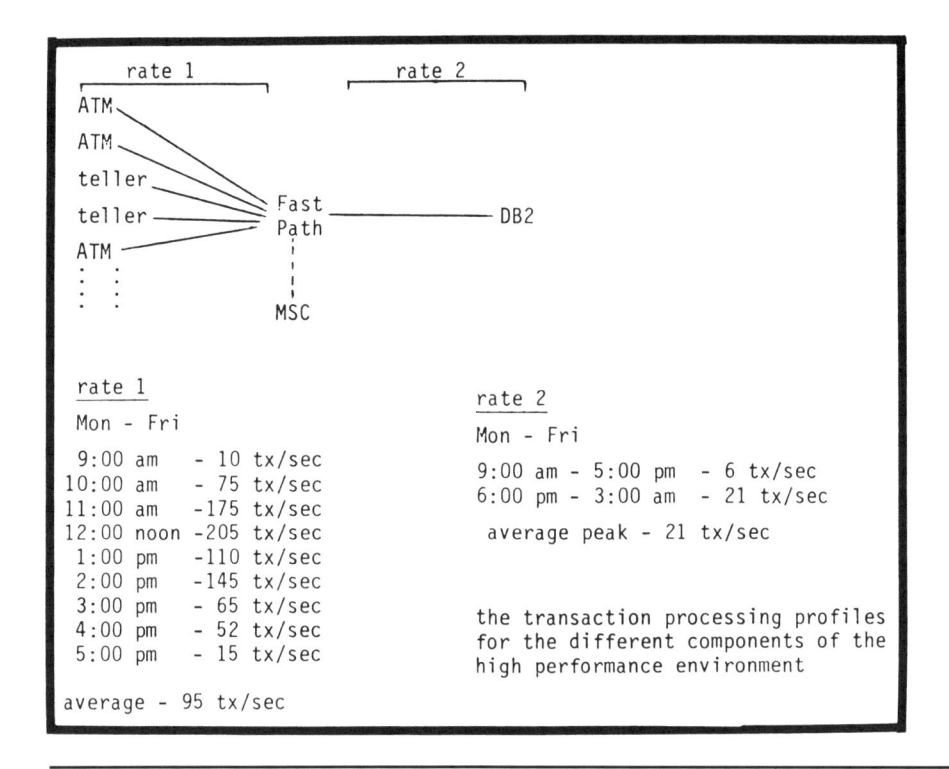

```
       rate 1              rate 2
    ┌─────────┐         ┌─────────┐
   ATM
   ATM
   teller
   teller ──── Fast ──────────── DB2
   ATM  ────── Path
    :  :        │
    :  :        │
              MSC

rate 1                      rate 2
Mon - Fri                   Mon - Fri

 9:00 am   -  10 tx/sec     9:00 am - 5:00 pm -  6 tx/sec
10:00 am   -  75 tx/sec     6:00 pm - 3:00 am - 21 tx/sec
11:00 am   - 175 tx/sec
12:00 noon - 205 tx/sec     average peak - 21 tx/sec
 1:00 pm   - 110 tx/sec
 2:00 pm   - 145 tx/sec
 3:00 pm   -  65 tx/sec
 4:00 pm   -  52 tx/sec     the transaction processing profiles
 5:00 pm   -  15 tx/sec     for the different components of the
                            high performance environment
average - 95 tx/sec
```

FIGURE 20-6. The transaction processing profiles for the different components of the high-performance environment.

24-hour day, the output of the MICR processing, or automated check-clearing processing, is delivered to DB2 for processing, but the stream from MICR is able to be regulated, unlike the stream of activities from ATMs and tellers).

The transaction arrival rate at different points in the system can be determined in several ways, such as—

- if a conversion to DB2 is being done, existing arrival rates may be used;
- if another bank is willing to share its demographic and operational information, the arrival rate can be extrapolated;
- if estimates must be made on other than empirical data, then the following variables (at the least!) must be factored into the estimated arrival rate: the number of customers to be served, the banking habits of the customers, the growth of the population, etc.

In any case, careful attention must be paid to BOTH the total number of transactions to be managed and the peak period transaction rate. The maximum transaction arrival rate is of interest even if the rate peaks sharply and then subsides. The maximum rate achieved causes transactions to enqueue even if the rate is sustained for only a short period of time.

Rate 1 is time-dependent on several factors—the time of day, the day of the month, and, to a small extent, the month of the year. The peak rates are shown in the table. During the evening, there is only a minimal amount of activity throughout the ATM/teller network. The average peak transaction arrival rate is 95 transactions per second with a peak around noon of a little over 200 transactions per second. During a peak day, approximately 3,100,000 transactions will be run.

Each ATM/teller transaction does not, however, result in a recordable activity for the bank. A recordable activity is one that changes the balance of an account in the system of record. One ATM transaction will verify an account's validity. Another ATM transaction will actually cause an account balance to change in the system of record. Still another ATM transaction will close off an ATM session with a card-holder in the case where a session is made up of multiple transactions.

Furthermore, a fair number of ATM transactions will result in no recordable activity at all. An account holder may request a withdrawal of more than the account balance. Another account holder may merely want to verify account balance, and so forth.

In general, every six ATM/teller transactions generate one recordable activity for the system of record that is maintained by DB2.

Rate 2 is for recordable activity only. All recordable activity is processed first from Fast Path to DB2, as all recordable activities are transacted against the system of record. Then, as the balance is adjusted against all daily activities, the balance is returned to Fast Path. The first part of the cycle occurs from 6:00 p.m. until 3:00 a.m. at a peak rate of 21 transactions per second. The second part of the posting cycle occurs from 3:00 a.m. to 5:30 a.m. at a peak transaction rate of 15 transactions per second.

There are, then, about 510,000 activities per day that need to be stored in the system of record. Throughout the day, Fast Path stores the activities for most accounts. (Some accounts are specially marked so that activity posting is done immediately by DB2. When DB2 refreshes data in Fast Path on a nightly basis, one piece of data stored by account is whether immediate posting should be done. The customer may request immediate posting, the account may be marked as a "trouble" account, the account may be a special upscale account, and so forth. However, no more than 2 percent of accounts are marked for immediate posting.) At the end of the business day, the DB2 accounts are posted based upon the stored transactions.

The peak processing time for posting is from 6:00 p.m. until 3:00 a.m. in the morning. During this time, a steady 21 transactions per second are run into DB2. Note that, unlike the ATM/teller processing, where the peak-period rate fluctuated, the Fast Path/DB2 rate does not fluctuate to any large extent. The transactions that flow into DB2 are highly "designed" (were they not "designed," DB2 would not be able to process the workload peaking at 21 transactions per second). Each transaction accesses and updates one row of data—the row where account balance is stored. The set processing of DB2 is severely constrained—i.e., limited to the accessing and processing of one row. Consequently, the physical I/O incurred by each of the transactions being passed from Fast Path/DB2 processing is minimized. Figure 20-7 illustrates the typical ACTIVITY jobs stream processing.

THE BANKING LIFE CYCLE

The full life cycle of a banking activity is shown by Figure 20-8.

In the morning, an ATM customer withdraws $50. The Fast Path database shows a balance of $400 at the time the request for withdrawal is made. The withdrawal is allowed. Since the account is normal and does not require immediate pass-through (i.e., immediate posting), it is held until the close of the business day. In the evening, the $50 is transacted against the DB2 system of record database,

```
                  retrieve account n
                  add/subtract to balance
   typical        replace account n
   activity         :   :   :   :
   processing       :   :   :   :
   in the DB2     retrieve account n+1
   environment    add/subtract to balance
   from the       replace account n+1
   Fast Path        :   :   :   :
   environment      :   :   :   :
```

FIGURE 20–7. Typical activity processing in the DB2 environment from the Fast Path environment.

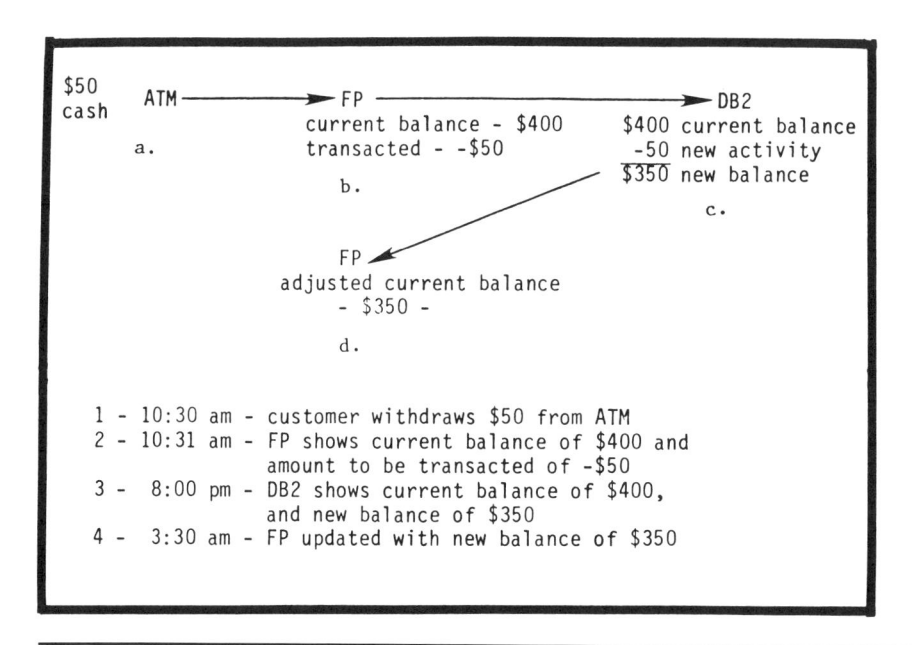

```
$50      ATM ─────────▶ FP ──────────────────▶ DB2
cash                    current balance - $400   $400 current balance
         a.             transacted - -$50        -50  new activity
                        b.                       $350 new balance
                                                              c.

                    FP ◀
                    adjusted current balance
                    - $350 -
                         d.


1 - 10:30 am - customer withdraws $50 from ATM
2 - 10:31 am - FP shows current balance of $400 and
               amount to be transacted of -$50
3 -  8:00 pm - DB2 shows current balance of $400,
               and new balance of $350
4 -  3:30 am - FP updated with new balance of $350
```

FIGURE 20-8. Full life cycle of banking activity.

making the balance in the system of record $350. After all daily transactions are run, the Fast Path databases are updated to reflect the new balances.

During the daytime, the DB2 processor is relatively untaxed, as far as activity run against it is concerned. There are two moderately high-volume activities that occur during the day—post MICR processing and customer statementing. One statement cycle is run each business day. (Actually, once or twice a month, depending on the calendar, holidays, etc., a statement cycle does not have to be run.) The only other major processing during the day occurs against account and customer activities, with the exception of DSS extract processing.

Depending on the workload and the day, some time is made available for DSS processing. The usual flow of activity for DSS processing is for extracts to be run against DB2 databases with the output of the extract being removed to another processing environment, such as the personal computer Lotus 1-2-3 spreadsheet environment. Very rarely does DSS analysis take place on the DB2 processor.

In general, the data flowing from the DB2 environment to the DSS environment flows directly into an atomic DSS database. An atomic DSS database provides a foundation for DSS processing. Atomic databases store more archival data than that normally found in the

DB2 environment and provide a basis for reconciliation of DSS processing when discrepancies occur. Furthermore, since atomic DSS databases are removed from the DSS processor(s), the workload (as far as DSS processing is concerned) on the DB2 processor is alleviated. (For an in-depth discussion of the architecture and the environment of atomic DSS databases, refer to *Information Engineering for the Practitioner*, Yourdon Press, Prentice-Hall, 1987.)

The Fast Path processor is a separate processor from the DB2 processor. The machines are physically separated, as are the databases.

EXTENSIBILITY OF THE ENVIRONMENT

One of the features of the design of the example being described is its extensibility. Should any component of the system become overtaxed with demands for resources, then more resources can be easily added. If an ATM begins to be heavily used, then two ATMs can be installed and attached to the Fast Path network. Should the ATM/teller link begin to reach its capacity, then another processor and another processing center can be installed. (In other words, a central processing center can be added to the northern and southern processing centers if there is need for expanded processing power.)

Should DB2 processing become a bottleneck, DB2 data and processing can be separated onto two (or more) processors. But long-term performance is not the only advantage of separating data by region. Availability of the system is enhanced as well. The multiple small databases that store the system of record provide a high degree of "uptime."

Should one small DB2 database go down and become unavailable, only a fraction of the data of the processing center is affected. Furthermore, restoring a small data base takes less time and effort than restoring a large database. The separation of the DB2 system of record data into small physical units enhances the availability posture of a system. The extreme flexibility and capacity of the configuration described paves the way for long term good, high performance.

The high degree of extensibility of the environment depends on several factors:

- Programs access data based first and generically on region differences (i.e., program code does not specifically code in only N or S, for example).

- The key structure of all databases first accommodates the regional differences of the data.
- ALL types of keys are qualified, either directly or indirectly on region.
- The partitioning of DB2 data is at the physical database level, not at the DB2 partition level.

An anomaly in the above criteria for the example has been developed. While account and activity data are certainly oriented towards the regionality of data, customer data has no such orientation in its key structure.

There are several ways to manage this anomaly. One way is to add an extra byte for regionality in the customer key. Another way is to rely upon the account/customer relationship to position the data accordingly. For example, a customer opens an account in the Northern part of the state. Both a customer record and an account record are established in the northern processing center. But only the key of the account explicitly shows in which center the data is domiciled.

Assuming that most of the processing for that customer will naturally occur in the northern center, when the account/customer linkage or the customer/account linkage needs to be made, then there is no need to cross the MSC path from one processing center to the next. Only during the odd occurrences, when activity first enters the processing network in a processing center other than the one where the data is domiciled (which should be only a small fraction of the time), will there be a need to switch processing from one center to the next.

The actual design of the DB2 tables for customer and account are of interest in that they show how the mid-level data model—the DIS (data item set)—is transformed into a physical database design.

Accounts are divided into four classes: loans, savings, bankcard, and DDA (checking). Loans are further divided into three types: home loans, commercial loans, and other loans. The mid-level for the data model (showing keys and a few representative data elements) looks like Figure 20-9.

KEY STRUCTURES

The underlying key structure of the physical databases are:

ACCOUNT—ABCxxx. . . , A = region, B = cycle number, C = account type

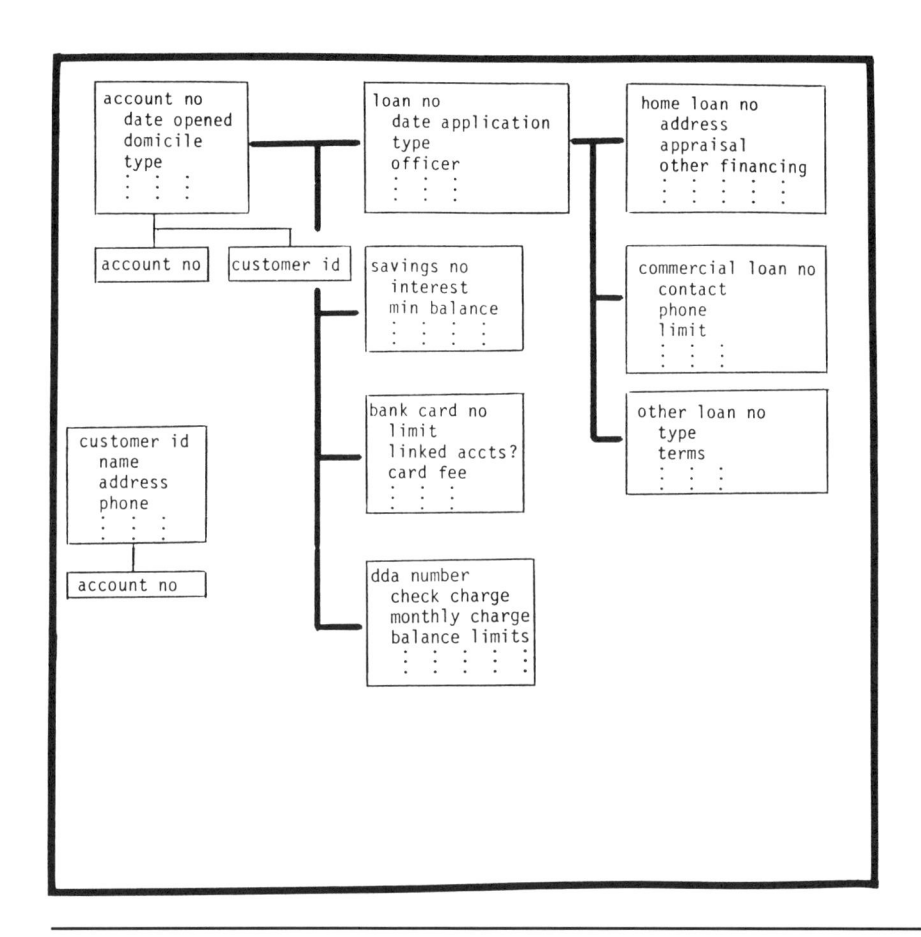

[Diagram showing boxes connected in a data model:
- account no / date opened / domicile / type
- loan no / date application / type / officer
- home loan no / address / appraisal / other financing
- account no
- customer id
- savings no / interest / min balance
- commercial loan no / contact / phone / limit
- customer id / name / address / phone
- bank card no / limit / linked accts? / card fee
- other loan no / type / terms
- account no
- dda number / check charge / monthly charge / balance limits]

FIGURE 20-9. The mid-level data model for customer and accounts in the banking environment (showing keys and some data elements).

LOAN ACCOUNT—ABCDxxx..., D = "L" signifying loan

HOME LOAN ACCOUNT—ABCDExxx..., E = "H" signifying home loan

COMMERCIAL LOAN ACCOUNT—ABCDExxx..., E = "C" signifying commercial loan account

OTHER LOAN ACCOUNT—ABCDExxx..., E = "O" signifying other loan account

SAVINGS ACCOUNT—ABCDxxx..., D = "S" signifying savings account

DDA ACCOUNT—ABCDxxx. . . , D = "D" signifying DDA account

BANKCARD ACCOUNT—ABCDxxx. . . , D = "B" signifying bankcard account

Using the DIS as a basis for physical design, the following DB2 tables are created, as shown in Figure 20-10.

Note that even though "account number" is the key for the vast majority of the tables shown, the contents of the tables are mutually

associate account table
- account no
- account no

account base table
- account no
- date opened
- domicile
- type
- ⋮

account/customer xref table
- account no
- customer id

loan table
- account no
- date application
- type
- officer
- ⋮

home loan table
- account no
- address
- appraisal
- other financing
- ⋮

savings table
- account no
- interest
- min balance
- ⋮

bankcard table
- account no
- limit
- linked account?
- card fee
- ⋮

commercial loan table
- account no
- contact
- phone
- limit
- ⋮

other loan table
- account no
- type
- terms
- ⋮

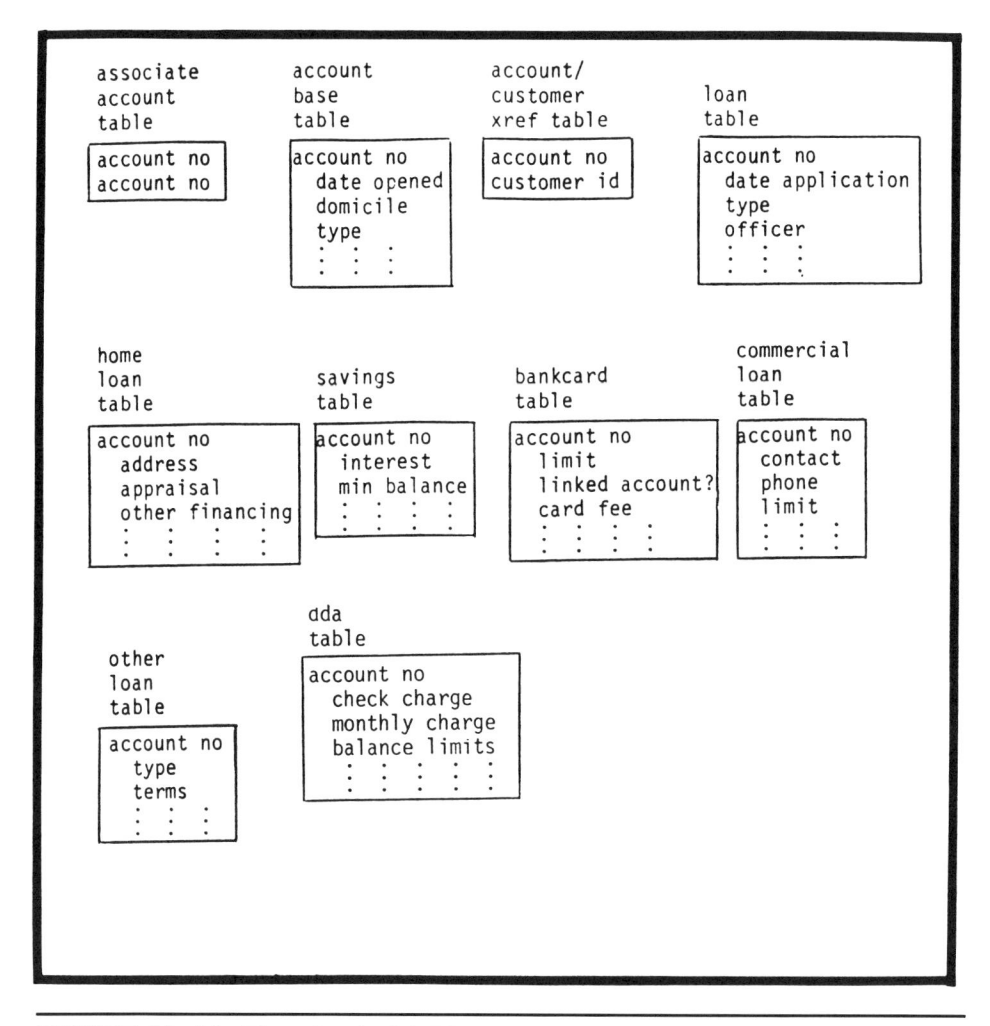

dda table
- account no
- check charge
- monthly charge
- balance limits
- ⋮

FIGURE 20–10. The physical DB2 tables that have been derived from the mid-level data model.

exclusive. Also note that the existence of the nonkey data depends directly on the existence of the type of key with which the data element is grouped.

From a performance perspective, it may make sense to group two or more tables together. But the frequency of access of each of the tables shown will be such that denormalization will buy very little. The data, once created, is not often deleted, changed, or accessed (relative to other data.) Consequently, denormalization does not apply to these tables.

DENORMALIZATION OF HIGH-PERFORMANCE DATA

There is a place where the techniques of denormalization do apply, however. Consider the field "balance." Every recordable activity will change the balance. On a nightly basis, it is likely that each balance will be changed (or a large percentage of the balances will have had at least one recordable activity transacted against them during the day).

One design technique to handle balance processing (which has a very different set of processing and access criteria than other logically related account fields) is to create a special table(s) for balance. Figure 20-10 shows two tables used for high-performance balance processing.

One table shows the balance table. There are only three fields in the balance table—account number (the key), balance, and conditions count. The other high-performance table contains variable-length rows and three data elements—account number (the higher portion of the key), condition count (the lower portion of the key), and condition description. Most accounts do not have any conditions, and their condition count equals zero. But when an account has unusual conditions, such as stop payment processing, immediate posting, special overdraft protection, etc., the conditions are described in the second table.

On a nightly basis, the balance data is accessed and the balance is modified accordingly. No reference is made to condition as long as condition count is not zero. When condition count is not zero, then another access may need to be made to the condition table. In short, the nightly processing against account is brief and unencumbered by excessive I/O.

Furthermore, because of the small size of each entry in the balance table, many balance rows can be stored in a block. The tight packing of data increases the probability of a buffer hit, especially when the recordable activities can be preprocessed and sorted prior to nightly balance processing.

Note that the design of the high-performance tables broke many of the rules of normalization. The need for high performance was greater than the need to adhere to the logical design practices.

SUMMARY

DB2 can be used in the high-performance environment if DB2 is properly positioned. The system architect needs to be especially sensitive to the maximum transaction arrival rate, ensuring that the enqueue condition is not reached.

In addition, the database designer can prepare for future growth by ensuring that data can be split at the application level. Once data can be split at the application level, the processing workload can be split across multiple machines.

There are two ways data can be split: at the application level and at the system level (by the partitioning of data). Each technique has its advantages and disadvantages. However, if a default option needs to be chosen, the default of splitting datas as the application level should be chosen.

The arrival rate of transactions coming into DB2 depends heavily on whether the transactions are "designed" or not. Undesigned transactions reduce DB2's maximum transaction arrival potential severely.

The splitting of data enhances not only performance but availability as well.

Glossary

1:n relationship. A relationship where a single component can relate to multiple other components.

ABEND. The abnormal termination of a program.

Archival. The storage of data (usually in bulk) for unknown future needs.

Arrays in a row. Multiple occurrences of the same field in a row.

Atomic database. The most granular data that is stored; used as a basis for DSS processing; each unit of atomic data is related to some moment in time; the atomic data is fed from operational or external data and feeds departmental data.

Audit. The verification of the accuracy of measurement of events.

Audit table. A table holding transaction audit trails.

Availability. The amount of time the system is up and running versus the amount of time the system ought to be up and running. Availability is a function of *all* the components in a system—hardware, software, application, database, etc.

"Average day" profile. The statistical profile of the database and TP parameters during a nonpeak day.

Batch processing. Long sequential processes, such as reports, merges, sorts, table scans, joins, etc.

Batch window. The time frame in which batch processing can be done. The nature of batch processing is such that it cannot be done in conjunction with online processing; usually, the batch window is during off hours; then there is little or no online processing to be done.

Bill of material. A manufacturing structure describing the assembly of products.

BTS. Batch terminal simulation; a software product for TSO execution of IMS database and TP calls.

Business transaction. A business-related unit of work. The logical limitations of a business transaction are determined by the work being done; in general, a business transaction is made up of one or more computer transactions.

Centralization. The configuration of processors in which all processors are centrally located and are usually tightly coupled.

Checkpointing. The process of periodically "freezing" a program so that backup can be done. A checkpoint prevents a process from needing to be completely rerun; processing may be restarted from the latest checkpoint.

CICS. A standard teleprocessor (TP) monitoring package that interfaces to many database packages.

Clustering. The processing of physically grouping rows in a table according to the values of a common column or columns.

COBOL. A common programming language oriented toward business use of the computer.

Code reuse. The practice of reusing code rather than writing code from scratch.

Column. A "field" in a table.

Computer transaction. A transaction as perceived by the computer. Every time a transaction goes through the queue and is entered into the computer, it is a computer transaction; a computer transaction is delimited by the hitting of the ENTER key or the PF key.

Continuous data. Time-variant data valid over a continuum of time.

Control database. A table containing non-application-oriented data such as terminal, security, audit data, and so forth.

Conversational processing. The mode of processing where multiple computer transactions are logically linked together by system software to form a single business transaction.

Conversion. The process of transforming data and processes from one environment into another environment.

CPU. Central processing unit; the computer.

Cross-reference table. The table needed to manage an m:n relationship.

CSP. Cross-system product.

Cursor stability. The facility of DB2 that allows data to be examined a row at a time and allows the data to be changed during the unit of recovery.

DASD. Disk storage; direct access storage.

Data administration. The organizational unit charged with looking after data as a corporate resource.

Database. The highest unit of storage of data in DB2; a database consists of one or more tablespaces.

Data dictionary. The repositioning of meta data. Typically included in the data dictionary are data layouts, control block specifications, data modeling documentation, definitions of data elements, and so forth.

Data independence. The property of data relating to a program. When data is independent of a program, the data can be changed without changing the program.

Data lock. The control of access and update of data at the page and tablespace level by DB2; the control of data to prevent more than one online user from overwriting the legitimate change of another online user.

Data model. The result of synthesis, collection, and abstraction of user requirements, focusing on the data.

DBEDIT. A utility for the quick construction of DB2 tables.

Debugging. The process of removing errors from hardware and/or software.

Decentralization. The configuration of processors in which the processors are geographically dispersed and are loosely coupled.

Derived data. Data that relates to multiple customers and/or multiple events. In general, derived data is summarized or otherwise refined; derived data has as its basis primitive data; derived data is usually used in DSS processing.

Development methodology. Procedures for development which include deliverables, schedules, order of development.

Downtime. The length of time a system is not available when, in fact, it should be available.

DROP. The DB2 activity of deallocating a table.

DSS. Decision Support Systems. DSS is typified by summarized data which is used to manage the organization.

Encryption/decryption. The algorithmic scrambling/ unscrambling of data for the purpose of protection.

End user. The ultimate user of the system being reviewed.

ENTER key. The key on the keyboard that, when depressed, causes a transaction to be submitted.

Entity. The highest abstraction of data; a paradigm about which information in needed.

Event discrete data. Time-variant data valid as of the passing of some event.

EXPLAIN function. A facility of DB2 that allows the programmer to see what options for execution DB2 has chosen.

Explosion. The traversal of a recursive structure from the top of the structure to the bottom of the structure, including all components that are one part of the manufacturing process of the highest level of recession.

External response time. The length of time from the moment when the transaction is sent from the originating terminal until the first of the output is sent to the receiving terminal. External response time includes both computer and data transmission time.

"Fire drill." The practice of recovering or reorganizing data when there is no real need (i.e., for practice). Operations learns how to execute recovery/reorganization utilities in a fire drill without the pressure of doing it live.

Flat arrival rate. The arrival rate that is achieved when all transactions arrive at a constant rate. In practice, the flat arrival rate is seldom if ever achieved; instead, it is a good theoretical baseline for online processing.

Foreign key. A field that allows two or more tables to be related.

FORTRAN. A common programming language.

FREEPAGE. The parameter that indicates what percent of each page is to be left free during the load process.

Generalized recursive structure. A recursive structure with a single definition of base data and multiple occurrences of "into" and "where from" positions.

GETPAGE. The DB2 operation of logically retrieving data. A GETPAGE can operate against data in the buffer area or data stored on DASD.

I/O. Input/Output operation; the activity done to put data into the computer or take data out of the computer. An I/O operates in terms of mechanical speeds that are significantly slower than the computer, which operates in terms of electronic speeds.

Image copy. The system activity of backing up data to some moment in time; at some moment in time, the contents of a table are "frozen," a snapshot is taken.

Implosion. The traversal of a recursive structure from the bottom of the structure to the top of the structure; the reverse of an explosion.

IMS (also IMS/DC). A standard teleprocessing/database package.

Index. A data structure allowing direct entry into a table based upon a key value found in the index.

Interactive processing. A mode of processing combining some aspects of online processing and some aspects of batch processing.

Interleaving. The application facility of placing data from different rows into the same page based on like key values.

Glossary

Internal response time. The amount of time from when a transaction first enters the computer until the transaction leaves the computer. Internal response time does not include data communications transmission time.

Join. The merging of two or more tables based on the value of one or more common columns.

Key. A data element that uniquely identifies a grouping of data elements.

Language. The medium in which programs are written, such as COBOL, PL-1, etc.

Line time. The length of time from the computer to the terminal or vice versa.

LOTUS 1-2-3. A popular spreadsheet software package.

m:n relationship. A relationship between two components that can be multivalued in either direction.

Mean. The statistical average.

Memory. Main storage.

MTAR (maximum transaction arrival rate). The peak rate of arrival of transactions at the computer.

Normalized table. A grouping of data in which the nonkey data elements depend logically for their existence on the key of the grouping of data.

NULL. The design option that allows a field to contain a null value.

NUMLKTS. A parameter that determines when page-locking escalates to tablespace-locking based on total number of pages per table that are locked.

NUMLKUS. A parameter that determines when page-locking escalates to tablespace-locking based on total number of pages across all tables.

Online. The environment in which data can be accessed/changed directly by the user. The online environment is usually characterized by terminal access to data.

Parallel batch runs. Multiple batch runs that can be run independently, either on the same machine or on separate machines.

Partitioned table. The organization of rows where rows are physically subdivided into separate tables.

PCTFREE. The parameter specifying what percentage of free space will be left during the load process.

Peak period. The moment in time at which the processing load is the heaviest. The peak period can be measured hourly, daily, weekly, monthly, or annually, or all of the above.

Performance. In the online environment— response time; in the batch environment—throughput. Performance is measured in terms of average performance and performance at peak periods.

Periodic discrete data. Time-variant data valid as of the periodic passing of time (i.e., hourly, daily, weekly, etc.).

Personal computer. A processor designed for individual access and manipulation of data.

PF (program function) key. A specially designated key that, when depressed, causes a transaction to be submitted; the submitted transaction is specially designed to be instigated by the PF key.

PL-1. A common programming language.

Primitive data. Detailed data used to run the day-to-day operations of the organization. Primitive data is data that relates to a single customer or a single event.

Processor. A computer.

Production systems. Typified by up-to-the-second, accurate, detailed data that is used to run the day-to-day operations of the organization.

Programming specifications. Instructions given to the programmer directing the programmer how to proceed to write code.

Prototyping. The building of a "shell" or scaled-down system.

Pseudo-conversational processing. The mode of processing where multiple computer transactions are logically linked together by application software.

Purging data. The physical removal of data from the system.

QMF. Query Management Facility. Software designed for unstructured end-user access to DB2 data. QMF runs in TSO only.

Query language. A language where the primary purpose is the selection and display of data from a database.

Read-only tables. Tables to which no update can be done once the tables are initialized.

READPAGE. The DB2 operation of physically retrieving data. A READPAGE occurs when data on DASD must be entered into the buffer area.

Recorder. The person in the design review responsible for taking notes. The recorder filters the conversations that are held during design review, removing extraneous information.

Recovery. The process of restoring data upon the occurrence of an error.

Recursive structure. A structure with an internal relationship.

Redundancy of data. The storage of the same data in multiple places.

Reorganization. The process of taking existing data and physically placing the data and its indexes in an optimal order.

Repeatable read. The facility of DB2 that allows data to be examined during a unit of recovery with no possibility of change during the unit of recovery.

Row. A single instance of a group of columns; an occurrence of data within a table; a tuple.

Scans. The sequential reading of a table.

Security table. A table whose purpose is the control of security.

Service level agreement. A covenant between the end user and the data processing department that specifies the response time once the system is in full operation.

Set processing. The access of data based on generic search criteria, where any number of occurrences of data may satisfy the criteria.

Simple table. The most basic organization of rows of data in DB2.

Software protocol. The format and structure of data in data communications that is required for one processor to communicate with another processor.

Sparse index. An index built at the application level containing only selected entries.

SQL calls. The calls issued to DB2 in an SQL format.

SQL. Structured Query Language, the DML of DB2.

SQLCA. SQL communications area.

Standard deviation. The statistical measurement of the deviation from the mean.

Static data. Time-variant data that has no moment in time associated with its validity.

System of record. The officially designated source of data; when data is stored redundantly there is a system of record. The system of record specifies one occurrence of data as the source. All other redundant copies of the data flow from the source. If there ever is a difference of opinion as to the values that are redundantly stored, the system of record is considered to be the authoritative source.

System software. Software needed to make the computer and its accessories run. System software is distinct from application software.

Table. A grouping of homogeneous data. A table is populated by rows of data; the contents of the rows are defined into columns.

Tablespace. One of the units of storage of data in DB2. A tablespace consists of one or more tables.

Terminal table. A table used for controlling terminal access to data.

Test environment. The computer facilities—hardware and software—designated for debugging application code.

Time-variant data. Data elements, each of which has a moment in time associated with it.

TP monitor (teleprocessing monitor). A piece of system software designed to interface the teleprocessing network to the operating system and the database management system.

Transaction. A unit of work done against one or more databases. These are business transactions and computer transactions.

Transaction arrival rate. The speed at which transactions arrive at the computer for processing.

Unique index. An index in which each value is unique.

User-view session. An interview of users in which the user expresses requirements.

Utility. A system program used to support a function such as backup, recovery, reorganization, etc.

Variable-length field. A field whose length can vary from one row to the next.

VIEW. The definition of one or more columns in one or more tables.

References

Astrahan, M., et al. (1979). System R: Relational Approach to Database Management. IEEE Computer Society: *Computer* 12(5).

Chen, P. (1977). *The Entity-Relationship Approach to Logical Data Base Design*, Data Base Monograph Series N (6). Wellesley, Mass.: QED Information Sciences Inc.

Codd EF, "Normalized Data Base Structures: A Brief Tutorial", *Proc 1971 ACM SIGFIDET Workshop on Data Description, Access and Control*

Date CJ, *AN INTRODUCTION TO DATA BASE SYSTEMS*, Addison-Wesley, Reading Ma 1974

Fagin, R. Normal Forms and Relational Database Operators, *Proc 1979 ACM SIGMOD International Conference on Management of Data*

IBM Manual, *Database 2 Application Programming Guides* (TSO—SC26-4081, IMS—SC26-4079, CICS—SC26-4080)

IBM Manual, *Database 2 Concepts and Facilities*, GC24-1582

IBM Manual, *Database 2 Data Base Planning and Administration Guide*, SC26-4077

IBM Manual, *Database 2 General Information*, GC26-4073

IBM Manual, *Database 2 General Information Guide*, GH24-5013

IBM Manual, *Database 2 Guide to Publications*, GC26-4111

IBM Manual, *Database 2 Installation*, SC26-4084

IBM Manual, *Database 2 Introduction to SQL*, GC26-4082

IBM Manual, *Database 2 Operation and Recovery Guide*, SC26-4083

IBM Manual, *Database 2 Performance and Tuning Guide*, GC24-1600

IBM Manual, *Database 2 Reference*, SC26-4078

IBM Manual, *Database 2 Reference Summary*, SX26-3740

IBM Manual, *Database 2 Sample Application Guide*, SC26-4113

IBM Manual, *Database 2 System Monitoring and Tuning Guide*, GG24-3005

IBM Manual, *Database 2 System Planning and Administration Guide*, SC26-4085

IBM Systems Journal Vol 23 No 2, 1984, G321-0076, "IBM Database 2 Performance: Design, Implementation and Tuning", JM Cheng, CR Looseley, A Shibayima, PS Worthington

Inmon, WH, INFORMATION ENGINEERING FOR THE PRACTITIONER, Yourdon Press, NY NY 1987

Inmon, WH, INFORMATION SYSTEMS ARCHITECTURE, Prentice-Hall, Englewood Cliffs, NJ 1986

Inmon, WH and Bird, TJ, DYNAMICS OF DATA BASE, Prentice-Hall, Englewood Cliffs, NJ 1986

Inmon, WH, EFFECTIVE DATA BASE DESIGN, Prentice-Hall, Englewood Cliffs, NJ 1980

Inmon, WH, "What Price Relational?", In-Depth, ComputerWorld, Nov 1984

James, M and Won, B, "Performance Management of Relational Database Systems", INFOIMS, Third Quarter 1983

James, M and Won, B, "Performance Management of Relational Database Systems—Part 2", INFOIMS, Fourth Quarter 1983

Kroenke, D, DATABASE PROCESSING: FUNDAMENTALS, MODELING, APPLICATIONS, Science Research Associates, Palo Alto, Ca 1977

Looseley, C, "Resource management in IBM DB2", Guide 65—Chicago—Illinios July 1986

Looseley, C, "Measuring IBM Database 2 Release 2", INFODB Vol 1 Number 2 1986

Martin, J COMPUTER DATA-BASE ORGANIZATION, Prentice-Hall, Englewood Cliffs NJ 1975

Perkinson, R, DATA ANALYSIS—THE KEY TO DATA BASE DESIGN, QED Information Sciences, Inc Wellesley Mass 1985

White, C, "DB2 Application Development: The Design Phase—Part 1", INFOIMS, First Quarter 1984

White, C, "DB2 Application Development: The Design Phase—Part 2", INFOIMS, Second Quarter 1984

Wiederhold, G, DATABASE DESIGN, McGraw-Hill, NY NY 1977

Zloof, M, "Operations on Hierarchical Data Bases", Proc NCC 45 1976

Answers

CHAPTER 1: THE DB2 ENVIRONMENT

1. The online mode, the interactive mode, the batch mode.
2. The online mode.
3. The interactive mode.
4. The batch mode.
5. All three modes.
6. The online, production mode.
7. Not really.
8. No.
9. Availability, accuracy of data, access of data across a large network, low level of detail of data.
10. The length of time from the initiation of a transaction until the output of the transaction reaches the output destination.
11. The input terminal, the communication line, the transaction queue, the transaction scheduler, the processor, the data bases, the buffer areas.
12. Peak period.
13. ACP (TPF), CICS, IMS/DC.
14. VM/CMS TSO.
15. Very important.

16. TSO.
17. IMS/DC CICS.
18. DXT.
19. PL1, FORTRAN.
20. Locking facility.
21. Tablespace, page, index, database, plan.
22. Read only, update.
23. BIND.
24. Commit, deallocation, unlock.
25. Tightly.
26. Can.
27. Field.
28. Rows.
29. Many.
30. Fixed length, no nulls allowed.
    Fixed length, null values allowed.
    Variable length, no null values allowed.
    Variable length, null values allowed.
31. Prefix.
32. Tuple.
33. Can.
34. One.
35. Pages.
36. Is.
37. Cannot.
38. 4k byte buffers, 32k byte buffers.
39. Zero.
40. Can.
41. Can.
42. False.
43. Reusable.
44. Tables, tablespaces.
45. Simple tablespaces, partitioned tablespaces.
46. Small tables, highly interrelated tables.

47. Large tables.
48. 64.
49. Randomly, sequentially.
50. Clustered.
51. Nonclustered.
52. Index.
53. One.
54. Three.
55. The root page level, the intermediate page level, the leaf page level.
56. Do not.
57. Leaf.
58. Page/entry.
59. Page.
60. Page prefix.
61. Allows.
62. Foreign keys.
63. Like value, common field.
64. Cannot.
65. Application programs.
66. Establishing the relationship, traversing the relationship.
67. Short running.
68. Long running.
69. Separation.
70. Do not.
71. Damage.
72. c or d.
73. a or c.
74. Will not.
75. Will not.
76. will not.
77. c. Precompiled only.
78. Will not.
79. Will not.

80. Will not.
81. Batch.
82. May.
83. Extend the batch window, preempting online processing.
84. Not do all the necessary processing.
85. Does.

CHAPTER 2: LOGICAL TO PHYSICAL DESIGN

1. Normalization.
2. Keys; elements.
3. Existence.
4. Is not.
5. Is.
6. Many.
7. Few.
8. Logical.
9. No.
10. A loss of.
11. Physical attributes.
12. CHAR (10); PIC '999'; DEC FIXED (15,2).
13. Process.
14. Sequencing of process; algorithms; merging of data; sorting of data.
15. SDM70; METHOD1; STRADIS.
16. Any answer.
17. Dynamically.
18. Set-at-a-time.
19. Resource.
20. Performance; availability.
21. True.
22. 10.
23. 24.
24. A.

Answers

25. 25.
26. 4.
27. 25.
28. 4.
29. Is not.
30. Is not.
31. Transaction.
32. Low level.
33. Physical.
34. Program.
35. Many.
36. Primary key; key.
37. Are not.
38. Is.
39. Usually.
40. Sometimes.
41. Can be.
42. First.
43. Separated.
44. WFI.
45. Requiring much time for loading; requiring much time for maintenance.
46. Tables.
47. Production; operational.
48. Decision support; end-user computing.
49. Does not.
50. Static.
51. Dynamic.
52. Less total resources are required; the primitive environment can be optimized for its patter of utilization and the derived environment can be optimized for its pattern of utilization.
53. I/O.
54. Does not.
55. 2 or more.

348 Answers

56. Redundancy; multiple copies.
57. Less.
58. True.
59. False.
60. Good.
61. Is.
62. Is.
63. Can.
64. Recover; reorganize.
65. Longer.
66. Does not affect.
67. Geographical boundaries; functional boundaries; by arbitrary key range.
68. Enhances.
69. Small; short.
70. By function; by limited accesses of data; by key range within transaction.
71. Enqueue.
72. Terminal database; audit database; security database.
73. Waits; is enqueued.
74. Establish a thread; initialize a thread.
75. Used often; popular; frequently executed.
76. Machines; processors.
77. True.
78. Higher.

CHAPTER 3: DB2 PERFORMANCE 1

1. Conceptual database design, logical database design.
2. Normalization, entity relationships (diagrams) (ERDS), data item sets (DIS), data modeling.
3. Identification of number of elements, volatility of data, growth patterns, system response time, estimation of peak workload, overnight batch window requirements, identification of monthly or annual requirements, creation/migration/conversion plans, system availability requirements.

Answers

4. Grouping.
5. Relational.
6. Key.
7. Removed.
8. Direct.
9. Relationships.
10. Rows, tables, tuples, tablespaces.
11. Many.
12. I/O, overhead, work.
13. Denormalized.
14. Does not necessarily introduce.
15. b. Often.
16. Enqueue.
17. Access.
18. Directly.
19. Sequentially.
20. Small.
21. Large.
22. 2.
23. Clustered.
24. 1.
25. Page.
26. Zero.
27. References, index entries, index references.
28. Maintenance.
29. Index.
30. Many.

CHAPTER 4: DB2 PERFORMANCE 2

1. Referential integrity.
2. Application, application programmer.
3. May.
4. False.

5. Batch.
6. Reorganization.
7. Recovery.
8. Reducing.
9. Does not necessarily.
10. Enhances.
11. True.
12. Removal.
13. Key.
14. Geography, random values, line of business, marketing classifications, many other ways.
15. Only a few.
16. Many, all, most.
17. Index.
18. 1.
19. Should not.
20. Will.
21. Are always.
22. Both are correct.
23. True.
24. True.
25. Fewer.
26. Saved.
27. Physical block size, block size—number of occurrences of data—pattern of access; access pattern—pattern of insertions/deletions.
28. False.
29. Unknown.
30. May not.
31. Single-record searches, massive manipulation.
32. Much.
33. Lowest.
34. Slower.

Answers

CHAPTER 5: DB2 PERFORMANCE 3

1. Variable-length field.
2. Are not.
3. True.
4. Is not.
5. Wasted.
6. Often.
7. Will help but not solve.
8. PCTFREE.
9. Page.
10. Control.
11. Terminal, security, audit, tables, variables.
12. Enqueue, enqueuing, locking, deadlock, deadly embrace.
13. Update.
14. True.
15. c. Sometimes applicable.
16. True.
17. May.
18. One.
19. True.
20. b. May be.
21. Recovery; reorganization.
22. Recovered.

CHAPTER 6: DB2 PERFORMANCE 4

1. True.
2. Internal cleanliness of data, changing index structure, changing row structure.
3. Unavailable.
4. Longer.
5. Should be.
6. Partitioning.
7. System; application.

352 Answers

8. Some.
9. Will not.
10. May cost or may save.
11. Symbolic; representative.
12. True.
13. Saves, prevents, minimizes.
14. Usage of data, size of data, variability of data size, many answers.

CHAPTER 7: DB2 TRANSACTION DESIGN FOR PERFORMANCE: PART 1

1. Establishment.
2. Are not.
3. Both.
4. Does not modify.
5. True.
6. May not.
7. a. Will never be allowed to run during peak hours.
8. Enqueue.
9. Enqueued.
10. Much larger.
11. b. I/Os.
12. Electronic.
13. Milli.
14. Nano.
15. True.
16. Is.
17. Is.
18. Is not.
19. Recognized.
20. Late.
21. Batch.
22. Unfriendly.
23. Buffers; data; network; internal protection; etc.
24. Data.

CHAPTER 8: DB2 TRANSACTION DESIGN FOR PERFORMANCE: PART 2

1. Operates; executes; runs; etc.
2. b. Very, very difficult.
3. Excessive; large; huge; monstrous; not worth it; etc.
4. Designed.
5. Undesigned.
6. Small; limited; etc.
7. True.
8. Function; purpose; use.
9. "Iterate"; repeat.
10. False.
11. True.
12. True.
13. True.
14. False.
15. False.
16. False.
17. True.
18. True.
19. True.
20. False.
21. True.

CHAPTER 9: DATA STRUCTURES AND DATA RELATIONSHIPS

1. Tables; indexes.
2. Simple; partitioned.
3. Multiple.
4. Clustered.
5. Application.
6. Field; element; key.
7. More.

8. SQL.
9. Index.
10. Scan; search.
11. Scan; search.
12. Cross.
13. Often.
14. True.
15. True.
16. May.
17. Intersection.
18. Both.
19. Inefficient; slow; awkward.
20. Places; locations; addresses.
21. Is not.
22. Application.
23. Only a few.
24. True.
25. Secondary.
26. A few.
27. False.
28. Named; defined; identified; declared.
29. Is not.
30. Stack.
31. Pointer; stack pointer; top of the stack.
32. Can.
33. Key; field; element.
34. Normalization; data analysis; data modeling.
35. Key.
36. May not.
37. Must.
38. c. Availability and performance are usually enhanced.
39. Itself.
40. The bill of material; the organization chart; the family tree.
41. Peer, hierarchical.

CHAPTER 10: REFERENTIAL INTEGRITY

1. Programmer; application; application program.
2. Foreign.
3. Cross-reference.
4. Causes.
5. Is incidental to.
6. True.
7. Occasional; little.
8. Many.
9. Can be.
10. Cannot be.
11. Integrity.
12. Batch.
13. May.
14. Enhancing; saving.
15. Conventions; techniques; controls.
16. Independent; external; outside.
17. False.
18. Design, programming, operating.
19. Infrequently.
20. Large.
21. Complexity.

CHAPTER 11: THE DB2 BATCH ENVIRONMENT

1. Batch.
2. Batch.
3. Always.
4. True.
5. True.
6. Substantially.
7. The entire batch environment.
8. True.

9. Some.
10. The same.
11. Utilities, batched updates, extracts, system software, undesigned transactions.
12. False.
13. Often.
14. Sorted.
15. Is not.
16. Separate, different, unique, etc.
17. Extract.
18. Individual.
19. Single.
20. Extra runs, more extracts, etc.
21. a. Can save unexpected processing.
22. Must.
23. Usually.
24. Prioritized.
25. Month; year.
26. True.

CHAPTER 12: THE DB2 TEST ENVIRONMENT

1. Is.
2. More.
3. Coding, logic, algorithms, resource consumption, performance.
4. False.
5. New, existing.
6. Input used to drive the test environment, databases on which testing is done, configuration of the TP monitor and DBMS.
7. Must.
8. Stress.
9. ALL.
10. Bringing down, killing, ABENDing.
11. Interrelationships, relationships.

Answers

12. Small.
13. Reinitialized.
14. Are not.
15. All (a,b,c,d,e).
16. May.
17. Execute the test input against live data.
18. Created.
19. 10 percent.
20. "Hot spots," bottlenecks.
21. True.
22. 25 percent.
23. False.
24. I/O, database calls.
25. Set-at-a-time.
26. Variable, volatile.
27. Total, complete.
28. GETPAGES.
29. READPAGES.
30. Buffer, main memory.
31. Teleprocessing monitor, database management system.
32. Display.
33. MVS console, DB2I, DSN processor.
34. Response time, queue lengths, arrival rates.
35. Should.
36. All (a,b,c,d,e).
37. 10 percent, 1/10th.
38. May.
39. Shutdown.
40. Joins.
41. Arithmetically.
42. Generate, issue, create.
43. TPNS; SURF.
44. TSO.
45. BTS.

358   Answers

46. Useful.
47. Unusual.
48. Damaging, disturbing, harming.
49. Two.
50. Preliminary.
51. Program logic, the first few tests run.
52. Reinitialized.
53. 10 percent.
54. One full set.
55. Is not.
56. May not.
57. Set.
58. 30–45.
59. Should.
60. Maximum.
61. Preliminary.
62. True.
63. Larger, community.
64. Many, lots of.
65. Test log.
66. Date of test, who conducted test, what data was altered.
67. Creating tables; granting, revoking authority; creating restore utilities; monitor size, usage of test data; moving table definitions from test to production; monitoring, administering naming conventions.

CHAPTER 12: TESTING PROGRAMS IN DB2

1. Does.
2. Know, predetermine.
3. Reset, reinitialize.
4. Database administrator, project manager.
5. Many, multiple, more than one.
6. Driver.

Answers 359

7. May.
8. Remove, takeout, disable.
9. Flow, sequence.
10. BTS traces, dumps of test databases, screen transmissions, reports, memory dumps.
11. Paths.
12. True.
13. Should.
14. True.
15. Force.
16. False.
17. Repeatable read.
18. Delete, inserts, update.
19. True.
20. Range, edit range.
21. Referential integrity.
22. True.
23. False (This may or may not be true).
24. Independent.
25. The same.
26. I/O Module.
27. Error module.
28. Simulated.
29. Foreign key; referential integrity.
30. Recursive.
31. May be able.
32. May not.
33. False.
34. Precompiler; compiler; dumps; BIND process; source listing; JCL listing; application program output; database management system/TP monitor output; BTS.
35. Stress.
36. Full.
37. Multiple; many; more than one.

360 Answers

38. How many resources; what resources; what consumption.
39. EXPLAIN.
40. Displayed; written out.
41. Joins.

CHAPTER 13: BILL OF MATERIALS PROCESSING

1. Bill of materials.
2. Relates.
3. Recursive.
4. Family tree; organization chart.
5. Nodes.
6. Hierarchical.
7. May be.
8. Downward.
9. Into.
10. Where from.
11. One.
12. Generalized.
13. Any; n; an indeterminate; an infinite; any number.
14. Subassemblies.
15. Unique.
16. Continuous.
17. Explosion.
18. Stack.
19. DB2 table; stack.
20. Stack pointer.
21. First in/first out (FIFO).
22. Implosion.
23. Are not.
24. Infinite loop.
25. Is not.
26. Stack.
27. Can.

28. Much memory.
29. Generalized.
30. Restrictive; inadequate; awkward.
31. Key.
32. Bad idea.
33. Tables.
34. Batch.
35. False.

CHAPTER 14: DENORMALIZATION

1. Relational.
2. Nonkey; key (in this order).
3. Many.
4. Dispersed; distributed; scattered.
5. Dynamically.
6. Apply.
7. Do not apply.
8. Data.
9. Row.
10. Always.
11. Common; like.
12. Occurrence.
13. No.
14. True.
15. Buffer.
16. High.
17. Clustered.
18. Clustering.
19. Never, under any conditions.
20. May.
21. Redundancy.
22. Update.
23. Stable.
24. Changes.

25. First.
26. Every.
27. Depends on.
28. Much.
29. Interleaving.
30. Is not.
31. False.
32. Does not restore.
33. Reload.

CHAPTER 15: HIGH AVAILABILITY

1. Length; frequency.
2. Quantifiable; measurable.
3. Recovery, reorganization.
4. Is.
5. Is not.
6. Reduce; shrink.
7. Unload/reload.
8. Three.
9. Discovery.
10. Is not.
11. Diagnostic.
12. True.
13. Formulated; laid; outlined.
14. Is.
15. True.
16. Large.
17. Prescriptive.
18. Is.
19. 2.3.
20. 2.3.
21. Two.
22. Internal; redefine.

Answers

23. True.
24. Is.
25. Size, structure.
26. Row size, overhead, freespace, free pages, index space.
27. Three.
28. Maximum.
29. Target.
30. Prototype.
31. False.
32. Probability.
33. Record.
34. Necessary.
35. Expensive.
36. Expensive.
37. Does not mean.
38. Expensive.
39. Slower.
40. Primitive; derived.
41. Large.
42. Administrative.
43. Is not.
44. True.
45. Applications.
46. Key.
47. Must.
48. Processors.
49. n; an indefinite; an indeterminate.
50. DB2; the system; the application.
51. Cannot.
52. False.
53. Independently.
54. True.
55. May.
56. Will not.

CHAPTER 16: EXTRACT PROCESSING IN DB2

1. Simple.
2. e. The volume of data and the resources used.
3. b. Undisciplined.
4. DASD; disk storage; storage.
5. By DXT; by application programs; by other utilities.
6. Parameter; values.
7. Operational; production.
8. Index.
9. Output file.
10. Summarized; consolidated; merged.
11. Report; decision support analysis; trend analysis; demographic analysis; exception reporting.
12. Transformation.
13. True.
14. Should not.
15. Should not.
16. Is.
17. Bulk; bulk storage.
18. Expensive; awkward; not easy to do; slow.
19. Expensive; wasteful.
20. Detail; summarization.
21. Extracted.
22. Consolidated; summarized, reordered.
23. Highest.
24. Usage.
25. Does not.
26. Does.
27. A modest amount; a small amount; a manageable amount.
28. Separate; split.
29. Scan, selection, extract; load.
30. CPU.
31. Consolidate.

Answers

32. True.
33. Sequentially.
34. Changed, been altered; been updated, created.
35. More.
36. More.
37. An important.
38. An index, indexing.
39. Time, I/O, DASD, disk storage.
40. Application; system, DBMS, database.
41. Does not.
42. Does.
43. False.
44. Application.
45. Reduce.
46. Increases.
47. False.
48. True.
49. Background.
50. Small.
51. I/O space; DASD, disk storage.
52. Reduces dramatically.
54. Implies.
55. Should not.
56. Is.

CHAPTER 17: DETAILED DESIGN AND TUNING

1. Save.
2. Does not control.
3. Index.
4. No.
5. No.
6. Possible, maybe, perhaps, etc.
7. Possible, maybe, perhaps, etc.

366   Answers

   8. No.
   9. No.
 10. Maybe, perhaps, possible, potentially.
 11. No.
 12. Maybe, perhaps, possible, potentially.
 13. No.
 14. No.
 15. No.
 16. Dependent.
 17. "JoebMohrBB".
 18. b. Maximum.
 19. c. End of row.
 20. True.
 21. True.
 22. Reduce.
 23. More.
 24. a. Data compression.
     b. Encoding
     c. Encryption
 25. No.
 26. CPU; CPU cycles; memory.
 27. 32K.
 28. 32K.
 29. Overhead; prefix; etc.

CHAPTER 18: DATA LOCKING IN DB2

   1. Data locking.
   2. Throughput.
   3. High performance, online, response sensitive.
   4. DB2
   5. Options.
   6. State.
   7. True.
   8. Row.

Answers

9. Pages.
10. May not.
11. Table.
12. Tablespace.
13. Database.
14. Unit of recovery.
15. ROLLBACK
16. Results table.
17. May not.
18. Cursor.
19. False.
20. Page, tablespace, index.
21. Time.
22. Mode.
23. Amount.
24. True.
25. False.
26. True.
27. Cannot.
28. Different.
29. SHARE; EXCLUSIVE; UPDATE.
30. DB2.
31. Passively.
32. Objects.
33. Level.
34. Levels.
35. Lowest.
36. Duration.
37. Duration.
38. Size; duration.
39. True.
40. May.
41. Page, tablespace.
42. Cursor stability, repeatable read.

368   **Answers**

43. Exclusive.
44. Shared intent, shared, exclusive intent, shared exclusive intent, exclusive.
45. Cursor positioning.
46. Concurrency.
47. Update, delete and insert activity.
48. False.
49. CHKP, ROLL, SYNC, or ROLB.
50. Execution; COMMIT; ROLLBACK.
51. Transaction, RETURN, SYNCPOINT, PSB, checkpoint.
52. Only those locks held by the program terminating.
53. True.
54. Few.
55. Minimal.
56. More.
57. Always.
58. Highest.
59. True.
60. False.
61. Yes.
62. True.
63. False.
64. Table.
65. TABLESPACE, PAGE, ANY.
66. PAGE, TABLESPACE.
67. PAGES.
68. NUMLKTS; NUMLKUS.
69. Cursor stability.
70. Repeatable read.
71. Cursor stability.
72. Backed out.
73. All.

Index

A

access path, 6, 79
access pattern, 67
ad hoc, 13, 14, 16, 18
aggregation of data, 52
algorithm, 81, 198, 199, 200, 201, 202
analytical modeling, 18
APL, 6
application designer, 49, 54, 61, 80
archival, 67, 68, 69
assembler, 6
availability, 48, 63, 223

B

batch, 3, 48, 62
batch window, 17, 147
BIND, 6, 7
blocksize, 67
buffer, 66, 80, 220, 269, 270
buffer pool, 7, 9

C

catalogue, 6
CHKP, 8, 286
CI (control interval), 9
CICS, 4, 8, 16
clustered (unclustered), 10, 63, 65, 66, 127, 213, 214
COBOL, 4, 6
column, 8, 9, 87, 259, 260, 262
commit, 6
commit point, 8
conceptual design, 47, 48
contention, 54, 76
control data base, 75, 76
conversion, 48
cross reference, 61

D

DASD, 52, 87
database, 4, 6
data driven, 97

369

370 Index

data encryption, 269
data item set (dis), 47
data manager, 7
data modeling, 47
DBA, 8, 18, 172
DBRM, 7
DDL, 86, 128
deallocation, 282, 286
derived data, 48
designed (undesigned) transactions, 16, 91, 96
DXT, 4, 16
dynamic SQL, 285

E

edit routines, 269
elapsed time, 85, 148
element, 49
embedded SQL, 4, 16
encoded data, 87–88
entity-relationship modeling, 47
ESDS, 7
existence dependency, 49, 50
extract, 182, 237

F

field, 9, 10, 65, 87
foreign key, 13, 61, 87
Fortran, 6
FREEPAGE, 74
free space, 74

G

growth (of data), 48

H

hierarchy of storage, 67

I

IMS, 4, 8, 16, 18
index, 6, 10, 11, 12, 54, 55, 56, 57, 119, 127, 269
initiation/shutdown, 148
integrity, 77
interactive, 3
intermediate page level, 10
I/O, 6, 52, 54, 55, 56, 57, 62, 79, 80, 81, 88, 89, 97, 129, 140, 148, 150, 151, 152, 155, 165, 166, 208, 214, 219, 259, 267, 269
IRLM, 6

J

join, 13, 14, 152

K

key, 48, 49, 63, 66, 68

L

leaf page level, 11, 12
literal, 260
locking, 5, 6, 54, 75
logical grouping of data, 50
loosely packed data, 74

M

machine time, 148
Media Manager, 7
migration, 48
MTAR, 17, 18

N

nonclustered, 11
normalization, 49, 50, 52, 54

Index

number of occurrences (of data), 48, 63, 67

O

online, 3

P

page, 6, 8, 9, 10, 11, 12, 75, 79
page entry, 12
paper/pencil estimates, 18
partition, 10, 85, 86, 87
partitioned table space, 10
PCTFREE, 74
peak period, 3, 6, 16, 17, 18, 19, 48, 147, 157
performance, 47, 52, 54, 134
physical device, 87
PLAN, 6, 7
PL-1, 4, 6
pointer, 12
precompiler, 7, 17
prefix, 8
primary key, 9
primary table, 57
primitive data, 18, 48
probability of access, 63
production processing, 16, 54
program development, 77
programmer, 61

Q

QMF, 4, 16, 181
query, 6, 55, 56, 121, 262

R

RDS, 7
read-only, 6
referential integrity, 61, 137
relational model, 49
release dependency, 263
reorganization, 74, 86, 87
replication, 76, 77
resource consumption, 14, 92, 127, 128
response time, 92, 93
root page level, 10
row, 8, 9, 63, 65, 66, 75, 211, 212, 213, 264

S

set-at-a-time, 68, 69
simple table space, 8, 10
sort, 5, 17, 81
SQL, 4, 7, 16, 17, 121, 122, 123, 169
static SQL, 285

T

table, 13, 17, 50, 52, 54, 207
table definition, 7
tablespace, 6, 9, 10, 75, 85
terminal access, 4
TP, 16
TPF, 3, 18
TSO, 3, 4
tuple, 8, 9

U

unlock, 6
user requirements, 47
utilities, 17, 85

V

variable length, 9, 73, 74, 264, 267
variable rows, 75
view, 17, 77, 78
VM, 3
volatility, 48, 74
VSAM, 7, 9

W

workload, 18, 48